ACCOUNTING:
The Language of Business

ELEVENTH EDITION
Copyright © 1974, 1975, 1977, 1979, 1982, 1984, 1987, 1990, 1994, 1999, 2005

Roman L. Weil, Ph.D., CPA, CMA
University of Chicago

Patricia C. O'Brien, Ph.D.
York University

In Collaboration With

Michael W. Maher, Ph.D., CPA
University of California, Davis

Clyde P. Stickney, DBA, CPA
Dartmouth College

Kathleen Fitzgerald, MBA, CPA
University of Chicago

D1310910

THOMAS HORTON AND DAUGHTERS
Glen Ridge, New Jersey 07028
www.hortondaughters.com

For Our Children

ISBN 0-913878-66-9

Library of Congress Cataloging in Publication Data

Weil, Roman L
   Accounting: the language of business, eleventh edition

1. Accounting-Terminology. 2. Accounting.

I. O'Brien Patricia C.   joint author.

III. Title.

HF5621.D28   657.03   94-5974

Composition by Progressive Information Technologies
Printed by Sheridan Books, Inc

Preface

Accounting is the language of business. We hope this book will assist the student in becoming familiar with the language required to understand business communications. The first edition appeared in 1974. Since that time feedback from readers about the contents of the book has enabled us to refine the presentation—adding here, deleting there—to suit the wishes of teacher and students as well as those earning a living in business. Although some of the material here will seem too advanced for the beginner, we think the book has something cost-effective for all interested in business.

WE ARE PROFIT-ORIENTED and are eager to learn from you how we can make the book more successful. We will pay the first person who makes a given suggestion incorporated in subsequent editions. Such suggestions might include typographical errors ($1), additional cross references ($1), errors of fact or substance ($5), and additional terms with their explanation ($5).

This edition contains the following sections.

Glossary. Accounting's vocabulary comprises many words that have other meanings in ordinary usage. Understanding the concepts and using accounting reports require that the reader know how to interpret the words used and their special meanings. Students of accounting and readers of accounting reports will find the tasks easier the sooner they learn, for example, the difference between the meanings of *revenue* and *receipt,* between *fund* and *reserve.* The Glossary defines these and some 1,400 other terms. A glossary is not a dictionary, so that we have given definitions of terms only as accounting uses them.

Students and readers of financial reports will not encounter all the terms in the Glossary. We have tried to include, however, the terms found in textbooks, problems, financial reports, financial periodicals, and newspapers.

The Glossary defines many words and phrases in terms of other entries in the Glossary. Terms in a given definition themselves explained elsewhere are *italicized.* Many of the entries in the Glossary are multiple-word phrases because much of the specialized terminology of accounting depends upon such phrases. We have tried to anticipate the most likely phrase that will occur to the reader and have used that phrase in the Glossary. Nevertheless, we probably have failed in some cases to put the explanation by the word or phrase that occurs to you. As Jim Schindler (our co-author before his death) used to say, "If you can't find what you're looking for under one listing, keep looking under others."

Words and phrases are alphabetized using the word-by-word principle. Thus, the following terms appear in the order shown: *account, account form, accountancy, accounting, accounting standards, accounts receivable turnover.*

A few words in accounting, for example *cost* and *expense,* mean different things to different people. We believe that the more precise the meaning of the words used, the easier is the understanding of accounting. Consequently, we give the restricted definition, for example, of *cost* that we think enhances the user's ability to understand. We also give the variants in meaning often used in practice. Further, certain terms used widely in the accounting profession, for example, *prepaid expenses* seem to us to be oxymorons given our preference for restricted and unambiguous definitions.

General Electric Company's Annual Report. GE's annual report is consistently among the best published. We reproduce GE's annual report issued in 2004 along with our own comments which should help in understanding it, and, we hope, other financial statements as well.

Tension in Reporting Income. Why do managers care about where an item appears on the income statement? Here we show why they care and how readers of the income statement use the information therein to estimate the firm's market value.

Corporate Scandals: The Accounting Underpinnings. Accounting scandals have captured everyone's attention. The accounting issues discussed in the financial press can confuse the accounting novice. The details can overwhelm even accounting professionals. This chapter explains the earnings management fundamentals behind the recent scandals to help both the novice and professional understand the current financial reporting environment.

Accounting for the Cost of Employee Stock Options: A Tale from Silicon Valley. No topic in recent years has caused as much controversy as has the accounting for employee stock options. The FASB's proposals here threatened to end standard-setting in the private sector. Here's a cautionary tale describing some of the FASB's opponents' lack of understanding of the issues.

Accounting Magic. This example shows how generally accepted accounting principles allow such a range of accounting treatments that two firms, exactly alike in all respects except for their accounting methods, report drastically different incomes.

We gratefully acknowledge the permission of The Dryden Press to reproduce material from our *Financial Accounting* and *Managerial Accounting* texts they publish.

Eli Worman designed the book and planned the layout. Progressive Information Technologies worked on the composition and layout for the 11th edition. We thank them for their help.

Table of Contents

Glossary

The definitions of many words and phrases in the glossary use other glossary terms. In a given definition, we *italicize* terms that themselves (or variants thereof) appear elsewhere under their own listings. The cross-references generally take one of two forms:

[1] **absorption costing.** See *full absorption costing.*

[2] **ABC.** *Activity-based costing.*

Form [1] refers you to another term for discussion of this **bold-faced** term. Form [2] tells you that this **bold-faced** term is synonymous with the *italicized* term, which you can consult for discussion if necessary.

A

AAA. *American Accounting Association.*

Abacus. A scholarly journal containing articles on theoretical aspects of accounting, published by Basil Blackwell for the Accounting Foundation of the University of Sydney.

abatement. A complete or partial cancellation of a levy imposed by a government unit.

ABC. *Activity-based costing.*

abnormal spoilage. Actual spoilage exceeding that expected when operations are normally efficient. Usual practice treats this cost as an *expense* of the period rather than as a *product cost.* Contrast with *normal spoilage.*

aboriginal cost. In public utility accounting, the *acquisition cost* of an *asset* incurred by the first *entity* devoting that asset to public use; the cost basis for most public utility regulation. If regulators used a different cost basis, then public utilities could exchange assets among themselves at ever-increasing prices in order to raise the rate base and, then, prices based on them.

absorbed overhead. *Overhead costs* allocated to individual products at some *overhead rate;* also called *applied overhead.*

absorption costing. See *full absorption costing.*

Abstracts of the EITF. See *Emerging Issues Task Force.*

accelerated cost recovery System (ACRS). A form of accelerated depreciation that Congress enacted in 1981 and amended in 1986, so that now most writers refer to it as *MACRS,* or *Modified Accelerated Cost Recovery System.* The system provides percentages of the asset's cost that a firm depreciates each year for tax purposes. The percentages derive, roughly, from 150-percent *declining-balance depreciation* methods. ACRS ignores salvage value. We do not generally use these amounts for *financial accounting.*

accelerated depreciation. In calculating *depreciation* charges, any method in which the charges become progressively smaller each period. Examples are *double declining-balance depreciation* and *sum-of-the-years'–digits depreciation* methods.

acceptance. A written promise to pay; equivalent to a *promissory note.*

account. A device for representing the amount (*balance*) for any line (or a part of a line) in the *balance sheet* or *income statement.* Because income statement accounts explain the changes in the balance sheet account Retained Earnings, the definition does not require the last three words of the preceding sentence. An account is any device for accumulating additions and subtractions relating to a single *asset, liability,* or *owners' equity* item, including *revenues* and *expenses.*

account analysis method. A method of separating *fixed costs* from *variable costs* based on the analyst's judgment of whether the cost is fixed or variable. Based on their names alone, the analyst might classify *direct labor (materials) costs* as variable and *depreciation* on a factory building as fixed. In our experience, this method results in too many fixed costs and not enough variable costs—that is, analysts have insufficient information to judge management's ability to reduce costs that appear to be fixed.

account form. The form of *balance sheet* in which *assets* appear on the left and *equities* appear on the right. Contrast with *report form*. See *T-account*.

accountability center. *Responsibility center.*

accountancy. The British word for *accounting*. In the United States, it means the theory and practice of accounting.

accountant's comments. Canada: a written communication issued by a public accountant at the conclusion of a review engagement. It consists of a description of the work performed and a statement that, under the terms of the engagement, the accountant has not performed an audit and consequently expresses no opinion. (Compare *auditor's report; denial of opinion.*)

accountant's opinion. *Auditor's report.*

accountant's report. *Auditor's report.*

accounting. A system conveying information about a specific *entity*. The information is in financial terms and will appear in accounting statements only if the accountant can measure it with reasonable precision. The *AICPA* defines accounting as a service activity whose "function is to provide quantitative information, primarily financial in nature, about economic entities that is intended to be useful in making economic decisions."

accounting adjustments. *Prior-period adjustments*, changes in accounting principles accounted for on a cumulative basis, and corrections of errors. See *accounting changes*. The *FASB* indicates that it will tend to call these items "accounting adjustments," not "accounting changes," when it requires the reporting of *comprehensive income*.

Accounting and Tax Index. A publication that indexes, in detail, the accounting literature of the period. Published by UMI, a subsidiary of Bell & Howell.

accounting changes. As defined by *APB Opinion No. 20*, a change in (1) an *accounting principle* (such as a switch from *FIFO* to *LIFO* or from *sum-of-the-years'–digits depreciation* to *straight-line depreciation*), (2) an accounting estimate (such as estimated useful lives or salvage value of depreciable assets and estimates of *warranty* costs or *uncollectible accounts*), or (3) the reporting *entity*. The firm should disclose changes of type (1). It should include in reported earnings for the period of change the cumulative effect of the change on *retained earnings* at the start of the period during which it made the change. The firm should treat changes of type (2) as affecting only the period of change and, if necessary, future periods. The firm should disclose reasons for changes of type (3) in statements reporting on operations of the period of the change, and it should show the effect of the change on all other periods, for comparative purposes. In some cases (such as a change from *LIFO* to other inventory *flow assumptions* or a change in the method of accounting for long-term construction contracts), *GAAP* treat changes of type (1) like changes of type (3). That is, for these changes the firm should restate all statements shown for prior periods to show the effect of adopting the change for those periods as well. See *all-inclusive (income) concept* and *accounting errors*.

accounting conventions. Methods or procedures used in accounting. Writers tend to use this term when the method or procedure has not yet received official authoritative sanction by a pronouncement of a group such as the *APB, EITF, FASB*, or *SEC*. Contrast with *accounting principles*.

accounting cycle. The sequence of accounting procedures starting with *journal entries* for various transactions and events and ending with the *financial statements* or, perhaps, the *post-closing trial balance*.

accounting deficiency. Canada: a failure to adhere to generally accepted *accounting principles* or to disclose essential information in *financial statements*.

accounting entity. See *entity*.

accounting equation. *Assets = Equities; Assets = Liabilities + Owners' Equity.*

accounting errors. Arithmetic errors and misapplications of *accounting principles* in previously published financial statements. The firm corrects these during the current period with direct *debits* or *credits* to *retained earnings*. In this regard, the firm treats them like *prior-period adjustments*, but technically *APB Opinion No. 9* does not classify them as prior-period adjustments. See *accounting changes,* and contrast with changes in accounting estimates as described there.

accounting event. Any occurrence that is recorded in the accounting records.

Accounting Horizons. A quarterly journal of the *American Accounting Association*.

accounting methods. *Accounting principles;* procedures for carrying out accounting principles.

accounting period. The time period between consecutive *balance sheets;* the time period for which the firm prepares *financial statements* that measure *flows*, such as the *income statement* and the *statement of cash flows*. See *interim statements*.

accounting policies. *Accounting principles* adopted by a specific *entity*.

accounting principles. The methods or procedures used in accounting for events reported in the *financial statements*. We tend to use this term when the method or procedure has received official authoritative sanction from a pronouncement of a group such as the *APB, EITF, FASB*, or *SEC*. Contrast with *accounting conventions* and *conceptual framework*.

Accounting Principles Board. See *APB*.

accounting procedures. See *accounting principles*. However, this term usually refers to the methods for implementing accounting principles.

accounting rate of return. Income for a period divided by average investment during the period; based on income, rather than discounted cash flows, and hence a poor decision-making aid or tool. See *ratio*.

Accounting Research Bulletin (ARB). The name of the official pronouncements of the former *Committee on Accounting*

Procedure (CAP) of the *AICPA*. The committee issued fifty-one bulletins between 1939 and 1959. *ARB No. 43* restated and codified the parts of the first forty-two bulletins not dealing solely with definitions.

Accounting Research Study (ARS). One of a series of studies published by the Director of Accounting Research of the *AICPA* and "designed to provide professional accountants and others interested in the development of accounting with a discussion and documentation of accounting problems." The AICPA published fifteen such studies in the period 1961–73.

Accounting Review. A journal of the *American Accounting Association*.

Accounting Series Release (ASR). See *SEC*.

accounting standards. *Accounting principles*.

Accounting Standards Executive Committee (AcSEC). The senior technical committee of the *AICPA* authorized to speak for the AICPA in the areas of *financial accounting* and reporting as well as *cost accounting*.

accounting system. The procedures for collecting and summarizing financial data in a firm.

Accounting Terminology Bulletin (ATB). One of four releases of the Committee on Terminology of the *AICPA* issued in the period 1953–57.

Accounting Trends and Techniques. An annual *AICPA* publication that surveys the reporting practices of 600 large corporations. It presents tabulations of specific practices, terminology, and disclosures along with illustrations taken from individual annual reports.

accounts payable. A *liability* representing an amount owed to a *creditor;* usually arising from the purchase of *merchandise* or materials and supplies, not necessarily due or past due; normally, a *current liability*.

accounts receivable. Claims against a *debtor;* usually arising from sales or services rendered, not necessarily due or past due; normally, a *current asset*.

accounts receivable turnover. Net sales on account divided by average accounts receivable. See *ratio*.

accretion. Occurs when a *book value* grows over time, such as a *bond* originally issued at a *discount;* the correct technical term is "accretion," not "amortization." This term also refers to an increase in economic worth through physical change caused by natural growth, usually said of a natural resource such as timber. Contrast with *appreciation*. See *amortization*.

accrual. Recognition of an *expense* (or *revenue*) and the related *liability* (or *asset*) resulting from an *accounting event*, frequently from the passage of time but not signaled by an explicit cash transaction; for example, the recognition of interest expense or revenue (or wages, salaries, or rent) at the end of a period even though the firm makes no explicit cash transaction at that time. Cash flow follows accounting recognition; contrast with *deferral*.

accrual basis of accounting. The method of recognizing *revenues* as a firm sells *goods* (or delivers them) and as it renders *services*, independent of the time when it receives cash. This system recognizes *expenses* in the period when it recognizes the related revenue, independent of the time when it pays cash. *SFAC No. 1* says, "Accrual accounting attempts to record the financial effects on an enterprise of transactions and other events and circumstances that have cash consequences for the enterprise in the periods in which those transactions, events, and circumstances occur rather than only in the periods in which cash is received or paid by the enterprise." Contrast with the *cash basis of accounting*. See *accrual* and *deferral*. We could more correctly call this "accrual/deferral" accounting.

accrue. See *accrued,* and contrast with *incur*.

accrued. Said of a *revenue (expense)* that the firm has earned (recognized) even though the related *receivable (payable)* has a future due date. We prefer not to use this adjective as part of an account title. Thus, we prefer to use Interest Receivable (Payable) as the account title rather than Accrued Interest Receivable (Payable). See *matching convention* and *accrual*. Contrast with *incur*.

accrued depreciation. An incorrect term for *accumulated depreciation*. Acquiring an asset with cash, capitalizing it, and then amortizing its cost over periods of use is a process of *deferral* and allocation, not of *accrual*.

accrued payable. A *payable* usually resulting from the passage of time. For example, *salaries* and *interest* accrue as time passes. See *accrued*.

accrued receivable. A *receivable* usually resulting from the passage of time. See *accrued*.

accumulated benefit obligation. See *projected benefit obligation* for definition and contrast.

accumulated depreciation. A preferred title for the asset *contra account* that shows the sum of *depreciation* charges on an asset since the time the firm acquired it. Other account titles are *allowance* for *depreciation* (acceptable term) and *reserve* for *depreciation* (unacceptable term).

accumulated other comprehensive income. *Balance sheet* amount in *owners' equity* showing the total of all *other comprehensive income* amounts from all prior periods.

accurate presentation. The qualitative accounting objective suggesting that information reported in financial statements should correspond as precisely as possible with the economic effects underlying transactions and events. See *fair presentation* and *full disclosure*.

acid test ratio. *Quick ratio*.

acquisition cost. Of an *asset*, the net *invoice* price plus all *expenditures* to place and ready the asset for its intended use. The other expenditures might include legal fees, transportation charges, and installation costs.

ACRS. *Accelerated Cost Recovery System*.

AcSEC. *Accounting Standards Executive Committee of the AICPA.*

activity accounting. *Responsibility accounting.*

activity-based costing (ABC). Method of assigning *indirect costs*, including nonmanufacturing *overhead costs,* to products and services. ABC assumes that almost all overhead costs associate with activities within the firm and vary with respect to the *drivers* of those activities. Some practitioners suggest that ABC attempts to find the drivers for all indirect costs; these people note that in the long run, all costs are *variable*, so *fixed* indirect costs do not occur. This method first assigns costs to activities and then to products based on the products' usage of the activities.

activity-based depreciation. *Production method (depreciation).*

activity-based management (ABM). Analysis and management of activities required to make a product or to produce a service. ABM focuses attention to enhance activities that add value to the customer and to reduce activities that do not. Its goal is to satisfy customer needs while making smaller demands on costly resources. Some refer to this as "activity management."

activity basis. *Costs* are *variable* or *fixed* (*incremental* or *unavoidable*) with respect to some activity, such as production of units (or the undertaking of some new project). Usage calls this activity the "activity basis."

activity center. Unit of the organization that performs a set of tasks.

activity variance. *Sales volume variance.*

actual cost (basis). *Acquisition* or *historical cost.* Also contrast with *standard cost.*

actual costing (system). Method of allocating costs to products using actual *direct materials*, actual *direct labor*, and actual *factory overhead.* Contrast with *normal costing* and *standard costing.*

actuarial. An adjective describing computations or analyses that involve both *compound interest* and probabilities, such as the computation of the *present value* of a life-contingent *annuity.* Some writers use the word even for computations involving only one of the two.

actuarial accrued liability. A 1981 report of the Joint Committee on Pension Terminology (of various actuarial societies) agreed to use this term rather than *prior service cost.*

ad valorem. A method of levying a tax or duty on goods by using their estimated value as the tax base.

additional paid-in capital. An alternative acceptable title for the *capital contributed in excess of par (or stated) value* account.

additional processing cost. *Costs* incurred in processing *joint products* after the *split-off point.*

adequate disclosure. An auditing standard that, to achieve *fair presentation* of *financial statements,* requires *disclosure* of *material* items. This *auditing standard* does not, however, require publicizing all information detrimental to a company. For example, the company may face a lawsuit, and disclosure might require a *debit* to a *loss* account and a *credit* to an *estimated liability.* But the court might view the making of this entry as an admission of liability, which could adversely affect the outcome of the suit. The firm should debit expense or loss for the expected loss, as required by *SFAS No. 5*, but need not use such accurate account titles that the court can spot an admission of liability.

adjunct account. An *account* that accumulates additions to another account. For example, Premium on Bonds Payable is adjunct to the liability Bonds Payable; the effective liability is the sum of the two account balances at a given date. Contrast with *contra account.*

adjusted acquisition (historical) cost. Sometimes said of the *book value* of a *plant asset*, that is, *acquisition cost* less *accumulated depreciation.* Also, cost adjusted to a *constant-dollar* amount to reflect *general price-level changes.*

adjusted bank balance of cash. The *balance* shown on the statement from the bank plus or minus amounts, such as for unrecorded deposits or outstanding checks, to reconcile the bank's balance with the correct cash balance. See *adjusted book balance of cash.*

adjusted basis. The *basis* used to compute gain or loss on the disposition of an *asset* for tax purposes. See also *book value.*

adjusted book balance of cash. The *balance* shown in the firm's account for cash in bank plus or minus amounts, such as for *notes* collected by the bank or bank service charges, to reconcile the account balance with the correct cash balance. See *adjusted bank balance of cash.*

adjusted trial balance. *Trial balance* taken after *adjusting entries* but before *closing entries.* Contrast with *pre-* and *postclosing trial balances.* See *unadjusted trial balance* and *postclosing trial balance.* See also *work sheet.*

adjusting entry. An entry made at the end of an *accounting period* to record a *transaction* or other *accounting event* that the firm has not yet recorded or has improperly recorded during the accounting period; an entry to update the accounts. See *work sheet.*

adjustment. An *account* change produced by an *adjusting entry.* Sometimes accountants use the term to refer to the process of restating *financial statement* amounts to *constant dollars.*

administrative costs (expenses). *Costs (expenses)* incurred for the firm as a whole, in contrast with specific functions such as manufacturing or selling; includes items such as salaries of top executives, general office rent, legal fees, and auditing fees.

admission of partner. Occurs when a new partner joins a *partnership.* Legally, the old partnership dissolves, and a new one comes into being. In practice, however, the firm may keep the old accounting records in use, and the accounting entries reflect

the manner in which the new partner joined the firm. If the new partner merely purchases the interest of another partner, the accounting changes the name for one capital account. If the new partner contributes *assets* and *liabilities* to the partnership, then the firm must recognize them. See *bonus method*.

ADR. See *asset depreciation range*.

advances from (by) customers. A preferred title for the *liability* account representing *receipts* of *cash* in advance of delivering the *goods* or rendering the *service*. After the firm delivers the goods or services, it will recognize *revenue*. Some refer to this as "deferred revenue" or "deferred income," terms likely to confuse the unwary because the item is not yet *revenue* or *income*.

advances to affiliates. *Loans* by a parent company to a *subsidiary;* frequently combined with "investment in subsidiary" as "investments and advances to subsidiary" and shown as a *noncurrent asset* on the parent's *balance sheet*. The consolidation process eliminates these advances in *consolidated financial statements*.

advances to suppliers. A preferred term for the *asset* account representing *disbursements* of cash in advance of receiving *assets* or *services*.

adverse opinion. An *auditor's report* stating that the financial statements are not fair or are not in accord with *GAAP*.

affiliated company. A company controlling or controlled by another company.

after closing. Post-closing; a *trial balance* at the end of the period.

after cost. *Expenditures* to be made after *revenue* recognition. For example, *expenditures* for *repairs* under warranty are after cost. Proper recognition of after cost involves a debit to expense at the time of the sale and a credit to an *estimated liability*. When the firm discharges the liability, it debits the estimated liability and credits the assets consumed.

AG (Aktiengesellschaft). Germany: the form of a German company whose shares can trade on the stock exchange.

agency cost. The *cost* to the *principal* caused by *agents* pursuing their own interests instead of the principal's interests. Includes both the costs incurred by principals to control agents' actions and the cost to the principals if agents pursue their own interests that are not in the interest of the principals.

agency fund. An account for *assets* received by governmental units in the capacity of trustee or agent.

agency theory. A branch of economics relating the behavior of *principals* (such as owner nonmanagers or bosses) and that of their *agents* (such as nonowner managers or subordinates). The principal assigns responsibility and authority to the agent, but the agent's own risks and preferences differ from those of the principal. The principal cannot observe all activities of the agent. Both the principal and the agent must consider the differing risks and preferences in designing incentive contracts.

agent. One authorized to transact business, including executing contracts, for another.

aging accounts receivable. The process of classifying *accounts receivable* by the time elapsed since the claim came into existence for the purpose of estimating the amount of uncollectible accounts receivable as of a given date. See *sales contra, estimated uncollectibles,* and *allowance for uncollectibles*.

aging schedule. A listing of *accounts receivable*, classified by age, used in *aging accounts receivable*.

AICPA (American Institute of Certified Public Accountants). The national organization that represents *CPAs*. See *AcSEC*. It oversees the writing and grading of the Uniform CPA Examination. Each state sets its own requirements for becoming a CPA in that state. See *certified public accountant*. Web Site: www.aicpa.org. While the AICPA sets many auditing and professional standards for public accountants, the *PCAOB* regulates auditing of public companies and the profession.

all-capital earnings rate. *Rate of return on assets*.

all-current method. *Foreign currency translation* in which all *financial statement* items are translated at the *current exchange rate*.

all-inclusive (income) concept. A concept that does not distinguish between *operating* and *nonoperating revenues* and *expenses*. Thus, the only entries to retained earnings are for *net income* and *dividends*. Under this concept, the *income statement* reports all *income*, *gains*, and *losses*; thus, net income includes events usually reported as *prior-period adjustments* and as *corrections of errors*. *GAAP* do not include this concept in its pure form, but *APB Opinions No. 9* and *No. 30* move far in this direction. They do permit retained earnings entries for prior-period adjustments and correction of errors.

allocate. To divide or spread a *cost* from one *account* into several accounts, to several products or activities, or to several periods.

allocation base. The systematic method that assigns *joint costs* to *cost objectives*. For example, a firm might assign the cost of a truck to periods based on miles driven during the period; the allocation base is miles. Or the firm might assign the cost of a factory supervisor to a product based on *direct labor* hours; the allocation base is direct labor hours.

allocation of income taxes. See *deferred income tax*.

allowance. A balance sheet *contra account* generally used for *receivables* and depreciable assets. See *sales* (or *purchase*) *allowance* for another use of this term.

allowance for funds used during construction. In accounting for public utilities, a *revenue* account *credited* for *implicit interest* earnings on *shareholders' equity* balances. One principle of public utility regulation and rate setting requires that customers should pay the full costs of producing the services (e.g., electricity) that they use, nothing more and nothing less. Thus, an electric utility must capitalize into an *asset* account the full costs, but no more, of producing a new electric power-generating plant. One of the costs of building a new plant is the *interest* cost on cash tied up during construction. If *funds* are explicitly borrowed by an ordinary business, the journal entry for interest of $1,000 is typically:

Interest Expense	1,000	
Interest Payable		1,000
Interest expense for the period.		

If the firm is constructing a new plant, then another entry would be made, capitalizing interest into the plant-under-construction account:

Construction Work in Progress	750	
Interest Expense.		750
Capitalize relevant portion of interest relating to construction work in progress into the asset account.		

The cost of the *plant asset* increases; when the firm uses the plant, it charges *depreciation*. The interest will become an expense through the depreciation process in the later periods of use, not currently as the firm pays for interest. Thus, the firm reports the full cost of the electricity generated during a given period as expense in that period. But suppose, as is common, that the electric utility does not explicitly borrow the funds but uses some of its own funds, including funds raised from equity issues as well as from debt. Even though the firm incurs no explicit interest expense or other explicit expense for capital, the funds have an *opportunity cost*. Put another way, the plant under construction will not have lower economic cost just because the firm used its own cash rather than borrowing. The public utility using its own funds, on which it would have to pay $750 of interest if it had explicitly borrowed the funds, will make the following entry:

Construction Work in Progress	750	
Allowance for Funds Used		
During Construction		750
Recognition of interest, an opportunity cost, on own funds used.		

The allowance account is a form of *revenue*, to appear on the income statement, and the firm will close it to Retained Earnings, increasing it. On the *statement of cash flows* it is an income or revenue item not producing funds, and so the firm must subtract it from net income in deriving *cash provided by operations*. *SFAS No. 34* specifically prohibits nonutility companies from capitalizing, into plant under construction, the opportunity cost (interest) on their own funds used.

allowance for uncollectibles (accounts receivable). A *contra account* that shows the estimated *accounts receivable* amount that the firm expects not to collect. When the firm uses such an allowance, the actual write-off of specific accounts receivable (*debit* allowance, *credit* specific customer's account) does not affect *revenue* or *expense* at the time of the write-off. The firm reduces revenue when it debits *bad debt expense* (or, our preference, a revenue contra account) and credits the allowance; the firm can base the amount of the credit to the allowance on a percentage of sales on account for a period of time or compute it from *aging accounts receivable*. This contra account enables the firm to show an estimated receivables amount that it expects to collect without identifying specific uncollectible accounts. See *allowance method*.

allowance method. A method of attempting to match all *expenses* of a transaction with their associated *revenues;* usually involves a debit to expense and a credit to an *estimated liability*, such as for estimated warranty expenditures, or a debit to a revenue (*contra*) account and a credit to an asset (*contra*) account, such as in some firms' accounting for uncollectible accounts. See *allowance for uncollectibles* for further explanation. When the firm uses the allowance method for *sales discounts*, the firm records sales at gross invoice prices (not reduced by the amounts of discounts made available). The firm *debits* an estimate of the amount of discounts to be taken to a revenue contra account and *credits* an allowance account, shown contra to *accounts receivable*.

American Accounting Association (AAA). An organization primarily for academic accountants but open to all interested in accounting. It publishes the *Accounting Review* and several other journals.

American Institute of Certified Public Accountants. See *AICPA*.

American Stock Exchange (AMEX) (ASE). A public market where various corporate *securities* are traded.

AMEX. *American Stock Exchange*.

amortization. Strictly speaking, the process of liquidating or extinguishing ("bringing to death") a *debt* with a series of payments to the *creditor* (or to a *sinking fund*). From that usage has evolved a related use involving the accounting for the payments themselves: "amortization schedule" for a mortgage, which is a table showing the allocation between *interest* and *principal*. The term has come to mean writing off ("liquidating") the cost of an asset. In this context it means the general process of *allocating* the *acquisition cost* of an asset either to the periods of benefit as an *expense* or to *inventory* accounts as a *product cost*. This is called *depreciation* for *plant assets, depletion* for *wasting assets* (natural resources), and "amortization" for *intangibles*. *SFAC No. 6* refers to amortization as "the accounting process of reducing an amount by periodic payments or write-downs." The expressions "unamortized debt discount or premium" and "to amortize debt discount or premium" relate to *accruals*, not to *deferrals*. The expressions "amortization of long-term assets" and "to amortize long-term assets" refer to deferrals, not accruals. Contrast with *accretion*.

amortized cost. A measure required by *SFAS No. 115* for *held-to-maturity securities*. This amount results from applying the method described at *effective interest method*. The firm records the security at its initial cost and computes the *effective interest rate* for the security. Whenever the firm receives cash from the issuer of the security or whenever the firm reaches the end of one of its own *accounting periods* (that is, reaches the time for its own *adjusting entries*), it takes the following steps. It multiplies the amount currently recorded on the books by the effective interest rate (which remains constant over the time the firm holds the security). It debits that amount to the debt security account and credits the amount to Interest Revenue. If the firm receives cash, it debits Cash and credits the debt security account. The firm recomputes the book value of the debt security as the book value before these entries plus the increase for the interest revenue less the decrease for the cash received. The resulting amount is the amortized cost for the end of that period.

analysis of variances. See *variance analysis*.

annual report. A report prepared once a year for shareholders and other interested parties. It includes a *balance sheet*, an *income statement*, a *statement of cash flows*, a reconciliation of changes in *owners' equity* accounts, a *summary of significant accounting principles*, other explanatory *notes*, the *auditor's report*, and comments from management about the year's events. See *10-K* and *financial statements*.

annuitant. One who receives an *annuity*.

annuity. A series of payments of equal amount, usually made at equally spaced time intervals.

annuity certain. An *annuity* payable for a definite number of periods. Contrast with *contingent annuity*.

annuity due. An *annuity* whose first payment occurs at the start of period 1 (or at the end of period 0). Contrast with *annuity in arrears*.

annuity in advance. An *annuity due*.

annuity in arrears. An *ordinary annuity* whose first payment occurs at the end of the first period.

annuity method of depreciation. See *compound interest depreciation*.

antidilutive. Said of a *potentially dilutive* security that will increase *earnings per share* if its holder *exercises* it or *converts* it into common stock. In computing *primary* and *fully diluted earnings per share*, the firm must assume that holders of antidilutive securities will not exercise their options or convert securities into common shares. The opposite assumption would lead to increased reported earnings per share in a given period.

APB. Accounting Principles Board of the *AICPA*. It set *accounting principles* from 1959 through 1973, issuing 31 *APB Opinions* and 4 *APB Statements*. The *FASB* superseded it.

APB Opinion. The name for the APB pronouncements that compose much of *generally accepted accounting principles*; the APB issued 31 *APB Opinions* from 1962 through 1973.

APB Statement. The *APB* issued four *APB Statements* between 1962 and 1970. The *Statements* were approved by at least two-thirds of the board, but they state recommendations, not requirements. For example, *Statement No. 3* (1969) suggested the publication of *constant-dollar* financial statements but did not require them.

APBs. An abbreviation used for *APB Opinions*.

applied cost. A *cost* that a firm has *allocated* to a department, product, or activity; not necessarily based on actual costs incurred.

applied overhead. *Overhead costs* charged to departments, products, or activities. Also called *absorbed overhead*.

appraisal. In valuing an *asset* or *liability,* a process that involves expert opinion rather than evaluation of explicit market transactions.

appraisal costs. *Costs* incurred to detect individual units of products that do not conform to specifications, including end-process sampling and field-testing. Also called "detection costs."

appraisal method of depreciation. The periodic *depreciation* charge that equals the difference between the beginning-of-period and the end-of-period appraised values of the *asset* if that difference is positive. If negative, there is no charge. Not based on *historical cost,* this method is thus not generally accepted.

appreciation. An increase in economic value caused by rising market prices for an *asset*. Contrast with *accretion*.

appropriated retained earnings. See *retained earnings, appropriated*.

appropriation. In governmental accounting, an *expenditure* authorized for a specified amount, purpose, and time.

appropriation account. In governmental accounting, an account set up to record specific authorizations to spend. The governmental unit credits this account with appropriation amounts. At the end of the period, the unit closes to (debits) this account all *expenditures* during the period and all *encumbrances* outstanding at the end of the period.

approximate net realizable value method. A method of assigning joint costs to *joint products* based on revenues minus *additional processing costs* of the end products.

ARB. Accounting Research Bulletin.

arbitrage. Strictly speaking, the simultaneous purchase in one market and sale in another of a *security* or commodity in hope of making a *profit* on price differences in the different markets. Often writers use this term loosely when a trader sells an item that is somewhat different from the item purchased; for example, the sale of shares of common stock and the simultaneous purchase of a *convertible bond* that is convertible into identical common shares. The trader hopes that the market will soon see that the similarities of the items should make them have equal market values. When the market values converge, the trader closes the positions and profits from the original difference in prices, less trading costs.

arbitrary. Having no causation basis. Accounting theorists and practitioners often, properly, say, "Some cost allocations are arbitrary." In that sense, the accountant does not mean that the allocations are capricious or haphazard but does mean that theory suggests no unique solution to the allocation problem at hand. Accountants require that arbitrary allocations be systematic, rational, and consistently followed over time.

arm's length. A transaction negotiated by unrelated parties, both acting in their own self-interests; the basis for a *fair market value* estimation or computation.

arrears. *Cumulative dividends* that the firm has not yet declared. See *annuity in arrears* for another context.

ARS. Accounting Research Study.

articles of incorporation. Document filed with state authorities by persons forming a corporation. When the state returns the document with a certificate of incorporation, the document becomes the corporation's *charter*.

articulate. The relation between any operating statement (for example, *income statement* or *statement of cash flows*) and comparative balance sheets, where the operating statement explains (or reconciles) the change in some major balance sheet category (for example, *retained earnings* or *working capital*).

ASE. *American Stock Exchange.*

ASR. *Accounting Series Release.*

assess. To value property for the purpose of property taxation; to levy a charge on the owner of property for improvements thereto, such as for sewers or sidewalks. The taxing authority computes the assessment.

assessed valuation. For real estate or other property, a dollar amount that a government uses as a basis for levying taxes. The amount need not have some relation to *market value*.

asset. *SFAC No. 6* defines assets as "probable future economic benefits obtained or controlled by a particular entity as a result of past transactions.... An asset has three essential characteristics: (a) it embodies a probable future benefit that involves a capacity, singly or in combination with other assets, to contribute directly or indirectly to future net cash inflows, (b) a particular entity can obtain the benefit and control others' access to it, and (c) the transaction or other event giving rise to the entity's right to or control of the benefit has already occurred." A footnote points out that "probable" means that which we can reasonably expect or believe but that is not certain or proved. You may understand condition (c) better if you think of it as requiring that a future benefit cannot be an asset if it arises from an *executory contract*, a mere exchange of promises. Receiving a purchase order from a customer provides a future benefit, but it is an executory contract, so the order cannot be an asset. An asset may be *tangible* or *intangible*, short-term (current) or long-term (noncurrent).

asset depreciation range (ADR). The range of *depreciable lives* allowed by the *Internal Revenue Service* for a specific depreciable *asset*.

asset securitization. S*ecuritization.*

asset turnover. Net sales divided by average assets. See *ratio*.

assignment of accounts receivable. Transfer of the legal ownership of an account receivable through its sale. Contrast with *pledging* accounts receivable, where the receivables serve as *collateral* for a *loan*.

ATB. *Accounting Terminology Bulletin.*

at par. A *bond* or *preferred shares* issued (or selling) at *face amount*.

attachment. The laying claim to the *assets* of a borrower (or debtor) by a lender (or creditor) when the borrower has failed to pay debts on time.

attest. An auditor's rendering of an *opinion* that the *financial statements* are fair. Common usage calls this procedure the "attest function" of the CPA. See *fair presentation*.

attestor. Typically independent *CPA*s, who *audit financial statements* prepared by management for the benefit of users. The *FASB* describes accounting's constituency as comprising preparers, attestors, and users.

attribute measured. The particular *cost* reported in the balance sheet. When making physical measurements, such as of a person, one needs to decide the units with which to measure, such as inches or centimeters or pounds or grams. One chooses the attribute height or weight independently of the measuring unit, English or metric. Conventional accounting uses *historical cost* as the attribute measured and *nominal dollars* as the measuring unit. Some theorists argue that accounting would better serve readers if it used *current cost* as the attribute measured. Others argue that accounting would better serve readers if it used *constant dollars* as the measuring unit. Some, including us, think accounting should change both the measuring unit and the attribute measured. One can measure the attribute historical cost in nominal dollars or in constant dollars. One can also measure the attribute current cost in nominal dollars or constant dollars. Choosing between the two attributes and the two measuring units implies four different accounting systems. Each of these four has its uses.

attribute(s) sampling. The use of sampling technique in which the observer assesses each item selected on the basis of whether it has a particular qualitative characteristic in order to ascertain the rate of occurrence of this characteristic in the population. See also *estimation sampling*. Compare *variables sampling*. Example of attributes sampling: take a sample population of people, note the fraction that is male (say, 40 percent), and then infer that the entire population contains 40 percent males. Example of variables sampling: take a sample population of people, observe the weight of each sample point, compute the mean of those sampled people's weights (say 160 pounds), and then infer that the mean weight of the entire population equals 160 pounds.

audit. Systematic inspection of accounting records involving analyses, tests, and *confirmations*. See *internal audit*.

audit committee. A committee of the board of directors of a *corporation*, usually comprising outside directors, who nominate the independent auditors and discuss the auditors' work with them. If the auditors believe the shareholders should know about certain matters, the auditors, in principle, first bring these matters to the attention of the audit committee; in practice, the auditors may notify management before they notify the audit committee.

Audit Guides. See *Industry Audit Guides*.

audit program. The procedures followed by the *auditor* in carrying out the *audit*.

audit trail. A reference accompanying an entry, or *post*, to an underlying source record or document. Efficiently checking the accuracy of accounting entries requires an audit trail. See *cross-reference*.

Auditing Research Monograph. Publication series of the *AICPA*.

auditing standards. Standards promulgated by the *PCAOB* for auditors to follow in carrying out their *attest* functions. The PCAOB began operations in earnest in 2003, and initially has said that it would use the standards originally promulgated by the *AICPA*, including general standards, standards of field work, and standards of reporting. According to the AICPA, these standards "deal with the measures of the quality of the performance and the objectives to be attained" rather than with specific auditing procedures. As time passes, the PCAOB will substitute its rules for those of the AICPA.

Auditing Standards Board. *AICPA* operating committee that promulgates auditing rules. The new operations of the PCAOB, after 2003, render uncertain what this Board will do.

auditor. Without a modifying adjective, usually refers to an external auditor—one who checks the accuracy, fairness, and general acceptability of accounting records and statements and then *attests* to them. See *internal auditor*.

auditor's opinion. *Auditor's report.*

auditor's report. The auditor's statement of the work done and an opinion of the *financial statements*. The auditor usually gives unqualified ("clean") opinions but may qualify them, or the auditor may disclaim an opinion in the report. Often called the "accountant's report." See *adverse opinion*.

AudSEC. The former Auditing Standards Executive Committee of the *AICPA*, now functioning as the *Auditing Standards Board*.

authorized capital stock. The number of *shares* of stock that a corporation can issue; specified by the *articles of incorporation*.

available for sale, securities. *Marketable securities* a firm holds that are classified as neither *trading securities* nor *held-to-maturity (debt) securities*. This classification is important in *SFAS No. 115*, which requires the owner to carry marketable equity securities on the balance sheet at market value, not at cost. Under *SFAS No. 115*, the income statement reports *holding gains and losses* on trading securities but not on securities available for sale. The required accounting *credits* (*debits*) holding gains (losses) on securities available for sale directly to an *owners' equity* account. On sale, the firm reports realized gain or loss as the difference between the selling price and the original cost, for trading securities, and as the difference between the selling price and the book value at the beginning of the period of sale, for securities available for sale and for debt securities held to maturity. By their nature, however, the firm will only rarely sell debt securities "held to maturity."

average. The arithmetic mean of a set of numbers; obtained by summing the items and dividing by the number of items.

average collection period of receivables. See *ratio*.

average-cost flow assumption. An inventory *flow assumption* in which the cost of units equals the *weighted average* cost of the *beginning inventory* and purchases. See *inventory equation*.

average tax rate. The rate found by dividing *income tax* expense by *net income* before taxes. Contrast with *marginal tax rate* and *statutory tax rate*.

avoidable cost. A *cost* that ceases if a firm discontinues an activity; an *incremental* or *variable cost*. See *programmed cost*.

B

backflush costing. A method of *allocating indirect costs* and *overhead;* used by companies that hope to have zero or small *work-in-process inventory* at the end of the period. The method *debits* all *product costs* to *cost of goods sold* (or *finished goods inventory*) during the period. To the extent that work in process actually exists at the end of the period, the method then debits work-in-process and *credits* cost of goods sold (or finished goods inventory). This method is "backflush" in the sense that costing systems ordinarily, but not in this case, allocate first to work-in-process and then forward to cost of goods sold or to finished goods. Here, the process allocates first to cost of goods sold (or finished goods) and then, later if necessary, to work-in-process.

backlog. Orders for which a firm has insufficient *inventory* on hand for current delivery and will fill in a later period.

backlog depreciation. In *current cost accounting*, a problem arising for the *accumulated depreciation* on *plant assets*. Consider an *asset* costing $10,000 with a 10-year life depreciated with the straight-line method. Assume that a similar asset has a current cost of $10,000 at the end of the first year but $12,000 at the end of the second year. Assume that the firm bases the depreciation charge on the average current cost during the year, $10,000 for the first year and $11,000 for the second. The depreciation charge for the first year is $1,000 and for the second is $1,100 (= .10 × $11,000), so the *accumulated depreciation account* is $2,100 after two years. Note that at the end of the second year, the firm has used 20 percent of the asset's future benefits, so the accounting records based on current costs must show a *net book value* of $9,600 (= .80 × $12,000), which results only if accumulated depreciation equals $2,400, so that book value equals $9,600 (= $12,000 – $2,400). But the sum of the depreciation charges equals only $2,100 (= $1,000 + $1,100). The *journal entry* to increase the accumulated depreciation account requires a *credit* to that account of $300. The backlog depreciation question arises: what account do we debit? Some theorists would *debit* an *income* account, and others would *debit* a *balance sheet owners' equity* account without reducing current-period earnings. The answer to the question of what to debit interrelates with how the firm records the *holding gains* on the asset. When the firm debits the asset account for $2,000 to increase the recorded amount from $10,000 to $12,000, it records a holding gain of $2,000 with a credit. Many theorists believe that whatever account the firm credits for the holding gain is the same account that the firm should debit for backlog depreciation. This is sometimes called "catch-up depreciation."

bad debt. An *uncollectible account;* see *bad debt expense* and *sales contra, estimated uncollectibles*.

bad debt expense. The name for an *account debited* in both the *allowance method* for *uncollectible accounts* and the *direct write-off method*. Under the allowance method, some prefer to treat the account as a revenue contra, not as an expense, and give it an account title such as Uncollectible Accounts Adjustment.

bad debt recovery. Collection, perhaps partial, of a specific account receivable previously written off as uncollectible. If a firm uses the *allowance method*, it will usually *credit* the *allowance* account, assuming that it has correctly assessed the amount of bad debts but has merely misjudged the identity of one of the nonpaying customers. If the firm decides that its charges for bad debts have been too large, it will credit the Bad Debt Expense account. If the firm uses the *direct write-off* method, it will credit a *revenue account*.

bailout period. In a *capital budgeting* context, the total time that elapses before accumulated cash inflows from a project, including the potential *salvage value* of assets at various times, equal or exceed the accumulated cash outflows. Contrast with *payback period*, which assumes completion of the project and uses terminal salvage value. Bailout, in contrast with payback, takes into account, at least to some degree, the *present value* of the cash flows after the termination date that the analyst is considering. The potential salvage value at any time includes some estimate of the flows that can occur after that time.

balance. As a noun, the opening balance in an *account* plus the amounts of increases less the amounts of decreases. (In the absence of a modifying adjective, the term means closing balance, in contrast to opening balance. The closing balance for a period becomes the opening balance for the next period.) As a verb, "balance" means to find the value of the arithmetic expression described above.

balance sheet. Statement of financial position that shows Total *Assets* = Total *Liabilities + Owners' Equity*. The *balance sheet* usually classifies Total Assets as (1) *current assets*, (2) *investments*, (3) *property, plant, and equipment*, or (4) *intangible assets*. The balance sheet accounts composing Total Liabilities usually appear under the headings Current Liabilities and Long-term Liabilities.

balance sheet account. An account that can appear on a balance sheet; a *permanent account*. Contrast with *temporary account*.

balanced scorecard. A set of performance targets, not all expressed in dollar amounts, for setting an organization's goals for its individual employees or groups or divisions. A community relations employee might, for example, set targets in terms of number of employee hours devoted to local charitable purposes.

balloon. Most *mortgage* and *installment loans* require relatively equal periodic payments. Sometimes the loan requires relatively equal periodic payments with a large final payment. Usage calls the large final payment a "balloon" payment and the loan, a "balloon" loan. Although a coupon bond meets this definition, usage seldom, if ever, applies this term to bond loans.

bank balance. The amount of the balance in a checking account shown on the *bank statement*. Compare with *adjusted bank balance of cash,* and see *bank reconciliation schedule*.

bank prime rate. See *prime rate*.

bank reconciliation schedule. A schedule that explains the difference between the book balance of the cash in a bank account and the bank's statement of that amount; takes into account the amount of items such as checks that have not cleared or deposits that have not been recorded by the bank, as well as errors made by the bank or the firm.

bank statement. A statement sent by the bank to a checking account customer showing deposits, checks cleared, and service charges for a period, usually one month.

bankrupt. Occurs when a company's *liabilities* exceed its *assets* and the firm or one of its creditors has filed a legal petition that the bankruptcy court has accepted under the bankruptcy law. A bankrupt firm is usually, but need not be, *insolvent*.

base stock method. A method of inventory valuation that assumes that a firm must keep on hand at all times a minimum normal, or base stock, of goods for effective continuity of operations. The firm values this base quantity at *acquisition cost* of the inventory on hand in the earliest period when inventory was on hand. Firms may not use this method, either for financial reporting or for tax reporting, but most theorists consider it to be the forerunner of the *LIFO* cost flow assumption.

basic accounting equation. *Accounting equation.*

basic cost-flow equation. *Cost-flow equation.*

basic earnings per share (BEPS). *Net income* to *common shareholders*, divided by the weighted average number of common shares *outstanding* during the period. Required by *SFAS No. 128* and by *IASB*. See *primary earnings per share (PEPS)* for contrast. Because BEPS does not deal with *common-stock equivalents,* it will almost always give a larger earnings-per-share figure than PEPS.

basis. *Acquisition cost*, or some substitute therefor, of an *asset* or *liability* used in computing gain or loss on disposition or retirement; *attribute measured*. This term appears in both *financial* and *tax reporting*, but the basis of a given item need not be the same for both purposes.

basis point. One one-hundreth (=1/100). Terminology usually quotes *interest rates* in percentage terms, such as "5.60 percent" or "5.67 percent." The difference between those two interest rates is described as "7 basis points" or seven one-hundreths of one percent. Financial writers often extend this usage to other contexts involving decimals. For example, if the mean grade point average in the class is 3.25 and a given student scores 3.30, we might say that the student scored "5 basis points" above the class average.

basket purchase. Purchase of a group of *assets* (and *liabilities*) for a single price; the acquiring firm must assign *costs* to each item so that it can record the individual items with their separate amounts in the *accounts*.

batch-level activities. Work required to ready equipment or people for a production run.

bear. One who believes that security prices will fall. A "bear market" refers to a time when stock prices are generally declining. Contrast with *bull*.

bearer bond. See *registered bond* for contrast and definition.

beginning inventory. Valuation of *inventory* on hand at the beginning of the *accounting period*, equals *ending inventory* from the preceding period.

behavioral congruence. *Goal congruence.*

benchmarking. Process of measuring a firm's performance, products, and services against standards based on best levels of performance achievable or, sometimes, achieved by other firms.

BEPS. *Basic earnings per share.*

betterment. An *improvement*, usually *capitalized*, not *expensed*.

bid. An offer to purchase, or the amount of the offer.

big bath. A *write-off* of a substantial amount of costs previously treated as *assets;* usually occurs when a corporation drops a business line that earlier required a large investment but that proved to be unprofitable. The term is sometimes used to describe a situation in which a corporation takes a large write-off in one period in order to free later periods of gradual write-offs of those amounts. In this sense it frequently occurs when the top management of the firm changes.

Big 4. Final 4. The four largest U.S. *public accounting* partnerships; in alphabetical order: Deloitte & Touche; Ernst & Young; KPMG Peat Marwick; and PricewaterhouseCoopers. See *Big N.*

Big N. The largest U.S. *public accounting* partnerships. When we first prepared this glossary, there were eight such partnerships, referred to as the "Big 8." See *Big 4.* The term "Big N" came into use when various of the *Big 8* proposed to merge with each other and the ultimate number of large partnerships was in doubt, which it still is, although we don't expect the number to change before 2010.

bill. An *invoice* of charges and *terms of sale* for *goods* and *services;* also, a piece of currency.

bill of materials. A specification of the quantities of *direct materials* that a firm expects to use to produce a given job or quantity of output.

blocked currency. Currency that the holder, by law, cannot withdraw from the issuing country or exchange for the currency of another country.

board. *Board of directors.*

board of directors. The governing body of a corporation; elected by the shareholders.

bond. A certificate to show evidence of debt. The *par value* is the *principal* or face amount of the bond payable at maturity. The *coupon rate* is the amount of the yearly payments divided by the principal amount. Coupon bonds have attached coupons that the holder can redeem at stated dates. Increasingly, firms issue not coupon bonds but registered bonds; the firm or its agent keeps track of the owners of registered bonds. Normally, bonds call for semiannual payments.

bond conversion. The act of exchanging *convertible bonds* for *preferred* or *common shares*.

bond discount. From the standpoint of the issuer of a *bond* at the issue date, the excess of the *par value* of a bond over its initial sales price and, at later dates, the excess of par over

the sum of the following two amounts: initial issue price and the portion of discount already *amortized;* from the standpoint of a bondholder, the difference between par value and selling price when the bond sells below par.

bond indenture. The contract between an issuer of *bonds* and the bondholders.

bond premium. Exactly parallel to *bond discount* except that the issue price (or current selling price) exceeds *par value*.

bond ratings. Corporate and *municipal bond* issue ratings, based on the issuer's existing *debt* level, its previous record of payment, the *coupon rate* on the bonds, and the safety of the *assets* or *revenues* that are committed to paying off *principal* and *interest*. Moody's Investors Service and Standard & Poor's Corporation publish bond ratings: Moody's top rating is Aaa; Standard & Poor's is AAA.

bond redemption. Retirement of *bonds*.

bond refunding. To incur *debt*, usually through the issue of new *bonds*, intending to use the proceeds to retire an *outstanding* bond issue.

bond sinking fund. See *sinking fund*.

bond table. A table showing the current price of a *bond* as a function of the *coupon rate*, current (remaining) term *maturity*, and effective *yield to maturity* (or *effective rate*).

bonus. Premium over normal *wage* or *salary*, paid usually for meritorious performance.

bonus method. One of two methods to recognize an excess, say $10,000, when a *partnership* admits a new partner and when the new partner's capital account is to show an amount larger than the amount of *tangible* assets that he or she contributes. First, the old partners may transfer $10,000 from themselves to the new partner. This is the bonus method. Second, the partnership may recognize goodwill in the amount of $10,000, with the credit to the new partner's capital account. This is the *goodwill method*. (Notice that the new partner's percentage of total ownership differs under the two methods.) If the new partner's capital account is to show an amount smaller than the tangible assets that he or she contributed, then the old partners will receive bonus or goodwill, depending on the method.

book. As a verb, to record a transaction; as a noun, usually plural, the *journals* and *ledgers*; as an adjective, see *book value*.

book cost. *Book value.*

book inventory. An *inventory* amount that results not from physical count but from the amount of beginning inventory plus *invoice* amounts of net purchases less invoice amounts of *requisitions* or withdrawals; implies a *perpetual inventory* method.

book of original entry. *Journal.*

book value. The amount shown in the books or in the *accounts* for an *asset, liability,* or *owners' equity* item. The term is generally used to refer to the *net* amount of an *asset* or group of assets shown in the account that records the asset and reductions, such as for *amortization*, in its cost. Of a firm, it refers to the excess of total assets over total liabilities; *net assets*.

book value per share of common stock. Common *shareholders' equity* divided by the number of shares of common stock outstanding. See *ratio*.

bookkeeping. The process of analyzing and recording transactions in the accounting records.

boot. The additional cash paid (or received) along with a used item in a trade-in or exchange transaction for another item. See *trade-in*.

borrower. See *loan*.

bottleneck. An operation in which the work to be performed equals or exceeds the available capacity, thus holding up further operations.

branch. A sales office or other unit of an enterprise physically separated from the home office of the enterprise but not organized as a legally separate *subsidiary*. Writers seldom use this term to refer to manufacturing units.

branch accounting. An accounting procedure that enables the firm to report the financial position and operations of each *branch* separately but later combine them for published statements.

brand. brand name. See *trademark* and *trademark right*.

breakeven analysis. See *breakeven chart*.

breakeven chart. Two kinds of breakeven charts appear here. The charts use the following information for one month. Revenue is $30 per unit.

Cost Classification	Variable Cost, Per Unit	Fixed Cost, Per Month
Manufacturing costs:		
Direct material	$ 4	—
Direct labor	9	—
Overhead	4	$3,060
Total manufacturing costs	$17	$3,060
Selling, general and administrative costs	5	1,740
Total costs	$22	$4,800

The cost-volume-profit graph presents the relation between changes in volume to the amount of *profit*, or *income*. Such a graph shows total *revenue* and total *costs* for each volume level, and the user reads profit or loss at any volume directly from the chart. The profit-volume graph does not show revenues and costs but more readily indicates profit (or loss) at various output levels. Keep in mind two caveats about these graphs:

1. Although the curve depicting *variable cost* and total cost appears as a straight line for its entire length, at low or high levels of output, variable cost will probably differ from $22 per unit. The variable cost figure usually results from studies of operations at some broad central area of production, called the *relevant range*. The chart will not usually provide accu-

(a) Cost-Volume-Profit Graph

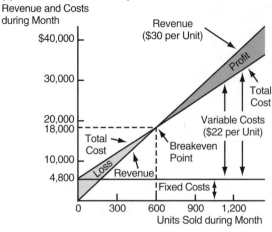

(b) Profit-Volume Graph

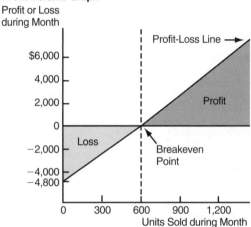

rate results for low (or high) levels of activity. For this reason, the total cost and the profit-loss curves sometimes appear as dotted lines at lower (or higher) volume levels.

2. This chart, simplistically, assumes a single-product firm. For a multiproduct firm, the horizontal axis would have to be stated in dollars rather than in physical units of output. Breakeven charts for multiproduct firms necessarily assume that the firm sells constant proportions of the several products, so that changes in this mixture, as well as in costs or selling prices, invalidate such a chart.

breakeven point. The volume of sales required so that total *revenues* equals total *costs;* may be expressed in units (*fixed costs/contribution per unit*) or in sales dollars [selling price per unit (fixed costs/contribution per unit)].

break-even time. Time required before the firm recovers the amounts it invested in developing a new product.

budget. A financial plan that a firm uses to estimate the results of future operations; frequently used to help control future operations. In governmental operations, budgets often become the law. See *standard costs* for further elaboration and contrast.

budgetary accounts. In governmental accounting, the accounts that reflect estimated operations and financial condition, as affected by estimated *revenues, appropriations,* and *encumbrances.* Contrast with *proprietary accounts,* which record the transactions.

budgetary control. Management of governmental (nongovernmental) unit in accordance with an official (approved) *budget* in order to keep total expenditures within authorized (planned) limits.

budgeted cost. See *standard costs* for definition and contrast.

budgeted statements. *Pro forma statements* prepared before the event or period occurs.

bull. One who believes that security prices will rise. A "bull market" refers to a time when stock prices are generally rising. Contrast with *bear*.

burden. See *overhead costs*.

burn rate. A new business usually begins life with cash-absorbing operating losses but with a limited amount of cash. The "burn rate" measures how long the new business can survive before operating losses must stop or the firm must receive a new infusion of cash. Writers usually express the burn rate in months.

business combination. As defined in *APB Opinion No. 16,* the bringing together into a single accounting *entity* of two or more incorporated or unincorporated businesses. The new entity will account for the *merger* either with the *purchase method* or, outside the US, with the *pooling-of-interests method.* See *conglomerate*.

business entity. *Entity; accounting entity.*

BV *(besloten vennootschap).* Netherlands: a private limited-liability company.

bylaws. The rules adopted by the shareholders of a corporation; specify the general methods for carrying out the functions of the corporation.

by-product. A *joint product* whose sales value is so small relative to the sales value of the other joint product(s) that it does not receive normal accounting treatment. The costs assigned to by-products reduce the costs of the main product(s). Accounting allocates by-products a share of joint costs such that the expected gain or loss at their sale is zero. Thus, by-products appear in the *accounts* at *net realizable value*.

C

C corporation. In tax terminology, a corporation paying its own income taxes. Contrast with *S corporation.*

CA. Chartered accountant.

call. An option to buy *shares* of a publicly traded corporation at a fixed price during a fixed time span. Contrast with *put*.

call premium. See *callable bond*.

call price. See *callable bond*.

callable bond. A *bond* for which the issuer reserves the right to pay a specific amount, the call price, to retire the obligation before its *maturity* date. If the issuer agrees to pay more than the *face amount* of the bond when called, the excess of the payment over the face amount is the "call premium."

called-up share capital. UK: *common stock* at *par value.*

Canadian Institute of Chartered Accountants. *The national organization that represents* chartered accountants *in Canada. Web Site: www.cica.ca.*

cancelable lease. See *lease*.

CAP. *Committee on Accounting Procedure.*

capacity. Stated in units of product, the amount that a firm can produce per unit of time; stated in units of input, such as *direct labor* hours, the amount of input that a firm can use in production per unit of time. A firm uses this measure of output or input in allocating *fixed costs* if the amounts producible are normal, rather than maximum, amounts.

capacity cost. A *fixed cost* incurred to provide a firm with the capacity to produce or to sell. Consists of *standby costs* and *enabling costs.* Contrast with *programmed costs.*

capacity variance. *Production volume variance.*

capital. *Owners' equity* in a business; often used, equally correctly, to mean the total assets of a business; sometimes used to mean *long-term assets.* Sometimes used to mean *funds* raised or all assets or long-term financing. This word causes confusion in accounting and finance. Uninformed users mix up the funds (and their uses) with the sources of the funds. Consider the following transactions. A firm raises $100 cash by issuing shares and uses the $100 to acquire *inventory* and *plant assets.* Did the investor "invest capital" of $100 or did the firm "invest capital" of $100 or both? You will hear "invest capital" used for both sides of that transaction. Now focus on the firm who issued the shares and received the cash. Some would say the first transaction, the issue of shares, "raised capital." (If you ask of a person who answers this way, "What is the *capital,* the increase in owners' equity or the increased cash?" you will not get a clear answer, consistent across all such people.) Others would say only the second transaction, spending the cash, raised capital and only then for the plant assets, not the inventory. When a regulator focuses on a bank's capital ratios, it looks to the right-hand side of the balance sheet, not to how the firm has invested its funds. Sometimes bank regulators will take the owners' equity total and subtract from that amount the amount of intangible assets, resulting in a total with no clear conception, which they call "tangible capital." See *cost of capital* for further discussion of the confusion between the cost of raising funds and the return to, or *opportunity cost* of, investing funds. The confusion is so prevalent that we tend to avoid using the word, except to mean *shareholders' equity.*

capital asset. Properly used, a designation, for income tax purposes, that describes property held by a taxpayer except *cash*, inventoriable *assets*, goods held primarily for sale, most depreciable property, *real estate, receivables*, certain *intangibles*, and a few other items. Sometimes writers use this term imprecisely to describe *plant* and *equipment*, which are clearly not capital assets under the income-tax definition. Writers often use the term to refer to an *investment* in *securities*.

capital budget. Plan of proposed outlays for acquiring long-term *assets* and the means of *financing* the acquisition.

capital budgeting. The process of choosing *investment* projects for an enterprise by considering the *present value* of cash flows and deciding how to raise the funds the investment requires.

capital consumption allowance. The term used for *depreciation expense* in national income accounting and the reporting of funds in the economy.

capital contributed in excess of par (or stated) value. A preferred title for the account that shows the amount received by the issuer for *capital stock* in excess of *par (or stated) value*.

capital expenditure (outlay). An *expenditure* to acquire long-term *assets*.

capital gain. The excess of proceeds over *cost*, or other *basis*, from the sale of a *capital asset* as defined by the Internal Revenue Code. If the taxpayer has held the capital asset for a sufficiently long time before sale, then the gain is taxed at a rate lower than that used for other gains and ordinary income.

capital lease. A *lease* treated by the *lessee* as both the borrowing of funds and the acquisition of an *asset* to be *amortized*. The lessee (tenant) recognizes both the *liability* and the asset on its balance sheet. Expenses consist of *interest* on the *debt* and *amortization* of the asset. The *lessor* (landlord) treats the lease as the sale of the asset in return for a series of future cash receipts. Contrast with *operating lease*.

capital loss. A negative capital gain; see *capital gain*.

capital rationing. In a *capital budgeting* context, the imposition of constraints on the amounts of total capital expenditures in each period.

capital stock. The ownership shares of a corporation. Consists of all classes of *common* and *preferred shares*.

capital structure. The composition of a corporation's equities; the relative proportions of short-term debt, long-term debt, and *owners' equity*.

capital surplus. An inferior term for *capital contributed in excess of par (or stated) value*.

capitalization of a corporation. A term used by investment analysts to indicate *shareholders' equity* plus bonds outstanding.

capitalization of earnings. The process of estimating the *fair value* of a firm by computing the *net present value* of the predicted *net income* (not *cash flows*) of the firm for the future.

capitalization rate. An *interest rate* used to convert a series of payments or receipts or earnings into a single *present value*.

capitalize. To record an *expenditure* that may benefit a future period as an *asset* rather than to treat the expenditure as an *expense* of the period of its occurrence. Whether expenditures for advertising or for research and development should be capitalized is controversial, but *SFAS No. 2* forbids capitalizing *R&D* costs. We believe GAAP should allow firms to capitalize expenditures when they lead to future benefits and thus meet the criterion to be an asset.

carryback, carryforward, carryover. The use of losses or tax credits in one period to reduce income taxes payable in other periods. Two common kinds of carrybacks exist: for net operating losses and for *capital losses*. They apply against taxable income. In general, carrybacks are for three years, with the earliest year first. The taxpayer can carry forward operating losses for fifteen years. Corporate capital loss carryforwards are for five years. Individuals can carry forward capital losses indefinitely.

carrying cost. Costs (such as property taxes and insurance) of holding, or storing, *inventory* from the time of purchase until the time of sale or use.

carrying value (amount). *Book value*.

CASB (Cost Accounting Standards Board). A board authorized by the U.S. Congress to "promulgate cost-accounting standards designed to achieve uniformity and consistency in the cost-accounting principles followed by defense contractors and subcontractors under federal contracts." The *principles* the CASB promulgated since 1970 have considerable weight in practice wherever the *FASB* has not established a standard. Congress allowed the CASB to go out of existence in 1980 but reinstated it in 1990.

cash. Currency and coins, negotiable checks, and balances in bank accounts. For the *statement of cash flows*, "cash" also includes *marketable securities* held as *current assets*.

cash basis of accounting. In contrast to the *accrual basis of accounting*, a system of accounting in which a firm recognizes *revenues* when it receives *cash* and recognizes *expenses* as it makes *disbursements*. The firm makes no attempt to match *revenues* and *expenses* in measuring income. See *modified cash basis*.

cash budget. A schedule of expected cash *receipts* and *disbursements*.

cash change equation. For any *period,* the change in *cash* equals the change in *liabilities* plus the change in *owners' equity* minus the change in noncash *assets*.

cash collection basis. The *installment method* for recognizing *revenue*. Do not confuse with the *cash basis of accounting*.

cash conversion cycle. *Cash cycle*.

cash cycle. The period of time during which a firm converts *cash* into *inventories*, inventories into *accounts receivable*, and *receivables* back into cash. Sometimes called *earnings cycle*.

cash disbursements journal. A specialized *journal* used to record *expenditures* by *cash* and by *check*. If a *check register* is also used, a cash disbursements journal records only expenditures of currency and coins.

cash discount. A sales or purchase price reduction allowed for prompt payment.

cash dividend. See *dividend*.

cash equivalent. According to *SFAS No. 95*, "short-term, highly liquid investments that are both readily convertible to known amounts of cash [and] so near their maturity that they present insignificant risk of changes in value because of changes in interest rates.... Examples of items commonly considered to be cash equivalents are Treasury bills, commercial paper, [and] money market funds."

cash equivalent value. A term used to describe the amount for which an *asset* could be sold. Sometimes called *market value* or *fair market price (value)*.

cash flow. Cash *receipts* minus *disbursements* from a given *asset*, or group of assets, for a given period. Financial analysts sometimes use this term to mean *net income + depreciation + depletion + amortization*. See also *operating cash flow* and *free cash flow*.

cash flow from operations. Receipts from customers and from investments less expenditures for inventory, labor, and services used in the usual activities of the firm, less interest expenditures. See *statement of cash flows* and *operations*. Same as *cash provided by operations*.

cash-flow hedge. A hedge of an exposure to variability in the cash flows of a recognized *asset* or *liability* or of a forecasted transaction, such as expected future foreign sales. The cash flows hedged do not themselves appear on the *balance sheet*. The hedging instrument itself is a *marketable security* and appears on the balance sheet at market value. If the firm uses hedge accounting and the hedging instrument is highly effective, then it will be able to report in *other comprehensive income* the *gains* and *losses*, so these amounts will not appear in periodic net income.

cash flow statement. *Statement of cash flows*.

cash provided by operations. An important subtotal in the *statement of cash flows*. This amount equals the total of revenues producing *cash* less *expenses* requiring cash. Often, the amount appears as *net income* plus expenses not requiring cash (such as depreciation charges) minus revenues not producing cash (such as revenues recognized under the *equity method* of accounting for a long-term investment). The statement of cash flows maintains the same distinctions between *continuing operations, discontinued operations*, and *income* or *loss* from *extraordinary items* as does the *income statement*.

cash receipts journal. A specialized *journal* used to record all *receipts* of *cash*.

cash (surrender) value of life insurance. An amount equal not to the face value of the policy to be paid in the event of death but to the amount that the owner could realize by immediately canceling the policy and returning it to the insurance company for cash. A firm owning a life insurance policy reports it as an asset at an amount equal to this value.

cash yield. See *yield*.

cashier's check. A bank's own *check* drawn on itself and signed by the cashier or other authorized official. It is a direct obligation of the bank. Compare with *certified check*.

catch-up depreciation. *Backlog depreciation*.

cause-and-effect analysis. An identification of potential causes of defects and taking actions to cure the problem found. To use this analysis, first define the effect and then identify the causes of the problem. The potential causes fall into four categories: human factors, methods and design factors, machine-related factors, and materials or components factors. As management identifies the prevailing causes, it develops and implements corrective measures.

CCA. *Current cost accounting; current value accounting*.

central corporate expenses. General *overhead expenses* incurred in running the corporate headquarters and related supporting activities of a corporation. Accounting treats these expenses as *period expenses*. Contrast with *manufacturing overhead*. *Line of business reporting* must decide how to treat these expenses—whether to allocate them to the individual segments and, if so, how to allocate them.

central processing unit (CPU). The computer system component that carries out the arithmetic, logic, and data transfer.

certificate. The document that is the physical embodiment of a *bond* or a *share of stock;* a term sometimes used for the *auditor's report*.

certificate of deposit. A form of *deposit* in a bank or thrift institution. Federal law constrains the rate of interest that banks can pay to their depositors. Current law allows banks to pay a rate higher than the one allowed on a *time deposit* if the depositor promises to leave funds on deposit for several months or more. When the bank receives such funds, it issues a certificate of deposit. The depositor can withdraw the funds before maturity by paying a penalty.

certified check. The *check* of a depositor drawn on a bank. The bank inserts the words "accepted" or "certified" on the face of the check, with the date and a signature of a bank official. The check then becomes an obligation of the bank. Compare with *cashier's check*.

certified financial statement. A financial statement attested to by an independent *auditor* who is a *CPA*.

certified internal auditor. See *CIA*.

certified management accountant. *CMA*.

certified public accountant (CPA). An accountant who has satisfied the statutory and administrative requirements of his or her jurisdiction to be registered or licensed as a public accountant. In addition to passing the Uniform CPA Examination administered by the *AICPA*, the CPA must meet certain educational, experience, and moral requirements that differ from jurisdiction to jurisdiction. The jurisdictions are the 50 states, the District of Columbia, Guam, Puerto Rico, and the Virgin Islands.

CFA. *Chartered Financial Analyst.*

CGA (Certified General Accountant). Canada: an accountant who has satisfied the experience, education, and examination requirements of the Certified General Accountants' Association.

chain discount. A series of *discount* percentages. For example, if a chain discount of 10 and 5 percent is quoted, then the actual, or *invoice*, price is the nominal, or list, price times .90 times .95, or 85.5, percent of invoice price.

change fund. Coins and currency issued to cashiers, delivery drivers, and so on.

changes, accounting. See *accounting changes*.

changes in financial position. See *statement of cash flows*.

channel stuffing. Assume a company's ordinary practices record *revenue* when it ships to customers goods previously ordered. A company engaging in channel-stuffing will ship goods not yet ordered but record them as *sales,* as though a real customer had ordered them. It might even get permission from the customer to ship, saying it will not bill the customer until next period and that the customer will get its usual grace period to pay the bill starting from that later date, next period. Often, sales staff eager to boost their own sales commissions will send a letter to the customer laying out the agreement: the customer will accept the shipment and if asked, confirm that it ordered the goods, but the seller will not send an invoice until later, and the customer need not pay until later or can return the goods. Such a letter is called a "side letter" and even honest managements have a hard time locating these. All a management can do is to be diligent and deal severely with employees found issuing side letters.

charge. As a noun, a *debit* to an account; as a verb, to debit.

charge off. To treat as a *loss* or *expense* an amount originally recorded as an *asset*; use of this term implies that the charge is not in accord with original expectations.

chart of accounts. A list of names and numbers, systematically organized, of *accounts*.

charter. Document issued by a state government authorizing the creation of a corporation.

chartered accountant(s) (CA). The title used in British Commonwealth countries, such as Australia, Canada, India, Scotland and New Zealand, for an accountant who has satisfied the requirements of the institute of his or her jurisdiction to be qualified to serve as a *public accountant*. In the UK other than Scotland, members use the initials ACA or FCA: *A* means Associate and *F* means Fellow; the Associate has less experience than does the Fellow. A partnership of chartered accountants signs its firm name with the letters *CA.* In Canada, each provincial institute or order has the right to administer the examination and set the standards of performance and ethics for Chartered Accountants in its province. For a number of years, however, the provincial organizations

have pooled their rights to qualify new members through the Inter-provincial Education Committee, and the result is that there are nationally set and graded examinations given in English and French. Deviation from the pass/fail grade awarded by the Board of Examiners (a subcommittee of the Inter-provincial Education Committee) is rare.

Chartered Financial Analyst (CFA). A person who has passed three examinations, over at least an 18-month period, covering topics in accounting, economics, financial economics, portfolio management, and security analysis. The Association for Investment Management and Research (AIMR) administers the program though its Institute of Chartered Financial Analysts. Beyond passing examinations, the person needs to have approved working experience and satisfy standards of professional conduct.

check. The Federal Reserve Board defines a check as "a *draft* or order upon a bank or banking house purporting to be drawn upon a deposit of funds for the payment at all events of a certain sum of money to a certain person therein named or to him or his order or to bearer and payable instantly on demand." It must contain the phrase "pay to the order of." The amount shown on the check must be clearly readable, and the check must have the signature of the drawer. The drawer need not date the check. In the accounts, the drawer usually reduces the *balance* in the *cash account* when it issues the check, not later when the check clears the bank. See *remittance advice*.

check register. A *journal* to record *checks* issued.

CIA (Certified Internal Auditor). One who has satisfied certain requirements of the *Institute of Internal Auditors* including experience, ethics, education, and passing examinations.

CICA. *Canadian Institute of Chartered Accountants.*

CIF (cost, insurance, and freight). In contracts, a term used along with the name of a given port, such as New Orleans, to indicate that the quoted price includes insurance, handling, and freight charges up to delivery by the seller at the given port.

circulating capital. *Working capital.*

clean opinion. See *auditor's report*.

clean surplus concept. The notion that all entries to the *retained earnings* account must record *net income* and *dividends*. See *comprehensive income*. Contrast with *current operating performance concept*. This concept, with minor exceptions, now controls *GAAP*. (See *APB Opinions No. 9* and *No. 30*.)

clearing account. An account containing amounts to be transferred to another account(s) before the end of the *accounting period*. Examples are the *income summary* account (whose balance transfers to *retained earnings*) and the purchases account (whose balance transfers to *inventory* or to *cost of goods sold*).

close. As a verb, to transfer the *balance* of a *temporary* or *contra* or *adjunct account* to the main account to which it relates; for example, to transfer *revenue* and *expense* accounts directly, or through the *income summary* account, to an *owners' equity* account or to transfer *purchase discounts* to purchases.

closed account. An *account* with equal *debits* and *credits*, usually as a result of a *closing entry*.

closing entries. The *entries* that accomplish the transfer of balances in *temporary accounts* to the related *balance sheet accounts*. See *work sheet*.

closing inventory. *Ending inventory*.

CMA (Certified Management Accountant) certificate. Awarded by the *Institute of Certified Management Accountants* of the *Institute of Management Accountants* to those who pass a set of examinations and meet certain experience and continuing-education requirements.

CoCoA. *Continuously Contemporary Accounting*.

coding of accounts. The numbering of *accounts*, as for a *chart of accounts*, that is necessary for computerized accounting.

coinsurance. Common condition of insurance policies that protect against hazards such as fire or water damage. These often specify that the owner of the property may not collect the full amount of insurance for a loss unless the insurance policy covers at least some specified "coinsurance" percentage, usually about 80 percent, of the *replacement cost* of the property. Coinsurance clauses induce the owner to carry full, or nearly full, coverage.

COLA. Cost-of-living adjustment. See *indexation*.

collateral. *Assets* pledged by a *borrower* who will surrender those assets if he or she fails to repay a *loan*.

collectible. Capable of being converted into *cash*—now if due, later otherwise.

collusion. Cooperative effort by employees to commit fraud or another unethical act.

combination. See *business combination*.

comfort letter. A letter in which an auditor conveys negative assurances as to unaudited financial statements in a prospectus or draft financial statements included in a preliminary prospectus.

commercial paper. Short-term notes issued by corporate borrowers.

commission. Employee remuneration, usually expressed as a percentage, based on an activity rate, such as sales.

committed costs. *Capacity costs*.

Committee on Accounting Procedure (CAP). Predecessor of the *APB*. The *AICPA's* principles-promulgating body from 1939 through 1959. Its 51 pronouncements are *Accounting Research Bulletins*.

common cost. *Cost* resulting from the use of *raw materials*, a facility (for example, plant or machines), or a service (for example, fire insurance) that benefits several products or departments. A firm must allocate this cost to those products or departments. Common costs result when two or more departments produce multiple products together even though the departments could produce them separately; *joint costs* occur when two or more departments must produce multiple products together. Many writers use "common costs" and "joint costs" synonymously. See *joint cost, indirect costs, overhead;* and *sterilized allocation*.

common-dollar accounting. *Constant-dollar accounting*.

common monetary measuring unit. For U.S. corporations, the dollar. See also *stable monetary unit assumption* and *constant-dollar accounting*.

common shares. *Shares* representing the class of owners who have residual claims on the *assets* and *earnings* of a *corporation* after the firm meets all *debt* and *preferred shareholders'* claims.

common-size statement. A *percentage statement* usually based on total *assets* or *net sales* or *revenues*.

common-stock equivalent. A *security* whose primary value arises from its holder's ability to exchange it for *common shares*; includes *stock options*, *warrants*, and also *convertible bonds* or *convertible preferred stock* whose *effective interest rate* at the time of issue is less than two-thirds the average Aa corporate bond yield. See *bond ratings*.

company-wide control. See *control system*.

comparative (financial) statements. *Financial statements* showing information for the same company for different times, usually two successive years for balance sheets and three for *income* and *cash flow statements*. Nearly all published financial statements are in this form. Contrast with *historical summary*.

compensating balance. The amount required to be left on deposit for a loan. When a bank lends funds to customers, it often requires that the customers keep on deposit in their checking accounts an amount equal to some percentage—say, 20 percent—of the loan. Such amounts effectively increase the *interest rate*. The borrower must disclose the amounts of such balances in *notes* to the *financial statements*.

completed contract method. Recognizing *revenues* and *expenses* for a job or order only when the firm finishes it, except that when the firm expects a loss on the contract, the firm must recognize all revenues and expenses in the period when the firm first foresees a loss. Accountants generally use this term only for long-term contracts. This method is otherwise equivalent to the *sales basis of revenue recognition*.

completed sales basis. See *sales basis of revenue recognition*.

compliance audit. Objectively obtaining and evaluating evidence regarding assertions, actions, and events to ascertain the degree of correspondence between them and established performance criteria.

compliance procedure. An *audit* procedure used to gain evidence as to whether the prescribed internal controls are operating effectively.

composite cost of capital. See *cost of capital.*

composite depreciation or **composite life method.** *Group depreciation* when the items are of unlike kind. The term also applies when the firm depreciates as a whole a single item (for example, a crane, which consists of separate units with differing service lives, such as the chassis, the motor, the lifting mechanism, and so on), rather than treating each of its components separately.

compound entry. A *journal entry* with more than one *debit* or more than one *credit* or both. See *trade-in transaction* for an example.

compound interest. *Interest* calculated on *principal* plus previously undistributed interest.

compound interest depreciation. A method designed to hold the *rate of return* on an asset constant. First find the *internal rate of return* on the cash inflows and outflows of the asset. The periodic depreciation charge equals the cash flow for the period less the internal rate of return multiplied by the asset's book value at the beginning of the period. When the cash flows from the asset are constant over time, usage sometimes refers to the method as the "annuity method" of depreciation.

compounding period. The time period, usually a year or a portion of a year, for which a firm calculates *interest.* At the end of the period, the borrower may pay interest to the lender or may add the interest (that is, convert it) to the principal for the next interest-earning period.

comprehensive budget. *Master budget.*

comprehensive income. Defined in *SFAC No. 3* as "the change in equity (net assets) of an entity during a period from transactions and other events and circumstances from nonowner sources. It includes all changes in equity during a period except those resulting from investments by owners and distributions to owners." In this definition, "equity" means *owners' equity* or *shareholders' equity. SFAS No. 130* requires firms to report comprehensive income as part of a statement showing *earnings* (primarily from realized transactions), comprehensive income (with additions for all other changes in owners' equity, primarily *holding gains and losses* and *foreign exchange gains and losses*), and comprehensive income plus *accounting adjustments.* The *FASB* encourages the discontinuation of the term "net income." The terms "earnings" and "comprehensive income" denote different concepts, with totals different from that of the old "net income." *SFAS No. 130* requires that the firm report comprehensive income in a format having the same prominence as other *financial statements.* We cannot predict which "income total"—earnings or comprehensive income—users of financial statements will focus on. See the accompanying exhibits for two formats the FASB suggests firms use. General Electric uses a different one, harder to follow.

comptroller. Same meaning and pronunciation as *controller.* Modern users, however, tend to use this form for government and not-for-profit entities and *controller* for profit-seeking ones.

conceptual framework. A coherent system of interrelated objectives and fundamentals, promulgated by the *FASB* primarily through its *SFAC* publications, expected to lead to consistent standards for *financial accounting* and reporting.

confidence level. The measure of probability that the actual characteristics of the population lie within the stated precision of the estimate derived from a sampling process. A sample estimate may be expressed in the following terms: "Based on the sample, we are 95 percent sure [confidence level] that the true population value is within the range of X to Y [precision]." See *precision.*

confirmation. A formal memorandum delivered by the customers or suppliers of a company to its independent *auditor* verifying the amounts shown as receivable or payable. The auditor originally sends the confirmation document to the customer. If the auditor asks that the customer return the document whether the *balance* is correct or incorrect, usage calls it a "positive confirmation." If the auditor asks that the customer return the document only if it contains an error, usage calls it a "negative confirmation."

conglomerate. *Holding company.* This term implies that the owned companies operate in dissimilar lines of business.

conservatism. A *reporting objective* that calls for anticipation of all *losses* and *expenses* but defers recognition of *gains* or *profits* until they are *realized* in *arm's-length* transactions. In the absence of certainty, report events to minimize cumulative income. Conservatism does not mean reporting low income in every *accounting period.* Over long-enough time spans, income is cash-in less cash-out. If a (conservative) reporting method shows low income in early periods, it must show higher income in some later period.

consignee. See *on consignment.*

consignment. See *on consignment.*

consignor. See *on consignment.*

consistency. Treatment of like *transactions* in the same way in consecutive periods so that financial statements will be more comparable than otherwise; the reporting policy implying that a reporting *entity*, once it adopts specified procedures, should follow them from period to period. See *accounting changes* for the treatment of inconsistencies.

consol. A *bond* that never matures; a *perpetuity* in the form of a bond; originally issued by Great Britain after the Napoleonic wars to consolidate debt issues of that period. The term arose as an abbreviation for "consolidated annuities."

consolidated financial statements. Statements that are issued by legally separate companies and that show financial position and income as they would appear if the companies were one economic *entity.*

constant dollar. A hypothetical unit of *general purchasing power*, denoted "C$" by the *FASB.*

constant-dollar accounting. Accounting that measures items in *constant dollars.* See *historical cost/constant-dollar accounting* and *current cost/nominal-dollar accounting.*

Reporting Comprehensive Income, Two Allowed Formats

ONE-STATEMENT APPROACH
Statement of Net Income and Comprehensive Income

Revenues		$100,000
Expenses		(25,000)
Gain on Sale of Securities		2,000
Other Gains and Losses		8,000
Earnings from Continuing Operations before Income Tax		$ 85,000
Income Tax Expense		(21,250)
Earnings before Discontinued Operations and Extraordinary Items		$ 63,750
Discontinued Operations, Net of Tax		30,000
Extraordinary Items, Net of Tax		(28,000)
Income before Cumulative Effect of Accounting Change		$ 65,750
Cumulative Effect of Accounting Change, Net of Tax		(2,500)
Net Income (or, as preferred by the FASB, Earnings)		**$ 63,250**
Other Comprehensive Income, Net of Tax:		
Foreign Currency Translation Adjstments		$ 7,000
Unrealized Gains and Losses on Securities:		
Unrealized Holding Gains Arising during Period	$13,000	
Less: Reclassification Adjustment for Gain Included in Net Income (Earnings)	(1,500)	11,500
Minimum Pension Liability Adjustment		(2,500)
Other Comprehensive Income (Loss)		**$ 16,000**
Comprehensive Income (Loss)		**$ 79,250**

TWO-STATEMENT APPROACH
Statement of Net Income

Revenues		$100,000
Expenses		(25,000)
Gain on Sale of Securities		2,000
Other Gains and Losses		8,000
Earnings from Continuing Operations before Income Tax		$ 85,000
Income Tax Expense		(21,250)
Earnings before Discontinued Operations and Extraordinary Items		$ 63,750
Discontinued Operations, Net of Tax		30,000
Extraordinary Items, Net of Tax		(28,000)
Income before Cumulative Effect of Accounting Change		$ 65,750
Cumulative Effect of Accounting Change, Net of Tax		(2,500)
Net Income (or, as preferred by the FASB, Earnings)		**$ 63,250**

Statement of Comprehensive Income

Net Income (or, as preferred by the FASB, Earnings)		**$ 63,250**
Other Comprehensive Income, Net of Tax:		
Foreign Currency Translation Adjstments		$ 7,000
Unrealized Gains and Losses on Securities:		
Unrealized Holding Gains Arising during Period	$13,000	
Less: Reclassification Adjustment for Gain Included in Net Income (Earnings)	(1,500)	11,500
Minimum Pension Liability Adjustment		(2,500)
Other Comprehensive Income (Loss)		**$ 16,000**
Comprehensive Income (Loss)		**$ 79,250**

Sometimes called "general price level–adjusted accounting" or "general purchasing-power accounting."

constant-dollar date. The time at which the *general purchasing power* of one *constant dollar* exactly equals the *general purchasing power* of one *nominal dollar*; that is, the date when C$1 = $1. When the constant-dollar date is midperiod, the nominal amounts of *revenues* and *expenses* spread evenly throughout the period equal their constant-dollar amounts but end-of-period *balance sheet* amounts measured in constant midperiod dollars differ from their nominal-dollar amounts. When the constant-dollar date is at the end of the period, the constant-dollar amounts equal the nominal-dollar amounts on a balance sheet for that date.

constrained share company. Canada: a public company whose *charter* specifies that people who are Canadian citizens or who are corporations resident in Canada must own a prescribed percentage of the shares.

constructive liability. *FASB's* term for an item recorded as an accounting *liability*, which the firm has no obligation to pay but intends to pay. An example is the liability with related *expense* that management establishes for future cash payments for severance payments for employees it intends to discharge in a restructuring.

constructive receipt. An item included in taxable income when the taxpayer can control funds whether or not it has received cash. For example, *interest* added to *principal* in a savings account is constructively received.

Consumer Price Index (CPI). A *price index* computed and issued monthly by the Bureau of Labor Statistics of the U.S. Department of Labor. The index attempts to track the price level of a group of goods and services purchased by the average consumer. The CPI is used in *constant-dollar accounting*.

contingency. A potential *liability*. If a specified event occurs, such as a firm's losing a lawsuit, it would recognize a liability. The notes disclose the contingency, but so long as it remains contingent, it does not appear in the balance sheet. *SFAS No. 5* requires treatment as a contingency until the outcome is "probable" and the amount of payment can be reasonably estimated, perhaps within a range. When the outcome becomes probable (the future event is "likely" to occur) and the firm can reasonably estimate the amount (using the lower end of a range if it can estimate only a range), then the firm recognizes a liability in the accounts, rather than just disclosing it. A *material* contingency may lead to a qualified, "*subject to*" auditor's opinion. Firms do not record *gain* contingencies in the accounts but merely disclose them in notes.

contingent annuity. An *annuity* whose number of payments depends on the outcome of an event whose timing is uncertain at the time the annuity begins; for example, an annuity payable until death of the *annuitant*. Contrast with *annuity certain*.

contingent issue (securities). Securities issuable to specific individuals at the occurrence of some event, such as the firm's attaining a specified level of earnings.

contingent liability. *Contingency*. Avoid this term because it refers to something not (yet) a *liability* on the *balance sheet*.

continuing appropriation. A governmental *appropriation* automatically renewed without further legislative action until altered or revoked or expended.

continuing operations. See *income from continuing operations*.

continuity of operations. The assumption in accounting that the business *entity* will continue to operate long enough to carry out its current plans. The *going-concern assumption*.

continuous budget. A *budget* that adds a future period as the current period ends. This budget, then, always reports on the same number of periods.

continuous compounding. *Compound interest* in which the *compounding period* is every instant of time. See *e* for the computation of the equivalent annual or periodic rate.

continuous flow processing. Mass production of homogeneous products in a continuous flow. Companies manufacturing with continuous flow processes use *process costing* to account for product costs.

continuous improvement. Modern *total quality management (TQM)* practitioners believe that the process of seeking quality is never complete. This attitude reflects that assumption, seeking always to improve activities.

continuous inventory method. The *perpetual inventory* method.

Continuously Contemporary Accounting (CoCoA). A name coined by the Australian theorist Raymond J. Chambers to indicate a combination of *current value accounting* in which the *measuring unit* is *constant dollars* and the *attribute measured* is *exit value*.

contra account. An *account*, such as *accumulated depreciation*, that accumulates subtractions from another account, such as machinery. Contrast with *adjunct account*.

contributed capital. Name for the *owners' equity* account that represents amounts paid in, usually in *cash*, by owners; the sum of the balances in *capital stock* accounts plus *capital contributed in excess of par (or stated) value* accounts. Contrast with *donated capital*.

contributed surplus. An inferior term for *capital contributed in excess of par value*.

contribution approach. *Income statement* preparation method that reports *contribution margin*, by separating *variable costs* from *fixed costs*, in order to emphasize the importance of cost-behavior patterns for purposes of planning and control.

contribution margin. *Revenue* from *sales* less all variable *expenses*. Contrast with *gross margin*.

contribution margin ratio. *Contribution margin* divided by *net sales*; usually measured from the price and cost of a single unit; sometimes measured in total for companies with multiple products.

contribution per unit. Selling price less *variable costs* per unit.

contributory. Said of a *pension plan* in which employees, as well as employers, make payments to a pension *fund*. Note that the provisions for *vesting* apply only to the employer's payments. Whatever the degree of vesting of the employer's payments, employees typically gets back all their payments, with interest, in case of death or other cessation of employment before retirement.

control (controlling) account. A summary *account* with totals equal to those of entries and balances that appear in individual accounts in a *subsidiary ledger*. Accounts Receivable is a control account backed up with an account for each customer. Do not change the balance in a control account unless you make a corresponding change in one of the subsidiary accounts.

control charts. Presentations of warning signals that help management distinguish between random or routine variations in quality and variations that it should investigate. The presentations show the results of statistical process-control measures for a sample, batch or some other unit. These presentations depict variation in a process and its behavior over time. Management specifies an acceptable level of variation and plans to investigate the causes of deviations beyond that level.

control system. A device used by top management to ensure that lower-level management carries out its plans or to safeguard assets. Control designed for a single function within the firm is "operational control"; control designed for autonomous segments that generally have responsibility for both revenues and costs is "divisional control"; control designed for activities of the firm as a whole is "company-wide control." Systems designed for safeguarding *assets* are "internal control" systems.

controllable cost. A *cost* influenced by the way a firm carries out operations. For example, marketing executives control advertising costs. These costs can be *fixed* or *variable*. See *programmed costs* and managed costs.

controlled company. A company in which an individual or corporation holds a majority of the voting shares. An owner can sometimes exercise effective control even though it owns less than 50 percent of the shares.

controller. A title for the chief accountant of an organization; often spelled *comptroller* when used to identify that person in a government or not-for-profit entity.

conversion. The act of exchanging a convertible security for another security.

conversion audit. An examination of changeover procedures, and new accounting procedures and files, that takes place when a significant change in the accounting system (e.g., a change from a manual to a computerized system or a change of computers) occurs.

conversion cost. *Direct labor* costs plus factory *overhead* costs incurred in producing a product; that is, the cost to convert raw materials to finished products. *Manufacturing cost*.

conversion period. *Compounding period;* also, period during which the holder of a *convertible bond* or *convertible preferred stock* can convert it into *common shares*.

convertible bond. A *bond* whose owner may convert it into a specified number of shares of *capital stock* during the *conversion period*.

convertible preferred stock. *Preferred shares* whose owner may convert them into a specified number of *common shares*.

cookie-jar accounting. A name, most prominently used by a chairman of the *SEC,* to indicate the practice of reporting lower *income* in an early period, so that management at its discretion, can report higher income in a later period. Consider, for example, the entry to estimate *warranty costs* for products sold. The *journal entry debits* an *expense account,* reducing income, and *credits* a *liability* account. In some later period, the firm can debit a warranty cost to the liability account, not to an expense account, relieving that later period of the income reduction that an expense would have caused. See *quality of earnings.* Often, users refer to the excess liability amount, the amount in the cookie jar, later available for income enhancement, as a "reserve." See *reserve* for our warnings about using that word in any context.

cooperative. An incorporated organization formed for the benefit of its members (owners), who are either producers or consumers, in order to acquire for them profits or savings that otherwise accrue to middlemen. Members exercise control on the basis of one vote per member.

coproduct. A product sharing production facilities with another product. For example, if an apparel manufacturer produces shirts and jeans on the same line, these are coproducts. Distinguish coproducts from *joint products* and *by-products* that, by their very nature, a firm must produce together, such as the various grades of wood a lumber factory produces.

copyright. Exclusive right granted by the government to an individual author, composer, playwright, or the like for the life of the individual plus 50 years. If a firm receives the copyright, then the right extends 75 years after the original publication. The *economic life* of a copyright can be less than the legal life, such as, for example, the copyright of this book.

core deposit intangible. A bank borrows funds from its customers, called "depositors," who open checking and savings accounts. Those depositors can take out their funds at any time, but usually don't. The amount that depositors leave on deposit for long periods of time are called "core deposits." The bank lends those funds to other customers, called "borrowers," at *interest rates* larger than the amount it pays the depositors for the funds. (For checking accounts, the rate the bank pays depositors is often zero.) The fact that the depositors can remove their funds at any time, but, on average, leave amounts on deposit relatively permanently means that the bank can lend those funds for relatively long periods of time, usually at higher interest rates, than it can charge for shorter-term loans. (See *yield curve.*) The bank's ability to borrow from some customers at a low rate and lend to other customers at a high rate creates wealth for the bank. Bankers and banking analysts call this wealth the "core deposit intangible." It represents an *asset* not recognized in the financial statements by the bank that created with wealth, although some *SEC*

25

commissioners have expressed the thought that accounting should recognize such items as assets. When one bank buys another in a *purchase*, however, it will pay for this asset and will record it as an asset. Usually, the acquiring bank does not use the specific account title "Core Deposit Intangible," but instead uses the account title *Goodwill*.

corner. The control, of a quantity of shares or a commodity, sufficiently large that the holder can control the market price.

corporation. A legal entity authorized by a state to operate under the rules of the entity's *charter*.

correcting entry. An *adjusting entry* that properly records a previously, improperly recorded *transaction*. Do not confuse with entries that correct *accounting errors*.

correction of errors. See *accounting errors*.

cost. The sacrifice, measured by the *price* paid or to be paid, to acquire *goods* or *services*. See *acquisition cost* and *replacement cost*. Terminology often uses "cost" when referring to the valuation of a good or service acquired. When writers use the word in this sense, a cost is an *asset*. When the benefits of the acquisition (the goods or services acquired) expire, the cost becomes an *expense* or *loss*. Some writers, however, use "cost" and "expense" as synonyms. Contrast with *expense*. The word "cost" appears in more than 50 accounting terms, each with sometimes subtle distinctions in meaning. See *cost terminology* for elaboration. Clarity requires that the user include with the word "cost" an adjective or phrase to be clear about intended meaning.

cost accounting. Classifying, summarizing, recording, reporting, and allocating current or predicted *costs;* a subset of *managerial accounting*.

Cost Accounting Standards Board. See *CASB*.

cost accumulation. Bringing together, usually in a single *account*, all *costs* of a specified activity. Contrast with *cost allocation*.

cost allocation. Assigning *costs* to individual products or time periods. Contrast with *cost accumulation*.

cost-based transfer price. A *transfer price* based on *historical costs*.

cost behavior. The functional relation between changes in activity and changes in *cost;* for example: *fixed* versus *variable costs*; *linear* versus *curvilinear cost*.

cost/benefit criterion. Some measure of *costs* compared with some measure of *benefits* for a proposed undertaking. If the costs exceed the benefits, then the analyst judges the undertaking not worthwhile. This criterion will not yield good decisions unless the analyst estimates all costs and benefits flowing from the undertaking.

cost center. A unit of activity for which a firm accumulates *expenditures* and *expenses*.

cost driver. A factor that causes an activity's costs. See *driver* and *activity basis*.

cost driver rate. Rate at which the *cost driver* causes *costs*.

cost-effective. Among alternatives, the one whose benefit, or payoff, per unit of cost is highest; sometimes said of an action whose expected benefits exceed expected costs whether or not other alternatives exist with larger benefit-cost ratios.

cost estimation. The process of measuring the functional relation between changes in activity levels and changes in cost.

cost flow assumption. See *flow assumption*.

cost-flow equation. Beginning Balance + Transfers In = Transfers Out + Ending Balance; BB + TI = TO + EB.

cost flows. Costs passing through various classifications within an entity. See *flow of costs* for a diagram.

cost hierarchy. Categorizes costs according to whether they are *capacity, product, customer, batch* or *unit costs*.

cost method (for investments). In accounting for an investment in the *capital stock* or *bonds* of another company, method in which the firm shows the investment at *acquisition cost* and treats only *dividends* declared or *interest receivable* as *revenue;* not allowed by *GAAP*.

cost method (for treasury stock). The method of showing *treasury stock* in a *contra account* to all other items of *shareholders' equity* in an amount equal to that paid to reacquire the stock.

cost object(ive). Any activity for which management desires a separate measurement of *costs*. Examples include departments, products, and territories.

cost of capital. *Opportunity cost* of funds invested in a business; the rate of return that rational owners require an asset to earn before they will devote that asset to a particular purpose; sometimes measured as the average annual rate that a company must pay for its *equities*. In *efficient capital markets*, this cost is the *discount rate* that equates the expected *present value* of all future cash flows to common shareholders with the market value of common stock at a given time. Analysts often measure the cost of capital by taking a *weighted average* of the firm's *debt* and various *equity securities*. We sometimes call the measurement so derived the "composite cost of capital," and some analysts confuse this measurement of the cost of capital with the cost of capital itself. For example, if the equities of a firm include substantial amounts for the *deferred income tax liability*, the composite cost of capital will underestimate the true cost of capital, the required rate of return on a firm's assets, because the deferred income tax liability has no explicit cost.

cost of goods manufactured. The sum of all costs allocated to products completed during a period, including materials, labor, and *overhead*.

cost of goods purchased. Net purchase price of goods acquired plus costs of storage and delivery to the place where the owner can productively use the items.

cost of goods sold. Inventoriable *costs* that firms *expense* because they sold the units; equals *beginning inventory* plus *cost of goods purchased* or *manufactured* minus *ending inventory*.

cost of sales. Generally refers to *cost of goods sold,* occasionally to *selling expenses*.

cost or market, whichever is lower. See *lower of cost or market*.

cost percentage. One less *markup percentage; cost* of *goods available for sale* divided by selling prices of goods available for sale (when FIFO is used); *cost* of *purchases* divided by selling prices of purchases (when LIFO is used). See *markup* for further detail on inclusions in the calculation of cost percentage.

cost-plus transfer pricing. *Transfer price* equal to the *cost* of the transferred product plus a *markup*.

cost pool. *Indirect cost pool;* groupings or aggregations of costs, usually for subsequent analysis.

cost principle. The *principle* that requires reporting *assets* at *historical* or *acquisition cost*, less accumulated *amortization*.

Cost Terminology: Distinctions among Terms Containing the Word "Cost"

Terms (Synonyms Given in Parentheses)			Distinctions and Comments
			1. The following pairs of terms distinguish the basis measured in accounting.
Historical Cost (Acquisition Cost)	v.	Current Cost	A distinction used in financial accounting. Current cost can be used more specifically to mean replacement cost, net realizable value, or present value of cash flows. "Current cost" is often used narrowly to mean replacement cost.
Historical Cost (Actual Cost)	v.	Standard Cost	The distinction between historical and standard costs arises in product costing for inventory valuation. Some systems record actual costs; others record the standard costs.
			2. The following pairs of terms denote various distinctions among historical costs. For each pair of terms, the sum of the two kinds of costs equals total historical cost used in financial reporting.
Variable Cost	v.	Fixed Cost (Constant Cost)	Distinction used in breakeven analysis and in the design of cost accounting systems, particularly for product costing. See (4), below, for a further subdivision of fixed costs and (5), below, for the economic distinction between marginal and average cost closely paralleling this one.
Traceable Cost	v.	Common Cost (Joint Cost)	Distinction arises in allocating manufacturing costs to product. Common costs are allocated to product, but the allocations are more or less arbitrary. The distinction also arises in preparing segment reports and in separating manufacturing from non-manufacturing costs.
Direct Cost	v.	Indirect Cost	Distinction arises in designing cost accounting systems and in product costing. Direct costs can be traced directly to a cost object (e.g., a product, a responsibility center), whereas indirect costs cannot.
Out-of-Pocket Cost (Outlay Cost; Cash Cost)	v.	Book Cost	Virtually all costs recorded in financial statements require a cash outlay at one time or another. The distinction here separates expenditures to occur in the future from those already made and is used in making decisions. Book costs, such as for depreciation, reduce income without requiring a future outlay of cash. The cash has already been spent. See future cost v. past cost in (5), below.
Incremental Cost (Marginal Cost; Differential Cost)	v.	Unavoidable Cost (Inescapable Cost; Sunk Cost)	Distinction used in making decisions. Incremental cost will be incurred (or saved) if a decision is made to go ahead (or to stop) some activity, but not otherwise. Unavoidable costs will be reported in financial statements whether the decision is made to go ahead or not, because cash has already been spent or committed. Not all unavoidable costs are book costs, as, for example, a salary promised but not yet earned and that will be paid even if a no-go decision is made.
			The economist restricts the term marginal cost to the cost of producing one more unit. Thus the next unit has a marginal cost; the next week's output has an incremental cost. If a firm produces and sells a new product, the related new costs would properly be called incremental, not marginal. If a factory is closed, the costs saved are incremental, not marginal.

(continued on next page)

Terms (Synonyms Given in Parentheses)			Distinctions and Comments
Escapable Cost	v.	Inescapable Cost (Unavoidable Cost)	Same distinction as incremental cost v. unavoidable cost, but this pair is used only when the decision maker is considering stopping something--ceasing to produce a product, closing a factory, or the like. See next pair.
Avoidable Cost	v.	Unavoidable Cost	A distinction sometimes used in discussing the merits of variable and absorption costing. Avoidable costs are treated as product costs and unavoidable costs are treated as period expenses under variable costing.
Controllable Cost	v.	Uncontrollable Cost	The distinction here is used in assigning responsibility and in setting bonus or incentive plans. All costs can be affected by someone in the entity; those who design incentive schemes attempt to hold a person responsible for a cost only if that person can influence the amount of the cost.

3. In each of the following pairs, used in historical cost accounting, the word "cost" appears in one of the terms where "expense" is meant.

Expired Cost	v.	Unexpired Cost	The distinction is between expense and asset.
Product Cost	v.	Period Cost	The terms distinguish product cost from period expense. When a given asset is used, is its cost converted into work in process and then finished goods on the balance sheet until the goods are sold or is it an expense shown on this period's income statement? Product costs appear on the income statement as part of cost of goods sold in the period when the goods are sold. Period expenses appear on the income statement with an appropriate caption for the item in the period when the cost is incurred or recognized.

4. The following subdivisions of fixed (historical) costs are used in analyzing operations. The relation between the components of fixed costs is as follows:

$$
\underbrace{\begin{array}{c}\text{Fixed} \\ \text{Costs}\end{array}}_{\substack{\text{Semifixed}\ +\ \text{Fixed} \\ \text{Costs}\quad\ \text{Portions} \\ +\qquad\text{of} \\ \text{``Pure''}\quad\text{Semi-} \\ \text{Fixed Costs}\ \text{variable} \\ \text{Costs}}} \quad = \quad \underbrace{\begin{array}{c}\text{Capacity} \\ \text{Costs}\end{array}}_{\begin{array}{c}\text{Standby} \\ \text{Costs}\end{array}}\ +\ \underbrace{\begin{array}{c}\text{Programmed} \\ \text{Costs}\end{array}}_{\begin{array}{c}\text{Enabling} \\ \text{Costs}\end{array}}
$$

Capacity Cost (Committed Cost)	v.	Programmed Cost (Managed Cost; Discretionary Cost)	Capacity costs give a firm the capability to produce or to sell Programmed costs, such as for advertising or research and development, may not be essential, but once a decision to incur them is made, they become fixed costs.
Standby Cost	v.	Enabling Cost	Standby costs will be incurred whether capacity, once acquired, is used or not, such as property taxes and depreciation on a factory. Enabling costs, such as for a security force, can be avoided if the capacity is unused.
Semifixed Cost	v.	Semivariable Cost	A cost fixed over a wide range but that can change at various levels is a semifixed cost or "step cost." An example is the cost of rail lines from the factory to the main rail line where fixed cost depends on whether there are one or two parallel lines, but are independent of the number of trains run per day. Semivariable costs combine a strictly fixed component cost plus a variable component. Telephone charges usually have a fixed monthly component plus a charge related to usage.

5. The following pairs of terms distinguish among economic uses or decision-making uses or regulatory uses of cost terms.

Fully Absorbed Cost	v.	Variable Cost (Direct Cost)	Fully absorbed costs refer to costs where fixed costs have been Allocated to units or departments as required by generally accepted accounting principles. Variable costs, in contrast, may be more relevant for making decisions, such as in setting prices.

Terms (Synonyms Given in Parentheses)			Distinctions and Comments
Fully Absorbed Cost	v.	Full Cost	In full costing, all costs, manufacturing costs as well as central corporate expenses (including financing expenses), are allocated to products or divisions. In full absorption costing, only manufacturing costs are allocated to products. Only in full costing will revenues, expenses, and income summed over all products or divisions equal corporate revenues, expenses, and income.
Opportunity Cost	v.	Outlay Cost (Out-of-Pocket Cost)	Opportunity cost refers to the economic benefit forgone by using a resource for one purpose instead of for another. The outlay cost of the resource will be recorded in financial records. The distinction arises because a resource is already in the possession of the entity with a recorded historical cost. Its economic value to the firm, opportunity cost, generally differs from the historical cost; it can be either larger or smaller.
Future Cost	v.	Past Cost	Effective decision making analyzes only present and future outlay costs, or out-of-pocket costs. Opportunity costs are relevant for profit maximizing; past costs are used in financial reporting.
Short-Run Cost	v.	Long-Run Cost	Short-run costs vary as output is varied for a given configuration of plant and equipment. Long-run costs can be incurred to change that configuration. This pair of terms is the economic analog of the accounting pair, see (2) above, variable and fixed costs. The analogy is not perfect because some short-run costs are fixed, such as property taxes on the factory, from the point of view of breakeven analysis.
Imputed Cost	v.	Book Cost	In a regulatory setting some costs, for example the cost of owners' equity capital, are calculated and used for various purposes; these are imputed costs. Imputed costs are not recorded in the historical costs accounting records for financial reporting. Book costs are recorded.
Average Cost	v.	Marginal Cost	The economic distinction equivalent to fully absorbed cost of product and variable cost of product. Average cost is total cost divided by number of units. Marginal cost is the cost to produce the next unit (or the last unit).
Differential Cost Incremental Cost)	v.	Variable Cost	Whether a cost changes or remains fixed depends on the activity basis being considered. Typically, but not invariably, costs are said to be variable or fixed with respect to an activity basis such as changes in production levels. Typically, but not invariably, costs are said to be incremental or not with respect to an activity basis such as the undertaking of some new venture. For example, consider the decision to undertake the production of food processors, rather than food blenders, which the manufacturer has been making. To produce processors requires the acquisition of a new machine tool. The cost of the new machine tool is incremental with respect to a decision to produce food processors instead of food blenders, but, once acquired, becomes a fixed cost of producing food processors. If costs of direct labor hours are going to be incurred for the production of food processors or food blenders, whichever is produced (in a scenario when not both are to be produced), such costs are variable with respect to production measured in units, but not incremental with respect to the decision to produce processors rather than blenders. This distinction is often blurred in practice, so a careful understanding of the activity basis being considered is necessary for understanding of the concepts being used in a particular application.

This principle relies on the assumption that cost equals *fair market value* at the date of acquisition and that subsequent changes are not likely to be significant.

cost-recovery-first method. A method of *revenue* recognition that *credits inventory* as the firm receives cash collections and continues until the firm has collected cash equal to the sum of all costs. Only after the firm has collected cash equal to costs does it recognize *income*. A firm may not use this method in financial reporting unless the total amount of collections is highly uncertain. It is never allowed for income tax reporting. Contrast with the *installment method*, allowed for oth book and tax, in which the firm credits *constant* proportions of each cash collection both to cost and to income.

cost sheet. Statement that shows all the elements composing the total cost of an item.

cost structure. For a given set of total costs, the percentages of fixed and variable costs, typically two percentages adding to 100 percent.

cost terminology. The word "cost" appears in many accounting terms. The accompanying exhibit classifies some of these terms according to the distinctions between the terms in accounting usage. Joel Dean was, to our knowledge, the first to attempt such distinctions; we have used some of his ideas here. We discuss some of the terms in more detail under their own listings.

cost-to-cost. The *percentage-of-completion* method in which the firm estimates the fraction of completion as the ratio of costs incurred to date divided by the total costs the firm expects to incur for the entire project.

cost-volume-profit analysis. A study of the sensitivity of *profits* to changes in units sold (or produced) or costs or prices.

cost-volume-profit graph (chart). A graph that shows the relation between *fixed costs, contribution per unit, breakeven point*, and *sales*. See *breakeven chart*.

costing. The process of calculating the cost of activities, products, or services; the British word for *cost accounting*.

counterparty. The term refers to the opposite party in a legal contract. In accounting and finance, a frequent usage arises when an entity purchases (or sells) a *derivative* financial contract, such as an *option, forward contract*, and *futures contract*.

coupon. That portion of a *bond* document redeemable at a specified date for payments. Its physical form resembles a series of tickets; each coupon has a date, and the holder either deposits it at a bank, just like a check, for collection or mails it to the issuer's agent for collection.

coupon rate. Of a *bond*, the total dollar amount of coupons paid in any one year divided by par value. Contrast with *effective rate*.

covenant. A promise with legal validity. A loan covenant specifies the terms under which the lender can force the borrower to repay funds otherwise not yet due. For example, a *bond* covenant might say that the *principal* of a bond issue falls due on December 31, 2010, unless the firm's *debt-equity ratio* falls below 40 percent, in which case the amount becomes due immediately.

CPA. See *certified public accountant*. The *AICPA* suggests that no periods appear in the abbreviation.

CPI. *Consumer price index*.

CPP. Current purchasing power; usually used, primarily in the UK, as an adjective modifying the word "accounting" to mean the accounting that produces *constant-dollar financial statements*.

Cr. Abbreviation for *credit*, always with initial capital letter. Quiz: what do you suppose *Cr.* stands for? For the answer, see *Dr.*

creative accounting. Selection of *accounting principles* and interpretation of transactions or events designed to manipulate, typically to increase but sometimes merely to smooth, reported *income from continuing operations;* one form of *fraudulent financial reporting*. Many attempts at creative accounting involve premature *revenue recognition*.

credit. As a noun, an entry on the right-hand side of an *account;* as a verb, to make an entry on the right-hand side of an account; records increases in *liabilities, owners' equity, revenues*, and *gains*; records decreases in *assets* and *expenses*. See *debit and credit conventions*. This term also refers to the ability or right to buy or borrow in return for a promise to pay later.

credit bureau. An organization that gathers and evaluates data on the ability of a person to meet financial obligations and sells this information to its clients.

credit loss. The amount of accounts receivable that the firm finds, or expects to find, *uncollectible*.

credit memorandum. A document used by a seller to inform a buyer that the seller is crediting (reducing) the buyer's account receivable because of *errors, returns*, or *allowances;* also, the document provided by a bank to a depositor to indicate that the bank is increasing the depositor's balance because of some event other than a deposit, such as the collection by the bank of the depositor's *note receivable*.

creditor. One who lends. In the UK, *account payable*.

critical accounting judgments. All numbers on a *balance sheet,* except the date, require some judgment or estimate. (The previous sentence passes for a joke in accounting.) The SEC requires that management in its annual report to shareholders identify the accounting issues whose judgments and estimates have potential for significant effect on *earnings* and *financial position*. Examples include *inventory valuation, measurement of goodwill impairment,* accounting for *hedges,* and *revenue recognition*.

critical path method (CPM). A method of *network analysis* in which the analyst estimates normal duration time for each activity within a project. The critical path identifies the shortest completion period based on the most time-consuming sequence of activities from the beginning to the end of the network. Compare *PERT*.

critical success factors. The important things a company must do to be successful; may vary from one company to another.

cross-reference (index). A number placed beside each *account* in a *journal entry* indicating the *ledger* account to which the record keeper posted the entry and placing in the ledger the page number of the journal where the record keeper first recorded the journal entry; used to link the *debit* and *credit* parts of an entry in the ledger accounts back to the original entry in the journal. See *audit trail*.

cross-section analysis. Analysis of *financial statements* of various firms for a single period of time; contrast with *time-series analysis,* in which analysts examine statements of a given firm for several periods of time.

Crown corporation. Canada and UK: a corporation that is ultimately accountable, through a minister of the Crown, to Parliament or a legislature for the conduct of its affairs.

cum div. (dividend). The condition of shares whose quoted market price includes a declared but unpaid dividend. This condition pertains between the declaration date of the dividend and the record date. Compare *ex div. (dividend)*.

cum rights. The condition of securities whose quoted market price includes the right to purchase new securities. Compare *ex rights*.

cumulative dividend. Preferred stock *dividends* that, if not paid, accrue as a commitment that the firm must pay before it can declare dividends to common shareholders.

cumulative preferred shares. *Preferred* shares with *cumulative dividend* rights.

current assets. *Cash* and other *assets* that a firm expects to turn into cash, sell, or exchange within the normal operating cycle of the firm or one year, whichever is longer. One year is the usual period for classifying asset balances on the balance sheet. Current assets include *cash, marketable securities, receivables, inventory,* and *current prepayments*.

current cost. *Cost* stated in terms of current values (of *productive capacity*) rather than in terms of *acquisition cost*. See *net realizable value* and *current selling price*.

current cost accounting. The *FASB's* term for *financial statements* in which the *attribute measured* is *current cost*.

current cost/nominal-dollar accounting. Accounting based on *current cost* valuations measured in *nominal dollars*. Components of *income* include an *operating margin* and *holding gains and losses*.

current exchange rate. The rate at which the holder of one unit of currency can convert it into another at the end of the *accounting period* being reported on or, for *revenues, expenses, gains*, and *losses*, the date of recognition of the transaction.

current exit value. *Exit value*.

current fund. In governmental accounting, a synonym for *general fund*.

current funds. *Cash* and other assets readily convertible into cash; in governmental accounting, funds spent for operating purposes during the current period; includes *general,* special revenue, *debt service,* and *enterprise funds*.

current (gross) margin. See *operating margin based on current costs*.

current liability. A debt or other obligation that a firm must discharge within a short time, usually the *earnings cycle* or one year, normally by expending *current assets*.

current operating performance concept. The notion that reported *income* for a period ought to reflect only ordinary, normal, and recurring operations of that period. A consequence is that *extraordinary* and nonrecurring items are entered directly in the Retained Earnings account. Contrast with *clean surplus concept*. This concept is no longer acceptable. (See *APB Opinion No. 9* and *No. 30*.)

current ratio. Sum of *current assets* divided by sum of *current liabilities*. See *ratio*.

current realizable value. *Realizable value*.

current replacement cost. Of an *asset*, the amount currently required to acquire an identical asset (in the same condition and with the same service potential) or an asset capable of rendering the same service at a current *fair market price*. If these two amounts differ, use the lower. Contrast with *reproduction cost*.

current selling price. The amount for which an *asset* could be sold as of a given time in an *arm's-length* transaction rather than in a forced sale.

current service costs. *Service costs* of a *pension plan*.

current value accounting. The form of accounting in which all assets appear at *current replacement cost (entry value)* or *current selling price* or *net realizable value (exit value)* and all *liabilities* appear at *present value*. Entry and exit values may differ from each other, so theorists have not agreed on the precise meaning of "current value accounting."

current yield. Of a *bond*, the annual amount of *coupons* divided by the current market price of the bond. Contrast with *yield to maturity*.

currently attainable standard cost. *Normal standard cost*.

curvilinear (variable) cost. A continuous, but not necessarily linear (straight-line), functional relation between activity levels and *costs*.

customer-level activities. Work performed to meet the needs of a specific customer, aggregated over all customers.

customer response time. Period that elapses from the moment a customer places an order for a product or requests service to the moment the firm delivers the product or service to the customer.

customers' ledger. The *ledger* that shows *accounts receivable* of individual customers. It is the *subsidiary ledger* for the *control account* Accounts Receivable.

cutoff rate. *Hurdle rate*.

D

data bank. An organized file of information, such as a customer name and address file, used in and kept up-to-date by a processing system.

database. A comprehensive collection of interrelated information stored together in computerized form to serve several applications.

database management system. Generalized software programs used to handle physical storage and manipulation of databases.

days of average inventory on hand. See *ratio*.

days of grace. The days allowed by law or contract for payment of a debt after its due date.

DCF. *Discounted cash flow*.

DDB. *Double declining-balance depreciation*.

debenture bond. A *bond* not secured with *collateral*.

debit. As a noun, an entry on the left-hand side of an *account;* as a verb, to make an entry on the left-hand side of an account; records increases in *assets* and *expenses*; records decreases in *liabilities, owners' equity*, and *revenues*. See *debit and credit conventions*.

debit and credit conventions. The conventional use of the *T-account* form and the rules for debit and credit in *balance sheet accounts* (see below). The equality of the two sides of the *accounting equation* results from recording equal amounts of *debits* and *credits* for each *transaction*.

Any Asset Account

Opening Balance Increase + Dr. Ending Balance	Decrease – Cr.

Any Liability Account

Decrease – Dr.	Opening Balance Increase + Cr. Ending Balance

Any Owners' Equity Account

Decrease – Dr.	Opening Balance Increase + Cr. Ending Balance

Revenue and expense accounts belong to the owners' equity group. The relation and the rules for debit and credit in these accounts take the following form:

Owners' Equity

Decrease – Dr. Expenses		Increase + Cr. Revenues	
Dr. + *	Cr. –	Dr. –	Cr. + *

* Normal balance prior to closing

debit memorandum. A document used by a seller to inform a buyer that the seller is debiting (increasing) the amount of the buyer's *accounts receivable*. Also, the document provided by a bank to a depositor to indicate that the bank is decreasing the depositor's *balance* because of some event other than payment for a *check*, such as monthly service charges or the printing of checks.

debt. An amount owed. The general name for *notes, bonds, mortgages*, and the like that provide evidence of amounts owed and have definite payment dates.

debt capital. *Noncurrent liabilities.* See *debt financing,* and contrast with *equity financing*.

debt-equity ratio. Total *liabilities* divided by total equities. See *ratio*. Some analysts put only total shareholders' equity in the denominator. Some analysts restrict the numerator to *long-term debt*.

debt financing. *Leverage.* Raising *funds* by issuing *bonds, mortgages*, or *notes*. Contrast with *equity financing*.

debt guarantee. See *guarantee*.

debt ratio. *Debt-equity ratio*.

debt service fund. In governmental accounting, a *fund* established to account for payment of *interest* and *principal* on all general-obligation *debt* other than that payable from special *assessments*.

debt service payment. The payment required by a lending agreement, such as periodic coupon payment on a bond or installment payment on a loan or a lease payment. It is sometimes called "interest payment," but this term will mislead the unwary. Only rarely will the amount of a debt service payment equal the interest expense for the period preceding the payment. A debt service payment will always include some amount for interest, but the payment will usually differ from the interest expense.

debt service requirement. The amount of cash required for payments of *interest*, current maturities of *principal* on outstanding *debt*, and payments to *sinking funds* (corporations) or to the debt service fund (governmental).

debtor. One who borrows; in the UK, *account receivable.*

decentralized decision making. Management practice in which a firm gives a manager of a business unit responsibility for that unit's *revenues* and *costs*, freeing the manager to make decisions about prices, sources of supply, and the like, as though the unit were a separate business that the manager owns. See *responsibility accounting* and *transfer price.*

declaration date. Time when the *board of directors* declares a *dividend.*

declining-balance depreciation. The method of calculating the periodic *depreciation* charge by multiplying the *book value* at the start of the period by a constant percentage. In pure declining-balance depreciation, the constant percentage is $1 - \sqrt[n]{s/c}$, where n is the *depreciable life*, s is *salvage value*, and c is *acquisition cost.* See *double declining-balance depreciation.*

deep discount bonds. Said of *bonds* selling much below (exactly how much is not clear) *par value.*

defalcation. Embezzlement.

default. Failure to pay *interest* or *principal* on a *debt* when due.

defeasance. Transaction with the economic effect of *debt retirement* that does not retire the debt. When *interest rates* increase, many firms find that the *market value* of their outstanding *debt* has dropped substantially below its *book value.* In *historical cost accounting* for debt retirements, retiring debt with a *cash* payment less than the book value of the debt results in a gain (generally, an *extraordinary item*). Many firms would like to retire the outstanding debt issues and report the gain. Two factors impede doing so: (1) the gain can be a taxable event generating adverse *income tax* consequences; and (2) the transaction costs in retiring all the debt can be large, in part because the firm cannot easily locate all the debt holders or persuade them to sell back their bonds to the issuer. The process of "defeasance" serves as the economic equivalent to retiring a debt issue while it saves the issuer from experiencing adverse tax consequences and from actually having to locate and retire the bonds. The process works as follows. The debt-issuing firm turns over to an independent trustee, such as a bank, amounts of cash or low-risk government bonds sufficient to make all debt service payments on the outstanding debt, including bond retirements, in return for the trustee's commitment to make all debt service payments. The debt issuer effectively retires the outstanding debt. It debits the liability account, credits Cash or Marketable Securities as appropriate, and credits Extraordinary Gain on Debt Retirement. The trustee can retire debt or make debt service payments, whichever it chooses. For income tax purposes, however, the firm's debt remains outstanding. The firm will have taxable interest *deductions* for its still-outstanding debt and taxable interest *revenue* on the investments held by the trustee for debt ser-

vice. In law, the term "defeasance" means "a rendering null and void." This process renders the outstanding debt economically null and void, without causing a taxable event.

defensive interval. A financial *ratio* equal to the number of days of normal cash *expenditures* covered by *quick assets.* It is defined as follows:

$$\frac{\text{Quick Assets}}{(\text{All Expenses Except Amortization and Others Not Using Funds}/365)}$$

The denominator of the ratio is the cash expenditure per day. Analysts have found this ratio useful in predicting *bankruptcy.*

deferral. The accounting process concerned with past *cash receipts* and *payments*; in contrast to *accrual;* recognizing a liability resulting from a current cash receipt (as for magazines to be delivered) or recognizing an asset from a current cash payment (as for prepaid insurance or a long-term depreciable asset).

deferral method. See *flow-through method* (of accounting for the *investment credit*) for definition and contrast.

deferred annuity. An *annuity* whose first payment occurs sometime after the end of the first period.

deferred asset. *Deferred charge.*

deferred charge. *Expenditure* not recognized as an *expense* of the period when made but carried forward as an *asset* to be *written off* in future periods, such as for advance rent payments or insurance premiums. See *deferral.*

deferred cost. *Deferred charge.*

deferred credit. Sometimes used to indicate *advances from customers.*

deferred debit. *Deferred charge.*

deferred expense. *Deferred charge.*

deferred gross margin. *Unrealized gross margin.*

deferred income. *Advances from customers.*

deferred income tax (liability). An *indeterminate-term liability* that arises when the pretax income shown on the tax return is less than what it would have been had the firm used the same *accounting principles* and *cost basis* for *assets* and *liabilities* in tax returns as it used for financial reporting. *SFAS No. 109* requires that the firm debit income tax *expense* and credit deferred income tax with the amount of the taxes delayed by using accounting principles in tax returns different from those used in financial reports. See *temporary difference, timing difference, permanent difference,* and *installment sales.* If, as a result of temporary differences, cumulative taxable income exceeds cumulative reported income before taxes, the deferred income tax account will have a *debit* balance, which the firm will report as a *deferred charge.*

deferred revenue. Sometimes used to indicate *advances from customers.*

deferred tax. See *deferred income tax.*

deficit. A *debit balance* in the Retained Earnings account; presented on the balance sheet in a *contra account* to shareholders' equity; sometimes used to mean negative *net income* for a period.

defined-benefit plan. A *pension plan* in which the employer promises specific dollar amounts to each eligible employee; the amounts usually depend on a formula that takes into account such things as the employee's earnings, years of employment, and age. The employer adjusts its cash contributions and pension expense to *actuarial* experience in the eligible employee group and investment performance of the pension *fund*. This is sometimes called a "fixed-benefit" pension plan. Contrast with *money purchase plan.*

defined-contribution plan. A *money purchase (pension) plan* or other arrangement, based on formula or discretion, in which the employer makes cash contributions to eligible individual employee *accounts* under the terms of a written plan document. The trustee of the funds in the account manages the funds, and the employee-beneficiary receives at retirement (or at some other agreed time) the amount in the fund. The employer makes no promise about that amount. Profit-sharing pension plans are of this type.

deflation. A period of declining *general price-level changes.*

Delphi technique. Forecasting method in which members of the forecasting group prepare individual forecasts, share them anonymously with the rest of the group, and only then compare forecasts and resolve differences.

demand deposit. *Funds* in a *checking account* at a bank.

demand loan. See *term loan* for definition and contrast.

denial of opinion. Canada: the statement that an *auditor*, for reasons arising in the *audit*, is unable to express an opinion on whether the *financial statement*s provide *fair presentation.*

denominator volume. Capacity measured in the number of units the firm expects to produce this period; when divided into *budgeted fixed costs*, results in fixed costs applied per unit of product.

department(al) allocation. Obtained by first accumulating *costs* in *cost pools* for each department and then, using separate rates, or sets of rates, for each department, allocating from each cost pool to products produced in that department.

dependent variable. See *regression analysis.*

depletion. Exhaustion or *amortization* of a *wasting asset* or *natural resource*. Also see *percentage depletion.*

depletion allowance. See *percentage depletion.*

deposit intangible. See *core deposit intangible.*

deposit, sinking fund. Payments made to a *sinking fund.*

deposit method (of revenue recognition). A method of *revenue* recognition that is the same as the *completed sale* or completed contract method. In some contexts, such as when the customer has the right to return goods for a full refund or in retail land sales, the customer must make substantial payments while still having the right to back out of the deal and receive a refund. When the seller cannot predict with reasonable precision the amount of cash it will ultimately collect and when it will receive cash, the seller must *credit* Deposits, a *liability account*, rather than *revenue*. (In this regard, the accounting differs from that in the completed contract method, in which the account credited offsets the *Work-in-Process* inventory account.) When the *sale* becomes complete, the firm credits a revenue account and *debits* the Deposits account.

deposits (by customers). A *liability* that the firm *credits* when receiving *cash* (as in a bank, or in a grocery store when the customer pays for soda-pop bottles with cash to be repaid when the customer returns the bottles) and when the firm intends to discharge the liability by returning the cash. Contrast with the liability account *Advances from Customers*, which the firm credits on receipt of cash, expecting later to discharge the liability by delivering goods or services. When the firm delivers the goods or services, it credits a *revenue* account.

deposits in transit. Deposits made by a firm but not yet reflected on the *bank statement.*

depreciable cost. That part of the *cost* of an asset, usually *acquisition cost* less *salvage value*, that the firm will charge off over the life of the asset through the process of *depreciation.*

depreciable life. For an *asset*, the time period or units of activity (such as miles driven for a truck) over which the firm allocates the *depreciable cost*. For tax returns, depreciable life may be shorter than estimated *service life.*

depreciation. *Amortization of plant assets*; the process of allocating the cost of an asset to the periods of benefit—the *depreciable life;* classified as a *production cost* or a *period expense*, depending on the asset and whether the firm uses *full absorption* or *variable costing*. Depreciation methods described in this glossary include the *annuity method, appraisal method, composite method, compound interest method, declining-balance method, production method, replacement method, retirement method, straight-line method, sinking fund method*, and *sum-of-the-years'–digits method.*

depreciation reserve. An inferior term for *accumulated depreciation*. See *reserve*. Do not confuse with a replacement *fund.*

derivative (financial instrument). A financial instrument, such as an option to purchase a share of stock, created from another, such as a share of stock; an instrument, such as a *swap,* whose value depends on the value of another asset called the "underlying"—for example, the right to receive the difference between the interest payments on a fixed-rate five-year loan for $1 million and the interest payments on a floating-rate five-year loan for $1 million. To qualify as a derivative under *FASB* rules, *SFAS No. 133*, the instrument has one or more underlyings, and one or more notional amounts or payment provisions or both, it either does not require an initial net investment or it requires one smaller than would be required for other types of contracts expected to have a similar response to changes in market factors, and its terms permit settlement for cash in lieu of physical delivery or the instrument itself trades on an exchange. See also *forward contract* and *futures contract.*

Descartes' rule of signs. In a *capital budgeting* context, a rule that says a series of cash flows will have a nonnegative number of *internal rates of return.* The number equals the number of variations in the sign of the cash flow series or is less than that number by an even integer. Consider the following series of cash flows, the first occurring now and the others at subsequent yearly intervals: –100, –100, +50, +175, –50, +100. The internal rates of return are the numbers for *r* that satisfy the following equation:

$$-100 - \frac{100}{(1+r)} + \frac{50}{(1+r)^2} + \frac{175}{(1+r)^3} - \frac{50}{(1+r)^4} + \frac{100}{(1+r)^5} = 0$$

The series of cash flows has three variations in sign: a change from minus to plus, a change from plus to minus, and a change from minus to plus. The rule says that this series must have either one or three internal rates of return; in fact, it has only one, about 12 percent. But also see *reinvestment rate.*

detection costs. See *appraisal costs.*

detective controls. *Internal controls* designed to detect, or maximize the chance of detection of, errors and other irregularities.

determination. See *determine.*

determine. A term often used (in our opinion, overused) by accountants and those who describe the accounting process. A leading dictionary associates the following meanings with the verb "determine": settle, decide, conclude, ascertain, cause, affect, control, impel, terminate, and decide upon. In addition, accounting writers can mean any one of the following: measure, allocate, report, calculate, compute, observe, choose, and legislate. In accounting, there are two distinct sets of meanings: those encompassed by the synonym "cause or legislate" and those encompassed by the synonym "measure." The first set of uses conveys the active notion of causing something to happen, and the second set of uses conveys the more passive notion of observing something that someone else has caused to happen. An accountant who speaks of cost or income "determination" generally means measurement or observation, not causation; management and economic conditions cause costs and income to be what they are. One who speaks of accounting principles "determination" can mean choosing or applying (as in "determining depreciation charges" from an allowable set) or causing to be acceptable (as in the *FASB*'s "determining" the accounting for *leases*). In the long run, income is cash-in less cash-out, so management and economic conditions "determine" (cause) income to be what it is. In the short run, reported income is a function of accounting principles chosen and applied, so the accountant "determines" (measures) income. A question such as "Who determines income?" has, therefore, no unambiguous answer. The meaning of "an accountant determining acceptable accounting principles" is also vague. Does the clause mean merely choosing one principle from the set of generally acceptable principles, or does it mean using professional judgment to decide that some of the generally accepted principles are not correct under the current circumstances? We try never to use "determine" unless we mean "cause." Otherwise we use "measure," "report," "calculate," "compute," or whatever

specific verb seems appropriate. We suggest that careful writers will always "determine" to use the most specific verb to convey meaning. "Determine" seldom best describes a process in which those who make decisions often differ from those who apply technique. The term *predetermined (factory) overhead rate* contains an appropriate use of the word.

development stage enterprise. As defined in *SFAS No. 7*, a firm whose planned principal *operations* have not commenced or, having commenced, have not generated significant *revenue*. The financial statements should identify such enterprises, but no special *accounting principles* apply to them.

diagnostic signal. See *warning signal* for definition and contrast.

differentiable cost. The cost increments associated with infinitesimal changes in volume. If a total cost curve is smooth (in mathematical terms, differentiable), then we say that the curve graphing the derivative of the total cost curve shows differentiable costs.

differential. An adjective used to describe the change (increase or decrease) in a *cost, expense, investment, cash flow, revenue, profit,* and the like as the firm produces or sells one or more additional (or fewer) units or undertakes (or ceases) an activity. This term has virtually the same meaning as *incremental*, but if the item declines, "decremental" better describes the change. Contrast with *marginal*, which means the change in cost or other item for a small (one unit or even less) change in number of units produced or sold.

differential analysis. Analysis of *differential costs, revenues, profits, investment, cash flow,* and the like.

differential cost. See *differential.*

differential cost analysis. See *relevant cost analysis.*

dilution. A potential reduction in *earnings per share* or *book value* per share by the potential *conversion* of securities or by the potential exercise of *warrants* or *options.*

dilutive. Said of a *security* that will reduce *earnings per share* if it is exchanged for *common shares.*

dip(ping) into LIFO layers. See *LIFO inventory layer.*

direct access. Access to computer storage where information can be located directly, regardless of its position in the storage file. Compare *sequential access.*

direct cost. Cost of *direct material* and *direct labor* incurred in producing a product. See *prime cost.* In some accounting literature, writers use this term to mean the same thing as *variable cost.*

direct costing. Another, less-preferred, term for *variable costing.*

direct-financing (capital) lease. See *sales-type (capital) lease* for definition and contrast.

direct labor (material) cost. Cost of labor (material) applied and assigned directly to a product; contrast with *indirect labor (material).*

direct labor variance. Difference between actual and *standard direct labor* allowed.

direct method. See *statement of cash flows*.

direct posting. A method of bookkeeping in which the firm makes *entries* directly in *ledger accounts*, without using a *journal*.

direct write-off method. See *write-off method*.

disbursement. Payment by *cash* or by *check*. See *expenditure*.

DISC (domestic international sales corporation). A U.S. *corporation*, usually a *subsidiary*, whose *income* results primarily from exports. The parent firm usually defers paying *income tax* on 50 percent of a DISC's income for a long period. Generally, this results in a lower overall corporate tax for the *parent* than would otherwise be incurred.

disclaimer of opinion. An *auditor's report* stating that the auditor cannot give an opinion on the *financial statements*. Usually results from *material* restrictions on the scope of the audit or from material uncertainties, which the firm has been unable to resolve by the time of the audit, about the accounts.

disclosure. The showing of facts in *financial statements, notes* thereto, or the *auditor's report*.

discontinued operations. See *income from discontinued operations*.

discount. In the context of *compound interest, bonds* and *notes*, the difference between *face amount* (or *future value*) and *present value* of a payment; in the context of *sales* and *purchases*, a reduction in price granted for prompt payment. See also *chain discount, quantity discount*, and *trade discount*.

discount factor. The reciprocal of one plus the *discount rate*. If the discount rate is 10 percent per period, the discount factor for three periods is $1/(1.10)^3 = (1.10)^{-3} = 0.75131$.

discount rate. *Interest rate* used to convert future payments to *present values*.

discounted bailout period. In a *capital budgeting* context, the total time that must elapse before discounted value of net accumulated cash flows from a project, including potential *salvage value* at various times of assets, equals or exceeds the *present value* of net accumulated cash outflows. Contrast with *discounted payback period*.

discounted cash flow (DCF). Using either the *net present value* or the *internal rate of return* in an analysis to measure the value of future expected cash *expenditures* and *receipts* at a common date. In discounted cash flow analysis, choosing the alternative with the largest *internal rate of return* may yield wrong answers given *mutually exclusive projects* with differing amounts of initial investment for two of the projects. Consider, to take an unrealistic example, a project involving an initial investment of $1, with an *IRR* of 60 percent, and another project involving an initial investment of $1 million, with an IRR of 40 percent. Under most conditions, most firms will prefer the second project to the first, but choosing the project with the larger IRR will lead to undertaking the first, not the

second. Usage calls this shortcoming of choosing between alternatives based on the magnitude of the internal rate of return, rather than based on the magnitude of the *net present value* of the cash flows, the "scale effect."

discounted payback period. The shortest amount of time that must elapse before the discounted *present value* of cash inflows from a project, excluding potential *salvage value*, equals the discounted present value of the cash outflows.

discounting a note. See *note receivable discounted* and *factoring*.

discounts lapsed (lost). The sum of *discounts* offered for prompt payment that the purchaser did not take because the discount period expired. See *terms of sale*.

discovery sampling. Acceptance sampling in which the analyst accepts an entire population if and only if the sample contains no disparities.

discovery value accounting. See *reserve recognition accounting*.

discretionary cost center. See *engineered cost center* for definition and contrast.

discretionary costs. *Programmed costs*.

Discussion Memorandum. A neutral discussion of all the issues concerning an accounting problem of current concern to the *FASB*. The publication of such a document usually signals that the FASB will consider issuing an *SFAS* or *SFAC* on this particular problem. The discussion memorandum brings together material about the particular problem to facilitate interaction and comment by those interested in the matter. A public hearing follows before the FASB will issue an *Exposure Draft*.

dishonored note. A *promissory note* whose maker does not repay the loan at *maturity*, for a *term loan*, or on demand, for a *demand loan*.

disintermediation. Moving funds from one interest-earning account to another, typically one promising a higher rate. Federal law regulates the maximum *interest rate* that both banks and savings-and-loan associations can pay for *time deposits*. When free-market interest rates exceed the regulated interest ceiling for such time deposits, some depositors withdraw their funds and invest them elsewhere at a higher interest rate. This process is known as "disintermediation."

distributable income. The portion of conventional accounting net income that the firm can distribute to owners (usually in the form of *dividends*) without impairing the physical capacity of the firm to continue operations at current levels. Pretax distributable income is conventional pretax income less the excess of *current cost* of goods sold and *depreciation* charges based on the replacement cost of *productive capacity* over cost of goods sold and depreciation on an *acquisition cost basis*. Contrast with *sustainable income*. See *inventory profit*.

distributable surplus. Canada and UK: the statutory designation to describe the portion of the proceeds of the issue of shares without *par value* not allocated to share capital.

distributed processing. Processing in a computer information network in which an individual location processes data relevant to it while the operating system transmits information required elsewhere, either to the central computer or to another local computer for further processing.

distribution expense. *Expense* of selling, advertising, and delivery activities.

dividend. A distribution of assets generated from *earnings* to owners of a corporation. The firm may distribute cash (cash dividend), stock (stock dividend), property, or other securities (dividend in kind). Dividends, except stock dividends, become a legal liability of the corporation when the corporation's board declares them. Hence, the owner of stock ordinarily recognizes *revenue* when the board of the corporation declares the dividend, except for stock dividends. See also *liquidating dividend* and *stock dividend*.

dividend yield. *Dividends* declared for the year divided by market price of the stock as of the time for which the analyst computes the yield.

dividends in arrears. Dividends on *cumulative preferred stock* that the corporation's board has not yet declared in accordance with the preferred stock contract. The corporation must usually clear such arrearages before it can declare dividends on *common shares*.

dividends in kind. See *dividend*.

division. A more or less self-contained business unit that is part of a larger family of business units under common control.

divisional control. See *control system*.

divisional reporting. See *segment reporting*.

division return on investment (ROI). Equals the *division profit* divided by the investment in the division.

dollar sign rules. In accounting statements or schedules, place a dollar sign beside the first figure in each column and beside any figure below a horizontal line drawn under the preceding figure.

dollar-value LIFO method. A form of *LIFO* inventory accounting with inventory quantities (*layers*) measured in dollar, rather than physical, terms. The method adjusts for changing prices by using specific price indexes appropriate for the kinds of items in the inventory.

domestic international sales corporation. See *DISC*.

donated capital. A *shareholders' equity* account credited when the company receives gifts, such as land or buildings, without issuing shares or other owners' equity interest in return. A city might donate a plant site hoping the firm will build a factory and employ local residents. Do not confuse with *contributed capital*.

double declining-balance depreciation (DDB). *Declining-balance depreciation* in which the constant percentage used to multiply by book value in computing the depreciation charge

for the year is $2/n$, where n is the *depreciable life* in periods. Omit *salvage value* from the depreciable amount. Thus if the asset cost $100 and has a depreciable life of five years, the depreciation in the first year would be $40 = 2/5 \times \$100$, in the second year would be $24 = 2/5 (\$100 - \$40)$, and in the third year would be $14.40 = 2/5 (\$100 - \$40 - \$24)$. By the fourth year, the remaining undepreciated cost could be depreciated under the straight-line method at $10.80 = 1/2 \times (\$100 - \$40 - \$24 - \$14.40)$ per year for tax purposes. Note that salvage value does not affect these computations except that the method will not depreciate the book value below salvage value.

double entry. In recording transactions, a system that maintains the equality of the accounting equation or the balance sheet. Each entry results in recording equal amounts of *debits* and *credits*.

double taxation. Occurs when the taxing authority (U.S. or state) taxes corporate income as earned (first tax) and then the same taxing authority taxes the aftertax income, distributed to owners as dividends, again as personal income tax (second tax).

doubtful accounts. *Accounts receivable* that the firm estimates to be *uncollectible*.

Dr. The abbreviation for *debit*, always with the initial capital letter. *Dr.* is a shortened from of the word *debitor*, and *Cr.* comes from the word *creditor*. In the early days of double-entry record keeping in the UK, the major asset was accounts receivable, called *creditors*, and the major liability was accounts payable, called *debitors*. Thus the *r* in *Cr.* does not refer to the *r* in *credit* but to the second *r* in *creditor*.

draft. A written order by the first party, called the drawer, instructing a second party, called the drawee (such as a bank) to pay a third party, called the payee. See also *check, cashier's check, certified check, NOW account, sight draft*, and *trade acceptance*.

drawee. See *draft*.

drawer. See *draft*.

drawing account. A *temporary account* used in *sole proprietorships* and *partnerships* to record payments to owners or partners during a period. At the end of the period, the firm closes the drawing account by crediting it and debiting the owner's or partner's share of income or, perhaps, his or her capital account.

drawings. Payments made to a *sole proprietor* or to a *partner* during a period. See *drawing account*.

driver, cost driver. A cause of costs incurred. Examples include processing orders, issuing an engineering change order, changing the production schedule, and stopping production to change machine settings. The notion arises primarily in product costing, particularly *activity-based costing*.

drop ship(ment). Occurs when a distributor asks a manufacturer to send an order directly to the customer (ordinarily a manufacturer sends goods to a distributor, who sends the goods to its customer). Usage calls the shipment a "drop shipment" and refers to the goods as "drop shipped."

dry-hole accounting. See *reserve recognition accounting* for definition and contrast.

dual-transactions assumption (fiction). Occurs when an analyst, in understanding cash flows, views transactions not involving *cash* as though the firm first generated cash and then used it. For example, the analyst might view the issue of *capital stock* in return for the *asset* land as though the firm issued stock for *cash* and then used cash to acquire the land. Other examples of transactions that could involve the dual-transaction assumption are the issue of a *mortgage* in return for a noncurrent asset and the issue of stock to bondholders on *conversion* of their *convertible bonds*.

dual transfer prices. Occurs when the *transfer price charged* to the buying *division* differs from that *credited* to the selling division. Such prices make sense when the selling division has excess capacity and, as usual, the *fair market value* exceeds the *incremental cost* to produce the goods or services being transferred.

duality. The *double entry* record-keeping axiom that every *transaction* must result in equal *debit* and *credit* amounts.

dumping. A foreign firm's selling a good or service in the United States at a price below market price at home or, in some contexts, below some measure of cost (which concept is not clearly defined). The practice is illegal in the United States if it harms (or threatens to harm) a U.S. industry.

E

e. The base of natural logarithms; 2.71828.... If *interest* compounds continuously during a period at stated rate of *r* per period, then the effective *interest rate* is equivalent to interest compounded once per period at rate *i* where $i = e^r - 1$. Tables of e^r are widely available. If 12 percent annual interest compounds continuously, the effective annual rate is $e^{.12} - 1 = 12.75$ percent. Interest compounded continuously at rate *r* for *d* days is $e^{rd/365} - 1$. For example, interest compounded for 92 days at 12 percent is $e^{.12 \times 92/365} - 1 = 3.07$ percent.

earn-out. For two merging firms, an agreement in which the amount paid by the acquiring firm to the acquired firm's shareholders depends on the future earnings of the acquired firm or, perhaps, of the *consolidated entity*.

earned surplus. A term that writers once used, but no longer use, for *retained earnings*.

earnings. A term with no precise meaning but used to mean *income* or sometimes *profit*. The *FASB*, in requiring that firms report *comprehensive income*, encouraged firms to use the term "earnings" for the total formerly reported as *net income*. Firms will likely only slowly change from using the term "net income" to the term "earnings."

earnings, retained. See *retained earnings*.

earnings cycle. The period of time, or the series of transactions, during which a given firm converts *cash* into *goods* and services, then sells goods and services to customers, and finally collects cash from customers. *Cash cycle*.

earnings per share (of common stock). *Net income* to common shareholders (net income minus *preferred dividends)* divided by the average number of *common shares* outstanding; see also *primary earnings per share* and *fully diluted earnings per share*. See *ratio*.

earnings per share (of preferred stock). *Net income* divided by the average number of *preferred shares* outstanding during the period. This ratio indicates how well income covers (or protects) the preferred dividends; it does not indicate a legal share of *earnings*. See *ratio*.

earnings statement. *Income statement.*

easement. The acquired right or privilege of one person to use, or have access to, certain property of another. For example, a public utility's right to lay pipes or lines under the property of another and to service those facilities.

EBIT. *Earnings* before *interest and (income) taxes;* acronym used by analysts.

EBITDA. *Earnings* before *interest, (income) taxes, depreciation,* and *amortization;* acronym used by analysts to focus on a particular measure of *cash flow* used in valuation. This is not the same as, but is similar in concept to, *cash flow from operations.* Some analysts exclude *nonrecurring* items from this total.

economic consequences. The *FASB* says that in setting *accounting principles,* it should take into account the real effects on various participants in the business world. It calls these effects "economic consequences."

economic depreciation. Decline in *current cost* (or *fair value)* of an *asset* during a period.

economic entity. See *entity*.

economic life. The time span over which the firm expects to receive the benefits of an *asset*. The economic life of a *patent, copyright,* or *franchise* may be less than the legal life. *Service life.*

economic order quantity (EOQ). In mathematical *inventory* analysis, the optimal amount of stock to order when demand reduces inventory to a level called the "reorder point." If *A* represents the *incremental cost* of placing a single order, *D* represents the total demand for a period of time in units, and *H* represents the incremental holding cost during the period per unit of inventory, then the economic order quantity is $EOQ = \sqrt{2AD/H}$. Usage sometimes calls *EOQ* the "optimal lot size."

economic transfer pricing rule. Transfer at the *differential outlay cost* to the selling division (typically *variable costs),* plus the *opportunity cost* to the company of making the internal transfers (\$0 if the seller has idle capacity, or selling price minus variable costs if the seller is operating at capacity).

economic value added (EVA®). The amount of earnings generated above the cost of funds invested to generate those earnings. To calculate economic value added, find the difference between (the net after-tax operating profit) and (the product of the weighted-average cost of capital multiplied by the investment in the economic unit).

ED. *Exposure Draft.*

EDGAR. Electronic Data, Gathering, Analysis, and Retrieval system; rules and systems adopted by the *SEC* in 1993 to ensure that all the paperwork involved in the filings submitted by more than 15,000 public companies are electronically submitted.

EDP. *Electronic data processing.*

effective interest method. In computing *interest expense* (or *revenue*), a systematic method that makes the interest expense (revenue) for each period divided by the amount of the net *liability (asset)* at the beginning of the period equal to the *yield rate* on the liability (asset) at the time of issue (acquisition). Interest for a period is the yield rate (at time of issue) multiplied by the net liability (asset) at the start of the period. The *amortization* of discount or premium is the *plug* to give equal *debits* and *credits.* (Interest expense is a debit, and the amount of debt service payment is a credit.)

effective (interest) rate. Of a liability such as a bond, the *internal rate of return* or *yield to maturity* at the time of issue. Contrast with *coupon rate.* If the borrower issues the bond for a price below *par*, the effective rate is higher than the coupon rate; if it issues the bond for a price greater than par, the effective rate is lower than the coupon rate. In the context of *compound interest*, the effective rate occurs when the *compounding period* on a *loan* differs from one year, such as a nominal interest rate of 12 percent compounded monthly. The effective interest is the single rate that one could use at the end of the year to multiply the *principal* at the beginning of the year and give the same amount as results from compounding interest each period during the year. For example, if 12 percent per year compounds monthly, the effective annual interest rate is 12.683 percent. That is, if you compound $100 each month at 1 percent per month, the $100 will grow to $112.68 at the end of the year. In general, if the nominal rate of *r* percent per year compounds *m* times per year, then the effective rate is $(1 + r/m)^m - 1$.

efficiency variance. A term used for the *quantity variance* for materials or labor or *variable overhead* in a *standard costing system.*

efficient capital market. A market in which security prices reflect all available information and react nearly instantaneously and in an unbiased fashion to new information.

efficient market hypothesis. The finance supposition that security prices trade in *efficient capital markets.*

EITF. *Emerging Issues Task Force.*

electronic data processing. Performing computations and other data-organizing steps in a computer, in contrast to doing these steps by hand or with mechanical calculators.

eligible. Under income tax legislation, a term that restricts or otherwise alters the meaning of another tax or accounting term, generally to signify that the related assets or operations may receive a specified tax treatment.

eliminations. In preparing *consolidated statements, work sheet* entries made to avoid duplicating the amounts of *assets, liabilities, owners' equity, revenues*, and *expenses* of the consolidated *entity* when the firm sums the accounts of the *parent* and *subsidiaries.*

Emerging Issues Task Force (EITF). A group convened by the *FASB* to deal more rapidly with accounting issues than the FASB's due-process procedures can allow. The task force comprises about 20 members from public accounting, industry, and several trade associations. It meets every six weeks. Several FASB board members usually attend and participate. The chief accountant of the *SEC* has indicated that the SEC will require that published financial statements follow guidelines set by a consensus of the EITF. The EITF requires that nearly all its members agree on a position before that position receives the label of "consensus." Such positions appear in *Abstracts of the EITF*, published by the FASB. Since 1984, the EITF has become one of the promulgators of *GAAP.*

employee stock option. See *stock option.*

Employee Stock Ownership Trust (or Plan). See *ESOT.*

employer, employee payroll taxes. See *payroll taxes.*

enabling costs. A type of *capacity cost* that a firm will stop incurring if it shuts down operations completely but will incur in full if it carries out operations at any level. Examples include costs of a security force or of a quality-control inspector for an assembly line. Contrast with *standby costs.*

encumbrance. In governmental accounting, an anticipated *expenditure* or *funds* restricted for an anticipated expenditure, such as for outstanding purchase orders. *Appropriations* less expenditures less outstanding encumbrances yields unencumbered balance.

ending inventory. The *cost* of *inventory* on hand at the end of the *accounting period;* often called "closing inventory." Ending inventory from the end of one period becomes the *beginning inventory* for the next period.

endorsee. See *endorser.*

endorsement. See *draft.* The *payee* signs the draft and transfers it to a fourth party, such as the payee's bank.

endorser. A *note* or *draft payee,* who signs the note after writing "Pay to the order of X," transfers the note to person X, and presumably receives some benefit, such as cash, in return. Usage refers to person X as the "endorsee." The endorsee then has the rights of the payee and may in turn become an endorser by endorsing the note to another endorsee.

engineered cost center. Responsibility center with sufficiently well-established relations between inputs and outputs that the analyst, given data on inputs, can predict the outputs or, conversely, given the outputs, can estimate the amounts of inputs that the process should have used. Consider the relation between pounds of flour (input) and loaves of bread (output). Contrast discretionary cost center, where such relations are so imprecise that analysts have no reliable way to relate inputs to outputs. Consider the relation between advertising the corporate logo or trademark (input) and future revenues (output).

engineering method (of cost estimation). To estimate unit cost of product from study of the materials, labor, and *overhead* components of the production process.

enterprise. Any business organization, usually defining the accounting *entity*.

enterprise fund. A *fund* that a governmental unit establishes to account for acquisition, operation, and maintenance of governmental services that the government intends to be self-supporting from user charges, such as for water or airports and some toll roads.

entity. A person, *partnership, corporation*, or other organization. The *accounting entity* that issues accounting statements may not be the same as the entity defined by law. For example, a *sole proprietorship* is an accounting entity, but the individual's combined business and personal assets are the legal entity in most jurisdictions. Several affiliated corporations may be separate legal entities but issue *consolidated financial statements* for the group of companies operating as a single economic entity.

entity theory. The corporation view that emphasizes the form of the *accounting equation* that says *assets = equities*. Contrast with *proprietorship theory*. The entity theory focuses less on the distinction between *liabilities* and *shareholders' equity* than does the proprietorship theory. The entity theory views all equities as coming to the corporation from outsiders who have claims of differing legal standings. The entity theory implies using a *multiple-step* income statement.

entry value. The *current cost* of acquiring an asset or service at a *fair market price. Replacement cost.*

EOQ. *Economic order quantity.*

EPS. *Earnings per share.*

EPVI. *Excess present value index.*

equalization reserve. An inferior title for the allowance or *estimated liability* account when the firm uses the *allowance method* for such things as maintenance expenses. Periodically, the accountant will debit maintenance *expense* and credit the allowance. As the firm makes *expenditures* for maintenance, it will debit the allowance and credit cash or the other asset used in maintenance.

equities. *Liabilities* plus *owners' equity*. See *equity*.

equity. A claim to *assets*; a source of assets. *SFAC No. 3* defines equity as "the residual interest in the assets of an entity that remains after deducting its liabilities." Thus, many knowledgeable people use "equity" to exclude liabilities and count only owners' equities. We prefer to use the term to mean all liabilities plus all owners' equity because there is no other single word that serves this useful purpose. We fight a losing battle.

equity financing. Raising *funds* by issuing *capital stock*. Contrast with *debt financing*.

equity method. In accounting for an *investment* in the stock of another company, a method that debits the proportionate share of the earnings of the other company to the investment account and credits that amount to a *revenue* account as earned.

When the investor receives *dividends*, it debits *cash* and credits the investment account. An investor who owns sufficient shares of stock of an unconsolidated company to exercise significant control over the actions of that company must use the equity method. It is one of the few instances in which the firm recognizes revenue without an increase in *working capital*.

equity ratio. *Shareholders' equity* divided by total *assets*. See *ratio*.

equivalent production. *Equivalent units*.

equivalent units (of work). The number of units of completed output that would require the same costs that a firm would actually incur for the production of completed and partially completed units during a period. For example, if at the beginning of a period the firm starts 100 units and by the end of the period has incurred costs for each of these equal to 75 percent of total costs to complete the units, then the equivalent units of work for the period would be 75. This is used primarily in *process costing* calculations to measure in uniform terms the output of a continuous process.

ERISA (Employee Retirement Income Security Act of 1974). The federal law that sets most *pension plan* requirements.

error accounting. See *accounting errors*.

escalator clause. Inserted in a purchase or rental contract, a clause that permits, under specified conditions, upward adjustments of price.

escapable cost. *Avoidable cost*.

ESOP (Employee Stock Ownership Plan). See *ESOT*.

ESOT (Employee Stock Ownership Trust). A trust *fund* that is created by a corporate employer and that can provide certain tax benefits to the corporation while providing for employee stock ownership. The corporate employer can contribute up to 25 percent of its payroll per year to the trust. The corporation may deduct the amount of the contribution from otherwise taxable income for federal *income tax* purposes. The trustee of the assets must use them for the benefit of employees—for example, to fund death or retirement benefits. The assets of the trust are usually the *common shares,* sometimes nonvoting, of the corporate employer. For an example of the potential *tax shelter*, consider the case of a corporation with $1 million of *debt* outstanding, which it wants to retire, and an annual payroll of $2 million. The corporation sells $1 million of common stock to the ESOT. The ESOT borrows $1 million with the loan guaranteed by, and therefore a *contingency* of, the corporation. The corporation uses the $1 million proceeds of the stock issue to retire its outstanding debt. (The debt of the corporation has been replaced with the debt of the ESOT.) The corporation can contribute $500,000 (= .25 × $2 million payroll) to the ESOT each year and treat the contribution as a deduction for tax purposes. After a little more than two years, the ESOT has received sufficient funds to retire its loan. The corporation has effectively repaid its original $1 million debt with pretax dollars. Assuming an income tax rate of 40 percent, it has saved $400,000 (= .40 × $1 million) of aftertax dollars *if* the $500,000 expense for the contribution to the ESOT for the pension benefits of employees would have been made, in one form or another, anyway. Observe that the corporation could use the proceeds ($1 million in the example) of the stock issued to the ESOT for any of several different purposes: financing expansion, replacing plant assets, or acquiring another company. Basically this same form of pretax-dollar financing through pensions is available with almost any corporate pension plan, with one important exception. The trustees of an ordinary pension trust must invest the assets prudently, and if they do not, they are personally liable to the employees. Current judgment about prudent investment requires diversification—trustees should invest pension trust assets in a wide variety of investment opportunities. (The trustee may not ordinarily invest more than 10 percent of a pension trust's assets in the parent's common stock.) Thus the ordinary pension trust cannot, in practice, invest all, or even most, of its assets in the parent corporation's stock. This constraint does not apply to the investments of an ESOT. The trustee may invest all ESOT assets in the parent company's stock. The ESOT also provides a means for closely held corporations to achieve wider ownership of shares without *going public*. The laws enabling ESOTs provide for the independent professional appraisal of shares not traded in public markets and for transactions between the corporation and the ESOT or between the ESOT and the employees to be based on the appraised values of the shares.

estate planning. The arrangement of an individual's affairs to facilitate the passage of assets to beneficiaries and to minimize taxes at death.

estimated expenses. See *after cost*.

estimated liability. The preferred terminology for estimated costs the firm will incur for such uncertain things as repairs under *warranty*. An estimated liability appears on the *balance sheet*. Contrast with *contingency*.

estimated revenue. A term used in governmental accounting to designate revenue expected to accrue during a period independent of whether the government will collect it during the period. The governmental unit usually establishes a *budgetary account* at the beginning of the budget period.

estimated salvage value. Synonymous with *salvage value* of an *asset* before its retirement.

estimates, changes in. See *accounting changes*.

estimation sampling. The use of sampling technique in which the sampler infers a qualitative (e.g., fraction female) or quantitative (e.g., mean weight) characteristic of the population from the occurrence of that characteristic in the sample drawn. See *attribute(s) sampling*; *variables sampling*.

EURL (entreprise unipersonnelle à responsabilité limitée). France: similar to *SARL* but having only one shareholder.

ex div. (dividend). Said of *shares* whose market price quoted in the market has been reduced by a *dividend* already declared but not yet paid. The *corporation* will send the dividend to the person who owned the share on the *record date*. One who buys the share ex dividend will not receive the dividend although the corporation has not yet paid it.

ex rights. The condition of securities whose quoted market price no longer includes the right to purchase new securities, such rights having expired or been retained by the seller. Compare *cum rights*.

except for. Qualification in *auditor's report*, usually caused by a change, approved by the auditor, from one acceptable accounting principle or procedure to another.

excess present value. In a *capital budgeting* context, *present value* (of anticipated net cash inflows minus cash outflows including initial cash outflow) for a project. The analyst uses the *cost of capital* as the *discount rate*.

excess present value index. *Present value* of future *cash* inflows divided by initial cash outlay.

exchange. The generic term for a transaction (or, more technically, a reciprocal transfer) between one entity and another; in another context, the name for a market, such as the New York Stock Exchange.

exchange gain or loss. The phrase used by the *FASB* for *foreign exchange gain or loss*.

exchange rate. The *price* of one country's currency in terms of another country's currency. For example, the British pound sterling might be worth U.S.$1.60 at a given time. The exchange rate would be stated as "one pound is worth one dollar and sixty cents" or "one dollar is worth £.625" (= £1/$1.60).

excise tax. Tax on the manufacture, sale, or consumption of a commodity.

executory contract. A mere exchange of promises; an agreement providing for payment by a payor to a payee on the performance of an act or service by the payee, such as a labor contract. Accounting does not recognize benefits arising from executory contracts as *assets*, nor does it recognize obligations arising from such contracts as *liabilities*. See *partially executory contract*.

exemption. A term used for various amounts subtracted from gross income in computing taxable income. Usage does not call all such subtractions "exemptions." See *tax deduction*.

exercise. Occurs when owners of an *option* or *warrant* purchase the security that the option entitles them to purchase.

exercise price. See *option*.

exit value. The proceeds that would be received if assets were disposed of in an *arm's-length transaction. Current selling price; net realizable value*.

expectancy theory. The notion that people act in ways to obtain rewards and prevent penalties.

expected value. The mean or arithmetic *average* of a statistical distribution or series of numbers.

expected value of (perfect) information. Expected *net benefits* from an undertaking with (perfect) information minus expected net benefits of the undertaking without (perfect) information.

expendable fund. In governmental accounting, a *fund* whose resources, *principal*, and earnings the governmental unit may distribute.

expenditure. Payment of *cash* for goods or services received. Payment may occur at the time the purchaser receives the goods or services or at a later time. Virtually synonymous with *disbursement* except that disbursement is a broader term and includes all payments for goods or services. Contrast with *expense*.

expense. As a noun, a decrease in *owners' equity* accompanying the decrease in *net assets* caused by selling goods or rendering services or by the passage of time; a "gone" (net) asset; an expired cost. Measure expense as the *cost* of the (net) assets used. Do not confuse with *expenditure* or *disbursement*, which may occur before, when, or after the firm recognizes the related expense. Use the word "cost" to refer to an item that still has service potential and is an asset. Use the word "expense" after the firm has used the asset's service potential. As a verb, "expense" means to designate an expenditure— past, current, or future—as a current expense.

expense account. An *account* to accumulate *expenses*; *closed* to *retained earnings* at the end of the accounting period; a *temporary owners' equity* account; also used to describe a listing of expenses that an employee submits to the employer for reimbursement.

experience rating. A term used in insurance, particularly unemployment insurance, to denote changes from ordinary rates to reflect extraordinarily large or small amounts of claims over time by the insured.

expired cost. An *expense* or a *loss*.

Exposure Draft (ED). A preliminary statement of the *FASB* (or the *APB* between 1962 and 1973) showing the contents of a pronouncement being considered for enactment by the board.

external failure costs. *Costs* that a firm *incurs* when it detects nonconforming products and services after delivering them to customers, including warranty repairs, product liability, marketing costs, and *sales allowances*.

external reporting. Reporting to shareholders and the public, as opposed to internal reporting for management's benefit. See *financial accounting,* and contrast with *managerial accounting*.

extraordinary item. A *material expense* or *revenue* item characterized both by its unusual nature and by its infrequency of occurrence; appears along with its income tax effects separately from ordinary income and *income from discontinued operations* on the *income statement*. Accountants would probably classify a *loss* from an earthquake as an extraordinary item. Accountants treat gain (or loss) on the retirement of *bonds* as an extraordinary item under the terms of *SFAS No. 4*.

extrinsic rewards. Rewards that come from outside the individual, such as rewards from a teacher, a parent, an organization, and a spouse; they include grades, money, praise, and prizes. Contrast with *intrinsic rewards*.

F

face amount (value). The nominal amount due at *maturity* from a *bond* or *note* not including the contractual periodic payment that may also come due on the same date. Good usage calls the corresponding amount of a stock certificate the *par* or *stated value*, whichever applies.

facility-level activities. Work that supports the entire organization. Examples include top management, human resources, and research and development.

factoring. The process of buying *notes* or *accounts receivable* at a *discount* from the holder owed the debt; from the holder's point of view, the selling of such notes or accounts. When the transaction involves a single note, usage calls the process "discounting a note."

factory. Used synonymously with *manufacturing* as an adjective.

factory burden. *Manufacturing overhead*.

factory cost. *Manufacturing cost*.

factory expense. *Manufacturing overhead. Expense* is a poor term in this context because the item is a *product cost*.

factory overhead. Usually an item of *manufacturing cost* other than *direct labor* or *direct materials*.

fair market price (value). See *fair value*.

fair presentation (fairness). One of the qualitative standards of financial reporting. When the *auditor's report* says that the *financial statements* "present fairly...," the auditor means that the accounting alternatives used by the entity all comply with *GAAP*. In recent years, however, courts have ruled that conformity with *generally accepted accounting principles* may be insufficient grounds for an opinion that the statements are fair. *SAS No. 5* requires that the auditor judge the accounting principles used in the statements to be "appropriate in the circumstances" before attesting to fair presentation.

fair value, fair market price (value). Price (value) negotiated at *arm's length* between a willing buyer and a willing seller, each acting rationally in his or her own self-interest. The accountant may estimate this amount in the absence of a monetary transaction. This is sometimes measured as the present value of expected cash flows.

fair-value hedge. A hedge of an exposure to changes in the *fair value* of a recognized *asset* or *liability* or of an unrecognized firm commitment. If the firm uses *hedge accounting,* it will report both the hedged item and the hedging instrument at fair value, with *gains* and *losses* reported in *net income*. If the hedge is effective, the gains and losses on these items will offset each other, although both will appear in net income.

FASAC. *Financial Accounting Standards Advisory Council.*

FASB (Financial Accounting Standards Board). An independent board responsible, since 1973, for establishing *gen-*

erally accepted accounting principles. Its official pronouncements are *Statements of Financial Accounting Concepts (SFAC), Statements of Financial Accounting Standards (SFAS),* and *FASB Interpretations.* See also *Discussion Memorandum* and *Technical Bulletin.* Web Site: www.fasb.org.

FASB Interpretation FIN. An official *FASB* statement interpreting the meaning of *Accounting Research Bulletins, APB Opinions,* and *Statements of Financial Accounting Standards. FIN 46,* for example, has curtailed the use of *off-balance-sheet financings.*

FASB Technical Bulletin. See *Technical Bulletin.*

favorable variance. An excess of actual *revenues* over expected revenues; an excess of *standard cost* over actual cost.

federal income tax. *Income tax* levied by the U.S. government on individuals and corporations.

Federal Insurance Contributions Act. See *FICA.*

Federal Unemployment Tax Act. See *FUTA.*

feedback. The process of informing employees about how their actual performance compares with the expected or desired level of performance, in the hope that the information will reinforce desired behavior and reduce unproductive behavior.

FEI. *Financial Executives Institute.*

FICA (Federal Insurance Contributions Act). The law that sets *Social Security taxes* and benefits.

fiduciary. Someone responsible for the custody or administration of property belonging to another; for example, an executor (of an estate), agent, receiver (in *bankruptcy*), or trustee (of a trust).

FIFO (first-in, first-out). The *inventory flow assumption* that firms use to compute *ending inventory* cost from most recent purchases and *cost of goods sold* from oldest purchases including beginning inventory. FIFO describes cost flow from the viewpoint of the income statement. From the balance sheet perspective, *LISH* (last-in, still-here) describes this same cost flow. Contrast with *LIFO.*

finance. As a verb, to supply with *funds* through the *issue* of stocks, bonds, notes, or mortgages or through the retention of earnings.

financial accounting. The accounting for *assets, equities, revenues,* and *expenses* of a business; primarily concerned with the historical reporting, to external users, of the *financial position* and operations of an *entity* on a regular, periodic basis. Contrast with *managerial accounting.*

Financial Accounting Foundation. The independent foundation (committee), governed by a board of trustees, that raises funds to support the *FASB* and *GASB.*

Financial Accounting Standards Advisory Council (FASAC). A committee of academics, preparers, attestors, and users giving advice to the *FASB* on matters of strategy and emerging issues. The council spends much of each meeting learning about current developments in standard-setting from the FASB staff.

Financial Accounting Standards Board. *FASB.*

Financial Executives Institute (FEI). An organization of financial executives, such as chief accountants, *controllers,* and treasurers, of large businesses. In recent years, the FEI has been a critic of the FASB because it views many of the FASB requirements as burdensome while not *cost-effective.*

financial expense. An *expense* incurred in raising or managing *funds.*

financial flexibility. As defined by *SFAC No. 5,* "the ability of an entity to take effective actions to alter amounts and timing of cash flows so it can respond to unexpected needs and opportunities."

financial forecast. See *financial projection* for definition and contrast.

financial instrument. The *FASB* defines this term as follows.: "Cash, evidence of an ownership interest in an entity, or a contract that both:
[a] imposes on one entity a contractual obligation (1) to deliver cash or another financial instrument to a second entity or (2) to exchange financial instruments on potentially unfavorable terms with the second entity, and
[b] conveys to that second entity a contractual right (1) to receive cash or another financial instrument from the first entity or (2) to exchange other financial instruments on potentially favorable terms with the first entity."

financial leverage. See *leverage.*

financial literacy. The *NYSE* and the *NASDAQ* have required that companies who list their shares with these groups have an audit committee comprising at least three independent board members who are financially literate. The organizations mention the ability to understand the *financial statements,* but leave the definition of financial literacy to the individual boards to define. We think financial literacy in this sense requires the ability to understand the transactions requiring critical accounting judgments or estimates; the accounting issues and choices for those judgments; what management chose, and why; and what opportunities management's choices provide for earnings management. See *critical accounting judgments.*

financial model. Model, typically expressed with arithmetic relations, that allows an organization to test the interaction of economic variables in a variety of settings.

financial position (condition). Statement of the *assets* and *equities* of a firm; displayed as a *balance sheet.*

financial projection. An estimate of *financial position,* results of *operations,* and changes in cash flows for one or more future periods based on a set of assumptions. If the assumptions do not represent the most likely outcomes, then auditors call the estimate a "projection." If the assumptions represent the most probable outcomes, then auditors call the estimate a "forecast." "Most probable" means that management has evaluated the assumptions and that they are management's judgment of the most likely set of conditions and most likely outcomes.

financial ratio. See *ratio*.

financial reporting objectives. Broad objectives that are intended to guide the development of specific *accounting standards;* set out by *FASB SFAC No. 1*.

Financial Reporting Release. Series of releases, issued by the SEC since 1982; replaces the *Accounting Series Release*. See *SEC*.

financial statements. The *balance sheet, income statement, statement of retained earnings, statement of cash flows*, statement of changes in *owners' equity accounts*, statement of *comprehensive income*, and *notes* thereto.

financial structure. *Capital structure*.

financial vice-president. Person in charge of the entire accounting and finance function; typically one of the three most influential people in the company.

financial year. Australia and UK: term for *fiscal year.*

financing activities. Obtaining resources from (a) owners and providing them with a return on and a return of their *investment* and (b) *creditors* and repaying amounts borrowed (or otherwise settling the obligation). See *statement of cash flows*.

financing lease. *Capital lease*.

finished goods (inventory account). Manufactured product ready for sale; a *current asset* (inventory) account.

firm. Informally, any business entity. (Strictly speaking, a firm is a *partnership*.)

firm commitment. The *FASB, in SFAS No. 133,* defines this as "an agreement with an unrelated party, binding on both parties and usually legally enforceable," which requires that the firm promise to pay a specified amount of a currency and that the firm has sufficient disincentives for nonpayment that the firm will probably make the payment. A firm commitment resembles a *liability,* but it is an *executory contract*, so is not a liability. *SFAS No. 133* allows the firm to recognize certain financial *hedges* in the balance sheet if they hedge firm commitments. The *FASB* first used the term in *SFAS No. 52* and *No. 80* but made the term more definite and more important in *SFAS No. 133*. This is an early, perhaps the first, step in changing the recognition criteria for assets and liabilities to exclude the test that the future benefit (asset) or obligation (liability) not arise from an executory contract.

first-in, first-out. See *FIFO*.

fiscal year. A period of 12 consecutive months chosen by a business as the *accounting period* for *annual reports*, not necessarily a *natural business year* or a calendar year.

FISH. An acronym, conceived by George H. Sorter, for *first-in, still-here*. FISH is the same cost flow assumption as *LIFO*. Many readers of accounting statements find it easier to think about inventory questions in terms of items still on hand.

Think of LIFO in connection with *cost of goods sold* but of FISH in connection with *ending inventory*. See *LISH*.

fixed assets. *Plant assets*.

fixed assets turnover. *Sales* divided by average total *fixed assets*.

fixed benefit plan. A *defined-benefit plan*.

fixed budget. A plan that provides for specified amounts of *expenditures* and *receipts* that do not vary with activity levels; sometimes called a "static budget." Contrast with *flexible budget*.

fixed charges earned (coverage) ratio. *Income* before *interest expense* and *income tax expense* divided by interest expense.

fixed cost (expense). An *expenditure* or *expense* that does not vary with volume of activity, at least in the short run. See *capacity costs*, which include *enabling costs* and *standby costs*, and *programmed costs* for various subdivisions of fixed costs. See *cost terminology*.

fixed cost price variance (spending variance). The difference between actual and *budgeted fixed costs.*

fixed interval sampling. A method of choosing a sample: the analyst selects the first item from the population randomly, drawing the remaining sample items at equally spaced intervals.

fixed liability. *Long-term* liability.

fixed manufacturing overhead applied. The portion of *fixed manufacturing overhead cost* allocated to units produced during a period.

fixed overhead variance. Difference between *actual fixed manufacturing costs* and fixed manufacturing costs applied to production in a *standard costing system*.

flexible budget. *Budget* that projects receipts and expenditures as a function of activity levels. Contrast with *fixed budget*.

flexible budget allowance. With respect to manufacturing overhead, the total cost that a firm should have incurred at the level of activity actually experienced during the period.

float. *Checks* whose amounts the bank has *added* to the depositor's bank account but whose amounts the bank has not yet reduced from the *drawer's* bank account.

flow. The change in the amount of an item over time. Contrast with *stock*.

flow assumption. An assumption used when the firm makes a *withdrawal* from *inventory*. The firm must compute the cost of the withdrawal by a flow assumption if the firm does not use the *specific identification* method. The usual flow assumptions are *FIFO, LIFO,* and *weighted average*.

flow of costs. *Costs* passing through various classifications within an *entity* engaging, at least in part, in manufacturing activities. See the accompanying diagram for a summary of *product* and *period cost* flows.

Flow of Costs (and Sales Revenue)

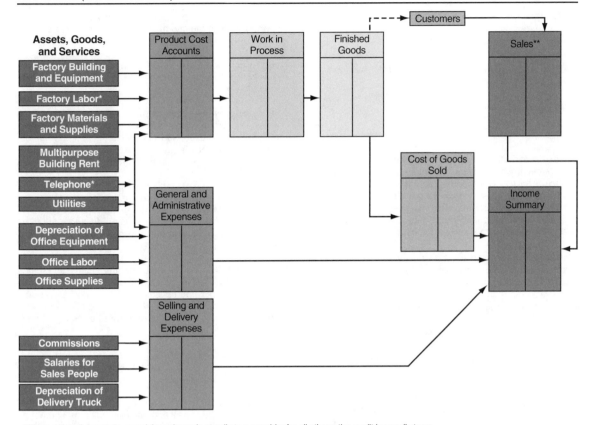

*The credit in the entry to record these items is usually to a payable; for all others, the credit is usually to an asset, or to an asset contra account.
**When the firm records sales to customers, it credits the Sales account. The debit is usually to Cash or

flow-through method. Accounting for the *investment credit* to show all income statement benefits of the credit in the year of acquisition rather than spreading them over the life of the asset acquired (called the "deferral method"). The *APB* preferred the deferral method in *Opinion No. 2* (1962) but accepted the flow-through method in *Opinion No. 4* (1964). The term also applies to *depreciation* accounting in which the firm uses the *straight-line method* for financial reporting and an *accelerated depreciation* method for tax reporting. Followers of the flow-through method would not recognize a *deferred tax liability. APB Opinion No. 11* prohibits the use of the flow-through approach in financial reporting, although some regulatory commissions have used it.

FOB. Free on board some location (for example, FOB shipping point, FOB destination). The *invoice* price includes delivery at seller's expense to that location. Title to goods usually passes from seller to buyer at the FOB location.

folio. A page number or other identifying reference used in posting to indicate the source of entry.

footing. Adding a column of figures.

footnotes. More detailed information than that provided in the *income statement, balance sheet, statement of retained earnings,* and *statement of cash flows.* These are an integral part of the statements, and the *auditor's report* covers them. They are sometimes called "notes."

forecast. See *financial projection* for definition and contrast.

foreclosure. Occurs when a lender takes possession of property for his or her own use or sale after the borrower fails to make a required payment on a *mortgage.* Assume that the lender sells the property but that the proceeds of the sale are too small to cover the outstanding balance on the loan at the time of foreclosure. Under the terms of most mortgages, the lender becomes an unsecured creditor of the borrower for the still-unrecovered balance of the loan.

foreign currency. For *financial statements* prepared in a given currency, any other currency.

foreign currency translation. Reporting in the currency used in financial statements the amounts denominated or measured in a different currency.

foreign exchange gain or loss. Gain or loss from holding *net* foreign *monetary items* during a period when the *exchange rate* changes.

foreign sales corporation. See *FSC.*

forfeited share. A share to which a subscriber has lost title because of nonpayment of a *call.*

Form 10-K. See *10-K.*

Form 20-F. See *20-F.*

forward contract. An agreement to purchase or sell a specific commodity or financial instrument for a specified price, the *forward price,* at a specified date. Contrast with *futures contract.* Typically, forward contracts are not traded on organized exchanges (unlike *futures contract*), so the parties to the agreement sacrifice liquidity but gain flexibility in setting contract quantities, qualities, and settlement dates.

forward-exchange contract. An agreement to exchange at a specified future date currencies of different countries at a specified rate called the "forward rate."

forward price. The price of a commodity for delivery at a specified future date; in contrast to the "spot price," the price of that commodity on the day of the price quotation.

franchise. A privilege granted or sold, such as to use a name or to sell products or services.

fraudulent conveyance. A transfer of goods or cash that a court finds illegal. *Creditors* of a *bankrupt* firm usually receive less than the firm owed them. For example, a creditor of a bankrupt firm might collect from the trustee of the bankrupt firm only $.60 for every dollar the bankrupt firm owed. Creditors, anticipating bankruptcy, sometimes attempt to persuade the firm to pay the debt in full before the firm declares bankruptcy, reducing the net assets available to other creditors. Bankruptcy laws have rules forbidding such transfers from a near-bankrupt firm to some of its creditors. Such a transfer is called a "fraudulent conveyance." Courts sometimes ask accountants to judge whether a firm had liabilities exceeding assets even before the firm went into bankruptcy. When the court can find that economic bankruptcy occurred before legal bankruptcy, it will declare transfers of assets to creditors after economic bankruptcy to be fraudulent conveyances and have the assets returned to the trustees (or to a legal entity called the "bankrupt's estate") for redistribution to all creditors.

fraudulent financial reporting. Intentional or reckless conduct that results in materially misleading *financial statements.* See *creative accounting.*

free cash flow. This term has no standard meaning. Some financial statement analysts use it to mean *cash flow from operations + interest expense + income tax expense.* Others mean the excess of cash flow from operations over cash flow for investing. Usage varies so much that you should ascertain the meaning intended in context by this phrase.

free on board. *FOB.*

freight-in. The *cost* of freight or shipping incurred in acquiring *inventory*, preferably treated as a part of the cost of *inventory;* often shown temporarily in an *adjunct account* that the acquirer closes at the end of the period with other purchase accounts to the inventory account.

freight-out. The *cost* of freight or shipping incurred in selling *inventory*, treated by the seller as a selling *expense* in the period of sale.

FSC (foreign sales corporation). A foreign *corporation* engaging in certain export activities, some of whose *income* the United States exempts from federal *income tax.* A U.S. corporation need pay no income taxes on *dividends* distributed by an FSC out of *earnings* attributable to certain foreign income.

full absorption costing. The *costing* method that assigns all types of manufacturing costs (*direct material, direct labor, fixed* and *variable overhead*) to units produced; required by *GAAP;* also called "absorption costing." Contrast with *variable costing.*

full costing, full costs. The total cost of producing and selling a unit; often used in *long-term* profitability and pricing decisions. Full cost per unit equals *full absorption cost* per unit plus *marketing, administrative, interest*, and other *central corporate expenses*, per unit. The sum of full costs for all units equals total costs of the firm.

full disclosure. The reporting policy requiring that all significant or *material* information appear in the financial statements. See *fair presentation.*

fully diluted earnings per share. For *common stock,* smallest *earnings per share* figure that one can obtain by computing an earnings per share for all possible combinations of assumed *exercise* or *conversion* of *potentially dilutive securities.* This figure must appear on the *income statement* if it is less than 97 percent of earnings available to common shareholders divided by the average number of common shares outstanding during the period.

fully vested. Said of a *pension plan* when an employee (or his or her estate) has rights to all the benefits purchased with the employer's contributions to the plan even if the employee does not work for this employer at the time of death or retirement.

function. In governmental accounting, said of a group of related activities for accomplishing a service or regulatory program for which the governmental unit has responsibility; in mathematics, a rule for associating a number, called the dependent variable, with another number (or numbers), called independent variable(s).

functional classification. *Income statement* reporting form that classifies *expenses* by function, that is, cost of goods sold, administrative expenses, financing expenses, selling expenses. Contrast with *natural classification.*

functional currency. Currency in which an entity carries out its principal economic activity.

fund. An *asset* or group of assets set aside for a specific purpose. See also *fund accounting.*

fund accounting. The accounting for resources, obligations, and *capital* balances, usually of a not-for-profit or governmental *entity*, which the entity has segregated into *accounts* representing logical groupings based on legal, donor, or administrative restrictions or requirements. The groupings are "funds." The accounts of each fund are *self-balancing*, and from them one can prepare a *balance sheet* and an operating statement for each fund. See *fund* and *fund balance*.

fund balance. In governmental accounting, the excess of assets of a *fund* over its liabilities and reserves; the not-for-profit equivalent of *owners' equity*.

funded. Said of a *pension plan* or other obligation when the firm has set aside *funds* for meeting the obligation when it comes due. The federal law for pension plans requires that the firm fund all *normal costs* when it recognizes them as expenses. In addition, the firm must fund *prior service cost* of pension plans over 30 or over 40 years, depending on the circumstances.

funding. Replacing *short-term* liabilities with *long-term* debt.

funds. Generally *working capital*; current assets less current liabilities; sometimes used to refer to *cash* or to cash and *marketable securities*.

funds provided by operations. See *cash provided by operations*.

funds statement. An informal name often used for the *statement of cash flows*.

funny money. Said of securities, such as *convertible preferred stock, convertible bonds, options*, and *warrants,* that have aspects of *common shares* but that did not reduce reported *earnings per share* before the issuance of *APB Opinion No. 9* in 1966 and *No. 15* in 1969.

FUTA (Federal Unemployment Tax Act). Provides for taxes to be collected at the federal level, to help subsidize the individual states' administration of their unemployment compensation programs.

future value. Value at a specified future date of a sum increased at a specified *interest rate*.

futures contract. An agreement to purchase or sell a specific commodity or financial instrument for a specified price, at a specific future time or during a specified future period. Contrast with *forward contract*. When traded on an organized exchange, the exchange sets the minimum contract size and expiration date(s). The exchange requires that the holder of the contract settle in cash each day the fluctuations in the value of the contract. That is, each day, the exchange marks the contract to market value, called the "(daily) settlement price." A contract holder who has lost during the day must put up more cash, and a holder who has gained receives cash.

G

GAAP. *Generally accepted accounting principles;* a plural noun. In the UK and elsewhere, this means "generally accepted accounting practices."

GAAS. *Generally accepted auditing standards;* a plural noun. Do not confuse with *GAS*.

gain. In *financial accounting* contexts, the increase in *owners' equity* caused by a transaction that is not part of a firm's typical, day-to-day operations and not part of owners' *investment* or *withdrawals*. Accounting distinguishes the meaning of the term "gain" (or *loss*) from that of related terms. First, gains (and losses) generally refer to nonoperating, incidental, peripheral, or nonroutine transactions: gain on sale of land in contrast to *gross margin* on *sale* of *inventory*. Second, gains and losses are *net* concepts, not gross concepts: gain or loss results from subtracting some measure of *cost* from the measure of inflow. *Revenues* and *expenses*, on the other hand, are gross concepts; their difference is a net concept. Gain is nonroutine and net, *profit* or *margin* is routine and net; revenue from *continuing operations* is routine and gross; revenue from *discontinued operations* is nonroutine and gross. Loss is net but can be either routine ("loss on sale of inventory") or not ("loss on disposal of segment of business").

In *managerial accounting* and lay contexts, the difference between some measure of *revenue* or *receipts* or *proceeds* and some measure of costs, such as direct costs or variable costs or fully absorbed costs or full costs (see *cost terminology*). Because the word can have so many different meanings, careful writers should be explicit to designate one.

gain contingency. See *contingency*.

GAS. *Goods available for sale*. Do not confuse with *GAAS*.

GASB (Governmental Accounting Standards Board). An independent body responsible, since 1984, for establishing accounting standards for state and local government units. It is part of the *Financial Accounting Foundation*, parallel to the *FASB*, and currently consists of five members.

GbR (Gesellschaft des bürgerlichen Rechtes). Germany: a *partnership* whose members agree to share in specific aspects of their own separate business pursuits, such as an office. This partnership has no legal form and is not a separate accounting *entity*.

GDP Implicit Price Deflator (index). A *price index* issued quarterly by the Office of Business Economics of the U.S. Department of Commerce. This index attempts to trace the price level of all *goods and services* composing the *gross domestic product*. Contrast with *Consumer Price Index*.

gearing. UK: *financial leverage*.

gearing adjustment. A *revenue* representing part of a *holding gain*. Consider a firm that has part of its assets financed by *non-current liabilities* and that has experienced *holding gains* on its *assets* during a period. All the increase in wealth caused by the holding gains belongs to the owners; none typically belongs to the lenders. Some British accounting authorities believe that published *income statements* should show part of the holding gain in *income* for the period. The part they would report in income is the fraction of the gain equal to the fraction that debt composes of total financing; for example, if debt equals 40 percent of total equities and the holding gain equals $100 for the period, the amount to appear in income for the period would be $40. Usage calls that part the "gearing adjustment."

general debt. A governmental unit's debt legally payable from general revenues and backed by the full faith and credit of the governmental unit.

general expenses. *Operating expenses* other than those specifically identified as cost of goods sold, selling, and administration.

general fixed asset (group of accounts). Accounts showing a governmental unit's long-term assets that are not accounted for in *enterprise, trust,* or intragovernmental service funds.

general fund. A nonprofit entity's assets and liabilities not specifically earmarked for other purposes; the primary operating fund of a governmental unit.

general journal. The formal record in which the firm records transactions, or summaries of similar transactions, in *journal entry* form as they occur. Use of the adjective "general" usually implies that the journal has only two columns for cash amounts or that the firm also uses various *special journals,* such as a *check register* or *sales journal.*

general ledger. The name for the formal *ledger* containing all the financial statement accounts. It has equal debits and credits, as evidenced by the *trial balance*. Some of the accounts in the general ledger may be *control accounts*, supported by details contained in *subsidiary ledgers*.

general partner. *Partnership* member who is personally liable for all debts of the partnership; contrast with *limited partner*.

general price index. A measure of the aggregate prices of a wide range of goods and services in the economy at one time relative to the prices during a base period. See *Consumer Price Index* and *GDP Implicit Price Deflator*. Contrast with *specific price index*.

general price level–adjusted statements. See *constant-dollar accounting*.

general price-level changes. Changes in the aggregate prices of a wide range of goods and services in the economy. These price measurements result from using a *general price index*. Contrast with *specific price changes*.

general purchasing power. The command of the dollar over a wide range of goods and services in the economy. The general purchasing power of the dollar is inversely related to changes in a general price index. See *general price index*.

general purchasing-power accounting. See *constant-dollar accounting*.

generally accepted accounting principles (GAAP). As previously defined by the *CAP, APB,* and now the *FASB*, the conventions, rules, and procedures necessary to define accepted accounting practice at a particular time; includes both broad guidelines and relatively detailed practices and procedures. In the United States the FASB defines GAAP to include accounting pronouncements of the *SEC* and other government agencies as well as a variety of authoritative sources, such as this book.

generally accepted auditing standards (GAAS). The *PCAOB* has explicitly stated that it began compiling its auditing promulgations with GAAS, as issued by the AICPA, but "a reference to generally accepted auditing standards in auditors' reports is no longer appropriate or necessary." The phrase has referred to the standards, as opposed to particular procedures, that the *AICPA* promulgated (in *Statements on Auditing Standards*) and that concern "the auditor's professional quantities" and "the judgment exercised by him in the performance of his examination and in his report." Currently, there have been ten such standards: three general ones (concerned with proficiency, independence, and degree of care to be exercised), three standards of field work, and four standards of reporting. The first standard of reporting requires that the *auditor's report* state whether the firm prepared the *financial statements* in accordance with *generally accepted accounting principles*. Thus, before the PCAOB became the auditing rulemaker, the typical auditor's report says that the auditor conducted the examination in accordance with generally accepted auditing standards and that the firm prepared the statements in accordance with generally accepted accounting principles. The report will not refer to the standards of the Public Company Accounting Oversight Board (United States). See *auditor's report*.

geographic segment. A single operation or a group of operations that are located in a particular geographic area and that generate revenue, incur costs, and have assets used in or associated with generating such revenue.

GIE (groupement d'intérêt économique). France: a joint venture, normally used for exports and research-and-development pooling.

GmbH (Gesellschaft mit beschränkter Haftung). Germany: a private company with an unlimited number of shareholders. Transfer of ownership can take place only with the consent of other shareholders. Contrast with *AG*.

goal congruence. The idea that all members of an organization have incentives to perform for a common interest, such as *shareholder* wealth maximization for a *corporation*.

going-concern assumption. For accounting purposes, accountants' assumption that a business will remain in operation long enough to carry out all its current plans. This assumption partially justifies the *acquisition cost* basis, rather than a *liquidation* or *exit value* basis, of accounting.

going public. Said of a business when its *shares* become widely traded rather than being closely held by relatively few shareholders; issuing shares to the general investing public.

goods. Items of merchandise, supplies, raw materials, or finished goods. Sometimes the meaning of "goods" is extended to include all *tangible* items, as in the phrase "goods and services."

goods available for sale. The sum of *beginning inventory* plus all acquisitions of merchandise or finished goods during an *accounting period*.

goods-in-process. *Work-in-process.*

goodwill. The excess of cost of an acquired firm (or operating unit) over the current *fair market value* of the separately identifiable *net assets* of the acquired unit. Before the acquiring firm can recognize goodwill, it must assign a *fair market value* to all identifiable assets, even when not recorded on the books of the acquired unit. For example, if a firm has developed a *patent* that does not appear on its books because of *SFAS No. 2,* if another company acquires the firm, the acquirer will recognize the patent at an amount equal to its estimated fair market value. The acquirer will compute the amount of goodwill only after assigning values to all assets it can identify. Informally, the term indicates the value of good customer relations, high employee morale, a well-respected business name, and so on, all of which the firm or analyst expects to result in greater-than-normal earning power.

goodwill method. A method of accounting for the *admission* of a new partner to a *partnership* when the new partner will receive a portion of capital different from the value of the *tangible* assets contributed as a fraction of tangible assets of the partnership. See *bonus method* for a description and contrast.

Governmental Accounting Standards Advisory Council. A group that consults with the *GASB* on agenda, technical issues, and the assignment of priorities to projects. It comprises more than a dozen members representing various areas of expertise.

Governmental Accounting Standards Board. *GASB.*

GPL (general price level). Usually used as an adjective modifying the word "accounting" to mean *constant-dollar accounting.*

GPLA (general price level–adjusted accounting). *Constant-dollar accounting.*

GPP (general purchasing power). Usually used as an adjective modifying the word "accounting" to mean *constant-dollar accounting.*

graded vesting. Said of a *pension plan* in which not all employees currently have fully *vested* benefits. By law, the benefits must vest according to one of several formulas as time passes.

grandfather clause. An exemption in new accounting *pronouncements* exempting transactions that occurred before a given date from the new accounting treatment. For example, *APB Opinion No. 17*, adopted in 1970, exempted *goodwill* acquired before 1970 from required *amortization.* The term "grandfather" appears in the title to *SFAS No. 10.*

gross. Not adjusted or reduced by deductions or subtractions. Contrast with *net,* and see *gain* for a description of how the difference between net and gross affects usage of the terms *revenue, gain, expense,* and *loss.*

gross domestic product (GDP). The market value of all goods and services produced by capital or labor within a country, regardless of who owns the capital or of the nationality of the labor; most widely used measure of production within a country. Contrast with gross national product (GNP), which measures the market value of all goods and services produced with capital owned by, and labor services supplied by, the residents of that country regardless of where they work or where they own capital. In the United States in recent years, the difference between GDP and GNP equals about two-tenths of 1 percent of GDP.

gross margin. *Net sales* minus *cost of goods sold.*

gross margin percent. 100 (1 – *cost of goods sold/net sales*) = 100 (*gross margin/net sales*).

gross national product (GNP). See *gross domestic product* for definition and contrast.

gross price method (of recording purchase or sales discounts). The firm records the *purchase* (or *sale*) at the *invoice price*, not deducting the amounts of *discounts* available. Later, it uses a *contra* account to purchases (or sales) to record the amounts of discounts taken. Since information on discounts lapsed will not emerge from this system, most firms should prefer the *net price method* of recording purchase discounts.

gross profit. *Gross margin.*

gross profit method. A method of estimating *ending inventory* amounts. First, the firm measures *cost of goods sold* as some fraction of sales; then, it uses the *inventory equation* to value *ending inventory.*

gross profit ratio. *Gross margin* divided by *net sales.*

gross sales. All *sales* at *invoice* prices, not reduced by *discounts, allowances, returns,* or other adjustments.

group depreciation. In calculating *depreciation* charges, a method that combines similar assets rather than depreciating them separately. It does not recognize gain or loss on retirement of items from the group until the firm sells or retires the last item in the group. See *composite life method.*

guarantee. A promise to answer for payment of debt or performance of some obligation if the person liable for the debt or obligation fails to perform. A guarantee is a *contingency* of the *entity* making the promise. Often, writers use the words "guarantee" and "warranty" to mean the same thing. In precise usage, however, "guarantee" means some person's promise to perform a contractual obligation such as to pay a sum of cash, whereas "warranty" refers to promises about pieces of machinery or other products. See *warranty.*

H

half-year convention. In *tax accounting* under *ACRS,* and sometimes in *financial accounting,* an assumption that the firm acquired *depreciable assets* at midyear of the year of acquisition. When the firm uses this convention, it computes the *depreciation charge* for the year as one-half the charge that it would have used if it had acquired the assets at the beginning of the year.

hardware. The physical equipment or devices forming a computer and peripheral equipment.

hash total. Used to establish accuracy of data processing; a control that takes the sum of data items not normally added together (e.g., the sum of a list of part numbers) and subsequently compares that sum with a computer-generated total of the same values. If the two sums are identical, then the analyst takes some comfort that the two lists are identical.

Hasselback. An annual directory of accounting faculty at colleges and universities; gives information about the faculty's training and fields of specialization. James R. Hasselback, of Florida State University, has compiled the directory since the 1970s; Prentice-Hall distributes it. On-line, you can find it at the Rutgers University accounting Web Site: *www.rutgers.edu/Accounting/.*

health-care benefits obligation. At any time, the present value of the non-pension benefits promised by an employer to employees during their retirement years.

hedge. To reduce, perhaps cancel altogether, one risk the entity already bears, by purchasing a security or other financial instrument. For example, a farmer growing corn runs the risk that corn prices may decline before the corn matures and can be brought to market. Such a farmer can arrange to sell the corn now for future delivery, hedging the risk of corn price changes. A firm may have a *receivable* denominated in Euros due in six months. It runs the risk that the exchange rate between the dollar and the Euro will change and the firm will receive a smaller number of dollars in the future than it would receive from the same number of marks received today. Such a firm may hedge its exposure to risk of changes in the exchange rate between dollars and Euros in a variety of ways. See *cash-flow hedge* and *fair-value hedge.* Do not confuse with *hedge accounting.*

hedge accounting. Firms may, but need not, use hedge accounting. If the firm elects hedge accounting and if its hedging instrument is highly effective, it will report *gains* and *losses* on hedging instruments for *cash-flow hedges* in *other comprehensive income*, rather than in *net income.* For *fair-value hedges,* the firm using hedge accounting will report the hedged *asset* or *liability* at *fair value;* it reports the hedging instrument at fair value in any event.

held-to-maturity securities. *Marketable debt securities* that a firm expects to, and has the ability to, hold to *maturity*; a classification important in *SFAS No. 115,* which generally requires the owner to carry marketable securities on the balance sheet at market value, not at cost. Under *SFAS No. 115,* the firm may show held-to-maturity debt securities at *amortized cost.* If the firm lacks either the expectation or the intent to hold the debt security to its maturity, then the firm will show that security at market value as a security *available for sale.*

hidden reserve. An amount by which a firm has understated *owners' equity*, perhaps deliberately. The understatement arises from an undervaluation of *assets* or overvaluation of *liabilities.* By undervaluing assets on this period's *balance sheet,* the firm can overstate *net income* in some future period by disposing of the asset: actual *revenues* less artificially low cost of assets sold yields artificially high net income. No *account* in the *ledger* has this title.

hire-purchase agreement (contract). UK: a *lease* containing a purchase *option.*

historical cost. *Acquisition cost; original cost; a sunk cost.*

historical cost/constant-dollar accounting. Accounting based on *historical cost* valuations measured in *constant dollars.* The method restates *nonmonetary items* to reflect changes in the *general purchasing power* of the dollar since the time the firm acquired specific *assets* or incurred specific *liabilities.* The method recognizes a *gain* or *loss* on *monetary items* as the firm holds them over time periods when the general purchasing power of the dollar changes.

historical exchange rate. The rate at which one currency converts into another at the date a transaction took place. Contrast with *current exchange rate.*

historical summary. A part of the *annual report* that shows items, such as *net income, revenues, expenses, asset* and *equity* totals, *earnings per share*, and the like, for five or ten periods including the current one. Usually not as much detail appears in the historical summary as in *comparative statements,* which typically report as much detail for the two preceding years as for the current year. Annual reports may contain both comparative statements and a historical summary.

holdback. Under the terms of a contract, a portion of the progress payments that the customer need not pay until the contractor has fulfilled the contract or satisfied financial obligations to subcontractors.

holding company. A company that confines its activities to owning *stock* in, and supervising management of, other companies. A holding company usually owns a controlling interest in—that is, more than 50 percent of the voting stock of—the companies whose stock it holds. Contrast with *mutual fund.* See *conglomerate.* In British usage, the term refers to any company with controlling interest in another company.

holding gain or loss. Difference between end-of-period price and beginning-of-period price of an asset held during the period. The financial statements ordinarily do not separately report realized holding gains and losses. Income does not usually report unrealized gains at all, except on *trading securities.* See *lower of cost or market.* See *inventory profit* for further refinement, including *gains* on *assets* sold during the period.

holding gain or loss net of inflation. Increase or decrease in the *current cost* of an asset while it is held; measured in units of *constant dollars.*

horizontal analysis. *Time-series analysis.*

horizontal integration. An organization's extension of activity in the same general line of business or its expansion into supplementary, complementary, or compatible products. Compare *vertical integration.*

house account. An account with a customer who does not pay sales commissions.

human resource accounting. A term used to describe a variety of proposals that seek to report the importance of human resources—knowledgeable, trained, and loyal employees—in a company's earning process and total assets.

hurdle rate. Required rate of return in a *discounted cash flow* analysis.

hybrid security. *Security*, such as a *convertible bond*, containing elements of both *debt* and *owners' equity*.

hypothecation. The *pledging* of property, without transfer of title or possession, to secure a loan.

I

IAA. *Interamerican Accounting Association*.

IASB. *International Accounting Standards Board*.

ICMA (Institute of Certified Management Accountants). See *CMA* and *Institute of Management Accountants*.

ideal standard costs. *Standard costs* set equal to those that a firm would incur under the best-possible conditions.

IFRS. International Financial Reporting Standard(s). Refers broadly to all the pronouncements of the *IASB* and, with numbers after the letters, to specific reporting standards issued by the IASB.

IIA. *Institute of Internal Auditors*.

IMA. *Institute of Management Accountants*.

impairment. Reduction in *market value* of an *asset*. When the firm has information indicating that its long-lived *assets*, such as *plant*, identifiable *intangibles*, and *goodwill*, have declined in *market value* or will provide a smaller future benefit that originally anticipated, it tests to see if the decline in value is so drastic that the expected future cash flows from the asset have declined below *book value*. If then-current book value exceeds the sum of expected cash flows, an asset impairment has occurred. At the time the firm judges that an impairment has occurred, the firm writes down the book value of the asset to its then-current *fair value*, which is the market value of the asset or, if the firm cannot assess the market value, the expected *net present value* of the future cash flows.

implicit interest. *Interest* not paid or received. See *interest, imputed*. All transactions involving the deferred payment or receipt of cash involve interest, whether explicitly stated or not. The implicit interest on a single-payment *note* equals the difference between the amount collected at maturity and the amount lent at the start of the loan. One can compute the implicit *interest rate* per year for loans with a single cash inflow and a single cash outflow from the following equation:

$$\left[\frac{\text{Cash Received at Maturity}}{\text{Cash Lent}}\right]^{(1/t)} - 1.$$

where t is the term of the loan in years; t need not be an integer.

imprest fund. *Petty cash fund*.

improvement. An *expenditure* to extend the useful life of an *asset* or to improve its performance (rate of output, cost) over that of the original asset; sometimes called "betterment." The firm capitalizes such expenditures as part of the asset's cost. Contrast with *maintenance* and *repair*.

imputed cost. A cost that does not appear in accounting records, such as the *interest* that a firm could earn on cash spent to acquire inventories rather than, say, government bonds. Or, consider a firm that owns the buildings it occupies. This firm has an imputed cost for rent in an amount equal to what it would have to pay to use similar buildings owned by another or equal to the amount it could collect from someone renting the premises from the firm. *Opportunity cost*.

imputed interest. See *interest, imputed*.

in the black (red). Operating at a profit (loss).

in-process R&D. When one firm acquires another, the acquired firm will often have *research and development* activities under way that, following *GAAP*, it has *expensed*. The acquiring firm will pay for these activities to the extent they have value and will then, following GAAP, write off the activities. For each dollar of in-process R&D the acquiring firm identifies and immediately *expenses*, it will have one less dollar of *goodwill* or other assets to *amortize*. Some acquirers have overstated the valuations of acquired in-process R&D in order to increase immediate *write-offs* and subsequent, recurring *income*.

incentive compatible compensation. Said of a compensation plan that induces managers to act for the interests of owners while acting also in their own interests. For example, consider that a time of rising prices and increasing inventories when using a *LIFO* cost flow assumption implies paying lower *income taxes* than using *FIFO*. A bonus scheme for managers based on accounting *net income* is not incentive-compatible because owners likely benefit more under LIFO, whereas managers benefit more if they report using FIFO. See *LIFO conformity rule* and *goal congruence*.

income. *Excess of revenues* and *gains* over *expenses* and *losses* for a period; *net income*. The term is sometimes used with an appropriate modifier to refer to the various intermediate amounts shown in a *multiple-step income statement* or to refer to revenues, as in "rental income." See *comprehensive income*.

income accounts. *Revenue* and *expense accounts*.

income before taxes. On the *income statement*, the difference between all *revenues* and *expenses* except *income tax* expense. Contrast with *net income*.

income determination. See *determine*.

income distribution account. *Temporary account* sometimes debited when the firm declares *dividends*; closed to *retained earnings*.

income from continuing operations. As defined by *APB Opinion No. 30*, all *revenues* less all *expenses* except for the following: results of operations (including *income tax* effects) that a firm has discontinued or will discontinue; *gains* or *losses*, including income tax effects, on disposal of segments of the business; gains or losses, including income tax effects, from *extraordinary items*; and the cumulative effect of *accounting changes*.

income from discontinued operations. *Income*, net of tax effects, from parts of the business that the firm has discontinued during the period or will discontinue in the near future. Accountants report such items on separate lines of the *income statement*, after *income from continuing operations* but before *extraordinary items*.

income (revenue) bond. See *special revenue debt*.

income smoothing. A method of timing business *transactions* or choosing *accounting principles* so that the firm reports smaller variations in *income* from year to year than it otherwise would. Although some managements set income smoothing as an objective, no standard-setter does.

income statement. The statement of *revenues, expenses, gains*, and *losses* for the period, ending with *net income* for the period. Accountants usually show the *earnings-per-share* amount on the income statement; the *reconciliation* of beginning and ending balances of *retained earnings* may also appear in a combined statement of income and retained earnings. See *income from continuing operations, income from discontinued operations, extraordinary items, multiple-step*, and *single-step*.

income summary. In problem solving, an *account* that serves as a surrogate for the *income statement*. In using an income summary, close all *revenue* accounts to the Income Summary as *credits* and all *expense* accounts as *debits*. The *balance* in the account, after you make all these *closing entries*, represents income or loss for the period. Then, close the income summary balance to retained earnings.

income tax. An annual tax levied by the federal and other governments on the income of an entity.

income tax allocation. See *deferred income tax (liability)* and *tax allocation:intra-statement*.

incremental. An adjective used to describe the increase in *cost, expense, investment, cash flow, revenue, profit*, and the like if the firm produces or sells one or more units or if it undertakes an activity. See *differential*.

incremental cost. See *incremental*.

incur. Said of an obligation of a firm, whether or not that obligation is *accrued*. For example, a firm incurs interest expense on a loan as time passes but accrues that interest only on payment dates or when it makes an *adjusting entry*.

indenture. See *bond indenture*.

independence. The mental attitude required of the *CPA* in performing the *attest* function. It implies that the CPA is impartial and that the members of the auditing CPA firm own no stock in the corporation being audited.

independent accountant. The *CPA* who performs the *attest* function for a firm.

independent variable. See *regression analysis*.

indeterminate-term liability. A *liability* lacking the criterion of being due at a definite time. This term is our own coinage to encompass the *minority interest*.

indexation. An attempt by lawmakers or parties to a contract to cope with the effects of *inflation*. Amounts fixed in law or contracts are "indexed" when these amounts change as a given measure of price changes. For example, a so-called escalator clause (COLA—cost of living allowance or adjustment) in a labor contract might provide that hourly wages will be increased as the *Consumer Price Index* increases. Many economists have suggested the indexation of numbers fixed in the *income tax* laws. If, for example, the personal *exemption* is \$2,500 at the start of the period, if prices rise by 10 percent during the period, and if the personal exemption is indexed, then the personal exemption would automatically rise to \$2,750 (= \$2,500 + .10 × \$2,500) at the end of the period.

indirect cost pool. Any grouping of individual costs that a firm does not identify with a *cost objective*.

indirect costs. Production costs not easily associated with the production of specific goods and services; *overhead costs*. Accountants may *allocate* them on some *arbitrary* basis to specific products or departments.

indirect labor (material) cost. An *indirect cost* for labor (material), such as for supervisors (supplies).

indirect method. See *statement of cash flows*.

individual proprietorship. *Sole proprietorship*.

Industry Audit Guides. A series of *AICPA* publications providing specific accounting and *auditing principles* for specialized situations. Audit guides have been issued covering government contractors, state and local government units, investment companies, finance companies, brokers and dealers in securities, and many other subjects.

inescapable cost. A *cost* that the firm or manager cannot avoid (see *avoidable*) because of an action. For example, if management shuts down two operating rooms in a hospital but still must employ security guards in unreduced numbers, the security costs are "inescapable" with respect to the decision to close the operating rooms.

inflation. A time of generally rising prices.

inflation accounting. Strictly speaking, *constant-dollar accounting*. Some writers incorrectly use the term to mean *current cost accounting*.

information circular. Canada: a document, accompanying the notice of a shareholders' meeting, prepared in connection with the solicitation of proxies by or on behalf of the management of the corporation. It contains information concerning the people making the solicitation, election of directors, appointment of auditors, and other matters to be acted on at the meeting.

information system. A system, sometimes formal and sometimes informal, for collecting, processing, and communicating data that are useful for the managerial functions of decision making, planning, and control and for financial reporting under the *attest* requirement.

inherent interest rate. *Implicit interest* rate.

initial cash flows. *Cash flows* associated with the beginning of an investment project. Often include *asset* cost, freight and installation costs, reduced by cash proceeds form disposing of existing assets made redundant or unnecessary by the new project, and *income tax* effect of *gain (loss)* on disposal of existing assets.

insolvent. Unable to pay debts when due; said of a company even though *assets* exceed *liabilities.*

installment. Partial payment of a debt or partial collection of a receivable, usually according to a contract.

installment contracts receivable. The name used for *accounts receivable* when the firm uses the *installment method* of recognizing revenue. Its *contra account, unrealized gross margin*, appears on the balance sheet as a subtraction from the amount receivable.

installment sales. Sales on account when the buyer promises to pay in several separate payments, called *installments*. The seller may, but need not, account for such sales using the *installment method*. If the seller accounts for installment sales with the sales *basis of revenue recognition* for financial reporting but with the installment method for income tax returns, then it will have *deferred income tax (liability).*

installment (sales) method. Recognizing *revenue* and *expense* (or *gross margin*) from a sales transaction in proportion to the fraction of the selling price collected during a period; allowed by the *IRS* for income tax reporting but acceptable in *GAAP* (*APB Opinion No. 10*) only when the firm cannot estimate cash collections with reasonable precision. See *realized* (and *unrealized*) *gross margin.*

Institute of Certified Management Accountants (ICMA). See *CMA* and *Institute of Management Accountants.*

Institute of Internal Auditors (IIA). The national association of accountants who are engaged in internal auditing and are employed by business firms; administers a comprehensive professional examination. Those who pass the exam qualify to be designated *CIA* (Certified Internal Auditor).

Institute of Management Accountants (IMA). Formerly, the National Association of Accountants, NAA; a society open to those engaged in management accounting; parent organization of the *ICMA*, which oversees the *CMA* program.

insurance. A contract for reimbursement of specific losses; purchased with insurance premiums. "Self-insurance" is not insurance but is merely the noninsured's willingness to assume the risk of incurring losses while saving the premium.

intangible asset. A nonphysical right that gives a firm an exclusive or preferred position in the marketplace. Examples are *copyright, patent, trademark, goodwill, organization costs, capitalized* advertising cost, computer programs, licenses for any of the preceding, government licenses (e.g., broadcasting or the right to sell liquor), *leases*, franchises, mailing lists, exploration permits, import and export permits, construction permits, and marketing quotas. Invariably, accountants define "intangible" using a "for example" list, as we have just done, because accounting has been unable to devise a definition of "intangible" that will include items such as those listed above but exclude stock and bond certificates. Accountants classify these items as tangibles, even though they give their holders a preferred position in receiving dividends and interest payments.

Interamerican Accounting Association (IAA). An organization, headquartered in Miami, devoted to facilitating interaction between accounting practitioners in the Americas.

intercompany elimination. See *eliminations.*

intercompany profit. Profit within an organization. If one *affiliated company* sells to another, and the goods remain in the second company's *inventory* at the end of the period, then the first company has not yet realized a *profit* by a sale to an outsider. The profit is "intercompany profit," and the accountant eliminates it from net *income* when preparing *consolidated income statements* or when the firm uses the *equity method.*

intercompany transaction. *Transaction* between a *parent company* and a *subsidiary* or between subsidiaries in a *consolidated entity;* the accountant must eliminate the effects of such a transaction when preparing *consolidated financial statements.* See *intercompany profit.*

intercorporate investment. Occurs when a given *corporation* owns *shares* or *debt* issued by another.

interdepartment monitoring. An *internal control* device. The advantage of allocating *service department costs* to *production departments* stems from the incentives that this gives those charged with the costs to control the costs incurred in the service department. That process of having one group monitor the performance of another is interdepartment monitoring.

interest. The charge or cost for using cash, usually borrowed funds. Interest on one's own cash used is an *opportunity cost, imputed interest.* The amount of interest for a loan is the total amount paid by a borrower to a lender less the amount paid by the lender to the borrower. Accounting seeks to allocate that interest over the time of the loan so that the interest rate (= interest charge/amount borrowed) stays constant each period See *interest rate* for discussion of the quoted amount. See *effective interest rate* and *nominal interest rate.*

interest, imputed. The difference between the face amount and the present value of a promise. If a borrower merely promises to pay a single amount, sometime later than the present, then the face amount the borrower will repay at *maturity* will exceed the present value (computed at a *fair market* interest rate, called the "imputed interest rate") of the promise. See also *imputed cost.*

interest factor. One plus the *interest* rate.

interest method. See *effective interest method.*

interest rate. A basis used for computing the cost of borrowing funds; usually expressed as a ratio between the number of currency units (e.g., dollars) charged for a period of time and the number of currency units borrowed for that same period of time. When the writers and speakers do not state a period, they almost always mean a period of one year. See *interest, simple interest, compound interest, effective (interest) rate,* and *nominal interest rate.*

interest rate swap. See *swap.*

interfund accounts. In governmental accounting, the accounts that show transactions between funds, especially interfund receivables and payables.

interim statements. Statements issued for periods less than the regular, annual *accounting period.* The *SEC* requires most corporations to issue interim statements on a quarterly basis. In preparing interim reports, a problem arises that the accountant can resolve only by understanding whether interim reports should report on the interim period (1) as a self-contained accounting period or (2) as an integral part of the year so that analysts can make forecasts of annual performance. For example, assume that at the end of the first quarter, a retailer has dipped into old LIFO layers, depleting its *inventory,* so that it computes *LIFO cost of goods sold* artificially low and *net income* artificially high, relative to the amounts the firm would have computed if it had made the "normal" purchases, equal to or greater than sales. The retailer expects to purchase inventory sufficiently large so that when it computes cost of goods sold for the year, there will be no *dips into old LIFO layers* and income will not be artificially high. The first approach will compute the quarterly income from low cost of goods sold using data for the dips that have actually occurred by the end of the quarter. The second approach will compute quarterly income from cost of goods sold assuming that purchases were equal to "normal" amounts and that the firm did not dip into old LIFO layers. *APB Opinion No. 28* and the *SEC* require that interim reports be constructed largely to satisfy the second purpose.

internal audit, internal auditor. An *audit* conducted by the firm's own employees, called "internal auditors," to ascertain whether the firm's *internal control* procedures work as planned. Contrast with an external audit conducted by a *CPA.*

internal controls. Policies and procedures designed to provide management with reasonable assurances that employees behave in a way that enables the firm to meet its organizational goals. See *control system.*

internal failure costs. *Costs incurred* when a firm detects nonconforming products and services before delivering them to customers; these include scrap, rework, and retesting.

internal rate of return (IRR). The discount rate that equates the net *present value* of a stream of cash outflows and inflows to zero.

internal reporting. Reporting for management's use in planning and control. Contrast with *external reporting* for financial statement users.

Internal Revenue Service (IRS). Agency of the U.S. Treasury Department responsible for administering the Internal Revenue Code and collecting income and certain other taxes.

International Accounting Standards Board (IASB). An organization that promotes the international convergence of accounting standards. Web Site: *www.iasb.org.* Successor to the International Accounting Standards Committee, IASC, which it superceded in 2001. A good site for tracing developments in international accounting is *www.iasplus.com*, maintained by the worldwide Deloitte firm, and recommended by the renowned

expert on international accounting, Professor Stephen A. Zeff of Rice University.

International Organization of Securities Commissions. *IOSCO.*

interperiod tax allocation. See *deferred income tax (liability).*

interpolation. The estimation of an unknown number intermediate between two (or more) known numbers.

Interpretations. See *FASB Interpretation.*

intrastatement tax allocation. See *tax allocation: intrastatement.*

intrinsic rewards. Rewards that come from within the individual, such as the satisfaction from studying hard, providing help to someone in need, or doing a good job. Contrast with *extrinsic rewards.*

inventoriable costs. *Costs* incurred that the firm adds to the cost of manufactured products; *product costs (assets)* as opposed to *period expenses.*

inventory. As a noun, the *balance* in an asset *account,* such as raw materials, supplies, work-in-process, and finished goods; as a verb, to calculate the *cost* of goods on hand at a given time or to count items on hand physically.

inventory equation. *Beginning inventory* + net additions − withdrawals = *ending inventory.* Ordinarily, additions are net purchases, and withdrawals are *cost of goods sold.* Notice that ending inventory, appearing on the balance sheet, and cost of goods sold, appearing on the income statement, must add to a fixed sum. The larger is one; the smaller must be the other. In valuing inventories, the firm usually knows beginning inventory and net purchases. Some inventory methods (for example, some applications of the *retail inventory method*) measure costs of goods sold and use the equation to find the cost of ending inventory. Most methods measure cost of ending inventory and use the equation to find the cost of goods sold (withdrawals). In *current cost* (in contrast to *historical cost*) *accounting,* additions (in the equation) include holding gains, whether realized or not. Thus the current cost inventory equation is as follows: Beginning Inventory (at Current Cost) + Purchases (where Current Cost is Historical Cost) + Holding Gains (whether Realized or Not) − Ending Inventory (at Current Cost) = Cost of Goods Sold (Current Cost).

inventory holding gains. See *inventory profit.*

inventory layer. See *LIFO inventory layer.*

inventory profit. A term with several possible meanings. Consider the data in the accompanying illustration. The firm uses a *FIFO cost flow assumption* and derives its *historical cost* data. The assumed *current cost* data resemble those that the FASB suggested in *SFAS No. 89.* The term *income from continuing operations* refers to revenues less expenses based on current, rather than historical, costs. To that subtotal, add realized holding gains to arrive at realized (conventional) income. To that, add unrealized holding gains to arrive at economic income. The term "inventory profit" often refers (for example in some *SEC* releases) to the realized holding gain,

Inventory Profit Illustration

	(Historical) Acquisition Cost Assuming FIFO	Current Cost
ASSUMED DATA		
Inventory, 1/1	$ 900	$1,100
Inventory, 12/31	1,160	1,550
Cost of Goods Sold for the Year . .	4,740	4,850
Sales for the Year	$5,200	$5,200
INCOME STATEMENT FOR THE YEAR		
Sales	$5,200	$5,200
Cost of Goods Sold	4,740	4,850
(1) Income from Continuing Operations		$ 350
Realized Holding Gains		$ 110[a]
(2) Realized Income = Conventional Net Income (under FIFO)	$ 460	$ 460
Unrealized Holding Gain		190[b]
(3) Economic Income		$ 650

[a]Realized holding gain during a period is current cost of goods sold less historical cost of goods sold; for the year the realized holding gain under FIFO is $110 = $4,850 2 $4,740. Some refer to this as "inventory profit."

[b]The total unrealized holding gain at any time is current cost of inventory on hand at that time less historical cost of that inventory. The unrealized holding gain during a period is the unrealized holding gain at the end of the period less the unrealized holding gain prior to this year. The unrealized holding gain at the beginning of the year in this example is: $200 = $1,100 – $900.

$110 in the illustration. The amount of inventory profit will usually be material when the firm uses FIFO and when prices rise. Other analysts, including us, prefer to use the term "inventory profit" to refer to the total *holding gain*, $300 (= $110 + $190, both realized and unrealized), but writers use this meaning less often. In periods of rising prices and increasing inventories, the realized holding gains under a FIFO cost flow assumption will exceed those under LIFO. In the illustration, for example, assume under LIFO that the historical cost of goods sold is $4,800, that historical LIFO cost of beginning inventory is $600, and that historical LIFO cost of ending inventory is $800. Then income from continuing operations, based on current costs, remains $350 (= $5,200 – $4,850), realized holding gains are $50 (= $4,850 – $4,800), realized income is $400 (= $350 + $50), the unrealized holding gain for the year is $250 [= ($1,550 – $800) – ($1,100 – $600)], and economic income is $650 (= $350 + $50 + $250). The cost flow assumption has only one real effect on this series of calculations: the split of the total holding gain into realized and unrealized portions. Thus, economic income does not depend on the cost flow assumption. Holding gains total

$300 in the illustration. The choice of cost flow assumption determines the portion reported as realized.

inventory turnover. Number of times the firm sells the average *inventory* during a period; *cost of goods sold* for a period divided by average inventory for the period. See *ratio*.

invested capital. *Contributed capital.*

investee. A company in which another entity, the "investor," owns stock.

investing activities. Acquiring and selling *securities* or productive *assets* expected to produce *revenue* over several *periods*.

investment. An *expenditure* to acquire property or other *assets* in order to produce *revenue*; the asset so acquired; hence a *current* expenditure made in anticipation of future income; said of other companies' *securities* held for the long term and appearing in a separate section of the *balance sheet*; in this context, contrast with *marketable securities*.

investment center. A *responsibility center*, with control over *revenues, costs,* and *assets*.

investment credit. A reduction in income tax liability sometimes granted by the federal government to firms that buy new equipment. This item is a credit in that the taxpayer deducts it from the tax bill, not from pretax income. The tax credit has been a given percentage of the purchase price of the assets purchased. The government has changed the actual rules and rates over the years. As of 1999, there is no investment credit. See *flow-through method* and *carryforward*.

investment decision. The decision whether to undertake an action involving production of goods or services; contrast with financing decision.

investment tax credit. *Investment credit.*

investment turnover ratio. A term that means the same thing as *total assets turnover ratio*.

investments. A balance sheet heading for tangible assets held for periods longer than the operating cycle and not used in revenue production (assets not meeting the definitions of *current assets* or *property, plant, and equipment*).

invoice. A document showing the details of a sale or purchase *transaction*.

IOSCO (International Organization of Securities Commissions). The name, since 1983, of a confederation of regulators of securities and futures markets. Members come from over 80 countries. The IOSCO encourages the *IASB* to eliminate accounting alternatives and to ensure that accounting standards are detailed and complete, with adequate disclosure requirements, and that financial statements are user-friendly.

I.O.U. An informal document acknowledging a debt, setting out the amount of the debt and signed by the debtor.

IRR. *Internal rate of return.*

IRS. *Internal Revenue Service.*

isoprofit line. On a graph showing feasible production possibilities of two products that require the use of the same, limited resources, a line showing all feasible production possibility combinations with the same *profit* or, perhaps, *contribution margin*.

issue. A corporation exchange of its stock (or *bonds*) for cash or other *assets*. Terminology says the corporation "issues," not "sells," that stock (or bonds). Also used in the context of withdrawing supplies or materials from inventory for use in operations and of drawing a *check*.

issued shares. Those shares of *authorized capital stock* that a *corporation* has distributed to the shareholders. See *issue*. Shares of *treasury stock* are legally issued but are not *outstanding* for the purpose of voting, *dividend declarations,* and *earnings-per-share* calculations.

J

JIT. See *just-in-time inventory.*

job cost sheet. A schedule showing actual or budgeted inputs for a special order.

job development credit. The name used for the *investment credit* in the 1971 tax law, since repealed, on this subject.

job (-order) costing. Accumulation of *costs* for a particular identifiable batch of product, known as a job, as it moves through production.

jobs. Customized products.

joint cost. Cost of simultaneously producing or otherwise acquiring two or more products, called joint products, that a firm must, by the nature of the process, produce or acquire together, such as the cost of beef and hides of cattle. Generally, accounting allocates the joint costs of production to the individual products in proportion to their respective sales value (or, sometimes and usually not preferred, their respective physical quantities) at the *split-off* point. Other examples include *central corporate expenses* and *overhead* of a department when it manufactures several products. See *common cost* and *sterilized allocation*.

joint cost allocation. See *joint cost*.

joint process. A process that converts a common input into several outputs.

joint product. One of two or more outputs with significant value that a firm must produce or acquire simultaneously. See *by-product* and *joint cost*.

journal. The place where the firm records transactions as they occur; the book of original entry.

journal entry. A dated *journal* recording, showing the accounts affected, of equal *debits* and *credits*, with an explanation of the *transaction*, if necessary.

Journal of Accountancy. A monthly publication of the *AICPA*.

Journal of Accounting and Economics. Scholarly journal published by the William E. Simon Graduate School of Business Administration of the University of Rochester.

Journal of Accounting Research. Scholarly journal containing articles on theoretical and empirical aspects of accounting; published by the Graduate School of Business of the University of Chicago.

journal voucher. A *voucher* documenting (and sometimes authorizing) a *transaction*, leading to an entry in the *journal*.

journalize. To make an entry in a *journal*.

judgment(al) sampling. A method of choosing a sample in which the analyst subjectively selects items for examination, in contrast to selecting them by statistical methods. Compare *random sampling*.

junk bond. A low-rated *bond* that lacks the merit and characteristics of an investment-grade bond. It offers high yields, typically in excess of 15 percent per year, but also possesses high risk of default. Sometimes writers, less pejoratively, call these "high-yield bonds." No clear line separates junk from nonjunk bonds.

just-in-time inventory (production) (JIT). In managing *inventory* for manufacturing, system in which a firm purchases or manufactures each component just before the firm uses it. Contrast with systems in which firms acquire or manufacture many parts in advance of needs. JIT systems have much smaller carrying costs for inventory, ideally none, but run higher risks of incurring *stockout* costs.

K

k. Two to the tenth power (2^{10} or 1,024), when referring to computer storage capacity. The one-letter abbreviation derives from the first letter of the prefix "kilo-" (which means 1,000 in decimal notation).

Kaizen costing. A management concept that seeks continuous improvements, likely occurring in small incremental amounts, by refinements of all components of a production process.

KG (Kommanditgesellschaft). Germany: similar to a general partnership (*OHG*) except that some of its members may limit their liability. One of the partners must be a *general partner* with unlimited liability.

kiting. A term with slightly different meanings in banking and auditing contexts. In both, however, it refers to the wrongful practice of taking advantage of the *float*, the time that elapses between the deposit of a *check* in one bank and its collection at another. In the banking context, an individual deposits in Bank A a check written on Bank B. He (or she) then writes checks against the deposit created in Bank A. Several days later, he deposits in Bank B a check written on Bank A, to cover the original check written on Bank B. Still later, he deposits in Bank A a check written on Bank B. The process of covering the deposit in Bank A with a check written on Bank B and vice versa continues until the person can arrange an actual deposit of cash. In the auditing context, kiting refers to a form of *window dressing* in which the firm makes the amount of the account Cash in Bank appear larger than it actually is by depositing in Bank A a check written on Bank B without recording the check written on Bank B in the *check register* until after the close of the *accounting period*.

know-how. Technical or business information that is of the type defined under *trade secret* but that a firm does not maintain as a secret. The rules of accounting for this *asset* are the same as for other *intangibles*.

L

labor efficiency variance. Measures labor productivity by multiplying the *standard* labor price times the difference between the standard labor hours and the actual labor hours.

labor price (or wage) variance. Measures the difference between the actual and *standard* labor prices (wage rates).

labor variances. The *price* (or *rate*) and *quantity* (or *usage*) *variances* for *direct labor* inputs in a *standard costing system*.

laid-down cost. Canada and UK: the sum of all direct costs incurred for procurement of goods up to the time of physical receipt, such as invoice cost plus customs and excise duties, freight and cartage.

land. An *asset* shown at *acquisition cost* plus the *cost* of any nondepreciable *improvements*; in accounting, implies use as a plant or office site rather than as a *natural resource*, such as timberland or farmland.

lapping (accounts receivable). The theft, by an employee, of cash sent in by a customer to discharge the latter's *payable*. The employee conceals the theft from the first customer by using cash received from a second customer. The employee conceals the theft from the second customer by using cash received from a third customer, and so on. The process continues until the thief returns the funds or can make the theft permanent by creating a fictitious *expense* or receivable write-off or until someone discovers the fraud.

lapse. To expire; said of, for example, an insurance policy or discounts that are made available for prompt payment and that the purchaser does not take.

last-in, first-out. See *LIFO*.

layer. See *LIFO inventory layer*.

lead time. The time that elapses between placing an order and receiving the *goods* or *services* ordered.

learning curve. A mathematical expression of the phenomenon that incremental unit costs to produce decrease as managers and labor gain experience from practice.

lease. A contract calling for the lessee (user) to pay the lessor (owner) for the use of an asset. A cancelable lease allows the lessee to cancel at any time. A noncancelable lease requires payments from the lessee for the life of the lease and usually shares many of the economic characteristics of *debt financing*. Most long-term noncancelable leases meet the usual criteria for classifying them as *liabilities,* and GAAP require the firm to show them as liabilities. *SFAS No. 13* and the *SEC* require disclosure, in notes to the financial statements, of the commitments for long-term noncancelable leases. See *capital lease* and *operating lease*.

leasehold. The *asset* representing the right of the lessee to use leased property. See *lease* and *leasehold improvement*.

leasehold improvement. An *improvement* to leased property. The firm should *amortize* it over the *service life* or the life of the lease, whichever is shorter.

least and latest rule. Paying the least amount of taxes as late as possible within the law to minimize the *present value* of tax payments for a given set of operations. Sensible taxpayers will follow this rule. When a taxpayer knows that tax rates will increase later, the taxpayer may reduce the present value of the tax burden by paying smaller taxes sooner. Each set of circumstances requires its own computations.

ledger. A book of accounts; book of final entry. See *general ledger* and *subsidiary ledger.* Contrast with *journal*.

legal capital. The amount of *contributed capital* that, according to state law, the firm must keep permanently in the firm as protection for creditors.

legal entity. See *entity*.

lender. See *loan*.

lessee. See *lease*.

lessor. See *lease*.

letter stock. Privately placed *common shares*; so called because the *SEC* requires the purchaser to sign a letter of intent not to resell the shares.

leverage. More than proportional result from extra effort or financing. Some measure of output increases faster than the measure of input. "Operating leverage" refers to the tendency of *net income* to rise at a faster rate than sales in the presence of *fixed costs*. A doubling of sales, for example, usually implies a more than doubling of net income. "Financial leverage" (or "capital leverage") refers to an increase in rate of return larger than the increase in explicit financing costs— the increased rate of return on *owners' equity* (see *ratio*) when an *investment* earns a return larger than the after-tax *interest rate* paid for *debt* financing. Because the interest charges on debt usually do not change, any *incremental* income benefits owners and none benefits debtors. When writers use the term "leverage" without a qualifying adjective, the term usually refers to financial leverage, the use of *long-term* debt in securing *funds* for the *entity*.

leveraged lease. A special form of lease involving three parties: a *lender*, a *lessor*, and a *lessee*. The lender, such as a bank or insurance company, lends a portion, say 80 percent, of the cash required for acquiring the *asset*. The lessor puts up the remainder, 20 percent, of the cash required. The lessor acquires the asset with the cash, using the asset as security for the loan, and leases it to the lessee on a *noncancelable* basis. The lessee makes periodic lease payments to the lessor, who in turn makes payments on the loan to the lender. Typically, the lessor has no obligation for the debt to the lender other than transferring a portion of the receipts from the lessee. If the lessee should default on the required lease payments, then the lender can repossess the leased asset. The lessor usually has the right to benefit from the tax deductions for *depreciation* on the asset, for *interest expense* on the loan from the lender, and for any *investment credit*. The lease is leveraged in the sense that the lessor, who takes most of the risks and enjoys most of the rewards of ownership, usually borrows most of the funds needed to acquire the asset. See *leverage*.

liability. An obligation to pay a definite (or reasonably definite) amount at a definite (or reasonably definite) time in return for a past or current benefit (that is, the obligation arises from a transaction that is not an *executory contract*); a probable future sacrifice of economic benefits arising from present obligations of a particular *entity* to *transfer assets* or to provide services to other entities in the future as a result of past *transactions* or events. *SFAC No. 6* says that "probable" refers to that which we can reasonably expect or believe but that is neither certain nor proved. A liability has three essential characteristics: (1) the obligation to transfer assets or services has a specified or knowable date, (2) the entity has little or no discretion to avoid the transfer, and (3) the event causing the obligation has already happened, that is, it is not executory.

lien. The right of person A to satisfy a claim against person B by holding B's property as security or by seizing B's property.

life annuity. A *contingent annuity* in which payments cease at the death of a specified person(s), usually the *annuitant(s)*.

LIFO (last-in, first-out). An *inventory* flow assumption in which the *cost of goods sold* equals the cost of the most recently acquired units and a firm computes the *ending inventory cost* from the costs of the oldest units. In periods of rising prices and increasing inventories, LIFO leads to higher reported expenses and therefore lower reported income and lower balance sheet inventories than does FIFO. Contrast with *FIFO*. See *FISH* and *inventory profit*.

LIFO conformity rule. The *IRS* rule requiring that companies that use a *LIFO cost flow assumption* for *income taxes* must also use LIFO in computing *income* reported in *financial statements* and forbidding the disclosure of *pro forma* results from using any other cost flow assumption.

LIFO, dollar-value method. See *dollar-value LIFO method*.

LIFO inventory layer. A portion of LIFO inventory cost on the *balance sheet*. The *ending inventory* in physical quantity will usually exceed the *beginning inventory*. The *LIFO cost flow assumption* assigns to this increase in physical quantities a cost computed from the prices of the earliest purchases during the year. The LIFO inventory then consists of layers, sometimes called "slices," which typically consist of relatively small amounts of physical quantities from each of the past

years when purchases in physical units exceeded sales in units. Each layer carries the prices from near the beginning of the period when the firm acquired it. The earliest layers will typically (in periods of rising prices) have prices much less than current prices. If inventory quantities should decline in a subsequent period—a "dip into old LIFO layers"—the latest layers enter cost of goods sold first.

LIFO reserve. *Unrealized holding gain* in *ending inventory*: current or *FIFO historical* cost of ending inventory less LIFO *historical cost*. A better term for this concept is "excess of current cost over LIFO historical cost." See *reserve*.

limited liability. The legal concept that shareholders of corporations are not personally liable for debts of the company.

limited partner. A *partnership* member who is not personally liable for debts of the partnership. Every partnership must have at least one *general partner,* who is fully liable.

line-of-business reporting. See *segment reporting*.

line of credit. An agreement with a bank or set of banks for short-term borrowings on demand.

linear programming. A mathematical tool for finding profit-maximizing (or cost-minimizing) combinations of products to produce when a firm has several products that it can produce but faces linear constraints on the resources available in the production processes or on maximum and minimum production requirements.

liquid. Said of a business with a substantial amount (the amount is unspecified) of *working capital*, especially *quick assets*.

liquid assets. *Cash, current marketable securities*, and sometimes, *current receivables*.

liquidating dividend. A *dividend* that a firm declares in the winding up of a business to distribute its assets to the shareholders. Usually the recipient treats this as a return of *investment*, not as *revenue*.

liquidation. Payment of a debt; sale of assets in closing down a business or a segment thereof.

liquidation value per share. The amount each *share* of stock will receive if the *board* dissolves a corporation; for *preferred stock* with a liquidation preference, a stated amount per share.

liquidity. Refers to the availability of *cash*, or near-cash resources, for meeting a firm's obligations.

LISH. An acronym, conceived by George H. Sorter, for *last-in, still-here*. LISH is the same cost flow assumption as *FIFO*. Many readers of accounting statements find it easier to think about inventory questions in terms of items still on hand. Think of FIFO in connection with *cost of goods sold* but of LISH in connection with *ending inventory*. See *FISH*.

list price. The published or nominally quoted price for goods.

list price method. See *trade-in transaction*.

loan. An arrangement in which the owner of property, called the lender, allows someone else, called the borrower, the use of the property for a period of time, which the agreement setting up the loan usually specifies. The borrower promises to return the property to the lender and, often, to make a payment for the use of the property. This term is generally used when the property is *cash* and the payment for its use is *interest*.

LOCOM. *Lower of cost or market.*

long-lived (term) asset. An asset whose benefits the firm expects to receive over several years; a *noncurrent* asset, usually includes *investments, plant assets*, and *intangibles*.

long run, long term. A term denoting a time or time periods in the future. How far in the future depends on context. For some securities traders, "long-term" can mean anything beyond the next hour or two. For most managers, it means the period of time long enough to allow change in total productive capacity. For government policymakers, it can mean anything beyond the next decade or two. For geologists, it can mean millions of years. In contrast to the *short run*. Use a hyphen when the phrase is an adjective, but no hyphen when it is a noun.

long-term (construction) contract accounting. The *percentage-of-completion method* of *revenue* recognition; sometimes used to mean the *completed contract method*.

long-term debt ratio. *Noncurrent liabilities* divided by total *assets*.

long-term liability (debt). *Noncurrent liability*.

long term. See *long run*.

long-term solvency risk. The risk that a firm will not have sufficient *cash* to pay its *debts* sometime in the *long run*.

loophole. Imprecise term meaning a technicality allowing a taxpayer (or *financial statements*) to circumvent the intent, without violating the letter, of the law (or *GAAP*).

loss. Excess of *cost* over net proceeds for a single transaction; negative *income* for a period; a cost expiration that produced no *revenue*. See *gain* for a discussion of related and contrasting terms and how to distinguish loss from *expense*.

loss contingency. See *contingency*.

lower of cost or market (LOCOM). A basis for valuation of *inventory* and, formerly in the US, of *marketable securities*. This basis sets inventory value at the lower of *acquisition cost* or *current replacement cost* (market), subject to the following constraints. First, the market value of an item used in the computation cannot exceed its *net realizable value*—an amount equal to selling price less reasonable costs to complete production and to sell the item. Second, the market value of an item used in the computation cannot be less than the net realizable value minus the normal *profit* ordinarily realized on disposition of completed items of this type. The basis chooses the lower-of-cost-or-market valuation as the lower of acquisition *cost* or replacement cost *(market)* subject to the upper and lower bounds on replacement cost established in the first two steps. Thus,

Market Value = Midvalue of (Replacement Cost, Net Realizable Value, Net Realizable Value less Normal Profit Margin)

Lower of Cost = Minimum (Acquisition Cost, Market or Market Value).
Valuation

The accompanying exhibit illustrates the calculation of the lower-of-cost-or-market valuation for four inventory items. Notice that each of the four possible outcomes occurs once in measuring lower of cost or market. Item 1 uses acquisition cost; item 2 uses net realizable value; item 3 uses replacement cost; and item 4 uses net realizable value less normal profit margin.

	Item			
	1	**2**	**3**	**4**
Calculation of Market Value				
(a) Replacement Cost	$92	$96	$92	$96
(b) Net Realizable Value ...	95	95	95	95
(c) Net Realizable Value Less Normal Profit Margin [= (b) − $9]	86	86	86	86
(d) Market = Midvalue [(a), (b), (c)]	92	95	92	95
Calculation of Lower of Cost or Market				
(e) Acquisition Cost	90	97	96	90
(f) Market [= (d)]	92	95	92	95
(g) Lower of Cost or Market = Minimum [(e), (f)]	90	95	92	90

A taxpayer may not use the lower-of-cost-or-market basis for inventory on tax returns in combination with a *LIFO cost flow assumption*. In the context of inventory, once the firm writes down the asset, it establishes a new "original cost" basis and ignores subsequent increases in market value in the accounts.

The firm may apply lower of cost or market to individual items of inventory or to groups (usually called *pools*) of items. The smaller the group, the more *conservative* the resulting valuation.

Omit hyphens when you use the term as a noun, but use them when you use the term as an adjectival phrase.

Ltd., Limited. UK: a private limited corporation. The name of a private limited company must include the word "Limited" or its abbreviation "Ltd."

lump-sum acquisition. *Basket purchase*.

M

MACRS. *Modified Accelerated Cost Recovery System*. See *Accelerated Cost Recovery System*. Since 1986, MACRS has been the accelerated depreciation method required for U.S. income tax purposes.

maintenance. *Expenditures* undertaken to preserve an *asset's* service potential for its originally intended life. These expenditures are *period expenses* or *product costs*. Contrast with *improvement,* and see *repair*.

make money. making money. Users of these words can mean any of the following: earn *income*; earn *other comprehensive income*; save *opportunity costs*; earn *revenues;* earn *gross margin;* sell for *cash;* and maybe others, as well. You can see that you should avoid these words in clear communications. See *money.*

make-or-buy decision. A managerial decision about whether the firm should produce a product internally or purchase it from others. Proper make-or-buy decisions in the short run result only when a firm considers *incremental costs* in the analysis.

maker (of note) (of check). One who signs a *note* to borrow; one who signs a *check*; in the latter context, synonymous with "drawer." See *draft.*

management. Executive authority that operates a business.

management accounting. See *managerial accounting.*

Management Accounting. Monthly publication of the *IMA.*

management audit. An audit conducted to ascertain whether a firm or one of its operating units properly carries out its objectives, policies, and procedures; generally applies only to activities for which accountants can specify qualitative standards. See *audit* and *internal audit.*

management by exception. A principle of management in which managers focus attention on performance only if it differs significantly from that expected.

management by objective (MBO). A management approach designed to focus on the definition and attainment of overall and individual objectives with the participation of all levels of management.

management information system (MIS). A system designed to provide all levels of management with timely and reliable information required for planning, control, and evaluation of performance.

management's discussion and analysis (MD&A). A discussion of management's views of the company's performance; required by the *SEC* to be included in the *10-K* and in the *annual report* to shareholders. The information typically contains discussion of such items as liquidity, results of *operations*, *segments*, and the effects of *inflation*.

managerial (management) accounting. Reporting designed to enhance the ability of management to do its job of decision making, planning, and control. Contrast with *financial accounting.*

manufacturing cost. Cost of producing goods, usually in a factory.

manufacturing expense. An imprecise, and generally incorrect, alternative title for *manufacturing overhead.* The term is generally incorrect because these costs are usually *product costs*, not expenses.

manufacturing overhead. General manufacturing *costs* that are not directly associated with identifiable units of product and that the firm incurs in providing a capacity to carry on productive activities. Accounting treats *fixed* manufacturing

overhead cost as a *product cost* under *full absorption costing* but as an *expense* of the period under *variable costing.*

margin. *Revenue* less specified expenses. See *contribution margin, gross margin*, and *current margin.*

margin of safety. Excess of actual, or budgeted, sales over *breakeven* sales; usually expressed in dollars but may be expressed in units of product.

marginal cost. The *incremental cost* or *differential cost* of the last unit added to production or the first unit subtracted from production. See *cost terminology* and *differential* for contrast.

marginal costing. *Variable costing.*

marginal revenue. The increment in *revenue* from the sale of one additional unit of product.

marginal tax rate. The amount, expressed as a percentage, by which income taxes increase when taxable income increases by one dollar. Contrast with *average tax rate.*

markdown. See *markup* for definition and contrast.

markdown cancellation. See *markup* for definition and contrast.

market-based transfer price. A *transfer price* based on external market data rather than internal company data.

market price. See *fair value.*

market rate. The rate of *interest* a company must pay to borrow *funds* currently. See *effective rate.*

market value. *Fair market value.*

marketable equity securities. *Marketable securities* representing *owners' equity* interest in other companies, rather than *loans* to them.

marketable securities. Other companies' *stocks* and *bonds* held that can be readily sold on stock exchanges or over-the-counter markets and that the company plans to sell as cash is needed; classified as *current assets* and as part of "cash" in preparing the *statement of cash flows.* If the firm holds these same securities for *long-term* purposes, it will classify them as *noncurrent assets. SFAS No. 115* requires that all marketable equity and all debt securities (except those debt securities the holder has the ability and intent to hold to maturity) appear at market value on the balance sheet. The firm reports changes in market value in income for *trading securities* but debits holding losses (or credits holding gains) directly to owners' equity accounts for *securities available for sale.*

marketing costs. Costs incurred to sell; includes locating customers, persuading them to buy, delivering the goods or services, and collecting the sales proceeds.

mark to market. As a verb, to record an item in the books at *current fair market value.* When used as an adjective, hyphenate the phrase.

markon. See *markup* for definition and contrast.

markup. The difference between the original selling price of items acquired for *inventory* and the cost. Precise usage calls this "markon," although many businesspeople use the term "markup." Because of confusion of this use of "markup" with its precise definition (see below), terminology sometimes uses "original markup." If the originally established retail price increases, the precise term for the amount of price increase is "markup," although terminology sometimes uses "additional markup." If a firm reduces selling price, terminology uses the terms "markdown" and "markup cancellation." "Markup cancellation" refers to reduction in price following "additional markups" and can, by definition, be no more than the amount of the additional markup; "cancellation of additional markup," although not used, is descriptive. "Markdown" refers to price reductions from the original retail price. A price increase after a markdown is a "markdown cancellation." If original cost is $12 and original selling price is $20, then markon (original markup) is $8; if the firm later increases the price to $24, the $4 increase is markup (additional markup); if the firm later lowers the price to $21, the $3 reduction is markup cancellation; if the firm further lowers the price to $17, the $4 reduction comprises $1 markup cancellation and $3 markdown; if the firm later increases the price to $22, the $5 increase comprises $3 of markdown cancellation and $2 of markup (additional markup). Accountants track markup cancellations and markdowns separately because they deduct the former (but not the latter) in computing the selling prices of goods available for sale for the denominator of the *cost percentage* used in the conventional *retail inventory method.*

markup cancellation. See *markup* for definition and contrast.

markup percentage. *Markup* divided by (acquisition cost plus *markup*).

master budget. A *budget* projecting all *financial statements* and their components.

matching convention. The concept of recognizing cost expirations *(expenses)* in the same accounting period during which the firm recognizes related *revenues;* combining or simultaneously recognizing the revenues and expenses that jointly result from the same *transactions* or other events.

material. As an adjective, it means relatively important, capable of influencing a decision (see *materiality*); as a noun, *raw material.*

materiality. The concept that accounting should disclose separately only those events that are relatively important (no operable definition yet exists) for the business or for understanding its statements. *SFAC No. 2* suggests that accounting information is material if "the judgment of a reasonable person relying on the information would have been changed or influenced by the omission or misstatement."

materials efficiency variance. Measures materials waste by multiplying the *standard* materials price times the difference between the standard materials quantity used and the actual materials quantity used.

materials price variance. Measures the difference between the actual and *standard* materials prices.

materials variances. *Price* and *quantity variances* for *direct materials* in *standard costing systems;* difference between actual cost and standard cost.

matrix. A rectangular array of numbers or mathematical symbols.

matrix inverse. For a given square *matrix* $\mathbf{A}$, the matrix, $\mathbf{A}^{-1}$ such that $\mathbf{AA}^{-1} = \mathbf{A}^{-1}\mathbf{A} = \mathbf{I}$, the identity matrix. Not all square matrices have inverses. Those that do not are "singular"; those that do are nonsingular.

maturity. The date at which an obligation, such as the *principal* of a *bond* or a *note*, becomes due.

maturity value. The amount expected to be collected when a loan reaches *maturity*. Depending on the context, the amount may be *principal* or principal and *interest.*

MBO. *Management by objective.*

MD&A. *Management's discussion and analysis* section of the *annual report.*

measuring unit. See *attribute measured* for definition and contrast.

merchandise. *Finished goods* bought by a retailer or wholesaler for resale; contrast with finished goods of a manufacturing business.

merchandise costs. Costs incurred to sell a product, such as commissions and advertising.

merchandise turnover. *Inventory turnover* for merchandise. See *ratio.*

merchandising business. As opposed to a manufacturing or service business, one that purchases (rather than manufactures) *finished goods* for resale.

merger. The joining of two or more businesses into a single *economic entity.* See *holding company.*

minority interest. A *balance sheet account* on *consolidated statements* showing the *equity* in a less-than-100-percent-owned *subsidiary* company; equity allocable to those who are not part of the controlling (majority) interest; may be classified either as shareholders' equity or as a liability of *indeterminate term* on the consolidated balance sheet. The *income statement* must subtract the minority interest in the current period's income of the less-than-100-percent-owned subsidiary to arrive at consolidated *net income* for the period.

minority investment. A holding of less than 50 percent of the *voting stock* in another corporation; accounted for with the *equity method* when the investor owns sufficient shares that it can exercise "significant influence" and as *marketable securities* otherwise. See *mutual fund.*

minutes book. A record of all actions authorized at corporate *board of directors* or shareholders' meetings.

MIS. *Management information system.*

mix variance. One of the *manufacturing variances.* Many *standard cost* systems specify combinations of inputs—for example, labor of a certain skill and materials of a certain quality grade. Sometimes combinations of inputs used differ from those contemplated by the standard. The mix variance attempts to report the cost difference caused by those changes in the combination of inputs.

mixed cost. A *semifixed* or a *semivariable* cost.

Modified Accelerated Cost Recovery System (MACRS). Name used for the *Accelerated Cost Recovery System,* originally passed by Congress in 1981 and amended by Congress in 1986.

modified cash basis. The *cash basis of accounting* with long-term assets accounted for using the *accrual basis of accounting.* Most users of the term "cash basis of accounting" actually mean "modified cash basis."

monetary assets and liabilities. See *monetary items.*

monetary gain or loss. The firm's *gain* or *loss* in *general purchasing power* as a result of its holding *monetary assets* or liabilities during a period when the *general purchasing power of the dollar* changes; explicitly reported in *constant-dollar accounting.* During periods of *inflation,* holders of net monetary assets lose, and holders of net monetary liabilities gain, general purchasing power. During periods of *deflation,* holders of net monetary assets gain, and holders of net monetary liabilities lose, general purchasing power.

monetary items. Amounts fixed in terms of dollars by statute or contract; *cash, accounts receivable, accounts payable*, and *debt*. The distinction between monetary and nonmonetary items is important for *constant-dollar accounting* and for *foreign exchange gain or loss* computations. In the foreign exchange context, account amounts denominated in dollars are not monetary items, whereas amounts denominated in any other currency are monetary.

monetary-nonmonetary method. *Foreign currency translation* that translates all *monetary items* at the *current exchange rate* and translates all *nonmonetary items* at the *historical rate.*

money. A word seldom used with precision in accounting, at least in part because economists have not yet agreed on its definition. Economists use the term to refer to both a medium of exchange and a store of value. See *cash* and *monetary items.*

Consider a different set of issues concerning the phrase, "making money." Lay terminology uses this to mean "earning *income*" whether, as a result, the firm increased its *cash* balances or other *net assets.* The user does not typically mean that the firm has increased cash equal to the amount of net income, although the unaware listeners often think the phrase means this. Given that usage equates "making money" with "earning income," in this sense "money" has a credit balance not a debit balance. Since cash typically has a debit balance, the phrase "making money" is even more troublesome. Consider the following language from the U.S. statutes on forfeitures required of some who commit illegal acts: "...the amount of money acquired through illegal transactions...." Does the law mean the cash left over after the lawbreaker has completed the illegal transactions the income earned from the transactions or something else? Sometimes "making money" means avoiding a cost, not recognized in financial accounting.

Consider the following sets of questions and see how you have to think to decide whether, in a given question, "money" refers to a debit or a credit. Assume I start with $10 in cash.

1. I took a cab and it cost $10; I spent money. Did the cabbie make money? Does the cabbie have money?
2. I decided to walk, so I didn't spend $10. Did I make money?
3. I canceled the trip. Did I make money?

"Money" sometimes refers to debits and sometimes to credits; "making money" sometimes means earning accounting income and sometimes avoiding a cost, not reported in accounting, so careful writing about accounting avoids the word.

In fact, "making money" can mean any of the following:

1. Earning *income*: "Microsoft made a lot of money last year."
2. Earning *other comprehensive income*: "I still hold the Microsoft shares I bought in 1990 and I've made a lot of money on them." This is an *unrealized holding gain*, an increase in wealth, but not an increase in cash.
3. Save *opportunity costs* or opportunity losses: "If I'd only sold those shares in 1999, I'd have made more money. I didn't sell the shares, so I lost money." Accounting does not recognize opportunity costs. This use of the term refers to the lost benefits from not doing something. You rightly feel you'd have been better off selling those shares. If you were to say, "I didn't sell; I lost money as a result," some people who use the phrase would argue you didn't lose money because you failed to make a transaction, but some people would agree with you.
4. Earn revenues: "George Forman has made a lot of money touting his cooking devices on TV." George earned income and received payments, but the user of the term this way subtracts no costs.
5. Earn gross margin: "We at the hardware store make more money selling those cooking devices than we do selling basic tools, because the cookers have a larger markup." The user understands we need to subtract some costs, but doesn't take into account the indirect costs such as occupancy costs, inventory holding costs, and shrinkage costs.
6. Sell for cash: "You didn't make any money yet from selling those cookers because the customer won't pay for another two months." This user would be better off to know the *allowance method for uncollectibles*. Net revenue, gross sales less expected uncollectibles, better describes what this user has in mind.
7. Generating cash flow from operations. Many companies can have positive income but negative cash flow from operations. Some analysts will say such a company made no money in such a year.
8. And, don't forget *counterfeiting*.

money purchase plan. A *pension plan* in which the employer contributes a specified amount of cash each year to each employee's pension fund; sometimes called a *defined-contribution plan;* contrast with *defined-benefit plan.* The plan does not specify the benefits ultimately received by the employee, since these benefits depend on the rate of return on the cash invested. As of the mid-1990s, most corporate pension plans were defined-benefit plans because both the law and *generally accepted accounting principles* for pensions made defined-benefit plans more attractive than money purchase plans. *ERISA* makes money purchase plans relatively more attractive than they had been. We expect the relative number of money purchase plans to continue to increase.

mortality table. Data of life expectancies or probabilities of death for persons of specified age and sex.

mortgage. A claim given by the borrower (mortgagor) to the lender (mortgagee) against the borrower's property in return for a loan.

moving average. An *average* computed on observations over time. As a new observation becomes available, analysts drop the oldest one so that they always compute the average for the same number of observations and use only the most recent ones.

moving average method. *Weighted-average inventory method.*

multiple-step. Said of an *income statement* that shows various subtotals of *expenses* and *losses* subtracted from *revenues* to show intermediate items such as *operating income*, income of the enterprise (operating income plus *interest* income), income to investors (income of the enterprise less *income taxes*), net income to shareholders (income to investors less interest charges), and income retained (net income to shareholders less dividends). See *entity theory*.

municipal bond. A *bond* issued by a village, town, or city. *Interest* on such bonds is generally exempt from federal *income taxes* and from some state income taxes. Because bonds issued by state and county governments often have these characteristics, terminology often calls such bonds "municipals" as well. These are also sometimes called "tax-exempts."

mutual fund. An investment company that issues its own stock to the public and uses the proceeds to invest in securities of other companies. A mutual fund usually owns less than 5 or 10 percent of the stock of any one company and accounts for its investments using current *market values*. Contrast with *holding company*.

mutually exclusive (investment) projects. Competing investment projects in which accepting one project eliminates the possibility of undertaking the remaining projects.

N

NAARS. *National Automated Accounting Research System.*

NASDAQ (National Association of Securities Dealers Automated Quotation System). A computerized system to provide brokers and dealers with price quotations for securities traded *over the counter* as well as for some *NYSE* securities.

National Association of Accountants (NAA). Former name for the *Institute of Management Accountants (IMA)*.

National Automated Accounting Research System (NAARS). A computer-based information-retrieval system containing, among other things, the complete text of most public corporate annual reports and *Forms 10-K*. Users may access the system through the *AICPA*.

natural business year. A 12-month period chosen as the reporting period so that the end of the period coincides with a low point in activity or inventories. See *ratio* for a discussion of analyses of financial statements of companies using a natural business year.

natural classification. *Income statement* reporting form that classifies *expenses* by nature of items acquired, that is, materials, wages, salaries, insurance, and taxes, as well as depreciation. Contrast with *functional classification*.

natural resources. Timberland, oil and gas wells, ore deposits, and other products of nature that have economic value. Terminology uses the term *depletion* to refer to the process of *amortizing* the cost of natural resources. Natural resources are "nonrenewable" (for example, oil, coal, gas, ore deposits) or "renewable" (timberland, sod fields); terminology often calls the former "wasting assets." See also *reserve recognition accounting* and *percentage depletion*.

negative confirmation. See *confirmation*.

negative goodwill. See *goodwill*. When a firm acquires another company, and the *fair market value* of the *net assets* acquired exceeds the purchase price, *APB Opinion No. 16* requires that the acquiring company reduce the valuation of noncurrent assets (except *investments* in *marketable securities*) until the purchase price equals the adjusted valuation of the fair market value of net assets acquired. If, after the acquiring company reduces the valuation of noncurrent assets to zero, the valuation of the remaining net assets acquired still exceeds the purchase price, then the difference appears as a credit balance on the balance sheet as negative goodwill. For negative goodwill to exist, someone must be willing to sell a company for less than the fair market value of net current assets and marketable securities. Because such bargain purchases are rare, one seldom sees negative goodwill in the financial statements. When it does appear, it generally signals unrecorded obligations, such as a contingency related to a pending lawsuit.

negotiable. Legally capable of being transferred by *endorsement*. Usually said of *checks* and *notes* and sometimes of *stocks* and *bearer bonds*.

negotiated transfer price. A *transfer price* set jointly by the buying and the selling divisions.

net. Reduced by all relevant deductions.

net assets. Total *assets* minus total *liabilities;* equals the amount of *owners' equity*. Often, we find it useful to split the balance sheet into two parts: owners' equity and all the rest. The "rest" is total assets less total liabilities. To take an example, consider one definition of *revenue*: the increase in owners' equity accompanying the net assets increase caused by selling goods or rendering services. An alternative, more cumbersome way to say the same thing is: the increase in owners' equity accompanying the assets increase or the liabilities decrease, or both, caused by selling goods or rendering services. Consider the definition of *goodwill*: the excess of purchase price over the fair market value of identifiable net assets acquired in a purchase transaction. Without the phrase "net assets," the definition might be as follows: the excess of purchase price over the fair market value of identifiable assets reduced by the fair market value of identifiable liabilities acquired in a purchase transaction.

net bank position. From a firm's point of view, *cash* in a specific bank less *loans* payable to that bank.

net book value. *Book value.*

net current asset value (per share). *Working capital* divided by the number of common shares outstanding. Some analysts think that when a common share trades in the market for an amount less than net current asset value, the shares are undervalued and investors should purchase them. We find this view naive because it ignores, generally, the efficiency of capital markets and, specifically, unrecorded obligations, such as for executory contracts and contingencies, not currently reported as *liabilities* in the *balance sheet* under *GAAP*.

net current assets. *Working capital = current assets – current liabilities.*

net income. The excess of all *revenues* and *gains* for a period over all *expenses* and *losses* of the period. The FASB is proposing to discontinue use of this term and substitute *earnings*. See *comprehensive income.*

net loss. The excess of all *expenses* and *losses* for a period over all *revenues* and *gains* of the period; negative *net income.*

net markup. In the context of *retail inventory methods, markups* less markup cancellations; a figure that usually ignores *markdowns* and markdown cancellations.

net of tax method. A nonsanctioned method for dealing with the problem of *income tax allocation*; described in *APB Opinion No. 11.* The method subtracts deferred tax items from specific *asset* amounts rather than showing them as a deferred credit or *liability.*

net of tax reporting. Reporting, such as for *income from discontinued operations, extraordinary items*, and *prior-period adjustments*, in which the firm adjusts the amounts presented in the *financial statements* for all income tax effects. For example, if an extraordinary loss amounted to $10,000, and the marginal tax rate was 40 percent, then the extraordinary item would appear "net of taxes" as a $6,000 loss. Hence, not all a firm's income taxes necessarily appear on one line of the income statement. The reporting allocates the total taxes among *income from continuing operations, income from discontinued operations, extraordinary items*, cumulative effects of *accounting changes*, and *prior-period adjustments.*

net operating profit. *Income from continuing operations.*

net present value. Discounted or *present value* of all cash inflows and outflows of a project or of an *investment* at a given *discount rate.*

net price method (of recording purchase or sales discounts). Method that records a *purchase* (or *sale*) at its *invoice* price less all *discounts* made available, under the assumption that the firm will take nearly all discounts offered. The purchaser debits, to an *expense* account, discounts lapsed through failure to pay promptly. For purchases, management usually prefers to know about the amount of discounts lost because of inefficient operations, not the amounts taken, so that most managers prefer the net price method to the *gross price method.*

net realizable (sales) value. Current selling price less reasonable costs to complete production and to sell the item. Also, a method for *allocating joint costs* in proportion to *realizable values* of the joint products. For example, joint products A and B together cost $100; A sells for $60, whereas B

sells for $90. Then a firm would allocate to A ($60/$150) × $100 = .40 x $100 = $40 of cost while it would allocate to B ($90/$150) x $100 = $60 of cost.

net sales. Sales (at gross invoice amount) less *returns, allowances*, freight paid for customers, and *discounts* taken.

net working capital. *Working capital;* the term "net" is redundant in accounting. Financial analysts sometimes mean *current assets* when they speak of working capital, so for them the "net" is not redundant.

net worth. A misleading term with the same meaning as *owners' equity*. Avoid using this term; accounting valuations at historical cost do not show economic worth.

network analysis. A project planning and scheduling method, usually displayed in a diagram, that enables management to identify the interrelated sequences that it must accomplish to complete the project.

new product development time. The period between a firm's first consideration of a product and delivery of it to the customer.

New York Stock Exchange (NYSE). A public market in which those who own seats (a seat is the right to participate) trade various corporate *securities.*

next-in, first-out. See *NIFO.*

NIFO (next-in, first-out). A *cost flow assumption,* one not allowed by GAAP. In making decisions, many managers consider *replacement costs* (rather than *historical costs*) and refer to them as NIFO costs.

no par. Said of *stock* without a *par value.*

nominal accounts. *Temporary accounts,* such as *revenue* and *expense* accounts; contrast with *balance sheet accounts.* The firm *closes* all nominal accounts at the end of each *accounting period.*

nominal amount (value). An amount stated in dollars, in contrast to an amount stated in *constant dollars*. Contrast with *real amount (value).*

nominal dollars. The measuring unit giving no consideration to differences in the *general purchasing power of the dollar* over time. The face amount of currency or coin, a *bond,* an *invoice,* or a *receivable* is a nominal-dollar amount. When the analyst adjusts that amount for changes in *general purchasing power*, it becomes a *constant-dollar* amount.

nominal interest rate. A rate specified on a *debt* instrument; usually differs from the market or *effective rate;* also, a rate of *interest* quoted for a year. If the interest compounds more often than annually, then the *effective interest rate* exceeds the nominal rate.

noncancelable. See *lease.*

nonconsolidated subsidiary. An *intercorporate investment* in which the parent owns more than 50 percent of the shares of the *subsidiary* but accounts for the investment with the *cost method*.

noncontributory. Said of a *pension plan* in which only the employer makes payments to a pension *fund*. Contrast with *contributory*.

noncontrollable cost. A cost that a particular manager cannot *control*.

noncurrent. Of a *liability*, due in more than one year (or more than one *operating cycle*); of an *asset*, the firm will enjoy the future benefit in more than one year (or more than one operating cycle).

nonexpendable fund. A governmental fund whose *principal*, and sometimes earnings, the entity may not spend.

noninterest-bearing note. A *note* that does not specify explicit interest. The *face value* of such a note will exceed its *present value* at any time before *maturity* value so long as *interest rates* are positive. *APB Opinion No. 21* requires that firms report the present value, not face value, of long-term noninterest-bearing notes as the *asset* or *liability* amount in financial statements. For this purpose, the firm uses the *historical interest rate*. See *interest, imputed*.

nonmanufacturing costs. All *costs* incurred other than those necessary to produce goods. Typically, only manufacturing firms use this designation.

nonmonetary items. All items that are not monetary. See *monetary items*.

nonoperating. In the *income statement* context, said of *revenues* and *expenses* arising from *transactions* incidental to the company's main line(s) of business; in the *statement of cash flows* context, said of all financing and investing sources or uses of cash in contrast to cash provided by operations. See *operations*.

nonprofit corporation. An incorporated *entity*, such as a hospital, with owners who do not share in the earnings. It usually emphasizes providing services rather than maximizing income.

nonrecurring. Said of an event that is not expected to happen often for a given firm. *APB Opinion No. 30* requires firms to disclose separately the effects of such events as part of *ordinary* items unless the event is also unusual. See *extraordinary* item.

nonvalue-added activity. An activity that causes costs without increasing a product's or service's value to the customer.

normal cost. Former name for *service cost* in accounting for pensions and other postemployment benefits.

normal costing. Method of charging costs to products using actual *direct materials*, actual *direct labor*, and predetermined *factory overhead* rates.

normal costing system. *Costing* based on *actual material* and *labor* costs but using *predetermined overhead* rates per unit of some *activity* basis (such as *direct labor hours* or machine

hours) to apply overhead to production. Management decides the rate to charge to production for overhead at the start of the period. At the end of the period the accounting multiplies this rate by the actual number of units of the base activity (such as actual direct labor hours worked or actual machine hours used during the period) to apply overhead to production.

normal spoilage. Costs incurred because of ordinary amounts of spoilage. Accounting prorates such costs to units produced as *product costs*. Contrast with *abnormal spoilage*.

normal standard cost, normal standards. The *cost* a firm expects to incur under reasonably efficient operating conditions with adequate provision for an average amount of rework, spoilage, and the like.

normal volume. The level of production that will, over a time span, usually one year, satisfy purchasers' demands and provide for reasonable *inventory* levels.

note. An unconditional written promise by the maker (borrower) to pay a certain amount on demand or at a certain future time.

note receivable discounted. A *note* assigned by the holder to another. The new holder of the note typically pays the old holder an amount less than the *face value* of the note, hence the word "discounted." If the old holder assigns the note to the new holder with recourse, the old holder has a *contingent liability* until the maker of the note pays the debt. See *factoring*.

notes. Some use this word instead of *footnotes* when referring to the detailed information included by management as an integral part of the *financial statements* and covered by the *auditor's report*.

NOW (negotiable order of withdrawal) account. Negotiable order of withdrawal. A *savings account* whose owner can draw an order to pay, much like a *check* but technically not a check, and give it to others, who can redeem the order at the savings institution.

number of days sales in inventory (or receivables). Days of average inventory on hand (or average collection period for receivables). See *ratio*.

NV (naamloze vennootschap). Netherlands: a public limited liability company.

NYSE. *New York Stock Exchange*.

O

OASD(H)I. *Old Age, Survivors, Disability, and (Hospital) Insurance*.

objective. See *reporting objectives* and *objectivity*.

objective function. In *linear programming*, the name of the profit (or cost) criterion the analyst wants to maximize (or minimize).

objectivity. The reporting policy implying that the firm will not give formal recognition to an event in financial statements until the firm can measure the magnitude of the events with reasonable accuracy and check that amount with independent verification.

obsolescence. An asset's *market value* decline caused by improved alternatives becoming available that will be more *cost-effective*. The decline in market value does not relate to physical changes in the asset itself. For example, computers become obsolete long before they wear out. See *partial obsolescence*.

Occupational Safety and Health Act. *OSHA.*

off-balance-sheet financing. A description often used for an obligation that meets all the tests to be classified a liability except that the obligation arises from an *executory contract* and, hence, is not a *liability*. Consider the following example. Miller Corporation desires to acquire land costing $25 million, on which it will build a shopping center. It could borrow the $25 million from its bank, paying interest at 12 percent, and buy the land outright from the seller. If so, both an asset and a liability will appear on the balance sheet. Instead, it borrows $5 million and purchases for $5 million from the seller an *option* to buy the land from the seller at any time within the next six years for a price of $20 million. The option costs Miller Corporation $5 million immediately and provides for continuing "option" payments of $2.4 million per year, which precisely equal Miller Corporation's borrowing rate multiplied by the remaining purchase price of the land: $2.4 million = .12 x $20 million. Although Miller Corporation need not continue payments and can let the option lapse at any time, it also has an obligation to begin developing on the site immediately. Because Miller Corporation has invested a substantial sum in the option, will invest more, and will begin immediately developing the land, Miller Corporation will almost certainly exercise its option before expiration. The seller of the land can take the option contract to the bank and borrow $20 million, paying interest at Miller Corporation's borrowing rate, 12 percent per year. The continuing option payments from Miller Corporation will be sufficient to enable the seller to make its payments to the bank. *Generally accepted accounting principles* view Miller Corporation as having acquired an option for $5 million rather than having acquired land costing $25 million in return for $25 million of debt. The firm will likely be able to structure this transaction so that it need not recognize debt on the balance sheet until it borrows more funds to exercise the option.

The *FASB* has curtailed the use of such financings with *FIN 46*. See also *variable interest entity*.

off-balance-sheet risk. A contract that exposes an entity to the possibility of loss but that does not appear in the financial statements. For example, a *forward-exchange contract* generally does not appear on the balance sheet because it is an *executory contract*. The contract may reduce or increase the entity's exposure to foreign-exchange risk (the chance of loss due to unfavorable changes in the foreign-exchange rate). It may also expose the entity to credit risk (the chance of loss that occurs when the *counterparty* to the contract cannot fulfill the contract terms). *SFAS No. 105* requires entities to describe contracts with off-balance-sheet risk.

OHG (Offene Handelsgesellschaft). Germany: a general *partnership*. The partners have unlimited *liability*.

Old Age, Survivors, Disability, and (Hospital) Insurance, or OASD(H)I. The technical name for Social Security under the Federal Insurance Contributions Act (*FICA*).

on consignment. Said of goods delivered by the owner (the consignor) to another (the consignee) to be sold by the consignee. On delivery of the goods from the consignor to the consignee, the consignor can, but need not, make an entry transferring the goods at cost from Finished Goods Inventory to another inventory account, such as Goods out on Consignment. The consignor recognizes revenue only when the consignee has sold the goods to customers. Under such an arrangement, the owner of the goods bears the inventory holding costs until the ultimate seller (consignee) sells them. The owner also bears the risk that the items will never sell to final customers, but manufacturers or distributors who provide generous return options to their customers can achieve this aspect of consignment sales in an outright sale. The consignment protects the consignor from the consignee's bankruptcy, as the arrangement entitles the owner either to the return of the property or to payment of a specified amount. The goods are assets of the consignor. Such arrangements provide the consignor with better protection than an outright sale on account to the consignee in bankruptcy. In event of bankruptcy, the ordinary seller, holding an account receivable, has no special claim to the return of the goods, whereas a consignor can reclaim the goods without going through bankruptcy proceedings, from which the consignor might recover only a fraction of the amounts owed to it.

on (open) account. Said of a *purchase* (or *sale*) when the seller expects payment sometime after delivery and the purchaser does not give a *note* evidencing the *debt*. The purchaser has generally signed an agreement sometime in the past promising to pay for such purchases according to an agreed time schedule. When the firm sells (purchases) on open account, it *debits* (*credits*) *Accounts Receivable (Payable)*.

one-line consolidation. Said of an *intercorporate investment* accounted for with the *equity method*. With this method, the *income* and *balance sheet* total *assets* and *equities* amounts are identical to those that would appear if the parent consolidated the investee firm, even though the income from the investment appears on a single line of the income statement and the net investment appears on a single line in the Assets section of the balance sheet.

one-write system. A system of bookkeeping that produces several records, including original documents, in one operation by the use of reproductive paper and equipment that provides for the proper alignment of the documents.

on-time performance. The firm delivers the product or service at the time scheduled for delivery.

open account. Any *account* with a nonzero *debit* or *credit* balance. See *on (open) account*.

operating. An adjective used to refer to *revenue* and *expense* items relating to the company's main line(s) of business. See *operations*.

operating accounts. *Revenue, expense,* and *production cost accounts.* Contrast with *balance sheet accounts.*

operating activities. For purposes of the *statement of cash flows*, all *transactions* and *events* that are neither *financing activities* nor *investing activities*. See *operations*.

operating budget. A formal *budget* for the *operating cycle* or for a year.

operating cash flow. *Cash flow from operations*. Financial statement analysts sometimes use this term to mean *cash flow from operations – capital expenditures – dividends*. This usage leads to such ambiguity that the reader should always confirm the definition that the writer uses before drawing inferences from the reported data.

operating cycle. *Earnings cycle*.

operating expenses. *Expenses* incurred in the course of *ordinary* activities of an *entity;* frequently, a classification including only *selling, general*, and *administrative expenses*, thereby excluding *cost of goods sold, interest*, and *income tax* expenses. See *operations*.

operating lease. A *lease* accounted for by the *lessee* without showing an *asset* for the lease rights (*leasehold*) or a *liability* for the lease payment obligations. The lessee reports only rental payments during the period, as *expenses* of the period. The asset remains on the lessor's *books,* where rental collections appear as *revenues*. Contrast with *capital lease*.

operating leverage. Usually said of a firm with a large proportion of *fixed costs* in its *total costs*. Consider a book publisher or a railroad: such a firm has large costs to produce the first unit of service; then, the *incremental costs* of producing another book or transporting another freight car are much less than the *average cost*, so the *gross margin* on the sale of the subsequent units is relatively large. Contrast this situation with that, for example, of a grocery store, where the *contribution margin* equals less than 5 percent of the selling price. For firms with equal profitability, however defined, we say that the one with the larger percentage increase in income from a given percentage increase in dollar sales has the larger operating leverage. See *leverage* for contrast of this term with "financial leverage." See *cost terminology* for definitions of terms involving the word "cost."

operating margin. *Revenues* from *sales* minus *cost of goods sold* and *operating expenses*.

operating margin based on current costs. *Revenues* from *sales* minus *current cost* of goods sold; a measure of operating efficiency that does not depend on the *cost flow assumption* for *inventory;* sometimes called "current (gross) margin." See *inventory profit* for illustrative computations.

operating ratio. See *ratio*.

operational control. See *control system*.

operational measures of time. Indicators of the speed and reliability with which organizations supply products and services to customer. Companies generally use two operational measures of time: *customer response time* and *on-time performance*.

operations. A word not precisely defined in *accounting*. Generally, analysts distinguish operating activities (producing and selling *goods* or *services*) from financing activities (raising funds) and *investing activities*. Acquiring goods on account and then paying for them one month later, though generally classified as an operating activity, has the characteristics of a financing activity. Or consider the transaction of selling plant assets for a price in excess of book value. On the *income statement*, the gain appears as part of income from operations ("continuing operations" or "discontinued" operations, depending on the circumstances), but the *statement of cash flows* reports all the funds received below the Cash from Operations section, as a nonoperating source of cash, "disposition of non-current assets." In income tax accounting, an "operating loss" results whenever deductions exceed taxable revenues.

opinion. The *auditor's report* containing an attestation or lack thereof; also, *APB Opinion*.

opinion paragraph. Section of *auditor's report*, generally following the *scope paragraph* and giving the auditor's conclusion that the *financial statements* are (rarely, are not) in accordance with *GAAP* and present fairly the *financial position*, changes in financial position, and the results of *operations*.

opportunity cost. The *present value* of the *income* (or *costs*) that a firm could earn (or save) from using an *asset* in its best alternative use to the one under consideration.

opportunity cost of capital. *Cost of capital*.

option. The legal right to buy or sell something during a specified period at a specified price, called the *exercise* price. If the right exists during a specified time interval, it is known as an "American option." If it exists for only one specific day, it is known as a "European option." Do not confuse employee stock options with *put* and *call* options, traded in various public markets.

ordinary annuity. An *annuity in arrears*.

ordinary income. For income tax purposes, reportable *income* not qualifying as *capital gains*.

organization costs. The *costs* incurred in planning and establishing an *entity*; example of an *intangible* asset. The firm must treat these costs as *expenses* of the period, even though the *expenditures* clearly provide future benefits and meet the test to be *assets*.

organization goals. Broad objectives for an organization established by management.

original cost. *Acquisition cost;* in public utility accounting, the acquisition cost of the *entity* first devoting the *asset* to public use. See *aboriginal cost*.

original entry. Entry in a *journal*.

OSHA (Occupational Safety and Health Act). The federal law that governs working conditions in commerce and industry.

other comprehensive income. According to the FASB, *comprehensive income* items that are not themselves part of earnings. See *comprehensive income*. To define comprehensive income does not convey its essence. To understand comprehensive income, you need to understand how it differs from *earnings* (or *net income*), the concept measured in the *earnings (income) statement*. The term *earnings* (or *net income*) refers to the sum of all components of comprehensive income *minus* the components of other comprehensive income.

outlay. The amount of an *expenditure*.

outlier. Said of an observation (or data point) that appears to differ significantly in some regard from other observations (or data points) of supposedly the same phenomenon; in a *regression analysis,* often used to describe an observation that falls far from the fitted regression equation (in two dimensions, line).

out-of-pocket. Said of an *expenditure* usually paid for with cash; an *incremental* cost.

out-of-stock cost. The estimated decrease in future *profit* as a result of losing customers because a firm has insufficient quantities of *inventory* currently on hand to meet customers' demands.

output. Physical quantity or monetary measurement of *goods* and *services* produced.

outside director. A corporate board of directors member who is not a company officer and does not participate in the corporation's day-to-day management.

outstanding. Unpaid or uncollected; when said of *stock,* refers to the shares issued less *treasury stock;* when said of *checks,* refers to a check issued that did not clear the *drawer's* bank prior to the *bank statement* date.

over-and-short. Title for an *expense account* used to account for small differences between book balances of cash and actual cash and vouchers or receipts in *petty cash* or *change funds.*

overapplied (overabsorbed) overhead. Costs applied, or *charged,* to product and exceeding actual *overhead costs* during the period; a *credit balance* in an overhead account after overhead is assigned to product.

overdraft. A *check* written on a checking account that contains funds less than the amount of the check.

overhead costs. Any *cost* not directly associated with the production or sale of identifiable goods and services; sometimes called "burden" or "indirect costs" and, in the UK, "oncosts"; frequently limited to manufacturing overhead. See *central corporate expenses* and *manufacturing overhead.*

overhead rate. Standard, or other predetermined rate, at which a firm applies *overhead costs* to products or to services.

over-the-counter. Said of a *security* traded in a negotiated transaction, as on *NASDAQ,* rather than in an auctioned one on an organized stock exchange, such as the *New York Stock Exchange.*

owners' equity. *Proprietorship; assets* minus *liabilities; paid-in capital* plus *retained earnings* of a corporation; partners' capital accounts in a *partnership*; owner's capital account in a *sole proprietorship.*

P

paid-in capital. Sum of balances in *capital stock* and *capital contributed in excess of par (or stated) value* accounts; same as *contributed capital* (minus *donated capital*). Some use the term to mean only *capital contributed in excess of par (or stated value).*

paid-in surplus. See *surplus*.

P&L. Profit-and-loss statement; *income statement.*

paper profit. A *gain* not yet realized through a *transaction;* an *unrealized holding gain.*

par. See *at par* and *face amount.*

par value. *Face amount* of a *security.*

par value method. In accounting for *treasury stock,* method that *debits* a common stock account with the *par value* of the shares required and allocates the remaining debits between the *Additional Paid-in Capital* and *Retained Earnings* accounts. Contrast with *cost method.*

parent company. Company owning more than 50 percent of the voting shares of another company, called the *subsidiary.*

Pareto chart. A graph of a skewed statistical distribution. In many business settings, a relatively small percentage of the potential population causes a relatively large percentage of the business activity. For example, some businesses find that the top 20 percent of the customers buy 80 percent of the goods sold. Or, the top 10 percent of products account for 60 percent of the revenues or 70 percent of the profits. The statistical distribution known as the Pareto distribution has this property of skewness, so a graph of a phenomenon with such skewness has come to be known as a Pareto chart, even if the underlying data do not actually well fit the Pareto distribution. Practitioners of *total quality management* find that in many businesses, a small number of processes account for a large fraction of the quality problems, so they advocate charting potential problems and actual occurrences of problems to identify the relatively small number of sources of trouble. They call such a chart a "Pareto chart."

partial obsolescence. One cause of decline in *market value* of an *asset.* As technology improves, the economic value of existing *assets* declines. In many cases, however, it will not pay a firm to replace the existing asset with a new one, even though it would acquire the new type rather than the old if it did make a new acquisition currently. In these cases, the accountant should theoretically recognize a loss from partial obsolescence from the firm's owning an old, out-of-date asset, but *GAAP* do not permit recognition of partial obsolescence until the sum of future cash flows from the asset total less than book value; see *impairment.* The firm will carry the old asset at *cost* less *accumulated depreciation* until the firm retires it from service so long as the *undiscounted* future *cash flows* from the asset exceed its book value. Thus management that uses an asset subject to partial obsolescence reports results inferior to those reported by a similar management that uses a new asset. See *obsolescence.*

partially executory contract. *Executory contract* in which one or both parties have done

something other than merely promise.

partially funded. Said of a *pension plan* in which the firm has not funded all earned benefits. See *funded* for funding requirements.

partially vested. Said of a *pension plan* in which not all employee benefits have *vested*. See *graded vesting*.

participating dividend. *Dividend* paid to preferred shareholders in addition to the minimum preferred dividends when the *preferred stock* contract provides for such sharing in earnings. Usually the contract specifies that dividends on *common shares* must reach a specified level before the preferred shares receive the participating dividend.

participating preferred stock. *Preferred stock* with rights to *participating dividends*.

participative budgeting. Using input from lower- and middle-management employees in setting goals.

partner's drawing. A payment made to a partner and debited against his or her share of income or capital. The name of a *temporary account,* closed to the partner's capital account, to record the debits when the partner receives such payments.

partnership. Contractual arrangement between individuals to share resources and operations in a jointly run business. See *general* and *limited partner* and *Uniform Partnership Act*.

patent. A right granted for up to 20 years by the federal government to exclude others from manufacturing, using, or selling a claimed design, product, or plant (e.g., a new breed of rose) or from using a claimed process or method of manufacture; an *asset* if the firm acquires it by purchase. If the firm develops it internally, current *GAAP* require the firm to *expense* the development costs when incurred.

payable. Unpaid but not necessarily due or past due.

pay-as-you-go. Said of an *income tax* scheme in which the taxpayer makes periodic payments of income taxes during the period when it earns the income to be taxed; in contrast to a scheme in which the taxpayer owes no payments until the end of, or after, the period when it earned the income being taxed (called PAYE—pay-as-you-earn—in the UK). The phrase is sometimes used to describe an *unfunded pension plan*, or retirement benefit plan, in which the firm makes payments to pension plan beneficiaries from general corporate funds, not from cash previously contributed to a fund. Under this method, the firm debits expense as it makes payments, not as it incurs the obligations. This is not acceptable as a method of accounting for pension plans, under *SFAS No. 87,* or as a method of *funding,* under *ERISA*.

payback period. Amount of time that must elapse before the cash inflows from a project equal the cash outflows.

payback reciprocal. One divided by the *payback period*. This number approximates the *internal rate of return* on a project when the project life exceeds twice the payback period and the cash inflows are identical in every period after the initial period.

PAYE (pay-as-you-earn). See *pay-as-you-go* for contrast.

payee. The person or entity who receives a cash payment or who will receive the stated amount of cash on a *check*. See *draft*.

payout ratio. *Common stock dividends* declared for a year divided by net *income* to common stock for the year; a term used by financial analysts. Contrast with *dividend yield*.

payroll taxes. Taxes levied because the taxpayer pays salaries or wages; for example, *FICA* and unemployment compensation insurance taxes. Typically, the employer pays a portion and withholds part of the employee's wages.

PCAOB. *Public Company Accounting Oversight Board.*

P/E ratio. *Price-earnings ratio.*

Pension Benefit Guarantee Corporation (PBGC). A federal corporation established under *ERISA* to guarantee basic pension benefits in covered pension plans by administering terminated pension plans and placing *liens* on corporate assets for certain unfunded pension liabilities.

pension fund. *Fund*, the assets of which the trustee will pay to retired ex-employees, usually as a *life annuity;* generally held by an independent trustee and thus not an *asset* of the employer.

pension plan. Details or provisions of employer's contract with employees for paying retirement *annuities* or other benefits. See *funded, vested, service cost, prior service cost, money purchase plan*, and *defined-benefit plan*.

per books. An expression used to refer to the *book value* of an item at a specific time.

percent. Any number, expressed as a decimal, multiplied by 100.

percentage depletion (allowance). Deductible *expense* allowed in some cases by the federal *income tax* regulations; computed as a percentage of gross income from a *natural resource* independent of the unamortized cost of the *asset*. Because the amount of the total deductions for tax purposes usually exceeds the cost of the asset being *depleted*, many people think the deduction is an unfair tax advantage or *loophole*.

percentage-of-completion method. Recognizing *revenues* and *expenses* on a job, order, or contract (1) in proportion to the *costs* incurred for the period divided by total costs expected to be incurred for the job or order ("cost to cost") or (2) in proportion to engineers' or architects' estimates of the incremental degree of completion of the job, order, or contract during the period. Contrast with *completed contract method*.

percentage statement. A statement containing, in addition to (or instead of) dollar amounts, ratios of dollar amounts to some base. In a percentage *income statement*, the base is usually either *net sales* or total *revenues,* and in a percentage *balance sheet*, the base is usually total *assets*.

period. *Accounting period.*

period cost. An inferior term for *period expense.*

period expense (charge). *Expenditure*, usually based on the passage of time, charged to operations of the accounting period rather than *capitalized* as an asset. Contrast with *product cost*.

periodic cash flows. *Cash flows* that occur during the life of an investment project. Often include *receipts* from *sales, expenditures* for *fixed* and *variable production costs,* and savings of *fixed* and *variable* production costs, to name a few. They do not include non-cash items, such as *financial accounting depreciation charges* or *allocated* items of *overhead* not requiring *differential* cash expenditures.

periodic inventory. In recording *inventory,* a method that uses data on beginning inventory, additions to inventories, and ending inventory to find the cost of withdrawals from inventory. Contrast with *perpetual inventory.*

periodic procedures. The process of making *adjusting entries* and *closing entries* and preparing the *financial statements,* usually by use of *trial balances* and *work sheets.*

permanent account. An account that appears on the *balance sheet.* Contrast with *temporary account.*

permanent difference. Difference between reported income and taxable income that will never reverse and, hence, requires no entry in the *deferred income tax (liability)* account; for example, nontaxable state and municipal *bond* interest that will appear on the financial statements. Contrast with *temporary difference.* See *deferred income tax liability.*

permanent file. The file of working papers that are prepared by a public accountant and that contain the information required for reference in successive professional engagements for a particular organization, as distinguished from working papers applicable only to a particular engagement.

perpetual annuity. *Perpetuity.*

perpetual inventory. *Inventory* quantity and amount records that the firm changes and makes current with each physical addition to or withdrawal from the stock of goods; an inventory so recorded. The records will show the physical quantities and, frequently, the dollar valuations that should be on hand at any time. Because the firm explicitly computes *cost of goods sold,* it can use the *inventory equation* to compute an amount for what *ending inventory* should be. It can then compare the computed amount of ending inventory with the actual amount of ending inventory as a *control* device to measure the amount of *shrinkages.* Contrast with *periodic inventory.*

perpetuity. An *annuity* whose payments continue forever. The *present value* of a perpetuity in *arrears* is p/r where p is the periodic payment and r is the *interest rate* per period. If a perpetuity promises $100 each year, in arrears, forever and the interest rate is 8 percent per year, then the perpetuity has a value of $1,250 = $100/.08.

perpetuity growth model. See *perpetuity.* A *perpetuity* whose cash flows grow at the rate g per period and thus has *present value* of $1/(r - g)$. Some call this the "Gordon Growth Model" because Myron Gordon wrote about applications of this formula and its variants in the 1950s. John Burr Williams wrote about them in the 1930s.

personal account. *Drawing account.*

PERT (Program Evaluation and Review Technique). A method of *network analysis* in which the analyst makes three time estimates for each activity—the optimistic time, the most likely time, and the pessimistic time—and gives an expected completion date for the project within a probability range.

petty cash fund. Currency and coins maintained for expenditures that the firm makes with cash on hand.

physical units method. A method of allocating a *joint cost* to the *joint products* based on a physical measure of the joint products; for example, allocating the cost of a cow to sirloin steak and to hamburger, based on the weight of the meat. This method usually provides nonsensical (see *sterilized allocation)* results unless the physical units of the joint products tend to have the same value.

physical verification. *Verification,* by an *auditor,* performed by actually inspecting items in *inventory, plant assets,* and the like, in contrast to merely checking the written records. The auditor may use statistical sampling procedures.

planning and control process. General name for the management techniques comprising the setting of organizational goals and *strategic plans, capital budgeting, operations* budgeting, comparison of plans with actual results, performance evaluation and corrective action, and revisions of goals, plans, and budgets.

plant. *Plant assets.*

plant asset turnover. Number of dollars of *sales* generated per dollar of *plant assets;* equal to sales divided by average *plant assets.*

plant assets. *Assets* used in the revenue-production process. Plant assets include buildings, machinery, equipment, land, and natural resources. The phrase "property, plant, and equipment" (though often appearing on balance sheets) is therefore a redundancy. In this context, "plant" used alone means buildings.

plantwide allocation method. A method for *allocating overhead costs* to product. First, use one *cost pool* for the entire plant. Then, allocate all costs from that pool to products using a single overhead *allocation* rate, or one set of rates, for all the products of the plant, independent of the number of departments in the plant.

PLC (public limited company). UK: a publicly held *corporation.* Contrast with *Ltd.*

pledging. The borrower assigns *assets* as security or *collateral* for repayment of a loan.

pledging of receivables. The process of using expected collections on *accounts receivable* as *collateral* for a loan. The borrower remains responsible for collecting the receivable but promises to use the proceeds for repaying the debt.

plow back. To retain *assets* generated by earnings for continued investment in the business.

plug. Process for finding an unknown amount. For any *account,* beginning balance + additions − deductions = ending balance; if you know any three of the four items, you can find the fourth with simple arithmetic, called "plugging." In making a *journal* *entry*, often you know all *debits* and all but one of the *credits* (or vice versa). Because *double-entry* bookkeeping requires equal debits and credits, you can compute the unknown quantity by subtracting the sum of the known credits from the sum of all the debits (or vice versa), also called "plugging." Accountants often call the unknown the "plug." For example, in amortizing a *discount* on *bonds payable* with the *straight-line depreciation* method, *interest expense* is a plug: interest expense = interest payable + *discount amortization*. See *trade-in transaction* for an example. The term sometimes has a bad connotation for accountants because plugging can occur in a slightly different context. During the process of preparing a *preclosing trial balance* (or *balance sheet*), often the sum of the debits does not equal the sum of the credits. Rather than find the error, some accountants are tempted to force equality by changing one of the amounts, with a plugged debit or credit to an account such as Other Expenses. No harm results from this procedure if the amount of the error is small compared with asset totals, since spending tens or hundreds of dollars in a bookkeeper's or accountant's time to find an error of a few dollars will not be *cost-effective*. Still, most accounting teachers rightly disallow this use of plugging because exercises and problems set for students provide enough information not to require it.

point of sale. The time, not the location, at which a *sale* occurs.

pooling-of-interests method. Accounting for a *business combination* by adding together the *book value* of the *assets* and *equities* of the combined firms; generally leads to a higher reported *net income* for the combined firms than results when the firm accounts for the business combination as a purchase because the *market values* of the merged assets generally exceed their book values. US GAAP do not allow this method, although it previously did, so financial statements still reflect the effects of pooling accounting. Contrast with *purchase method*. Called *uniting-of-interests method* by the *IASB*.

population. The entire set of numbers or items from which the analyst samples or performs some other analysis.

positive confirmation. See *confirmation*.

post. To record entries in an *account* to a *ledger*, usually as transfers from a *journal*.

post-closing trial balance. *Trial balance* taken after the accountant has *closed* all *temporary accounts*.

post-statement events. Events that have *material* impact and that occur between the end of the *accounting period* and the formal publication of the *financial statements*. Even though the events occur after the end of the period being reported on, the firm must disclose such events in notes if the auditor is to give a *clean opinion*.

potentially dilutive. A *security* that its holder may convert into, or exchange for, common stock and thereby reduce reported *earnings per share; options, warrants, convertible bonds*, and *convertible preferred stock*.

PPB. *Program budgeting*. The second "P" stands for "plan."

practical capacity. Maximum level at which a plant or department can operate efficiently.

precision. The degree of accuracy for an estimate derived from a sampling process, usually expressed as a range of values around the estimate. The analyst might express a sample estimate in the following terms: "Based on the sample, we are 95 percent sure [confidence level] that the true population value is within the range of X to Y [precision]." See *confidence level*.

preclosing trial balance. *Trial balance* taken at the end of the period before *closing entries;* in this sense, an *adjusted trial balance;* sometimes taken before *adjusting entries* and then synonymous with *unadjusted trial balance*.

predatory prices. Setting prices below some measure of cost in an effort to drive out competitors with the hope of recouping losses later by charging monopoly prices. Illegal in the United States if the prices set are below long-run variable costs. We know of no empirical evidence that firms are successful at recoupment.

predetermined (factory) overhead rate. Rate used in applying *overhead costs* to products or departments developed at the start of a period. Compute the rate as estimated overhead cost divided by the estimated number of units of the overhead allocation base (or *denominator volume*) activity. See *normal costing*.

preemptive right. The privilege of a *shareholder* to maintain a proportionate share of ownership by purchasing a proportionate share of any new stock issues. Most state corporation laws allow corporations to pay shareholders to waive their preemptive rights or state that preemptive rights exist only if the *corporation charter* explicitly grants them. In practice, then, preemptive rights are the exception rather than the rule.

preference as to assets. The rights of *preferred shareholders* to receive certain payments before common shareholders receive payments in case the board dissolves the corporation.

preferred shares. *Capital stock* with a claim to *income* or *assets* after *bondholders* but before *common shares*. Dividends on preferred shares are *income distributions*, not *expenses*. See *cumulative preferred stock*.

premium. The excess of issue (or market) price over *par value*. For a different context, see *insurance*.

premium on capital stock. Alternative but inferior title for *capital contributed in excess of par (or stated) value*.

prepaid expense. An *expenditure* that leads to a *deferred charge* or *prepayment*. Strictly speaking, this is a contradiction in terms because an *expense* is a gone asset, and this title refers to past *expenditures*, such as for rent or insurance premiums, that still have future benefits and thus are *assets*. We try to avoid this term and use "prepayment" instead.

prepaid income. An inferior alternative title for *advances from customers*. Do not call an item *revenue* or *income* until the firm earns it by delivering goods or rendering services.

prepayments. *Deferred charges;* assets representing *expenditures* for future benefits. Rent and insurance premiums paid in advance are usually current prepayments.

present value. Value today (or at some specific date) of an amount or amounts to be paid or received later (or at other, different dates), discounted at some *interest* or *discount rate*; an amount that, if invested today at the specified rate, will grow to the amount to be paid or received in the future.

prevention costs. *Costs incurred* to prevent defects in the products or services they produce, including procurement inspection, processing control (inspection), design, quality training and machine inspection.

price. The quantity of one *good* or *service*, usually *cash*, asked in return for a unit of another good or service. See *fair value*.

price-earnings (P/E) ratio. At a given time, the market value of a company's *common share*, per share, divided by the *earnings per* common *share* for the past year. The analyst usually bases the denominator on *income from continuing operations* or, if the analyst thinks the current figure for that amount does not represent a usual situation—such as when the number is negative or, if positive, close to zero—on some estimate of the number. See *ratio*.

price index. A series of numbers, one for each period, that purports to represent some *average* of prices for a series of periods, relative to a base period.

price level. The number from a *price index* series for a given period or date.

price level–adjusted statements. *Financial statements* expressed in terms of dollars of uniform purchasing power. The statements restate *nonmonetary* items to reflect changes in general *price levels* since the time the firm acquired specific *assets* and incurred *liabilities*. The statements recognize a *gain* or *loss* on *monetary items* as the firm holds them over time periods when the general *price level changes*. Conventional financial statements show *historical costs* and ignore differences in purchasing power in different periods.

price variance. In accounting for *standard costs*, an amount equal to (actual cost per unit − standard cost per unit) times actual quantity.

primary earnings per share (PEPS). Net *income* to common shareholders plus *interest* (net of tax effects) or *dividends* paid on *common-stock equivalents* divided by (weighted average of common shares outstanding plus the net increase in the number of common shares that would become *outstanding* if the holders of all common stock equivalents were to exchange them for common shares with cash proceeds, if any, used to retire common shares). As of 1997 and *SFAS No. 128,* replaced with *basic earnings per share.*

prime cost. Sum of *direct materials* plus *direct labor* costs assigned to product.

prime rate. The loan rate charged by commercial banks to their creditworthy customers. Some customers pay even less than the prime rate and others, more. The *Federal Reserve Bulletin* is the authoritative source of information about historical prime rates.

principal. An amount on which *interest* accrues, either as *expense* (for the borrower) or as *revenue* (for the lender); the *face amount* of a *loan;* also, the absent owner (principal) who hires the manager (agent) in a "principal-agent" relationship.

principle. See *generally accepted accounting principles.*

prior-period adjustment. A *debit* or *credit* that is made directly to *retained earnings* (and that does not affect *income* for the period) to adjust earnings as calculated for prior periods. Such adjustments are now rare. Theory suggests that accounting should correct for errors in accounting estimates (such as the *depreciable life* or *salvage value* of an asset) by adjusting retained earnings so that statements for future periods will show correct amounts. But *GAAP* require that corrections of such estimates flow through current, and perhaps future, *income statements*. See *accounting changes* and *accounting errors*.

prior service cost. *Present value* at a given time of a *pension plan's* retroactive *benefits*. "Unrecognized prior service cost" refers to that portion of prior service cost not yet *debited* to *expense*. See *actuarial accrued liability* and *funded.* Contrast with *normal cost.*

pro forma income. See *pro forma statements.*

pro forma statements. Hypothetical statements; financial statements as they would appear if some event, such as a *merger* or increased production and sales, had occurred or were to occur; sometimes spelled as one word, "proforma." The phrase "pro forma income" has come to disrepute, as some companies have published pro forma income statements showing their good news, their recurring income, and omitting the bad news, as non-recurring. They have attempted to focus the investment community on their own presentation of this good news, de-emphasizing GAAP net income. The *SEC* and others have attempted to make these disclosures less misleading.

probable. In many of its definitions, the *FASB* uses the term "probable." See, for example, *asset, firm commitment, liability.* A survey of practicing accountants revealed that the average of the probabilities that those surveyed had in mind when they used the term "probable" was 85 percent. Some accountants think that any event whose outcome is greater than 50 percent should be called "probable." The FASB uses the phrase "more likely than not" when it means greater than 50 percent.

proceeds. The *funds* received from the disposition of assets or from the issue of securities.

process costing. A method of *cost accounting* based on average costs (total cost divided by the *equivalent units* of work done in a period); typically used for assembly lines or for products that the firm produces in a series of steps that are more continuous than discrete.

product. *Goods* or *services* produced.

product cost. Any *manufacturing cost* that the firm can—or, in some contexts, should—debit to an *inventory* account. See *flow of costs,* for example. Contrast with *period expenses*.

product life cycle. Time span between initial concept (typically starting with research and development) of a good or service and the time when the firm ceases to support customers who have purchased the good or service.

production cost. *Manufacturing cost.*

production cost account. A *temporary account* for accumulating *manufacturing costs* during a period.

production department. A department producing salable *goods* or *services*; contrast with *service department.*

production method (depreciation). One form of *straight-line depreciation.* The firm assigns to the depreciable asset (e.g., a truck) a *depreciable life* measured not in elapsed time but in units of output (e.g., miles) or perhaps in units of time of expected use. Then the *depreciation* charge for a period is a portion of depreciable cost equal to a fraction computed as the actual output produced during the period divided by the expected total output to be produced over the life of the asset. This method is sometimes called the "units-of-production (or output) method."

production method (revenue recognition). *Percentage-of-completion method* for recognizing *revenue.*

production volume variance. Standard fixed *overhead* rate per unit of normal *capacity* (or base activity) times (units of base activity budgeted or planned for a period minus actual units of base activity worked or assigned to product during the period); often called a "volume variance."

productive capacity. One *attribute measured* for *assets.* The *current cost* of *long-term assets* means the cost of reproducing the productive capacity (for example, the ability to manufacture one million units a year), not the cost of reproducing the actual physical assets currently used (see *reproduction cost*). *Replacement cost* of productive capacity will be the same as reproduction cost of assets only in the unusual case when no technological improvement in production processes has occurred and the relative prices of goods and services used in production have remained approximately the same as when the firm acquired the currently used goods and services.

product-level activities. Work that supports a particular product or service line. Examples include design work, supervision, and advertising that are specific to each type of product or service.

production cycle efficiency. Measures the efficiency of the production cycle by computing the ratio of the time spent processing a unit divided by the *production cycle time.* The higher the percentage, the less the time and costs spent on *non-value-added activities,* such as moving and storage.

production cycle time. The total time to produce a unit. Includes processing, moving, storing, and inspecting.

profit. Excess of *revenues* over *expenses* for a *transaction*; sometimes used synonymously with *net income* for the period.

profit and loss account. UK: *retained earnings.*

profit-and-loss sharing ratio. The fraction of *net income* or loss allocable to a partner in a *partnership;.* need not be the same fraction as the partner's share of capital.

profit-and-loss statement. *Income statement.*

profit center. A *responsibility center* for which a firm accumulates both *revenues* and *expenses.* Contrast with *cost center.*

profit margin. *Sales* minus all *expenses.*

profit margin percentage. *Profit margin* divided by *net sales.*

profit maximization. The doctrine that the firm should account for a given set of operations so as to make reported *net income* as large as possible; contrast with *conservatism.* This concept in accounting differs from the profit-maximizing concept in economics, which states that the firm should manage operations to maximize the present value of the firm's wealth, generally by equating *marginal costs* and *marginal revenues.*

profit plan. The *income statement* portion of a *master budget.*

profit-sharing plan. A *defined-contribution plan* in which the employer contributes amounts based on *net income.*

profit variance analysis. Analysis of the causes of the difference between budgeted profit in the *master budget* and the profits earned.

profit-volume analysis (equation). Analysis of effects, on *profits,* caused by changes in volume or *contribution margin* per unit or *fixed costs.* See *breakeven chart.*

profit-volume graph. See *breakeven chart.*

profit-volume ratio. *Net income* divided by net sales in dollars.

profitability accounting. *Responsibility accounting.*

program budgeting (PPB). Specification and analysis of inputs, outputs, costs, and alternatives that link plans to *budgets.*

programmed cost. A *fixed cost* not essential for carrying out operations. For example, a firm can control costs for research and development and advertising designed to generate new business, but once it commits to incur them, they become fixed costs. These costs are sometimes called managed costs or *discretionary costs.* Contrast with *capacity costs.*

progressive tax. Tax for which the rate increases as the taxed base, such as income, increases. Contrast with *regressive tax.*

project financing arrangement. As defined by *SFAS No. 47,* the financing of an investment project in which the lender looks principally to the *cash flows* and *earnings* of the project as the source of funds for repayment and to the *assets* of the project as *collateral* for the loan. The general *credit* of the project entity usually does not affect the terms of the financing either because the borrowing entity is a *corporation* without other assets or because the financing provides that the lender has no direct *recourse* to the entity's owners.

projected benefit obligation. The *actuarial present value* at a given date of all pension benefits attributed by a *defined-benefit pension* formula to employee service rendered before that date. The analyst measures the obligation using assumptions as to future compensation levels if the formula incorporates future compensation, as happens, for example, when the plan bases the eventual pension benefit on wages of the last several years of employees' work lives. Contrast to "accumulated benefit obligation," where the analyst measures the obligation using employee compensation levels at the time of the measurement date.

projected financial statement. *Pro forma* financial statement.

projection. See *financial projection* for definition and contrast.

promissory note. An unconditional written promise to pay a specified sum of cash on demand or at a specified date.

proof of journal. The process of checking the arithmetic accuracy of *journal entries* by testing for the equality of all *debits* and all *credits* since the last previous proof.

property dividend. A *dividend in kind*.

property, plant, and equipment. See *plant assets*.

proportionate consolidation. Canada: a presentation of the *financial statements* of any investor-investment relationship, whereby the investor's pro rata share of each *asset, liability, income* item, and *expense* item appears in the *financial statements* of the investor under the various *balance sheet* and *income statement* headings.

proprietary accounts. See *budgetary accounts* for definition and contrast in the context of governmental accounting.

proprietorship. *Assets* minus *liabilities* of an *entity*; equals *contributed capital* plus *retained earnings*.

proprietorship theory. The corporation view that emphasizes the form of the *accounting equation* that says *assets – liabilities = owners' equity*; contrast with *entity theory*. The major implication of a choice between these theories deals with the treatment of *subsidiaries*. For example, the proprietorship theory views *minority interest* as an *indeterminate-term liability*. The proprietorship theory implies using a *single-step income statement*.

prorate. To *allocate* in proportion to some base; for example, to allocate *service department* costs in proportion to hours of service used by the benefited department or to allocate *manufacturing variances* to product sold and to product added to *ending inventory*.

prorating variances. See *prorate*.

prospectus. Formal written document describing *securities* a firm will issue. See *proxy*.

protest fee. Fee charged by banks or other financial agencies when the bank cannot collect items (such as *checks*) presented for collection.

provision. Part of an *account* title. Often the firm must recognize an *expense* even though it cannot be sure of the exact amount. The entry for the estimated expense, such as for *income taxes* or expected costs under *warranty*, is as follows:

Expense (Estimated).............	X	
Liability (Estimated)		X

American terminology often uses "provision" in the expense account title of the above entry. Thus, Provision for Income Taxes means the estimate of income tax expense. (British terminology uses "provision" in the title for the estimated liability of the above entry, so that Provision for Income Taxes is a balance sheet account.)

proxy. Written authorization given by one person to another so that the second person can act for the first, such as to vote shares of stock; of particular significance to accountants because the *SEC* presumes that management distributes financial information along with its proxy solicitations.

public accountant. Generally, this term is synonymous with *certified public accountant*. Some jurisdictions, however, license individuals who are not CPAs as public accountants.

public accounting. That portion of accounting primarily involving the *attest* function, culminating in the *auditor's report*.

Public Company Accounting Oversight Board. PCAOB. A board established by the Sarbanes-Oxley Act of 2002 which regulates the auditing profession and sets standards for audits of public companies. The *SEC* appoints its members.

PuPU. Acronym for *p*urchasing *p*ower *u*nit; conceived by John C. Burton, former chief accountant of the *SEC*. Those who think that *constant-dollar accounting* is not particularly useful poke fun at it by calling it "PuPU accounting."

purchase allowance. A reduction in sales *invoice price* usually granted because the purchaser received *goods* not exactly as ordered. The purchaser does not return the goods but agrees to keep them for a price lower than originally agreed upon.

purchase discount. A reduction in purchase *invoice price* granted for prompt payment. See *sales discount* and *terms of sale*.

purchase investigation. An investigation of the financial affairs of a company for the purpose of disclosing matters that may influence the terms or conclusion of a potential acquisition.

purchase method. Accounting for a *business combination* by adding the acquired company's assets at the price paid for them to the acquiring company's assets. Contrast with *pooling-of-interests method*. The firm adds the acquired assets to the books at current values rather than original costs; the subsequent *amortization expenses* usually exceed those (and reported income is smaller than that) for the same business combination accounted for as a pooling of interests. US *GAAP* now require that the acquirer use the purchase method, but other countries still allow poolings.

purchase order. Document issued by a buyer authorizing a seller to deliver goods, with the buyer to make payment later.

purchasing power gain or loss. *Monetary gain or loss*.

push-down accounting. An accounting method used in some *purchase transactions*. Assume that Company A purchases substantially all the *common shares* of Company B but that Company B must still issue its own *financial statements*. The question arises, shall Company B change the *basis* for its *assets* and *equities* on its own books to the same updated amounts at which they appear on Company A's *consolidated* *financial statements*? Company B uses "push-down accounting" when it shows the new asset and equity bases reflecting Company A's purchase, because the method "pushes down" the new bases from Company A (where *GAAP* require them) to Company B (where the new bases would not appear in *historical cost accounting*). Since 1983, the *SEC* has required push-down accounting under some circumstances.

put. An option to sell *shares* of a publicly traded corporation at a fixed price during a fixed time span. Contrast with *call*.

Q

qualified report (opinion). *Auditor's report* containing a statement that the auditor was unable to complete a satisfactory examination of all things considered relevant or that the auditor has doubts about the financial impact of some *material* item reported in the financial statements. See *except for* and *subject to*.

quality. In modern usage, a product or service has quality to the extent it conforms to specifications or provides customers the characteristics promised them.

quality of earnings. A phrase with no single, agreed-upon meaning. Some who use the phrase use it with different meanings on different occasions. "Quality of earnings" has an accounting aspect and a business cycle aspect.

In its accounting aspect, managers have choices in measuring and reporting *earnings*. This discretion can involve any of the following: selecting *accounting principles* or standards when *GAAP* allow a choice; making estimates in the application of accounting principles; and timing transactions to allow recognizing *nonrecurring* items in earnings. In some instances the range of choices has a large impact on reported earnings and in others, small. (1) Some use the phrase "quality of earnings" to mean the degree to which management can affect reported income by its choices of accounting estimates even though the choices recur every period. These users judge, for example, insurance companies to have low-quality earnings. Insurance company management must reestimate its liabilities for future payments to the insured each period, thereby having an opportunity to report periodic earnings within a wide range. (2) Others use the phrase to mean the degree to which management actually takes advantage of its flexibility. For them, an insurance company that does not vary its methods and estimating techniques, even though it has the opportunity to do so, has high-quality earnings. (3) Some have in mind the proximity in time between *revenue* recognition and cash collection. For them, the smaller the time delay, the higher will be the quality. (4) Still others use the phrase to mean the degree to which managers who have a choice among the items with large influence on earnings choose the ones that result in income measures that are more likely to recur. For them, the more likely an item of earnings is to recur, the higher will be its quality. Often these last two groups trade off with each other. Consider a dealer leasing a car on a long-term *lease*, receiving monthly collections. The dealer who uses *sales-type lease* accounting scores low on proximity of revenue recognition (all at the time of signing the lease) to cash collection but highlights the nonrepetitive nature of the transaction. The leasing dealer who uses *operating lease* accounting has perfectly matching revenue recognition and cash collection, but the *recurring* nature of the revenue gives a misleading picture of a repet-

itive transaction. The phrase "item of earnings" in (4) is ambiguous. The writer could mean the underlying economic event (which occurs when the lease for the car is signed) or the revenue recognition (which occurs every time the dealer using operating lease accounting receives cash). Hence, you should try to understand what other speakers and writers mean by "quality of earnings" when you interpret what they say and write. Some who refer to "earnings quality" suspect that managers will usually make choices that enhance current earnings and present the firm in the best light, independent of the ability of the firm to generate similar earnings in the future.

In the business cycle aspect, management's action often has no impact on the stability and recurrence of earnings. Compare a company that sells consumer products and likely has sales repeating every week with a construction company that builds to order. Companies in noncyclical businesses, such as some public utilities, likely have more stable earnings than ones in cyclical businesses, such as steel. Some use "quality of earnings" to refer to the stability and recurrence of basic revenue-generating activities. Those who use the phrase this way rarely associate earnings quality with accounting issues.

quality of financial position. Because of the *articulation* of the *income statement* with the *balance sheet,* the factors that imply a high (or low) *quality of earnings* also affect the balance sheet. Users of this phrase have in mind the same accounting issues as they have in mind when they use the phrase "quality of earnings."

quantitative performance measure. A measure of output based on an objectively observable quantity, such as units produced or *direct costs* incurred, rather than on an unobservable quantity or a quantity observable only nonobjectively, like quality of service provided.

quantity discount. A reduction in purchase price as quantity purchased increases. The Robinson-Patman Act constrains the amount of the discount. Do not confuse with *purchase discount*.

quantity variance. *Efficiency variance;* in *standard cost* systems, the standard price per unit times (actual quantity used minus standard quantity that should be used).

quasi-reorganization. A *reorganization* in which no new company emerges or no court has intervened, as would happen in *bankruptcy*. The primary purpose is to rid the balance sheet of a *deficit* (negative *retained earnings*) and give the firm a "fresh start."

quick assets. *Assets* readily convertible into *cash*; includes cash, current marketable securities, and current receivables.

quick ratio. Sum of (cash, current marketable securities, and current receivables) divided by *current liabilities;* often called the "acid test ratio." The analyst may exclude some nonliquid receivables from the numerator. See *ratio*.

R

R^2. The proportion of the statistical variance of a *dependent variable* explained by the equation fit to *independent variable(s)* in a *regression analysis*.

Summary of Financial Statement Ratios

Ratio	Numerator	Denominator
Profitability Ratios		
Rate of Return on Assets	Net Income + Interest Expense (net of tax effects)[a]	Average Total Assets during the Period[b]
Profit Margin for ROA (before interest effects)	Net Income + Interest Expense (net of tax effects)[a]	Sales
Various Expense Ratios	Various Expenses	Sales
Total Assets Turnover Ratio	Sales	Average Total Assets during the Period
Accounts Receivable Turnover Ratio	Sales	Average Accounts Receivable during the Period
Inventory Turnover Ratio	Cost of Goods Sold	Average Inventory during the Period
Fixed Asset Turnover Ratio	Sales	Average Fixed Assets during the Period
Rate of Return on Common Shareholders' Equity	Net Income - Preferred Stock Dividends	Average Common Shareholders' Equity During the Period
Profit Margin for ROCE (after interest expense and preferred dividends)	Net Income - Preferred Stock Dividends	Sales
Capital Structure Leverage Ratio	Average Total Assets during the period	Average Common Shareholders' Equity during the Period
Earnings per Share of Common Stock[b]	Net Income - Preferred Stock Dividends	Weighted-Average Number of Common Shares Outstanding

[a]If the parent company does not own all of a consolidated subsidiary, the calculation also adds back to net income the minority interest share of earnings.

[b]This calculation is more complicated when there are convertible securities, options, or warrants outstanding.

Railroad Accounting Principles Board (RAPB). A board brought into existence by the Staggers Rail Act of 1980 to advise the Interstate Commerce Commission on accounting matters affecting railroads. The RAPB was the only cost-accounting body authorized by the government during the decade of the 1980s (because Congress ceased funding the CASB during the 1980s). The RAPB incorporated the pronouncements of the CASB and became the government's authority on cost accounting principles.

R&D. See *research and development*.

random number sampling. For choosing a sample, a method in which the analyst selects items from the *population* by using a random number table or generator.

random sampling. For choosing a sample, a method in which all items in the population have an equal chance of being selected. Compare *judgment(al) sampling*.

RAPB. *Railroad Accounting Principles Board*.

rate of return on assets. *Return on assets*.

rate of return on common stock equity. See *ratio*.

rate of return on shareholders' (owners') equity. See *ratio*.

rate of return (on total capital). See *ratio* and *return on assets*.

rate variance. *Price variance*, usually for *direct labor costs*.

ratio. The number resulting when one number divides another. Analysts generally use ratios to assess aspects of profitability, solvency, and liquidity. The commonly used financial ratios fall into three categories: (1) those that summarize some aspect of *operations* for a period, usually a year, (2) those that summarize some aspect of *financial position* at a given moment—the moment for which a balance sheet

Summary of Financial Statement Ratios

Ratio	Numerator	Denominator
Short-term Liquidity Ratios		
Current Ratio	Current Assets	Current Liabilities
Quick or Acid Test Ratio	Highly Liquid Assets (cash, marketable securities, and receivables)[c]	Current Liabilities
Cash Flow from Operations to Current Liabilities Ratio	Cash Flow from Operations	Average Current Liabilities during the Period
Accounts Payable Turnover Ratio	Purchases[d]	Average Accounts Payable during the Period
Days Accounts Receivable Outstanding	365 days	Accounts Receivable Turnover Ratio
Days Inventories Held	365 days	Inventory Turnover Ratio
Days Accounts Payable Outstanding	365 days	Accounts Payable Turnover Ratio
Long-term Liquidity Ratios		
Long-term Debt Ratio	Total Long-term Debt	Total Long-term Debt Plus Shareholders' Equity
Debt-Equity Ratio	Total Liabilities	Total Equities (total liabilities plus shareholders' equity)
Cash Flow from Operations to Total Liabilities Ratio	Cash Flow from Operations	Average Total Liabilities during the Period
Interest Coverage Ratio	Income before Interest and Income Taxes	Interest Expense

[c]The calculation could conceivably exclude receivables for some firms and include inventories for others.
[d]Purchases = Cost of Goods Sold + Ending Inventories − Beginning Inventories.

reports, and (3) those that relate some aspect of operations to some aspect of financial position. The accompanying exhibit lists common financial ratios and shows separately both the numerator and the denominator for each ratio.

For all ratios that require an average balance during the period, the analyst often derives the average as one half the sum of the beginning and the ending balances. Sophisticated analysts recognize, however, that particularly when companies use a fiscal year different from the calendar year, this averaging of beginning and ending balances may mislead. Consider, for example, the rate of *return on assets* of Sears, Roebuck & Company, whose fiscal year ends on January 31. Sears chooses a January 31 closing date at least in part because inventories are at a low level and are therefore easy to count—it has sold the Christmas merchandise, and the Easter merchandise has not yet all arrived. Furthermore, by January 31, Sears has collected for most Christmas sales, so receivable amounts are not unusually large. Thus at January 31, the amount of total assets is lower than at many other times during the year. Consequently, the denominator of the rate of return on assets, total assets, for Sears more likely represents the smallest amount of total assets on hand during the year rather than the average amount. The return on assets rate for Sears and other companies that choose a fiscal year-end to coincide with low points in the inventory cycle

is likely to exceed the ratio measured with a more accurate estimate of the average amounts of total assets.

raw material. Goods purchased for use in manufacturing a product.

reacquired stock. *Treasury shares.*

real accounts. *Balance sheet accounts,* as opposed to *nominal accounts.* See *permanent accounts.*

real amount (value). An amount stated in *constant dollars.* For example, if the firm sells an investment costing $100 for $130 after a period of 10 percent general *inflation,* the *nominal amount* of *gain* is $30 (= $130 − $100) but the real amount of gain is C$20 (= $130 − 1.10 $100), where "C$" denotes constant dollars of purchasing power on the date of sale.

real estate. *Land* and its *improvements,* such as landscaping and roads, but not buildings.

real interest rate. Interest rate reflecting the productivity of capital, not including a premium for inflation anticipated over the life of the loan.

realizable value. *Fair value* or, sometimes, *net realizable (sales) value.*

realization convention. The accounting practice of delaying the recognition of *gains* and *losses* from changes in the market price of *assets* until the firm sells the assets. However, the firm recognizes unrealized losses on *inventory* (or *marketable securities* classified as *trading securities*) prior to sale when the firm uses the *lower-of-cost-or-market* valuation basis for inventory (or the *fair value* basis for marketable securities).

realize. To convert into *funds;* when applied to a *gain* or *loss*, implies that an *arm's-length transaction* has taken place. Contrast with *recognize*; the firm may recognize a loss (as, for example, on *marketable equity securities*) in the financial statements even though it has not yet realized the loss via a transaction.

realized gain (or loss) on marketable equity securities. An income statement account title for the difference between the proceeds of disposition and the *original cost* of *marketable equity securities.*

realized holding gain. See *inventory profit* for definition and an example.

rearrangement costs. Costs of reinstalling assets, perhaps in a different location. The firm may, but need not, *capitalize* them as part of the assets cost, just as is done with original installation cost. The firm will *expense* these costs if they merely maintain the asset's future benefits at their originally intended level before the relocation.

recapitalization. *Reorganization.*

recapture. Name for one kind of tax payment. Various provisions of the *income tax* rules require a refund by the taxpayer (recapture by the government) of various tax advantages under certain conditions. For example, the taxpayer must repay tax savings provided by *accelerated depreciation* if the taxpayer prematurely retires the item providing the tax savings.

receipt. Acquisition of *cash.*

receivable. Any *collectible,* whether or not it is currently due.

receivable turnover. See *ratio.*

reciprocal holdings. Company A owns stock of Company B, and Company B owns stock of Company A; or Company B owns stock of Company C, which owns stock of Company A.

recognize. To enter a transaction in the accounts; not synonymous with *realize.*

reconciliation. A calculation that shows how one balance or figure derives from another, such as a reconciliation of retained earnings or a *bank reconciliation schedule.* See *articulate.*

record date. The date at which the firm pays *dividends* on payment date to those who own the stock.

recourse. The rights of the lender if a borrower does not repay as promised. A recourse loan gives the lender the right to take

any of the borrower's assets not exempted from such taking by the contract. See also *note receivable discounted.*

recovery of unrealized loss on trading securities. An *income statement account title* for the *gain* during the current period on *trading securities.*

recurring. Occurring again; occurring repetitively; in accounting, an adjective often used in describing *revenue* or *earnings.* In some contexts, the term "recurring revenue" is ambiguous. Consider a construction contractor who accounts for a single long-term project with the *installment method,* with revenue recognized at the time of each cash collection from the customer. The recognized revenue is recurring, but the transaction leading to the revenue is not. See *quality of earnings.*

redemption. Retirement by the issuer, usually by a purchase or *call,* of *stocks* or *bonds.*

redemption premium. *Call premium.*

redemption value. The price a corporation will pay to retire *bonds* or *preferred stock* if it calls them before *maturity.*

refinancing. An adjustment in the *capital structure* of a *corporation,* involving changes in the nature and amounts of the various classes of *debt* and, in some cases, *capital* as well as other components of *shareholders' equity. Asset* carrying values in the accounts remain unchanged.

refunding bond issue. Said of a *bond* issue whose proceeds the firm uses to retire bonds already *outstanding.*

register. A collection of consecutive entries, or other information, in chronological order, such as a check register or an insurance register that lists all insurance policies owned. If the firm records entries in the register, it can serve as a *journal.*

registered bond. A bond for which the issuer will pay the *principal* and *interest,* if registered as to interest, to the owner listed on the books of the issuer; as opposed to a bearer bond, in which the issuer must pay the possessor of the bond.

registrar. An *agent,* usually a bank or trust company, appointed by a corporation to keep track of the names of shareholders and distributions to them.

registration statement. Required by the Securities Act of 1933, statement of most companies that want to have owners of their securities trade the securities in public markets. The statement discloses financial data and other items of interest to potential investors.

regression analysis. A method of *cost estimation* based on statistical techniques for fitting a line (or its equivalent in higher mathematical dimensions) to an observed series of data points, usually by minimizing the sum of squared deviations of the observed data from the fitted line. Common usage calls the cost that the analysis explains the "dependent variable"; it calls the variable(s) we use to estimate cost behavior "independent variable(s)." If we use more than one independent variable, the term for the analysis is "multiple regression analysis." See R^2, *standard error,* and *t-value.*

regressive tax. Tax for which the rate decreases as the taxed base, such as income, increases. Contrast with *progressive tax.*

Regulation S-K. The *SEC's* standardization of nonfinancial statement disclosure requirements for documents filed with the SEC.

Regulation S-T. The *SEC's* regulations specifying formats for electronic filing and the *EDGAR* system.

Regulation S-X. The *SEC's* principal accounting regulation, which specifies the form and content of financial reports to the SEC.

rehabilitation. The improving of a used *asset* via an extensive repair. Ordinary *repairs* and *maintenance* restore or maintain expected *service potential* of an asset, and the firm treats them as *expenses.* A rehabilitation improves the asset beyond its current service potential, enhancing the service potential to a significantly higher level than before the rehabilitation. Once rehabilitated, the asset may be better, but need not be, than it was when new. The firm will *capitalize expenditures* for rehabilitation, like those for *betterments* and *improvements.*

reinvestment rate. In a *capital budgeting* context, the rate at which the firm invests cash inflows from a project occurring before the project's completion. Once the analyst assumes such a rate, no project can ever have multiple *internal rates of return.* See *Descartes' rule of signs.*

relative performance evaluation. Setting performance targets and, sometimes, compensation in relation to the performance of others, perhaps in different firms or divisions, who face a similar environment.

relative sales value method. See *net realizable (sales) value.*

relevant cost. Cost used by an analyst in making a decision. *Incremental cost; opportunity cost.*

relevant cost analysis. Identifies the *costs* (or *revenues*) relevant to the decision to be made. A cost or revenue is relevant only if an amount differs between alternatives. Also called *differential cost analysis*

relevant range. Activity levels over which costs are linear or for which *flexible budget* estimates and *breakeven charts* will remain valid.

remit earnings. An expression likely to confuse a reader without a firm understanding of accounting basics. A firm generates *net assets* by earning *income* and retains net assets if it does not declare *dividends* in the amount of net income. When a firm declares dividends and pays the cash (or other net assets), some writers would say the firm "remits earnings." We think the student learns better by conceiving earnings as a *credit balance.* When a firm pays dividends it sends net assets, things with debit balances, not something with a credit balance, to the recipient. When writers say firms "remit earnings," they mean the firms send assets (or net assets) that previous earnings have generated and reduce *retained earnings.*

remittance advice. Information on a *check stub,* or on a document attached to a check by the *drawer,* that tells the *payee* why a payment is being made.

rent. A charge for use of land, buildings, or other assets.

reorganization. In the *capital structure* of a corporation, a major change that leads to changes in the rights, interests, and implied ownership of the various security owners; usually results from a *merger* or an agreement by senior security holders to take action to forestall *bankruptcy.*

repair. An *expenditure* to restore an *asset's* service potential after damage or after prolonged use. In the second sense, after prolonged use, the difference between repairs and maintenance is one of degree and not of kind. A repair is treated as an *expense* of the period when incurred. Because the firm treats repairs and maintenance similarly in this regard, the distinction is not important. A repair helps to maintain capacity at the levels planned when the firm acquired the *asset.* Contrast with *improvement.*

replacement cost. For an asset, the current fair market price to purchase another, similar asset (with the same future benefit or service potential). *Current cost.* See *reproduction cost* and *productive capacity.* See also *distributable income* and *inventory profit.*

replacement cost method of depreciation. Method in which the analyst augments the original-cost *depreciation* charge with an amount based on a portion of the difference between the *current replacement cost* of the asset and its *original cost.*

replacement system of depreciation. See *retirement method of depreciation* for definition and contrast.

report. *Financial statement; auditor's report.*

report form. *Balance sheet* form that typically shows *assets* minus *liabilities* as one total. Then, below that total appears the components of *owners' equity* summing to the same total. Often, the top section shows *current* assets less current liabilities before *noncurrent assets* less noncurrent liabilities. Contrast with *account form.*

reporting objectives (policies). The general purposes for which the firm prepares *financial statements.* The *FASB* has discussed these in *SFAC No. 1.*

representative item sampling. Sampling in which the analyst believes the sample selected is typical of the entire population from which it comes. Compare *specific item sampling.*

reproduction cost. The *cost* necessary to acquire an *asset* similar in all physical respects to another asset for which the analyst requires a *current value.* See *replacement cost* and *productive capacity* for contrast.

required rate of return (RRR). *Cost of capital.*

requisition. A formal written order or request, such as for withdrawal of supplies from the storeroom.

resale value. *Exit value; net realizable value.*

research and development (R&D). A form of economic activity with special accounting rules. Firms engage in research in hopes of discovering new knowledge that will create a new product, process, or service or of improving a present product, process, or service. Development translates research findings or other knowledge into a new or improved product, process, or service. *SFAS No. 2* requires that firms expense costs of such activities as incurred on the grounds that the future benefits are too uncertain to warrant *capitalization* as an asset. This treatment seems questionable to us because we wonder why firms would continue to undertake R&D if there was no expectation of future benefit; if future benefits exist, then R&D *costs* should be assets that appear, like other assets, at *historical cost.*

reserve. The worst word in accounting because almost everyone not trained in accounting, and some who are, misunderstand it. The common confusion is that "reserves" represent a pool of *cash* or other *assets* available when the firm needs them. Wrong. Cash always has a *debit balance.* Reserves always have a *credit* balance. When properly used in accounting, "reserves" refer to an account that appropriates *retained earnings* and restricts dividend declarations. Appropriating retained earnings is itself a poor and vanishing practice, so the word should seldom appear in accounting. In addition, "reserve" was used in the past to indicate an asset *contra account* (for example, "reserve for depreciation") or an *estimated liability* (for example, "reserve for warranty costs"). In any case, reserve accounts have *credit* balances and are not pools of *funds,* as the unwary reader might infer. If a company has set aside a pool of *cash* (or *marketable securities*) to serve some specific purpose such as paying for a new factory, then it will call that cash a *fund.* No other word in accounting causes so much misunderstanding by nonexperts as well as by "experts" who should know better. A leading unabridged dictionary defines "reserve" as "cash, or assets readily convertible into cash, held aside, as by a corporation, bank, state or national government, etc. to meet expected or unexpected demands." This definition is absolutely wrong in accounting. Reserves are not funds. For example, the firm creates a contingency fund of $10,000 by depositing cash in a fund and makes the following entry:

Dr. Contingency Fund	10,000	
Cr. Cash		10,000

The following entry may accompany this entry, if the firm wants to appropriate retained earnings:

Dr. Retained Earnings	10,000	
Cr. Reserve for Contingencies . . .		10,000

The transaction leading to the first entry has economic significance. The second entry has little economic impact for most firms. The problem with the word "reserve" arises because the firm can make the second entry without the first—a company can create a reserve, that is, appropriate retained earnings, without creating a fund. The problem results, at least in part, from the fact that in common usage, "reserve" means a pool of assets, as in the phrase "oil reserves." The *Internal Revenue Service* does not help in dispelling confusion about the term "reserves." The federal *income tax* return for corporations uses the title "Reserve for Bad Debts" to mean "Allowance for Uncollectible Accounts" and speaks of the "Reserve Method" in referring to the *allowance method* for estimating *revenue* or *income* reductions from estimated *uncollectibles.*

reserve recognition accounting (RRA). One form of *accounting* for natural resources. In exploration for natural resources,

the problem arises of how to treat the expenditures for exploration, both before the firm knows the outcome of the efforts and after it knows the outcome. Suppose that the firm spends $10 million to drill 10 holes ($1 million each) and that nine of them are dry whereas one is a gusher containing oil with a *net realizable value* of $40 million. Dry hole, or *successful efforts,* accounting would expense $9 million and *capitalize* $1 million, which the firm will *deplete* as it lifts the oil from the ground. *SFAS No. 19,* now suspended, required *successful efforts costing.* Full costing would expense nothing but would capitalize the $10 million of drilling costs that the firm will deplete as it lifts the oil from the single productive well. Reserve recognition accounting would capitalize $40 million, which the firm will deplete as it lifts the oil, with a $30 million *credit* to *income* or *contributed capital.* The *balance sheet* shows the *net realizable value* of proven oil and gas reserves. The *income statement* has three sorts of items: (1) current income resulting from production or "lifting profit," which is the *revenue* from sales of oil and gas less the expense based on the current valuation amount at which these items have appeared on the balance sheet, (2) profit or loss from exploration efforts in which the current value of new discoveries is revenue and all the exploration cost is expense, and (3) gain or loss on changes in current value during the year, which accountants in other contexts call a *holding gain or loss.*

reset bond. A bond, typically a *junk bond,* that specifies that periodically the issuer will reset the coupon rate so that the bond sells at *par* in the market. Investment bankers created this type of instrument to help ensure the purchasers of such bonds of getting a fair rate of return, given the riskiness of the issuer. If the issuer gets into financial trouble, its bonds will trade for less than par in the market. The issuer of a reset bond promises to raise the interest rate and preserve the value of the bond. Ironically, the reset feature has often had just the opposite effect. The default risk of many issuers of reset bonds has deteriorated so much that the bonds have dropped to less than 50 percent of par. To raise the value to par, the issuer would have to raise the interest rate to more than 25 percent per year. That rate is so large that issuers have declared bankruptcy rather than attempt to make the new large interest payments; this then reduces the market value of the bonds rather than increases them.

residual income. In an external reporting context, a term that refers to *net income* to *common shares* (= net income less *preferred stock dividends*). In *managerial accounting,* this term refers to the excess of income for a *division* or *segment* of a company over the product of the *cost of capital* for the company multiplied by the average amount of capital invested in the division during the period over which the division earned the income.

residual security. A *potentially dilutive security.* Options, *warrants, convertible bonds,* and *convertible preferred stock.*

residual value. At any time, the estimated or actual *net realizable value* (that is, proceeds less removal costs) of an *asset,* usually a depreciable *plant asset.* In the context of depreciation accounting, this term is equivalent to *salvage value* and is preferred to *scrap value* because the firm need not scrap the asset. It is sometimes used to mean net *book value.* In the context of a *noncancelable* lease, it is the estimated value of the leased asset at the end of the lease period. See *lease.*

resources supplied. *Expenditures* made for an activity.

resources used. *Cost driver* rate times cost driver volume.

responsibility accounting. Accounting for a business by considering various units as separate entities, or *profit centers*, giving management of each unit responsibility for the unit's *revenues* and *expenses*. See *transfer price*.

responsibility center. An organization part or *segment* that top management holds accountable for a specified set of activities. Also called "accountability center." See *cost center*, *investment center*, *profit center*, and *revenue center*.

restricted assets. Governmental resources restricted by legal or contractual requirements for specific purpose.

restricted retained earnings. That part of *retained earnings* not legally available for *dividends*. See *retained earnings, appropriated*. Bond indentures and other loan contracts can curtail the legal ability of the corporation to declare dividends without formally requiring a retained earnings appropriation, but the firm must disclose such restrictions.

retail inventory method. Ascertaining cost amounts of *ending inventory* as follows (assuming *FIFO*): cost of ending inventory = (selling price of *goods available for sale* – sales) *cost percentage*. The analyst then computes cost of goods sold from the inventory equation; costs of beginning inventory, purchases, and ending inventory are all known. (When the firm uses *LIFO*, the method resembles the *dollar-value LIFO method*.) See *markup*.

retail terminology. See *markup*.

retained earnings. Net *income* over the life of a corporation less all *dividends* (including capitalization through *stock dividends*); *owners' equity* less *contributed capital*.

retained earnings, appropriated. An *account* set up by crediting it and debiting *retained earnings;* used to indicate that a portion of retained earnings is not available for dividends. The practice of appropriating retained earnings is misleading unless the firm marks all capital with its use, which is not practicable, nor sensible, since capital is fungible—all the *equities* jointly fund all the *assets*. The use of formal retained earnings appropriations is declining.

retained earnings statement. A *reconciliation* of the beginning and the ending balances in the *retained earnings account;* required by *generally accepted accounting principles* whenever the firm presents *comparative balance sheets* and an *income statement.* This reconciliation can appear in a separate statement, in a combined statement of income and retained earnings, or in the balance sheet.

retirement method of depreciation. A method in which the firm records no entry for *depreciation expense* until it retires an *asset* from service. Then, it makes an entry *debiting* depreciation expense and *crediting* the asset account for the cost of the asset retired. If the retired asset has a *salvage value*, the firm reduces the amount of the debit to depreciation expense by the amount of salvage value with a corresponding debit to cash, receivables, or salvaged materials. The "replacement system of depreciation" is similar, except that the debit to depreciation expense equals the cost of the new asset less the salvage value, if any, of the old asset. Some public utilities

used these methods. For example, if the firm acquired ten telephone poles in Year 1 for $60 each and replaces them in Year 10 for $100 each when the salvage value of the old poles is $5 each, the accounting would be as follows:

Retirement Method.

Plant Assets......................	600	
Cash........................		600
To acquire assets in Year 1.		
Depreciation Expense..............	550	
Salvage Receivable................	50	
Plant Assets......................		600
To record retirement and depreciation in Year 10.		
Plant Assets......................	1,000	
Cash........................		1,000
To record acquisition of new assets in Year 10.		

Replacement Method.

Plant Assets......................	600	
Cash........................		600
To acquire assets in Year 1.		
Depreciation Expense..............	950	
Salvage Receivable................	50	
Cash........................		1,000
To record depreciation on old asset in amount quantified by net cost of replacement asset in Year 10.		

The retirement method is like *FIFO* in that it records the cost of the first assets as depreciation and puts the cost of the second assets on the balance sheet. The replacement method is like *LIFO* in that it records the cost of the second assets as depreciation expense and leaves the cost of the first assets on the balance sheet.

retirement plan. *Pension plan.*

retroactive benefits. In initiating or amending a *defined-benefit pension plan,* benefits that the benefit formula attributes to employee services rendered in periods prior to the initiation or amendment. See *prior service costs.*

return. A schedule of information required by governmental bodies, such as the tax return required by the *Internal Revenue Service;* also the physical return of merchandise. See also *return on investment.*

return on assets (ROA). *Net income* plus after-tax *interest charges* plus *minority interest* in income divided by average total *assets;* perhaps the single most useful ratio for assessing management's overall operating performance. Most financial economists would subtract average noninterest-bearing *liabilities* from the denominator. Economists realize that when liabilities do not provide for explicit interest charges, the creditor adjusts the terms of contract, such as setting a higher selling price or lower discount, to those who do not pay cash immediately. (To take an extreme example, consider how much higher salary a worker who receives a salary once per year, rather than once per month, would demand.) This ratio requires in the numerator the income amount before the firm accrues any charges to suppliers of funds. We cannot measure the interest charges implicit in the noninterest-bearing liabilities because they cause items such as cost of goods sold and salary expense to be somewhat larger, since the interest is implicit. Subtracting their amounts from the denominator adjusts for their implicit cost. Such subtraction assumes that assets financed with noninterest-bearing liabilities have the same rate of return as all the other assets.

return on investment (ROI), return on capital. *Income* (before distributions to suppliers of capital) for a period; as a rate, this amount divided by average total assets. The analyst should add back *interest*, net of tax effects, to *net income* for the numerator. See *ratio*.

revenue. The *owners' equity* increase accompanying the *net assets* increase caused by selling goods or rendering services; in short, a service rendered; *sales* of products, merchandise, and services and earnings from *interest*, *dividends*, *rents*, and the like. Measure revenue as the expected *net present value* of the net assets the firm will receive. Do not confuse with *receipt* of *funds*, which may occur before, when, or after revenue is recognized. Contrast with *gain* and *income*. See also *holding gain*. Some writers use the term *gross income* synonymously with *revenue*; avoid such usage.

revenue center. Within a firm, a *responsibility center* that has control only over revenues generated. Contrast with *cost center*. See *profit center*.

revenue expenditure. A term sometimes used to mean an *expense*, in contrast to a capital *expenditure* to acquire an *asset* or to discharge a *liability*. Avoid using this term; use *period expense* instead.

revenue received in advance. An inferior term for *advances from customers*.

reversal (reversing) entry. An *entry* in which all *debits* and *credits* are the credits and debits, respectively, of another entry, and in the same amounts. The accountant usually records a reversal entry on the first day of an *accounting period* to reverse a previous *adjusting entry*, usually an *accrual*. The purpose of such entries is to make the bookkeeper's tasks easier. Suppose that the firm pays salaries every other Friday, with paychecks compensating employees for the two weeks just ended. Total salaries accrue at the rate of $5,000 per five-day workweek. The bookkeeper is accustomed to making the following entry every other Friday:

(1) Salary Expense	10,000	
Cash.		10,000

To record salary expense and salary payments.

If the firm delivers paychecks to employees on Friday, November 25, then the *adjusting entry* made on November 30 (or perhaps later) to record accrued salaries for November 28, 29, and 30 would be as follows:

(2) Salary Expense	3,000	
Salaries Payable		3,000

To charge November operations with all salaries earned in November.

The firm would close the Salary Expense account as part of the November 30 closing entries. On the next payday, December 9, the salary entry would be as follows:

(3) Salary Expense	7,000	
Salaries Payable	3,000	
Cash.		10,000

To record salary payments split between expense for December (7 days) and liability carried over from November.

To make entry (3), the bookkeeper must look back into the records to see how much of the debit is to Salaries Payable accrued from the previous month in order to split the total debits between December expense and the liability carried over from November. Notice that this entry forces the bookkeeper both (a) to refer to balances in old accounts and (b) to make an entry different from the one customarily made, entry (1). The reversing entry, made just after the books have been closed for the second quarter, makes the salary entry for December 9 the same as that made on all other Friday paydays. The reversing entry merely *reverses* the adjusting entry (2):

(4) Salaries Payable	3,000	
Salary Expense.		3,000

To reverse the adjusting entry.

This entry results in a zero balance in the Salaries Payable account and a credit balance in the Salary Expense account. If the firm makes entry (4) just after it closes the books for November, then the entry on December 9 will be the customary entry (1). Entries (4) and (1) together have exactly the same effect as entry (3).

The procedure for using reversal entries is as follows: the firm makes the required adjustment to record an accrual (*payable* or *receivable*) at the end of an *accounting period*; it makes the closing entry as usual; as of the first day of the following period, it makes an entry reversing the adjusting entry; when the firm makes (or receives) a payment, it records the entry as though it had not recorded an adjusting entry at the end of the preceding period. Whether a firm uses reversal entries affects the record-keeping procedures but not the financial statements.

This term is also used to describe the entry reversing an incorrect entry before recording the correct entry.

reverse stock split. A stock split in which the firm decreases the number of shares *outstanding*. See *stock split*.

revolving fund. A fund whose amounts the firm continually spends and replenishes; for example, a *petty cash fund*.

revolving loan. A *loan* that both the borrower and the lender expect to renew at *maturity*.

right. The privilege to subscribe to new *stock* issues or to purchase stock. Usually, securities called *warrants* contain the rights, and the owner of the warrants may sell them. See also *preemptive right*.

risk. A measure of the variability of the *return on investment*. For a given expected amount of return, most people prefer less risk to more risk. Therefore, in rational markets, investments with more risk usually promise, or investors expect to receive, a higher rate of return than investments with lower risk. Most people use "risk" and "uncertainty" as synonyms. In technical language, however, these terms have different meanings. We use "risk" when we know the probabilities attached to the various outcomes, such as the probabilities of heads or tails in the flip of a fair coin. "Uncertainty" refers to an event for which we can only estimate the probabilities of the outcomes, such as winning or losing a lawsuit.

risk-adjusted discount rate. Rate used in discounting cash flows for projects more or less risky than the firm's average. In a *capital budgeting* context, a decision analyst compares projects by comparing their net *present values* for a given *interest* rate, usually the cost of capital. If the analyst considers a given project's outcome to be much more or much less risky than the normal undertakings of the company, then the analyst will use a larger interest rate (if the project is riskier) or a smaller interest rate (if less risky) in discounting, and the rate used is "risk-adjusted."

risk-free rate. An interest rate reflecting only the pure interest rate plus an amount to compensate for inflation anticipated over the life of a loan, excluding a premium for the risk of default by the borrower. Financial economists usually measure the risk-free rate in the United States from U.S. government securities, such as Treasury bills and notes.

risk premium. Extra compensation paid to employees or extra *interest* paid to lenders, over amounts usually considered normal, in return for their undertaking to engage in activities riskier than normal.

ROA. *Return on assets.*

ROI. *Return on investment*; usually used to refer to a single project and expressed as a ratio: *income* divided by average *cost* of *assets* devoted to the project.

royalty. Compensation for the use of property, usually a patent, copyrighted material, or natural resources. The amount is often expressed as a percentage of receipts from using the property or as an amount per unit produced.

RRA. *Reserve recognition accounting.*

RRR. Required rate of return. See *cost of capital.*

rule of 69. Rule stating that an amount of cash invested at r percent per period will double in $69/r + .35$ periods. This approximation is accurate to one-tenth of a period for interest rates between ¼ and 100 percent per period. For example, at 10 percent per period, the rule says that a given sum will double in $^{69}/_{10} + .35 = 7.25$ periods. At 10 percent per period, a given sum actually doubles in 7.27+ periods.

rule of 72. Rule stating that an amount of cash invested at r percent per period will double in $72/r$ periods. A reasonable approximation for interest rates between 4 and 10 percent but not nearly as accurate as the *rule of 69* for interest rates outside that range. For example, at 10 percent per period, the rule says that a given sum will double in $72/10 = 7.2$ periods.

rule of 78. The rule followed by many finance companies for allocating earnings on *loans* among the months of a year on the sum-of-the-months'–digits basis when the borrower makes equal monthly payments to the lender. The sum of the digits

from 1 through 12 is 78, so the rule allocates $^{12}/_{78}$ of the year's earnings to the first month, $^{11}/_{78}$ to the second month, and so on. This approximation allocates more of the early payments to interest and less to principal than does the correct, compound-interest method. Hence, lenders still use this method even though present-day computers can make the compound-interest computation as easily as they can carry out the approximation. See *sum-of- the-years'–digits depreciation.*

ruling (and balancing) an account. The process of summarizing a series of entries in an *account* by computing a new *balance* and drawing double lines to indicate that the new balance summarizes the information above the double lines. An illustration appears below. The steps are as follows: (1) Compute the sum of all *debit* entries including opening debit balance, if any—$1,464.16. (2) Compute the sum of all credit entries including opening credit balance, if any—$413.57. (3) If the amount in (1) exceeds the amount in (2), then write the excess as a credit with a checkmark—$1,464.16 – $413.57 = $1,050.59. (4) Add both debit and credit columns, which should both now sum to the same amount, and show that identical total at the foot of both columns. (5) Draw double lines under those numbers and write the excess of debits over credits as the new debit balance with a checkmark. (6) If the amount in (2) exceeds the amount in (1), then write the excess as a debit with a checkmark. (7) Do steps (4) and (5) except that the excess becomes the new credit balance. (8) If the amount in (1) equals the amount in (2), then the balance is zero, and only the totals with the double lines beneath them need appear.

Rutgers Accounting Web Site. See http://www.rutgers.edu/ Accounting/ for a useful compendium of accounting information.

S

S corporation. A corporation taxed like a *partnership.* Corporation (or partnership) agreements allocate the periodic *income* to the individual shareholders (or partners) who report these amounts on their individual *income tax* returns. Contrast with *C corporation.*

SA (société anonyme). France: A *corporation.*

SAB. *Staff Accounting Bulletin* of the *SEC.*

safe-harbor lease. A form of *tax-transfer lease.*

safety stock. Extra items of *inventory* kept on hand to protect against running out.

salary. Compensation earned by managers, administrators, and professionals, not based on an hourly rate. Contrast with *wage.*

sale. A *revenue* transaction in which the firm delivers *goods* or *services* to a customer in return for cash or a contractual obligation to pay.

sale and leaseback. A *financing* transaction in which the firm sells improved property but takes it back for use on a long-term *lease.* Such transactions often have advantageous income

An Open Account, Ruled and Balanced
(Steps indicated in parentheses correspond to steps described in "ruling an account.")

	Date 2005	Explanation	Ref.	Debit (1)	Date 2005	Explanation	Ref.	Credit (2)	
	Jan. 2	Balance	✓	100.00					
	Jan. 13		VR	121.37	Sept. 15		J	.42	
	Mar. 20		VR	56.42	Nov. 12		J	413.15	
	June 5		J	1,138.09	Dec. 31	Balance	✓	1,050.59	(3)
	Aug. 18		J	1.21					
	Nov. 20		VR	38.43					
	Dec. 7		VR	8.64					
(4)	2006			1,464.16	2006			1,464.16	(4)
(5)	Jan. 1	Balance	✓	1,050.59					

tax effects but usually have no effect on *financial statement income*.

sales activity variance. *Sales volume variance.*

sales allowance. A sales *invoice* price reduction that a seller grants to a buyer because the seller delivered *goods* different from, perhaps because of damage, those the buyer ordered. The seller often accumulates amounts of such adjustments in a temporary *revenue contra account* having this, or a similar, title. See *sales discount.*

sales basis of revenue recognition. Recognition of *revenue* not when a firm produces goods or when it receives orders but only when it has completed the sale by delivering the goods or services and has received cash or a claim to cash. Most firms recognize revenue on this basis. Compare with the *percentage-of-completion method* and the *installment method.* This is identical with the *completed contract method,* but the latter term ordinarily applies only to *long-term* construction projects.

sales contra, estimated uncollectibles. A title for the contra-revenue account to recognize estimated reductions in income caused by *accounts receivable* that will not be collected. See *bad debt expense, allowance for uncollectibles,* and *allowance method.*

sales discount. A sales *invoice* price reduction usually offered for prompt payment. See *terms of sale* and *²⁄₁₀, n/30.*

sales return. The physical return of merchandise. The seller often accumulates amounts of such returns in a temporary revenue contra account.

sales-type (capital) lease. A form of *lease.* See *capital lease.* When a manufacturer (or other firm) that ordinarily sells goods enters a capital lease as *lessor,* the lease is a "sales-type lease." When a financial firm, such as a bank or insurance company or leasing company, acquires the asset from the manufacturer and then enters a capital lease as lessor, the lease is a "direct-financing-type lease." The manufacturer recognizes its ordinary profit (sales price less *cost of goods sold,* where sales price is the *present value* of the contractual lease

payments plus any down payment) on executing the sales-type capital lease, but the financial firm does not recognize profit on executing a capital lease of the direct-financing type.

sales value method. *Relative sales value method.* See *net realizable value method.*

sales volume variance. Budgeted *contribution margin* per unit times (planned sales volume minus actual sales volume).

salvage value. Actual or estimated selling price, net of removal or disposal costs, of a used *plant asset* that the firm expects to sell or otherwise retire. See *residual value.*

SAR. *Summary annual report.*

Sarbanes-Oxley Act. The law, passed in 2002 in the wake of the Enron and related scandals, to stiffen the requirements for corporate governance, including accounting issues. It speaks, among other things, to the regulation of the accounting profession, the standards for audit committees of public companies, the certifications managements must sign, and standards of internal control that companies must meet.

SARL (société à responsabilité limitée). France: a *corporation* with limited liability and a life of no more than 99 years; must have at least two and no more than 50 *shareholders.*

SAS. *Statement on Auditing Standards* of the *AICPA.*

scale effect. See *discounted cash flow.*

scatter diagram. A graphic representation of the relation between two or more variables within a population.

schedule. A supporting set of calculations, with explanations, that show how to derive figures in a *financial statement* or tax return.

scientific method. *Effective interest method* of amortizing *bond discount* or *premium.*

scrap value. *Salvage value* assuming the owner intends to junk the item. A *net realizable value. Residual value.*

SEC (Securities and Exchange Commission). An agency authorized by the U.S. Congress to regulate, among other things, the financial reporting practices of most public corporations. The SEC has indicated that it will usually allow the *FASB* to set accounting principles, but it often requires more disclosure than the FASB requires. The SEC states its accounting requirements in its *Accounting Series Releases (ASR—* replaced in 1982 by the following two*), Financial Reporting Releases, Accounting and Auditing Enforcement Releases, Staff Accounting Bulletins* (these are, strictly speaking, interpretations by the accounting staff, not rules of the commissioners themselves), and *Regulation S-X and Regulation S-K.* See also *registration statement, 10-K,* and *20-F.*

secret reserve. *Hidden reserve.*

Securities and Exchange Commission. *SEC.*

securitization. The process of bundling together a group of like *assets,* for example *accounts receivable,* into a single portfolio, then selling that portfolio or partial ownership shares in it. This has roughly the same economic effect as using the assets as *collateral* for a borrowing, but the securitization transaction removes the assets from the *balance sheet.*

security. Document that indicates ownership, such as a *share* of *stock,* or indebtedness, such as a *bond,* or potential ownership, such as an *option* or *warrant.*

security available for sale. According to *SFAS No. 115* (1993), a *debt* or *equity security* that is not a *trading security,* or a debt security that is not a *security held to maturity.*

security held to maturity. According to *SFAS No. 115* (1993), a *debt security* the holder has both the ability and the intent to hold to *maturity;* valued in the *balance sheet* at amortized acquisition cost: the book value of the security at the end of each period is the book value at the beginning of the period multiplied by the historical *yield* on the security (measured as of the time of purchase) less any cash the holder receives at the end of this period from the security.

segment (of a business). As defined by *APB Opinion No. 30,* "a component of an *entity* whose activities represent a separate major line of business or class of customer.... [It may be] a *subsidiary,* a division, or a department,... provided that its *assets,* results of *operations,* and activities can be clearly distinguished, physically and operationally for financial reporting purposes, from the other assets, results of operations, and activities of the entity." In *SFAS No. 14,* a segment is defined as a "component of an enterprise engaged in promoting a product or service or a group of related products and services primarily to unaffiliated customers ... for a profit." *SFAS No. 131* defines operating segments using the "management approach" as components of the enterprise engaging in revenue- and expense-generating business activities "whose operating results are regularly reviewed by the enterprise's chief operating decision maker to make decisions about resources... and asset performance."

segment reporting. Reporting of *sales, income,* and *assets* by *segments of a business,* usually classified by nature of products sold but sometimes by geographical area where the firm produces or sells goods or by type of customers; sometimes called "line of business reporting." The accounting for segment income does not allocate *central corporate expenses* to the segments.

self-balancing. A set of records with equal *debits* and *credits* such as the *ledger* (but not individual accounts), the *balance sheet,* and a *fund* in nonprofit accounting.

self-check(ing) digit. A digit forming part of an account or code number, normally the last digit of the number, which is mathematically derived from the other numbers of the code and is used to detect errors in transcribing the code number. For example, assume the last digit of the account number is the remainder after summing the preceding digits and dividing that sum by nine. Suppose the computer encounters the account numbers 7027261-7 and 9445229-7. The program can tell that something has gone wrong with the encoding of the second account number because the sum of the first seven digits is 35, whose remainder on division by 9 is 8, not 7. The first account number does not show such an error because the sum of the first seven digits is 25, whose remainder on division by 9 is, indeed, 7. The first account number may be in error, but the second surely is.

self-insurance. See *insurance.*

self-sustaining foreign operation. A foreign operation both financially and operationally independent of the reporting enterprise (owner) so that the owner's exposure to exchange-rate changes results only from the owner's net investment in the foreign entity.

selling and administrative expenses. *Expenses* not specifically identifiable with, or assigned to, production.

semifixed costs. *Costs* that increase with activity as a step function.

semivariable costs. *Costs* that increase strictly linearly with activity but that are positive at zero activity level. Royalty fees of 2 percent of sales are variable; royalty fees of $1,000 per year plus 2 percent of sales are semivariable.

senior securities. *Bonds* as opposed to *preferred stock; preferred stock* as opposed to *common stock.* The firm must meet the senior security claim against *earnings* or *assets* before meeting the claims of less-senior securities.

sensitivity analysis. A study of how the outcome of a decision-making process changes as one or more of the assumptions change.

sequential access. Computer-storage access in which the analyst can locate information only by a sequential search of the storage file. Compare *direct access.*

serial bonds. An *issue* of *bonds* that mature in part at one date, another part on another date, and so on. The various maturity dates usually occur at equally spaced intervals. Contrast with *term bonds.*

service basis of depreciation. *Production method.*

service bureau. A commercial data-processing center providing service to various customers.

service cost, (current) service cost. *Pension plan expenses incurred* during an *accounting period* for employment services performed during that period. Contrast with *prior service cost.* See *funded.*

service department. A department, such as the personnel or computer department, that provides services to other departments rather than direct work on a salable product. Contrast with *production department.* A firm must allocate costs of service departments whose services benefit manufacturing operations to *product costs* under *full absorption costing.*

service department cost allocation. A procedure in which firms *allocate* the *costs* of operating service departments to other departments.

service life. Period of expected usefulness of an asset; may differ from *depreciable life* for income tax purposes.

service potential. The future benefits that cause an item to be classified as an *asset.* Without service potential, an item has no future benefits, and accounting will not classify the item as an asset. *SFAC No. 6* suggests that the primary characteristic of service potential is the ability to generate future net cash inflows.

services. Useful work done by a person, a machine, or an organization. See *goods.*

setup. The time or costs required to prepare production equipment for doing a job.

SFAC. *Statement of Financial Accounting Concepts* of the *FASB.*

SFAS. *Statement of Financial Accounting Standards.* See *FASB.*

shadow price. An opportunity cost. A *linear programming* analysis provides as one of its outputs the potential value of having available more of the scarce resources that constrain the production process, for example, the value of having more time available on a machine tool critical to the production of two products. Common terminology refers to this value as the "shadow price" or the "dual value" of the scarce resource.

share. A unit of *stock* representing ownership in a corporation.

share premium. UK: *additional paid-in capital* or *capital contributed in excess of par value.*

shareholders' equity. *Proprietorship* or *owners' equity* of a corporation. Because *stock* means inventory in Australia, the UK, and Canada, their writers use the term "shareholders' equity" rather than the term "stockholders' equity."

short run, short term. Contrast with *long run.* Managers mean a period of time long enough to allow change the level of production or other activity within the constraints of current total productive capacity. In a *balance sheet* context, it means *current,* ordinarily due within one year. Use a hyphen when the phrase is an adjective, but no hyphen when it is a noun.

short-term liquidity risk. The risk that an *entity* will not have enough *cash* in the *short run* to pay its *debts.*

short-term operating budget. Management's quantitative action plan for the coming year.

shrinkage. An excess of *inventory* shown on the *books* over actual physical quantities on hand; can result from theft or shoplifting as well as from evaporation or general wear and tear. Some accountants, in an attempt to downplay their own errors, use the term to mean record-keeping mistakes that they later must correct, with some embarrassment, and that result in material changes in reported income. One should not use the term "shrinkage" for the correction of mistakes because adequate terminology exists for describing mistakes.

shutdown cost. Those fixed costs that the firm continues to incur after it has ceased production; the costs of closing down a particular production facility.

side letter. See *channel stuffing.*

sight draft. A demand for payment drawn by Person A to whom Person B owes cash. Person A presents the *draft* to Person B's (the debtor's) bank in expectation that Person B will authorize his or her bank to disburse the funds. Sellers often use such drafts when selling goods to a new customer in a different city. The seller is uncertain whether the buyer will pay the bill. The seller sends the *bill* of lading, or other evidence of ownership of the goods, along with a sight draft to the buyer's bank. Before the warehouse holding the goods can release them to the buyer, the buyer must instruct its bank to honor the sight draft by withdrawing funds from the buyer's account. Once the bank honors the sight draft, it hands to the buyer the bill of lading or other document evidencing ownership, and the goods become the property of the buyer.

simple interest. *Interest* calculated on *principal* where interest earned during periods before maturity of the loan does not increase the principal amount earning interest for the subsequent periods and the lender cannot withdraw the funds before maturity. Interest = principal x interest rate x time, where the rate is a rate per period (typically a year) and time is expressed in units of that period. For example, if the *rate* is annual and the time is two months, then in the formula, use $\frac{2}{12}$ for *time.* Simple interest is seldom used in economic calculations except for periods of less than one year and then only for computational convenience. Contrast with *compound interest.*

single-entry accounting. Accounting that is neither *self-balancing* nor *articulated.* That is, it does not rely on equal *debits* and *credits.* The firm makes no *journal entries* and must *plug* to derive *owners' equity* for the *balance sheet.*

single proprietorship. *Sole proprietorship.*

single-step. Said of an *income statement* in which *ordinary revenue* and *gain* items appear first, with their total. Then come all ordinary *expenses* and *losses,* with their total. The difference between these two totals, plus the effect of *income from discontinued operations* and *extraordinary items,* appears as *net income.* Contrast with *multiple-step* and see *proprietorship theory.*

sinking fund. *Assets* and their earnings earmarked for the retirement of bonds or other long-term obligations. Earnings of sinking fund investments become taxable income of the company.

sinking fund method of depreciation. Method in which the periodic charge is an equal amount each period so that the *future value* of the charges, considered as an *annuity,* will accumulate at the end of the depreciable life to an amount equal to the *acquisition cost* of the asset. The firm does not necessarily, or even usually, accumulate a *fund* of cash. Firms rarely use this method.

skeleton account. *T-account.*

slide. The name of the error made by a bookkeeper in recording the digits of a number correctly with the decimal point misplaced; for example, recording $123.40 as $1,234.00 or as $12.34. If the only errors in a *trial balance* result from one or more slides, then the difference between the sum of the *debits* and the sum of the *credits* will be divisible by nine. Not all such differences divisible by nine result from slides. See *transposition error*.

SMAC (Society of Management Accountants of Canada). The national association of accountants whose provincial associations engage in industrial and governmental accounting. The association undertakes research and administers an educational program and comprehensive examinations; those who pass qualify to be designated CMA (Certified Management Accountants), formerly called RIA (Registered Industrial Accountant).

SNC (société en nom collectif). France: a *partnership*.

soak-up method. The *equity method*.

Social Security taxes. Taxes levied by the federal government on both employers and employees to provide *funds* to pay retired persons (or their survivors) who are entitled to receive such payments, either because they paid Social Security taxes themselves or because Congress has declared them eligible. Unlike a *pension plan*, the Social Security system does not collect funds and invest them for many years. The tax collections in a given year pay primarily for benefits distributed that year. At any given time the system has a multitrillion-dollar unfunded obligation to current workers for their eventual retirement benefits. See *Old Age, Survivors, Disability, and (Hospital) Insurance*.

software. The programming aids, such as compilers, sort and report programs, and generators, that extend the capabilities of and simplify the use of the computer, as well as certain operating systems and other control programs. Compare *hardware*.

sole proprietorship. A firm in which all *owners' equity* belongs to one person.

solvent. Able to meet debts when due.

SOP. *Statement of Position* (of the *AcSEC* of the *AICPA*).

sound value. A phrase used mainly in appraisals of *fixed assets* to mean *fair market price (value)* or *replacement cost* in present condition.

source of funds. Any *transaction* that increases *cash* and *marketable securities* held as *current assets*.

sources and uses statement. *Statement of cash flows*.

SOYD. *Sum-of-the years'–digits depreciation*.

SP (société en participation). France: a silent *partnership* in which the managing partner acts for the partnership as an individual in transacting with others who need not know that the person represents a partnership.

special assessment. A compulsory levy made by a governmental unit on property to pay the costs of a specific improvement or service presumed not to benefit the general public but only the owners of the property so assessed; accounted for in a special assessment fund.

special journal. A *journal*, such as a sales journal or cash disbursements journal, to record *transactions* of a similar nature that occur frequently.

special purpose entity. The name for a business now known as a *variable interest entity. GAAP* never defined this name, but brought it into existence with an *EITF* consensus in 1990. The Enron financial manipulations depended in part on use of these entities to achieve *off-balance-sheet financing*.

special revenue debt. A governmental unit's debt backed only by revenues from specific sources, such as tolls from a bridge.

specific identification method. Method for valuing *ending inventory* and *cost of goods sold* by identifying actual units sold and remaining in inventory and summing the actual costs of those individual units; usually used for items with large unit values, such as precious jewelry, automobiles, and fur coats.

specific item sampling. Sampling in which the analyst selects particular items because of their nature, value, or method of recording. Compare *representative item sampling*.

specific price changes. Changes in the market prices of specific *goods* and *services*. Contrast with *general price-level changes*.

specific price index. A measure of the price of a specific good or service, or a small group of similar goods or services, at one time relative to the price during a base period. Contrast with *general price index*. See *dollar-value LIFO method*.

spending variance. In *standard cost systems*, the *rate* or *price variance* for *overhead costs*.

split. *Stock split*. Sometimes called "split-up."

split-off point. In accumulating and allocating costs for *joint products*, the point at which all costs are no longer *joint costs* but at which an analyst can identify costs associated with individual products or perhaps with a smaller number of *joint products*.

spoilage. See *abnormal spoilage* and *normal spoilage*.

spot price. The price of a commodity for delivery on the day of the price quotation. See *forward price* for contrast.

spreadsheet. For many years, a term that referred specifically to a *work sheet* organized like a *matrix* that provides a two-way classification of accounting data. The rows and columns both have labels, which are *account* titles. An entry in a row represents a *debit*, whereas an entry in a column represents a *credit*. Thus, the number "100" in the "cash" row and the "accounts receivable" column records an entry debiting cash and crediting accounts receivable for $100. A given row total indicates all debit entries to the account represented by that row, and a given column total indicates the sum of all credit entries to the account represented by the column. Since personal-computer software has become widespread, this term has come to refer to any file created by programs such as Lotus 1-2-3® and Microsoft Excel®. Such files have rows and columns, but they need not represent debits and credits. Moreover, they can have more than two dimensions.

squeeze. A term sometimes used for *plug*.

SSARS. *Statement on Standards for Accounting and Review Services*.

stabilized accounting. *Constant-dollar accounting.*

stable monetary unit assumption. In spite of *inflation*, which appears to be a way of life, the assumption that underlies historical cost/nominal-dollar accounting—namely that one can meaningfully add together current dollars and dollars of previous years. The assumption gives no specific recognition to changing values of the dollar in the usual *financial statements*. See *constant-dollar accounting*.

Staff Accounting Bulletin. An interpretation issued by the staff of the Chief Accountant of the *SEC* "suggesting" how the accountants should apply various *Accounting Series Releases* in practice. The suggestions are part of *GAAP*.

stakeholder. An individual or group, such as employees, suppliers, customers, and shareholders, who have an interest in the corporation's activities and outcomes.

standard cost. Anticipated *cost* of producing a unit of output; a predetermined cost to be assigned to products produced. Standard cost implies a norm—what costs should be. Budgeted cost implies a forecast—something likely, but not necessarily, a "should," as implied by a norm. Firms use standard costs as the benchmark for gauging good and bad performance. Although a firm may similarly use a budget, it need not. A budget may be a planning document, subject to changes whenever plans change, whereas standard costs usually change annually or when technology significantly changes or when costs of labor and materials significantly change.

standard costing. *Costing* based on *standard costs*.

standard costing system. *Product costing* using *standard costs* rather than actual costs. The firm may use either *full absorption* or *variable costing* principles.

standard error (of regression coefficients). A measure of the uncertainty about the magnitude of the estimated parameters of an equation fit with a *regression analysis*.

standard manufacturing overhead. *Overhead costs* expected to be incurred per unit of time and per unit produced.

standard price (rate). Unit price established for materials or labor used in *standard cost systems*.

standard quantity allowed. The direct material or direct labor (inputs) quantity that production should have used if it had produced the units of output in accordance with preset *standards*.

standby costs. A type of *capacity cost*, such as property taxes, incurred even if a firm shuts down operations completely. Contrast with *enabling costs*.

stated capital. Amount of capital contributed by shareholders; sometimes used to mean *legal capital*.

stated value. A term sometimes used for the *face amount of capital stock*, when the *board* has not designated a *par value*. Where there is stated value per share, capital *contributed in excess of stated value* may come into being.

statement of affairs. A *balance sheet* showing immediate *liquidation* amounts rather than *historical costs*, usually prepared when *insolvency* or *bankruptcy* is imminent. Such a statement specifically does not use the *going-concern assumption*.

statement of cash flows. A schedule of *cash receipts* and *payments*, classified by *investing*, *financing*, and *operating activities;* required by the *FASB* for all for-profit companies. Companies may report operating activities with either the direct method (which shows only receipts and payments of cash) or the indirect method (which starts with *net income* and shows adjustments for *revenues* not currently producing cash and for *expenses* not currently using cash). "Cash" includes cash equivalents such as Treasury bills, commercial paper, and *marketable securities* held as *current assets*. This is sometimes called the "funds statement." Before 1987, the FASB required the presentation of a similar statement called the *statement of changes in financial position*, which tended to emphasize *working capital*, not cash.

statement of changes in financial position. As defined by *APB Opinion No. 19*, a statement that explains the changes in *working capital* (or cash) balances during a period and shows the changes in the working capital (or cash) accounts themselves. The *statement of cash flows* has replaced this statement.

statement of charge and discharge. A financial statement, showing *net assets* or *income*, drawn up by an executor or administrator, to account for receipts and dispositions of cash or other assets in an estate or trust.

Statement of Financial Accounting Concepts (SFAC). One of a series of *FASB* publications in its *conceptual framework* for *financial accounting* and reporting. Such statements set forth objectives and fundamentals to be the basis for specific financial accounting and reporting standards.

Statement of Financial Accounting Standards (SFAS). See *FASB*.

statement of financial position. *Balance sheet*.

Statement of Position (SOP). A recommendation, on an emerging accounting problem, issued by the *AcSEC* of the *AICPA*. The AICPA's Code of Professional Ethics specifically states that *CPAs* need not treat *SOPs* as they do rules from the

FASB, but a CPA would be wary of departing from the recommendations of an *SOP*.

statement of retained earnings (income). A statement that reconciles the beginning-of-period and the end-of-period balances in the *retained earnings* account. It shows the effects of *earnings, dividend declarations*, and *prior-period adjustments*.

statement of significant accounting policies (principles). A summary of the significant *accounting principles* used in compiling an *annual report;* required by *APB Opinion No. 22.* This summary may be a separate exhibit or the first *note* to the financial statements.

Statement on Auditing Standards (SAS). A series addressing specific auditing standards and procedures. *No. 1* (1973) of this series codifies all statements on auditing standards previously promulgated by the *AICPA*.

Statement on Standards for Accounting and Review Services (SSARS). Pronouncements issued by the *AICPA* on unaudited *financial statements* and unaudited financial information of nonpublic entities.

static budget. *Fixed budget*. Budget developed for a set level of the driving variable, such as production or sales, which the analyst does not change if the actual level deviates from the level set at the outset of the analysis.

status quo. Events or cost incurrences that will happen or that a firm expects to happen in the absence of taking some contemplated action.

statutory tax rate. The tax rate specified in the *income tax* law for each type of income (for example, *ordinary income, capital gain or loss).*

step allocation method. *Step-down method.*

step cost. *Semifixed cost.*

step-down method. In *allocating service department* costs, a method that starts by allocating one service department's costs to *production departments* and to all other service departments. Then the firm allocates a second service department's costs, including costs allocated from the first, to production departments and to all other service departments except the first one. In this fashion, a firm may allocate all service departments costs, including previous allocations, to production departments and to those service departments whose costs it has not yet allocated.

step method. *Step-down method.*

step(ped) cost. *Semifixed cost.*

sterilized allocation. Desirable characteristics of cost allocation methods. Optimal decisions result from considering *incremental costs* only. Optimal decisions never require *allocations* of *joint* or *common costs*. A "sterilized allocation" causes the optimal decision choice not to differ from the one that occurs when the accountant does not allocate joint or common costs "sterilized" with respect to that decision. Arthur L. Thomas first used the term in this context. Because *absorption costing* requires that product costs absorb all manufacturing costs

and because some allocations can lead to bad decisions, Thomas (and we) advocate that the analyst choose a sterilized allocation scheme that will not alter the otherwise optimal decision. No single allocation scheme is always sterilized with respect to all decisions. Thus, Thomas (and we) advocate that decisions be made on the basis of incremental costs before any allocations.

stewardship. Principle by which management is accountable for an *entity's* resources, for their efficient use, and for protecting them from adverse impact. Some theorists believe that accounting has as a primary goal aiding users of *financial statements* in their assessment of management's performance in stewardship.

stock. A measure of the amount of something on hand at a specific time. In this sense, contrast with *flow*. See *inventory* and *capital stock.*

stock appreciation rights. An employer's promise to pay to the employee an amount of *cash* on a certain future date, with the amount of cash being the difference between the *market value* of a specified number of *shares* of *stock* in the employer's company on the given future date and some base price set on the date the rights are granted. Firms sometimes use this form of compensation because changes in tax laws in recent years have made *stock options* relatively less attractive. *GAAP* compute compensation based on the difference between the market value of the shares and the base price set at the time of the grant.

stock dividend. A so-called *dividend* in which the firm distributes additional *shares* of *capital stock* without cash payments to existing shareholders. It results in a *debit* to *retained earnings* in the amount of the market value of the shares issued and a *credit* to *capital stock* accounts. Firms ordinarily use stock dividends to indicate that they have permanently reinvested earnings in the business. Contrast with a *stock split*, which requires no entry in the capital stock accounts other than a notation that the *par* or *stated value* per share has changed.

stock option. The right to purchase or sell a specified number of shares of *stock* for a specified price at specified times. Employee stock options are purchase rights granted by a corporation to employees, a form of compensation. Traded stock options are *derivative* securities, rights created and traded by investors, independent of the corporation whose stock is optioned. Contrast with *warrant*.

stock right. See *right*.

stock split(-up). Increase in the number of common shares outstanding resulting from the issuance of additional shares to existing shareholders without additional capital contributions by them. Does not increase the total *value* (or *stated value*) of *common shares* outstanding because the *board* reduces the par (or stated) value per share in inverse proportion. A three-for-one stock split reduces par (or stated) value per share to one-third of its former amount. A stock split usually implies a distribution that increases the number of shares outstanding by 20 percent or more. Compare with *stock dividend*.

stock subscriptions. See *subscription* and *subscribed stock*.

stock warrant. See *warrant*.

stockholders' equity. See *shareholders' equity*.

stockout. Occurs when a firm needs a unit of *inventory* to use in production or to sell to a customer but has none available.

stockout costs. *Contribution margin* or other measure of *profits* not earned because a seller has run out of *inventory* and cannot fill a customer's order. A firm may incur an extra cost because of delay in filling an order.

stores. *Raw materials*, parts, and supplies.

straight-debt value. An estimate of the *market value* of a *convertible bond* if the bond did not contain a conversion privilege.

straight-line depreciation. Method in which, if the *depreciable life* is *n* periods, the periodic *depreciation* charge is $1/n$ of the *depreciable cost;* results in equal periodic charges. Accountants sometimes call it "straight-time depreciation."

strategic plan. A statement of the method for achieving an organization's goals.

stratified sampling. In choosing a *sample,* a method in which the investigator first divides the entire *population* into relatively homogeneous subgroups (strata) and then selects random samples from these subgroups.

street security. A stock certificate in immediately transferable form, most commonly because the issuing firm has registered it in the name of the broker, who has endorsed it with "payee" left blank.

Subchapter S corporation. A firm legally organized as a *corporation* but taxed as if it were a *partnership*. Tax terminology calls the corporations paying their own income taxes *C corporations*.

subject to. In an *auditor's report,* qualifications usually caused by a *material* uncertainty in the valuation of an item, such as future promised payments from a foreign government or outcome of pending litigation.

subordinated. *Debt* whose claim on income or assets has lower priority than claims of other debt.

subscribed stock. A *shareholders' equity* account showing the capital that the firm will receive as soon as the share-purchaser pays the subscription price. A subscription is a legal contract, so once the share-purchaser signs it, the firm makes an entry *debiting* an *owners' equity contra account* and *crediting* subscribed stock.

subscription. Agreement to buy a *security* or to purchase periodicals, such as magazines.

subsequent events. *Poststatement events.*

subsidiary. A company in which another company owns more than 50 percent of the voting shares.

subsidiary ledger. The *ledger* that contains the detailed accounts whose total appears in a *controlling account* of the *general ledger*.

subsidiary (ledger) accounts. The *accounts* in a *subsidiary ledger*.

successful efforts costing. In petroleum accounting, the *capitalization* of the drilling costs of only those wells that contain gas or oil. See *reserve recognition accounting* for an example.

summary annual report (SAR). Condensed financial statements distributed in lieu of the usual *annual report*. Since 1987, the *SEC* has allowed firms to include such statements in the annual report to shareholders as long as the firm includes full, detailed statements in SEC filings and in *proxy* materials sent to shareholders.

summary of significant accounting principles. *Statement of significant accounting policies (principles).*

sum-of-the-years'–digits depreciation (SYD, SOYD). An *accelerated depreciation* method for an asset with *depreciable life* of *n* years where the charge in period i ($i = 1, \ldots, n$) is the fraction $(n + 1 - i)/[n(n + 1)/2]$ of the *depreciable cost*. If an asset has a depreciable cost of \$15,000 and a five-year depreciable life, for example, the depreciation charges would be \$5,000 (= $\frac{5}{15}$ \$15,000) in the first year, \$4,000 in the second, \$3,000 in the third, \$2,000 in the fourth, and \$1,000 in the fifth. The name derives from the fact that the denominator in the fraction is the sum of the digits 1 through *n*.

sunk cost. Past *costs* that current and future decisions cannot affect and, hence, that are irrelevant for decision making aside from *income tax* effects. Contrast with *incremental costs* and *imputed costs*. For example, the *acquisition cost* of machinery is irrelevant to a decision of whether to scrap the machinery. The current *exit value* of the machinery is the *opportunity cost* of continuing to own it, and the cost of, say, the electricity to run the machinery is an incremental cost of its operation. Sunk costs become relevant for decision making when the analysis requires taking *income taxes (gain* or *loss* on disposal of asset) into account, since the cash payment for income taxes depends on the tax basis of the asset. Avoid this term in careful writing because it is ambiguous. Consider, for example, a machine costing \$100,000 with current *salvage value* of \$20,000. Some (including us) would say that \$100,000 (the *gross* amount) is "sunk"; others would say that only \$80,000 (the *net* amount) is "sunk."

supplementary statements (schedules). Statements (schedules) in addition to the four basic *financial statements* (*balance sheet, income statement, statement of cash flows,* and the *statement of retained earnings*).

surplus. A word once used but now considered poor terminology; prefaced by "earned" to mean *retained earnings* and prefaced by "capital" to mean *capital contributed in excess of par* (*or stated*) *value*.

surplus reserves. *Appropriated retained earnings.* A phrase with nothing to recommend it: of all the words in accounting, *reserve* is the most objectionable, and *surplus* is the second-most objectionable.

suspense account. A *temporary account* used to record part of a transaction before final analysis of that transaction. For example, if a business regularly classifies all sales into a dozen or more different categories but wants to deposit the proceeds of cash sales every day, it may credit a sales suspense account pending detailed classification of all sales into Durable Goods Sales, Women's Clothing Sales, Men's Clothing Sales, Housewares Sales, and so on.

sustainable income. The part of *distributable income* (computed from *current cost* data) that the firm can expect to earn in the next accounting period if it continues operations at the same levels as were maintained during the current period. *Income from discontinued operations*, for example, may be distributable but not sustainable.

swap. A currency swap is a financial instrument in which the holder promises to pay to (or receive from) the *counterparty* the difference between *debt* denominated in one currency (such as U.S. dollars) and the payments on debt denominated in another currency (such as German marks). An interest-rate swap typically obligates the party and counterparty to exchange the difference between fixed- and floating-rate interest payments on otherwise similar loans.

S-X. See *Regulation S-X*.

SYD. *Sum-of-the-years'–digits depreciation*.

T

T-account. Account form shaped like the letter T with the title above the horizontal line. *Debits* appear on the left of the vertical line, *credits* on the right.

take-home pay. The amount of a paycheck; earned wages or *salary* reduced by deductions for *income taxes, Social Security taxes*, contributions to fringe-benefit plans, union dues, and so on. Take-home pay might be as little as half of earned compensation.

take-or-pay contract. As defined by *SFAS No. 47*, a purchaser-seller agreement that provides for the purchaser to pay specified amounts periodically in return for products or services. The purchaser must make specified minimum payments even if it does not take delivery of the contracted products or services.

taking a bath. To incur a large loss. See *big bath*.

tangible. Having physical form. Accounting has never satisfactorily defined the distinction between tangible and intangible assets. Typically, accountants define intangibles by giving an exhaustive list, and everything not on the list is defined as tangible. See *intangible asset* for such a list.

target cost. *Standard cost*. Sometimes, target price less expected profit margin.

target price. Selling price based on customers' value in use of a good or service, constrained by competitors' prices of similar items.

tax. A nonpenal, but compulsory, charge levied by a government on income, consumption, wealth, or other basis, for the benefit of all those governed. The term does not include fines or specific charges for benefits accruing only to those paying the charges, such as licenses, permits, special assessments, admission fees, and tolls.

tax allocation: interperiod. See *deferred income tax liability*.

tax allocation: intrastatement. The showing of income tax effects on *extraordinary items, income from discontinued operations*, and *prior-period adjustments,* along with these items, separately from income taxes on other income. See *net-of-tax reporting*.

tax avoidance. See *tax shelter* and *loophole*.

tax basis of assets and liabilities. A concept important for applying *SFAS No. 109* on *deferred income taxes*. Two *assets* will generally have different *book values* if the firm paid different amounts for them, *amortizes* them on a different schedule, or both. Similarly a single asset will generally have a book value different from what it will have for tax purposes if the firm recorded different *acquisition* amounts for the asset for book and for tax purposes, amortizes it differently for book and for tax purposes, or both. The difference between financial book value and income tax basis becomes important in computing deferred income tax amounts. The adjusted cost in the financial records is the "book basis," and the adjusted amount in the tax records is the "tax basis." Differences between book and tax basis can arise for *liabilities* as well as for assets.

tax credit. A subtraction from taxes otherwise payable. Contrast with *tax deduction*.

tax deduction. A subtraction from *revenues* and *gains* to arrive at taxable income. Tax deductions differ technically from tax *exemptions*, but both reduce gross income in computing taxable income. Both differ from *tax credits*, which reduce the computed tax itself in computing taxes payable. If the tax rate is the fraction *t* of pretax income, then a *tax credit* of \$1 is worth \$1/*t* of *tax deductions*.

tax evasion. The fraudulent understatement of taxable revenues or overstatement of deductions and expenses or both. Contrast with *tax shelter* and *loophole*.

tax-exempts. See *municipal bonds*.

tax shelter. The legal avoidance of, or reduction in, *income taxes* resulting from a careful reading of the complex income-tax regulations and the subsequent rearrangement of financial affairs to take advantage of the regulations. Often writers use the term pejoratively, but the courts have long held that a taxpayer has no obligation to pay taxes any larger than the legal minimum. If the public concludes that a given tax shelter is "unfair," then Congress can, and has, changed the laws and regulations. The term is sometimes used to refer to the investment that permits tax avoidance. See *loophole*.

tax shield. The amount of an *expense*, such as *depreciation,* that reduces taxable income but does not require *working capital*. Sometimes this term includes expenses that reduce taxable income and use working capital. A depreciation deduction (or *R&D expense* in the expanded sense) of $10,000 provides a tax shield of $3,700 when the marginal tax rate is 37 percent.

taxable income. *Income* computed according to *IRS* regulations and subject to *income taxes*. Contrast with income, net income, income before taxes (in the *income statement*), and *comprehensive income* (a *financial reporting* concept). Use the term "pretax income" to refer to income before taxes on the income statement in financial reports.

tax-transfer lease. One form of *capital lease*. Congress has in the past provided business with an incentive to invest in qualifying *plant and equipment* by granting an *investment credit*, which, though it occurs as a reduction in *income taxes* otherwise payable, effectively reduces the purchase price of the assets. Similarly, Congress continues to grant an incentive to acquire such assets by allowing the *Modified Accelerated Cost Recovery System* (*MACRS*, form of unusually *accelerated depreciation*). Accelerated depreciation for tax purposes allows a reduction of taxes paid in the early years of an asset's life, providing the firm with an increased *net present value* of *cash flows*. The *IRS* administers both of these incentives through the income tax laws, rather than paying an outright cash payment. A business with no taxable income in many cases had difficulty reaping the benefits of the investment credit or of accelerated depreciation because Congress had not provided for tax refunds to those who acquire qualifying assets but who have no taxable income. In principle, a company without taxable income could lease from another firm with taxable income an asset that it would otherwise purchase. The second firm acquires the asset, gets the tax-reduction benefits from the acquisition, and becomes a lessor, leasing the asset (presumably at a lower price reflecting its own costs lowered by the tax reductions) to the unprofitable company. Before 1981, tax laws discouraged such leases. That is, although firms could enter into such leases, they could not legally transfer the tax benefits. Under certain restrictive conditions, the tax law now allows a profitable firm to earn tax credits and take deductions while leasing to the firm without tax liability in such leases. These are sometimes called "safe-harbor leases."

Technical Bulletin. The *FASB* has authorized its staff to issue bulletins to provide guidance on financial accounting and reporting problems. Although the FASB does not formally approve the contents of the bulletins, their contents are part of *GAAP*.

technology. The sum of a firm's technical *trade secrets* and *know-how*, as distinct from its *patents*.

temporary account. *Account* that does not appear on the *balance sheet; revenue* and *expense* accounts, their *adjuncts* and *contras, production cost accounts, dividend distribution accounts*, and purchases-related accounts (which close to the various inventories); sometimes called a "nominal account."

temporary difference. According to the *SFAS No. 109* (1992) definition: "A difference between the tax basis of an asset or liability and its reported amount in the financial statements that will result in taxable or deductible amounts in future years." Temporary differences include *timing differences* and differences between *taxable income* and pretax income caused

by different cost bases for assets. For example, a plant asset might have a cost of $10,000 for financial reporting but a basis of $7,000 for income tax purposes. This temporary difference might arise because the firm has used an accelerated depreciation method for tax but straight-line for book, or the firm may have purchased the asset in a transaction in which the fair value of the asset exceeded its tax basis. Both situations create a temporary difference.

temporary investments. Investments in *marketable securities* that the owner intends to sell within a short time, usually one year, and hence classifies as *current assets*.

10-K. The name of the annual report that the *SEC* requires of nearly all publicly held corporations.

term bonds. A *bond issue* whose component bonds all mature at the same time. Contrast with *serial bonds*.

terminal cash flows. *Cash flows* that occur at the end of an *investment* project. Often include proceeds of *salvage* of equipment and tax on *gain (loss)* on disposal.

term loan. A loan with a *maturity* date, as opposed to a demand loan, which is due whenever the lender requests payment. In practice, bankers and auditors use this phrase only for loans for a year or more.

term structure. A phrase with different meanings in *accounting* and *financial economics*. In accounting, it refers to the pattern of times that must elapse before *assets* turn into, or produce, *cash* and the pattern of times that must elapse before *liabilities* require cash. In financial economics, the phrase refers to the pattern of interest rates as a function of the time that elapses for loans to come due. For example, if six-month loans cost 6 percent per year and 10-year loans cost 9 percent per year, this is called a "normal" term structure because the longer-term loan carries a higher rate. If the six-month loan costs 9 percent per year and the 10-year loan costs 6 percent per year, the term structure is said to be "inverted." See *yield curve*.

terms of sale. The conditions governing payment for a sale. For example, the terms ²/₁₀, *n(et)/30* mean that if the purchaser makes payment within 10 days of the invoice date, it can take a *discount* of 2 percent from *invoice* price; the purchaser must pay the invoice amount, in any event, within 30 days, or it becomes overdue.

theory of constraints (TOC). Concept of improving operations by identifying and reducing bottlenecks in process flows.

thin capitalization. A state of having a high *debt-equity ratio*. Under income tax legislation, the term has a special meaning.

throughput contract. As defined by *SFAS No. 47*, an agreement that is signed by a shipper (processor) and by the owner of a transportation facility (such as an oil or natural gas pipeline or a ship) or a manufacturing facility and that provides for the shipper (processor) to pay specified amounts periodically in return for the transportation (processing) of a product. The shipper (processor) must make cash payments even if it does not ship (process) the contracted quantities.

throughput contribution. Sales dollars minus the sum of all short-run variable costs.

tickler file. A collection of *vouchers* or other memoranda arranged chronologically to remind the person in charge of certain duties to make payments (or to do other tasks) as scheduled.

time-adjusted rate of return. *Internal rate of return.*

time cost. *Period cost.*

time deposit. Cash in bank earning interest. Contrast with *demand deposit.*

time-series analysis. See *cross-section analysis* for definition and contrast.

times-interest (charges) earned. Ratio of pretax *income* plus *interest* charges to interest charges. See *ratio.*

timing difference. The major type of *temporary difference* between taxable income and pretax income reported to shareholders; reverses in a subsequent period and requires an entry in the *deferred income tax* account; for example, the use of *accelerated depreciation* for tax returns and *straight-line depreciation* for financial reporting. Contrast with *permanent difference.*

Toronto Stock Exchange (TSX). A public market where various corporate securities trade.

total assets turnover. *Sales* divided by average total *assets.*

total quality management (TQM). Concept of organizing a company to excel in all its activities in order to increase the quality of products and services.

traceable cost. A *cost* that a firm can identify with or assign to a specific product. Contrast with a *joint cost.*

trade acceptance. A *draft* that a seller presents for signature (acceptance) to the buyer at the time it sells goods. The draft then becomes the equivalent of a *note receivable* of the seller and a *note payable* of the buyer.

trade credit. Occurs when one business allows another to buy from it in return for a promise to pay later. Contrast with "consumer credit," which occurs when a business extends a retail customer the privilege of paying later.

trade discount. A *list price discount* offered to all customers of a given type. Contrast with a *discount* offered for prompt payment and with *quantity discount.*

trade-in. Acquiring a new *asset* in exchange for a used one and perhaps additional cash. See *boot* and *trade-in transaction.*

trade-in transaction. The accounting for a trade-in; depends on whether the firm receives an asset "similar" to (and used in the same line of business as) the asset traded in and whether the accounting is for *financial statements* or for *income tax* returns. Assume that an old asset cost $5,000, has $3,000 of *accumulated depreciation* (after recording depreciation to the

date of the trade-in), and hence has a *book value* of $2,000. The old asset appears to have a market value of $1,500, according to price quotations in used asset markets. The firm trades in the old asset on a new asset with a list price of $10,000. The firm gives up the old asset and $5,500 cash *(boot)* for the new asset. The generic entry for the trade-in transaction is as follows:

New Asset	A		
Accumulated Depreciation (Old Asset)	3,000		
Adjustment on Exchange of Asset	B or	B	
Old Asset			5,000
Cash			5,500

(1) The *list price* method of accounting for trade-ins rests on the assumption that the list price of the new asset closely approximates its market value. The firm records the new asset at its list price (A = $10,000 in the example); B is a *plug* (= $2,500 credit in the example). If B requires a *debit* plug, the Adjustment on Exchange of Asset is a *loss*; if B requires a *credit* plug (as in the example), the adjustment is a *gain*.

(2) Another theoretically sound method of accounting for trade-ins rests on the assumption that the price quotation from used-asset markets gives a market value of the old asset that is a more reliable measure than the market value of the new asset determined by list price. This method uses the *fair market price (value)* of the old asset, $1,500 in the example, to determine B (= $2,000 book value – $1,500 assumed proceeds on disposition = $500 debit or loss). The exchange results in a loss if the book value of the old asset exceeds its market value and in a gain if the market value exceeds the book value. The firm records the new asset on the books by plugging for A (= $7,000 in the example).

(3) For income tax reporting, the taxpayer must recognize neither gain nor loss on the trade-in. Thus the taxpayer records the new asset for tax purposes by assuming B is zero and plugging for A (= $7,500 in the example). In practice, firms that want to recognize the loss currently will sell the old asset directly, rather than trading it in, and acquire the new asset entirely for cash.

(4) *Generally accepted accounting principles (APB Opinion No. 29)* require a variant of these methods. The basic method is (1) or (2), depending on whether the list price of the new asset (1) or the quotation of the old asset's market value (2) provides the more reliable indication of market value. If the basic method requires a debit entry, or loss, for the Adjustment on Exchange of Asset, then the firm records the trade-in as in (1) or (2) and recognizes the full amount of the loss currently. If, however, the basic method requires a credit entry, or gain, for the Adjustment on Exchange of Asset, then the firm recognizes the gain currently if the old asset and the new asset are not "similar." If the assets are similar and the party trading in receives no cash, then it recognizes no gain and the treatment resembles that in (3); that is B = 0, plug for A. If the assets are similar and the firm trading in receives cash—a rare case—then it recognizes a portion of the gain currently. The portion of the gain recognized currently is the fraction cash received/fair market value of total consideration received. (When the firm uses the list price method, (1), it assumes that the market value of the old asset is the list price of the new asset plus the amount of cash received by the party trading in.)

A summary of the results of applying *GAAP* to the example follows.

More Reliable Information As to Fair Market Value	Old Asset Compared with New Asset	
	Similar	**Not Similar**
New Asset . . . . A = $7,500		A = $10,000
List Price . . . . B = 0		B = 2,500 gain
Old Asset . . . . A = $7,000		A = $ 7,000
Market Price . . . . B = 500 loss		B = 500 loss

trade payables (receivables). *Payables (receivables)* arising in the ordinary course of business transactions. Most *accounts payable (receivable)* are of this kind.

trade secret. Technical or business information such as formulas, recipes, computer programs, and marketing data not generally known by competitors and maintained by the firm as a secret; theoretically capable of having an indefinite, finite life. A famous example is the secret process for Coca-Cola® (a registered *trademark* of the company). Compare with *know-how*. The firm will capitalize this intangible asset only if purchased. If this *intangible* has a finite, expected useful life, GAAP require amortization over that estimate of its life. If the right has indefinite life, then GAAP require no amortization, but annual tests for *impairment*. If the firm develops the intangible internally, the firm will *expense* the costs as incurred and show no asset.

trademark. A distinctive word or symbol that is affixed to a product, its package, or its dispenser and that uniquely identifies the firm's products and services. See *trademark right*.

trademark right. The right to exclude competitors in sales or advertising from using words or symbols that are so similar to the firm's *trademarks* as possibly to confuse consumers. Trademark rights last as long as the firm continues to use the trademarks in question. In the United States, trademark rights arise from use and not from government registration. They therefore have a legal life independent of the life of a registration. Registrations last 20 years, and the holder may renew them as long as the holder uses the trademark. If this *intangible* has a finite, expected useful life, GAAP require amortization over that estimate of its life. If the right has indefinite life, then GAAP require no amortization, but annual tests for *impairment*. Under *SFAS No. 2*, the firm must *expense* internally developed trademark rights.

trading on the equity. Said of a firm engaging in *debt financing*; frequently said of a firm doing so to a degree considered abnormal for a firm of its kind. *Leverage*.

trading securities. *Marketable securities* that a firm holds and expects to sell within a relatively short time; a classification important in *SFAS No. 115*, which requires the owner to carry marketable equity securities on the balance sheet at market value, not at cost. Contrast with *available for sale, securities* and *held-to-maturity securities*. Under *SFAS No. 115*, the balance sheet reports trading securities at market value on the balance sheet date, and the income statement reports *holding gains and losses* on trading securities. When the firm sells the securities, it reports realized gain or loss as the difference between the selling price and the market value at the last balance sheet date.

transaction. A *transfer* (of more than promises—see *executory contract*) between the accounting *entity* and another party or parties.

transfer. Under *SFAC No. 6,* consists of two types: "reciprocal" and "nonreciprocal." In a reciprocal transfer, or "exchange," the entity both receives and sacrifices. In a nonreciprocal transfer, the entity sacrifices but does not receive (examples include gifts, distributions to owners) or receives but does not sacrifice (investment by owner in entity). *SFAC No. 6* suggests that the term "internal transfer" is self-contradictory and that writers should use the term "internal event" instead.

transfer agent. Usually a bank or trust company designated by a corporation to make legal transfers of *stock (bonds)* and, perhaps, to pay *dividends (coupons)*.

transfer price. A substitute for a *market*, or *arm's-length*, price used in *profit*, or *responsibility center*, *accounting* when one segment of the business "sells" to another segment. Incentives of profit center managers will not coincide with the best interests of the entire business unless a firm sets transfer prices properly.

transfer-pricing problem. The problem of setting *transfer prices* so that both buyer and seller have *goal congruence* with respect to the parent organization's goals.

translation adjustment. The effect of *exchange-rate* changes caused by converting the value of a net investment denominated in a *foreign currency* to the entity's reporting currency. *SFAS No. 52* requires firms to translate their net investment in relatively self-contained foreign operations at the *balance sheet* date. Year-to-year changes in value caused by exchange-rate changes accumulate in an *owners' equity* account, sometimes called the "cumulative translation adjustment."

translation gain (or loss). *Foreign exchange gain (or loss)*.

transportation-in. *Freight-in*.

transposition error. An error in record keeping resulting from reversing the order of digits in a number, such as recording "32" for "23." If the only errors in a *trial balance* result from one or more transposition errors, then the difference between the sum of the *debits* and the sum of the *credits* will be divisible by nine. Not all such differences result from transposition errors. See *slide*.

treasurer. The financial officer responsible for managing cash and raising funds.

treasury bond. A bond issued by a corporation and then reacquired. Such bonds are treated as retired when reacquired, and an *extraordinary gain or loss* on reacquisition is recognized. This term also refers to a *bond* issued by the U.S. Treasury Department.

treasury shares. *Capital stock* issued and then reacquired by the corporation. Such reacquisitions result in a reduction of *shareholders' equity* and usually appear on the balance sheet as contra to shareholders' equity. Accounting recognizes neither *gain* nor *loss* on transactions involving treasury stock. The accounting debits (if positive) or credits (if negative) any difference between the amounts paid and received for treasury stock transactions to *additional paid-in capital*. See *cost method* and *par value method*.

treasury stock. *Treasury shares.*

trend analysis. Investigation of sales or other economic trends. Can range from a simple visual extrapolation of points on a graph to a sophisticated computerized time series analysis.

trial balance. A two-column listing of *account balances*. The left-hand column shows all accounts with *debit* balances and their total. The right-hand column shows all accounts with *credit* balances and their total. The two totals should be equal. Accountants compute trial balances as a partial check of the arithmetic accuracy of the entries previously made. See *adjusted, preclosing, post-closing, unadjusted trial balance, plug, slide*, and *transposition error.*

troubled debt restructuring. As defined in *SFAS No. 15*, a concession (changing of the terms of a *debt*) that is granted by a *creditor* for economic or legal reasons related to the *debtor's* financial difficulty and that the creditor would not otherwise consider.

TSE. *Toronto Stock Exchange.*

t-statistic. For an estimated *regression* coefficient, the estimated coefficient divided by the *standard error* of the estimate.

turnover. The number of times that *assets*, such as *inventory* or *accounts receivable*, are replaced on average during the period. Accounts receivable turnover, for example, is total sales on account for a period divided by the average accounts receivable balance for the period. See *ratio*. In the UK, "turnover" means *sales*.

turnover of plant and equipment. See *ratio*.

t-value. In *regression analysis*, the ratio of an estimated regression coefficient divided by its *standard error*.

20-F. Form required by the *SEC* for foreign companies issuing or trading their securities in the United States. This form reconciles the foreign accounting amounts resulting from using foreign *GAAP* to amounts resulting from using U.S. GAAP.

two T-account method. A method for computing either (1) *foreign-exchange gains and losses* or (2) *monetary gains or losses* for constant-dollar accounting statements. The left-hand *T-account* shows actual net balances of *monetary items*, and the right-hand T-account shows implied (common) dollar amounts.

2/10, n(et)/30. See *terms of sale*.

U

unadjusted trial balance. *Trial balance* taken before the accountant makes *adjusting* and *closing entries* at the end of the period.

unappropriated retained earnings. *Retained earnings* not appropriated and therefore against which the *board* can declare *dividends* in the absence of retained earnings restrictions. See *restricted retained earnings*.

unavoidable cost. A *cost* that is not an *avoidable cost*.

uncertainty. See *risk* for definition and contrast.

uncollectible account. An *account receivable* that the *debtor* will not pay. If the firm uses the preferable *allowance method*, the entry on judging a specific account to be uncollectible *debits* the allowance for uncollectible accounts and *credits* the specific account receivable. See *bad debt expense* and *sales contra, estimated uncollectibles*.

unconsolidated subsidiary. A *subsidiary* not consolidated and, hence, not accounted for in the *equity method*.

uncontrollable cost. The opposite of *controllable cost*.

underapplied (underabsorbed) overhead. An excess of actual *overhead costs* for a period over costs applied, or charged, to products produced during the period; a *debit balance* remaining in an overhead account after the accounting assigns overhead to product.

underlying document. The record, memorandum, *voucher*, or other signal that is the authority for making an *entry* into a *journal*.

underwriter. One who agrees to purchase an entire *security issue* for a specified price, usually for resale to others.

undistributed earnings. *Retained earnings*. Typically, this term refers to that amount retained for a given year.

unearned income (revenue). *Advances from customers*; strictly speaking, a contradiction in terms because the terms "income" and "revenue" mean earned.

unemployment tax. See *FUTA*.

unencumbered appropriation. In governmental accounting, portion of an *appropriation* not yet spent or encumbered.

unexpired cost. An *asset*.

unfavorable variance. In *standard cost* accounting, an excess of expected revenue over actual revenue or an excess of actual cost over standard cost.

unfunded. Not *funded*. An obligation or *liability*, usually for *pension costs*, exists, but no *funds* have been set aside to discharge the obligation or liability.

Uniform Partnership Act. A model law, enacted by many states, to govern the relations between partners when the *partnership* agreement fails to specify the agreed-upon treatment.

unissued capital stock. *Stock* authorized but not yet issued.

uniting-of-interests method. The IASB's term for the *pooling-of-interests method*. The IASB allows uniting of interests only when the merging firms are roughly equal in size and the shareholders retain substantially the same, relative to each other, voting rights and interests in the combined entity after the combination as before.

unit-level activities. Work that converts resources into individual products. Examples include *direct materials, direct labor,* and energy to run the machines.

units-of-production method. The *production method of depreciation.*

unlimited liability. The legal obligation of *general partners* or the sole proprietor for all debts of the *partnership* or *sole proprietorship.*

unqualified opinion. See *auditor's report.*

unrealized appreciation. An *unrealized holding gain*; frequently used in the context of *marketable securities.*

unrealized gain (loss) on marketable securities. An *income statement account* title for the amount of *gain (loss)* during the current period on the portfolio of *marketable securities* held as *trading securities. SFAS No. 115* requires the firm to recognize, in the income statement, gains and losses caused by changes in market values, even though the firm has not yet *realized* them.

unrealized gross margin (profit). A *contra account* to *installment accounts receivable* used with the *installment method* of revenue recognition; shows the amount of profit that the firm will eventually realize when it collects the receivable. Some accountants show this account as a *liability.*

unrealized holding gain. See *inventory profit* for the definition and an example.

unrecovered cost. *Book value* of an *asset.*

unused capacity. The difference between resources supplied and resources used.

usage variance. *Efficiency variance.*

use of funds. Any transaction that reduces funds (however "funds" is defined).

useful life. *Service life.*

valuation account. A *contra account* or *adjunct account.* When the firm reports *accounts receivable* at expected collectible amounts, it will credit any expected uncollectible amounts to the *allowance for uncollectibles,* a valuation account. In this way, the firm can show both the gross receivables amount and the amount it expects to collect. *SFAC No. 6* says a valuation account is "a separate item that reduces and increases the carrying amount" of an asset (or liability). The accounts are part of the related assets (or liabilities) and are not assets (or liabilities) in their own right.

value. Monetary worth. This term is usually so vague that you should not use it without a modifying adjective unless most people would agree on the amount. Do not confuse with cost. See *fair market price (value), entry value,* and *exit value.*

value added. *Cost* of a product or *work-in-process* minus the cost of the material purchased for the product or work-in-process.

value-added activity. Any activity that increases the usefulness to a customer of a product or service.

value chain. The set of business functions that increase the usefulness to the customer of a product or service; typically including research and development, design of products and services, production, marketing, distribution, and customer service.

value engineering. An evaluation of the activities in the value chain to reduce costs.

value variance. *Price variance.*

variable annuity. An *annuity* whose periodic payments depend on some uncertain outcome, such as stock market prices.

variable budget. *Flexible budget.*

variable costing. In allocating costs, a method that assigns only *variable manufacturing costs* to products and treats *fixed manufacturing costs* as *period expenses.* Contrast with *full absorption costing.*

variable costs. *Costs* that change as activity levels change. Strictly speaking, variable costs are zero when the activity level is zero. See *semivariable costs.* In accounting, this term most often means the sum of *direct costs* and variable *overhead.*

variable interest entity. VIE. An entity arranged so that one cannot analyze controlling financial interest by analyzing voting interest, because the entity has insufficient *owners' equity* at risk, which means it cannot finance its operations without additional financial support, such as the promises of another entity. The entity's owners' equity lacks attributes associated with equity: the ability to absorb losses, the right to receive residual returns, and the ability, conveyed by voting rights, to make decisions. The entity may, but need not, have a "primary beneficiary," which absorbs (or receives) a majority of the variability of outcomes of the entity. If there is a primary beneficiary, that business will consolidate the VIE, regardless of ownership.

variable overhead efficiency variance. The difference between the *actual* and *standard cost driver* volume times the standard cost driver rate.

variable overhead price variance. The difference between the *actual* and *standard cost driver* rate times the actual cost driver volume.

variable overhead variance. Difference between actual and *standard variable overhead costs.*

variable rate debt. *Debt* whose interest rate results from the periodic application of a formula, such as "three-month LIBOR [London Interbank Offered Rate] plus 1 percent [one hundred basis points] set on the 8th day of each February, May, August, and November."

variables sampling. The use of a sampling technique in which the sampler infers a particular quantitative characteristic of an entire population from a sample (e.g., mean amount of accounts receivable). See also *estimation sampling*. See *attribute(s) sampling* for contrast and further examples.

variance. Difference between actual and *standard costs* or between *budgeted* and actual *expenditures* or, sometimes, *expenses*. The word has completely different meanings in accounting and in statistics, where it means a measure of dispersion of a distribution.

variance analysis. *Variance investigation*. This term's meaning differs in statistics.

variance investigation. A step in managerial control processes. *Standard costing systems* produce *variance* numbers of various sorts. These numbers seldom exactly equal zero. Management must decide when a variance differs sufficiently from zero to study its cause. This term refers both to the decision about when to study the cause and to the study itself.

variation analysis. Analysis of the causes of changes in financial statement items of interest such as *net income* or *gross margin*.

VAT (Value-added tax). A tax levied on the market value of a firm's outputs less the market value of its purchased inputs.

vendor. A seller; sometimes spelled "vender."

verifiable. A qualitative *objective* of financial reporting specifying that accountants can trace items in *financial statements* back to *underlying documents*—supporting *invoices*, canceled *checks*, and other physical pieces of evidence.

verification. The auditor's act of reviewing or checking items in *financial statements* by tracing back to *underlying documents*—supporting *invoices*, canceled *checks*, and other business documents—or sending out *confirmations* to be returned. Compare with *physical verification*.

vertical analysis. Analysis of the financial statements of a single firm or across several firms for a particular time, as opposed to *horizontal* or *time-series analysis*, in which the analyst compares items over time for a single firm or across firms.

vertical integration. The extension of activity by an organization into business directly related to the production or distribution of the organization's end products. Although a firm may sell products to others at various stages, a vertically integrated firm devotes the substantial portion of the output at each stage to the production of the next stage or to end products. Compare *horizontal integration*.

vested. An employee's *pension plan* benefits that are not contingent on the employee's continuing to work for the employer.

VIE. *Variable interest entity.*

visual curve fitting method. One crude form of cost *estimation*. Sometimes, when a firm needs only rough approximations of the amounts of *fixed* and *variable costs*, management need not perform a formal *regression analysis* but can plot the data and draw a line that seems to fit the data. Then it can use the parameters of that line for the rough approximations.

volume variance. *Production volume variance*; less often, used to mean *sales volume variance*.

voucher. A document that signals recognition of a *liability* and authorizes the disbursement of cash; sometimes used to refer to the written evidence documenting an *accounting entry*, as in the term *journal voucher*.

voucher system. In controlling *cash*, a method that requires someone in the firm to authorize each *check* with an approved *voucher*. The firm makes no *disbursements* of currency or coins except from *petty cash funds*.

vouching. The function performed by an *auditor* to ascertain that underlying data or documents support a *journal entry*.

W

wage. Compensation of employees based on time worked or output of product for manual labor. But see *take-home pay*.

warning signal. Tool used to identify quality-control problems; only signals a problem. Contrast with *diagnostic signal*, which both signals a problem and suggests its cause.

warrant. A certificate entitling the owner to buy a specified number of shares at a specified time(s) for a specified price; differs from a *stock option* only in that the firm grants options to employees and issues warrants to the public. See *right*.

warranty. A promise by a seller to correct deficiencies in products sold. When the seller gives warranties, proper accounting practice recognizes an estimate of warranty *expense* and an *estimated liability* at the time of sale. See *guarantee* for contrast in proper usage.

wash sale. The sale and purchase of the same or similar *asset* within a short time period. For *income tax* purposes, the taxpayer may not recognize *losses* on a sale of stock if the taxpayer purchases equivalent stock within 30 days before or after the date of sale.

waste. Material that is a residue from manufacturing operations and that has no sale value. Frequently, this has negative value because a firm must incur additional costs for disposal.

wasting asset. A *natural resource* that has a limited *useful life* and, hence, is subject to *amortization*, called *depletion*. Examples are timberland, oil and gas wells, and ore deposits.

watered stock. Shares issued for *assets* with *fair market price (value)* less than *par* or *stated value*. The firm records the assets on the books at the overstated values. In the law, for shares to be considered watered, the *board of directors* must have acted in bad faith or fraudulently in issuing the shares under these circumstances. The term originated from a former practice of cattle owners who fed cattle ("stock") large quantities of salt to make them thirsty. The cattle then drank much water before their owner took them to market. The owners did this to make the cattle appear heavier and more valuable than otherwise.

weighted average. An average computed by counting each occurrence of each value, not merely a single occurrence of each value. For example, if a firm purchases one unit for $1 and two units for $2 each, then the simple average of the purchase prices is $1.50, but the weighted average price per unit is $5/3 = $1.67. Contrast with *moving average*.

weighted-average cost of capital. Measured as the *weighted-average* of the *after-tax cost* of *long-term debt* and the cost of *equity.*

weighted-average inventory method. Valuing either *withdrawals* or *ending inventory* at the *weighted-average* purchase price of all units on hand at the time of withdrawal or of computation of ending inventory. The firm uses the *inventory equation* to calculate the other quantity. If a firm uses the *perpetual inventory* method, accountants often call it the *moving average method.*

where-got, where-gone statement. A term allegedly used in the 1920s by W. M. Cole for a statement much like the *statement of cash flows*. Noted accounting historian S. Zeff reports that Cole actually used the term "where-got-gone" statement.

wind up. To bring to an end, such as the life of a corporation. The *board* winds up the life of a corporation by following the winding-up provisions of applicable statutes, by surrendering the charter, or by following *bankruptcy* proceedings. See also *liquidation.*

window dressing. The attempt to make financial statements show *operating* results, or a *financial position*, more favorable than they would otherwise show.

with recourse. See *note receivable discounted.*

withdrawals. *Assets* distributed to an owner. *Partner's drawings.* See *inventory equation* for another context.

withholding. Deductions that are taken from *salaries* or *wages*, usually for *income taxes*, and that the employer remits, in the employee's name, to the taxing authority.

without recourse. See *note receivable discounted.*

work sheet (program). (1) A computer program designed to combine explanations and calculations. This type of program helps in preparing *financial statements* and *schedules.* (2) A tabular schedule for convenient summary of *adjusting* and *closing entries*. The work sheet usually begins with an *unadjusted trial balance.* Adjusting entries appear in the next two columns, one for *debits* and one for *credits.* The work sheet carries the horizontal sum of each line to the right into either the *income statement* or the *balance sheet* column, as appropriate. The *plug* to equate the income statement column totals is, if a debit, the income or, if a credit, a loss for the period. That income will close retained earnings on the balance sheet. The income statement credit columns are the revenues for the

period, and the debit columns are the expenses (and revenue contras) that appear on the income statement. "Work sheet" also refers to *schedules* for ascertaining other items that appear on the *financial statements* and that require adjustment or compilation.

working capital. *Current assets* minus *current liabilities;* sometimes called "net working capital" or "net current assets."

work(ing) papers. The schedules and analyses prepared by the *auditor* in carrying out investigations before issuing an *opinion* on *financial statements.*

work-in-process (inventory account). Partially completed product; appears on the balance sheet as *inventory.*

worth. *Value.* See *net worth.*

worth-debt ratio. Reciprocal of the *debt-equity ratio.* See *ratio.*

write down. To *write off,* except that the firm does not charge all the *asset*'s cost to *expense* or *loss;* generally used for nonrecurring items.

write off. To *charge* an *asset* to *expense* or *loss;* that is, to *debit* expense (or loss) and *credit* the asset.

write-off method. For treating *uncollectible accounts,* a method that *debits bad debt expense* and *credits* accounts receivable of specific customers as the firm identifies specific accounts as uncollectible. The firm cannot use this method when it can estimate uncollectible amounts and they are significant. See *bad debt expense, sales contra, estimated uncollectibles,* and the *allowance method* for contrast.

write up. To increase the recorded *cost* of an *asset* with no corresponding *disbursement* of *funds;* that is, to *debit* asset and *credit revenue* or, perhaps, *owners' equity;* seldom done in the United States because currently accepted accounting principles await actual transactions before recording asset increases. An exception occurs in accounting for *marketable equity securities.*

X

XBRL. eXtensible Business Reporting Language. A language created by over thirty partners, including the *AICPA*, to promote automated processing of business information by software on a computer. The main idea is that financial data get coded labels, called "tags," not locations in a financial statement, so that the user can access only the data needed for a particular use, without downloading and extracting the needed data from a *balance sheet.* For example, if you download a company's *annual report,* you can go to the balance sheet and copy out the amounts for *current assets* and *current liabilities*, then divide the first by the second to get the *current ratio.* Using XBRL, you'd write an arithmetic expression such as:

tag for current assets[particular company]/tag for current liabilities[same company]

Then XBRL would extract from the data just the two numbers, corresponding to the two tags you programmed.

The initiative to construct XBRL began around 2000; Microsoft was the first to prepare, in 2002, financial statement data available for public use in XBRL; and the *SEC*, in 2005, has allowed companies to file financial data at the SEC using XBRL. In 2005, the *PCAOB* issued guidelines for the audit of such XBRL filings at the SEC. We guess that use of XBRL will mushroom over the next decade. It serves users' needs in a way no other widely available system does.

Y

yield. *Internal rate of return* of a stream of cash flows. Cash yield is cash flow divided by book value. See also *dividend yield*.

yield curve. The relation between *interest rates* and the term to maturity of loans. Ordinarily, longer-term loans have higher interest rates than shorter-term loans. This is called a "normal" yield curve. Sometimes long-term and short-term rates are approximately the same—a "flat" yield curve. Sometimes short-term loans have a higher rate than long-term ones—an "inverted" yield curve. *Term structure* of interest rates.

yield to maturity. At a given time, the *internal rate of return* of a series of cash flows; usually said of a *bond;* sometimes called the "effective rate."

yield variance. Measures the input-output relation while holding the standard mix of inputs constant: (standard price multiplied by actual amount of input used in the standard mix) –

(standard price multiplied by standard quantity allowed for the actual output). It is the part of the *efficiency variance* not called the *mix variance*.

Z

zero-base(d) budgeting (ZBB). One philosophy for setting budgets. In preparing an ordinary budget for the next period, a manager starts with the budget for the current period and makes adjustments as seem necessary because of changed conditions for the next period. Since most managers like to increase the scope of the activities managed and since most prices increase most of the time, amounts in budgets prepared in the ordinary, incremental way seem to increase period after period. The authority approving the budget assumes that managers will carry out operations in the same way as in the past and that next period's expenditures will have to be at least as large as those of the current period. Thus, this authority tends to study only the increments to the current period's budget. In ZBB, the authority questions the process for carrying out a program and the entire budget for the next period. The authority studies every dollar in the budget, not just the dollars incremental to the previous period's amounts. The advocates of ZBB claim that in this way, (1) management will more likely delete programs or divisions of marginal benefit to the business or governmental unit, rather than continuing with costs at least as large as the present ones, and (2) management may discover and implement alternative, more cost-effective ways of carrying out programs. ZBB implies questioning the existence of programs and the fundamental nature of the way that firms carry them out, not merely the amounts used to fund them. Experts appear to divide evenly as to whether the middle word should be "base" or "based."

General Electric
2003 Annual Report

Authors' Introduction

GE's Annual Reports consistently rank among the best we see. We can think of no better way to learn financial accounting than to try to understand all that appears in GE's statements. In this annotated excerpt from GE's 2003 Annual Report, we comment on various aspects of the financial statements in numbered footnotes keyed to the report.

We leave the original report's page numbers intact. References, both in the report and in our comments, use these numbers. We have inserted circled numbers — known as call-outs — in the annual report to refer to our comments. Comments begin at the bottom of this page, and generally appear on a page facing (or near) the relevant call-outs. The Glossary explains accounting terms we use in our comments; here as elsewhere in the book we indicate glossary entries with *italicized text*. As we went to press, GE restated some numbers from its annual report. We discuss this in our comment 22.

Most readers of this book can access the GE annual reports and notes thereto on GE's web site. We do not attempt to reproduce all that information. Instead, we reproduce material where we think we can help you understand complications and subtleties in the annual report. Use the following URL addresses to access the original GE information.

http://www.ge.com/ar2003/tools_guide.jsp

This URL has two links: Understanding Annual Reports, and Glossary of Terms. The first link provides an overview of the components of the annual report and the second provides explanations of terms GE uses in its report. Many, but not all, of these terms appear also in the Glossary of this book.

http://www.ge.com/files/usa/en/ar2003/ge_ar2003_full_book_v1.pdf

This URL provides the entire Annual Report, from which we excerpt and on which we comment. If GE re-organizes its website, the above URLs may not work. In this case, start from GE's main page, www.ge.com, and search for investor information.

Authors' Comments on General Electric Annual Report

(1) This begins our numbered comments. Notice the GE corporate symbol — a trademark of General Electric Company — as it appears on the front cover of the annual report. GE calls it "the meatball." This symbol may be the Company's single most valuable asset, but in accordance with *generally accepted accounting principles* (GAAP), this asset does not appear anywhere in the financial statements.

(2) These paragraphs, which appear on page 42 of the annual report, indicate that management takes responsibility for the financial statements' preparation.

GENERAL ELECTRIC 2003 ANNUAL REPORT

GROWING
IN AN *UNCERTAIN*
WORLD

GENERAL ELECTRIC 2003 ANNUAL REPORT

High quality financial reporting is an excellent measure of a company and its management. We demonstrate our commitment to high quality reporting by adopting appropriate accounting policies, devoting our full, unyielding commitment to ensuring that those policies are applied properly and consistently, and presenting our results in a manner that is complete and clear. We welcome suggestions from those who use our reports.

Rigorous Management Oversight

Members of our corporate leadership team review each of our businesses constantly, on matters that range from overall strategy and financial performance to staffing and compliance. Our business leaders constantly monitor real-time financial and operating systems, enabling us to identify potential opportunities and concerns at an early stage, and positioning us to develop and execute rapid responses. Our Board of Directors oversees management's business conduct, and our Audit Committee, which consists entirely of independent directors, oversees our system of controls and procedures. We continually examine our governance practices in an effort to enhance investor trust and improve the board's overall effectiveness. Our Presiding Director, who conducts at least three meetings per year with non-employee directors, has helped us to set more focused and effective meeting agendas. We changed compensation policies for our executives, including modifying CEO compensation to award equity grants only if key performance metrics are met, thereby aligning leadership's interests with the long-term interests of GE investors.

Dedication to Controllership

We maintain a dynamic system of controls and procedures — including internal controls over financial reporting — designed to ensure reliable financial record-keeping, transparent financial reporting and disclosure, protection of physical and intellectual property, and efficient, effective use of resources. We recruit, develop and retain a world-class financial team, including 520 internal auditors who conduct thousands of financial, compliance and process improvement audits each year, in every geographic area, at every GE business. The Audit Committee oversees the scope and results of these reviews. Our global integrity policies — the "Spirit & Letter" — require compliance with law and policy, and pertain to such vital issues as upholding financial integrity and avoiding conflicts of interest. These integrity policies are available in 27 languages, and we have provided them to every one of GE's more than 300,000 global employees, holding each of these individuals — from our top management on down — personally accountable for compliance. Our integrity policies serve to reinforce key employee responsibilities around the world, and we inquire extensively about compliance. Our strong compliance culture reinforces these efforts by requiring employees to raise any compliance concerns and by prohibiting retribution for doing so. We hold our consultants, agents and independent contractors to the same integrity standards.

Visibility to Investors

We are keenly aware of the importance of full and open presentation of our financial position and operating results. To facilitate this, we maintain a Disclosure Committee, which includes senior executives with exceptional knowledge of our businesses and the related needs of our investors. We ask this committee to evaluate the fairness of our financial and non-financial disclosures, and to report their findings to us and to the Audit Committee. We further ensure strong disclosure by holding more than 250 analyst and investor meetings every year, and by communicating any material information covered in those meetings to the public. In testament to the effectiveness of our stringent disclosure policies, investors surveyed annually by *Investor Relations* magazine have given us 19 awards in the last eight years, including Best Overall Investor Relations Program by a mega-cap company for six of those years. We are in regular contact with representatives of the major rating agencies, and our debt continues to receive their highest ratings. We welcome the strong oversight of our financial reporting activities by our independent audit firm, KPMG LLP, who are engaged by and report directly to the Audit Committee. Their report for 2003 appears on page 43.

A Great Company

GE continues to earn the admiration of the business world. We were named "The World's Most Respected Company" for the sixth consecutive year in the *Financial Times* annual CEO survey, ranking first for governance and integrity.

Great companies are built on the foundation of reliable financial information and compliance with the law. For GE, the financial disclosures in this report are a vital part of that foundation. We present this information proudly, with the expectation that those who use it will understand our company, recognize our commitment to performance with integrity, and share our confidence in GE's future.

Jeff Immelt

Jeffrey R. Immelt
Chairman of the Board and
Chief Executive Officer

Keith S. Sherin

Keith S. Sherin
Senior Vice President, Finance, and
Chief Financial Officer

February 6, 2004

**To Shareowners and Board of Directors of
General Electric Company**

We have audited the accompanying statement of financial position of General Electric Company and consolidated affiliates ("GE") as of December 31, 2003 and 2002, and the related statements of earnings, changes in shareowners' equity and cash flows for each of the years in the three-year period ended December 31, 2003. These consolidated financial statements are the responsibility of GE management. Our responsibility is to express an opinion on these consolidated financial statements based on our audits.

We conducted our audits in accordance with auditing standards generally accepted in the United States of America. Those standards require that we plan and perform the audit to obtain reasonable assurance about whether the financial statements are free of material misstatement. An audit includes examining, on a test basis, evidence supporting the amounts and disclosures in the financial statements. An audit also includes assessing the accounting principles used and significant estimates made by management, as well as evaluating the overall financial statement presentation. We believe that our audits provide a reasonable basis for our opinion.

In our opinion, the aforementioned financial statements appearing on pages 70, 72, 74, 48 and 76-113 present fairly, in all material respects, the financial position of General Electric Company and consolidated affiliates at December 31, 2003 and 2002, and the results of their operations and their cash flows for each of the years in the three-year period ended December 31, 2003, in conformity with accounting principles generally accepted in the United States of America.

As discussed in note 1 to the consolidated financial statements, GE in 2003 changed its methods of accounting for variable interest entities and asset retirement obligations, in 2002 changed its methods of accounting for goodwill and other intangible assets and for stock-based compensation, and in 2001 changed its methods of accounting for derivative instruments and hedging activities and impairment of certain beneficial interests in securitized assets.

Our audits were made for the purpose of forming an opinion on the consolidated financial statements taken as a whole. The accompanying consolidating information appearing on pages 71, 73 and 75 is presented for purposes of additional analysis of the consolidated financial statements rather than to present the financial position, results of operations and cash flows of the individual entities. The consolidating information has been subjected to the auditing procedures applied in the audits of the consolidated financial statements and, in our opinion, is fairly stated in all material respects in relation to the consolidated financial statements taken as a whole.

KPMG LLP

KPMG LLP
Stamford, Connecticut

February 6, 2004, except as to page 48 and notes 10, 12, 13, 16 and 27, which are as of March 29, 2004.

GE'S TOTAL BACKLOG of firm unfilled orders at the end of 2003 was $31.2 billion, a decrease of 12% from year-end 2002, reflecting softening demand for new equipment in the power generation business at Energy and at Transportation, partially offset by higher backlog at Healthcare. Of the total backlog, $21.2 billion related to products, of which 63% was scheduled for delivery in 2004. Product services orders, included in this reported backlog for only the succeeding 12 months, were $10.0 billion at the end of 2003. Orders constituting this backlog may be canceled or deferred by customers, subject in certain cases to penalties. See Segment Operations beginning on page 49 for further information.

(4) CRITICAL ACCOUNTING ESTIMATES

Accounting estimates and assumptions discussed in this section are those that we consider to be the most critical to an understanding of our financial statements because they inherently involve significant judgments and uncertainties. For all of these estimates, we caution that future events rarely develop exactly as forecast, and the best estimates routinely require adjustment.

LOSSES ON FINANCING RECEIVABLES are recognized when they are incurred. Our best estimate of such probable losses requires consideration of historical loss experience, adjusted for current conditions, and judgments about the probable effects of relevant observable data, including present economic conditions such as delinquency rates, financial health of specific customers and market sectors, collateral values, and the present and expected future levels of interest rates. Our lending and leasing experience and the extensive data we accumulate and analyze facilitate estimates that have been reliable over time. Our actual loss experience was in line with expectations for 2003, 2002 and 2001. While losses depend to a large degree on future economic conditions, we do not anticipate significant adverse credit development in 2004. Further information is provided in the financing receivables section on page 57, and in notes 1, 12, 13 and, for special purpose entities, in note 29.

REVENUE RECOGNITION ON LONG-TERM AGREEMENTS to provide product services (product services agreements) requires estimates of profits over the multiple-year terms of such agreements, considering factors such as the frequency and extent of future monitoring, maintenance and overhaul events; the amount of personnel, spare parts and other resources required to perform the services; and future cost changes. We routinely review estimates under product services agreements and regularly revise them to adjust for changes in outlook. Revisions that affect a product services agreement's total estimated profitability will also result in an immediate adjustment of earnings. We provide for probable losses. We also regularly assess customer credit risk inherent in the carrying amounts of contract costs and estimated earnings. We gain insight into future utilization and cost trends, as well as credit risk, through our knowledge of the installed base of equipment and the close interaction with our customers that comes with supplying critical services and parts over extended periods. Carrying amounts for product services agreements in progress at December 31, 2003 and 2002, were $3.2 billion and $2.9 billion, respectively, and are included in the line, "Contract costs and estimated earnings" in note 17. Adjustments to earnings resulting from revisions to estimates on product services agreements have been insignificant for each of the years in the three-year period ended December 31, 2003.

ASSET IMPAIRMENT assessment involves various estimates and assumptions as follows:

INVESTMENTS We regularly review investment securities for impairment based on criteria that include the extent to which the investment's carrying value exceeds its related market value, the duration of the market decline, our ability to hold to recovery and the financial strength and specific prospects of the issuer of the security. We perform comprehensive market research and analysis and monitor market conditions to identify potential impairments. Further information about actual and potential impairment losses is provided on page 57 and in note 9.

LONG-LIVED ASSETS We review long-lived assets for impairment whenever events or changes in circumstances indicate that the related carrying amounts may not be recoverable. Determining whether an impairment has occurred typically requires various estimates and assumptions, including determining which cash flows are directly related to the potentially impaired asset, the useful life over which cash flows will occur, their amount, and the asset's residual value, if any. In turn, measurement of an impairment loss requires a determination of fair value, which is based on the best information available. We use internal discounted cash flow estimates, quoted market prices when available and independent appraisals as appropriate to determine fair value. We derive the required cash flow estimates from our historical experience and our internal business plans and apply an appropriate discount rate.

Commercial aircraft are a significant concentration of assets in our Commercial Finance business, and are particularly subject to market fluctuations. Therefore we test recoverability of each aircraft in our operating lease portfolio at least annually. Additionally we perform quarterly evaluations in circumstances such as when aircraft are re-leased, current lease terms have changed or a specific lessee's credit standing changes. Future rentals and residual values are based on historical experience and information received routinely from independent appraisers. Estimated cash flows from future leases are reduced for expected downtime between leases and for estimated technical costs required to prepare aircraft to be redeployed. Fair value used to measure impairment is based on current market values from independent appraisers.

GOODWILL AND OTHER IDENTIFIED INTANGIBLE ASSETS We test goodwill for impairment annually and whenever events or circumstances make it more likely than not that an impairment may have occurred, such as a significant adverse change in the business climate or a decision to sell or dispose of a reporting unit. Determining whether an impairment has occurred requires valuation of the respective reporting unit, which we estimate using a discounted cash flow methodology. When available and as appropriate, we use comparative market multiples to corroborate discounted cash flow results. In applying this methodology, we rely on a number of factors, including actual operating results, future business plans, economic projections and market data.

If this analysis indicates goodwill is impaired, measuring its impairment requires a fair value estimate of each identified tangible and intangible asset. In this case we supplement the cash flow approach discussed above with independent appraisals, as appropriate.

We test other identified intangible assets with defined useful lives and subject to amortization by comparing the carrying amount to the sum of undiscounted cash flows expected to be generated by the asset. We test intangible assets with indefinite lives annually for impairment using a fair value methodology such as discounted cash flows.

Further information is provided on page 58 and in notes 1, 9, 15 and 16.

INSURANCE LIABILITIES AND RESERVES differ for short and long-duration insurance contracts. Short-duration contracts such as property and casualty policies are accounted for based on actuarial estimates of losses inherent in that period's claims, including losses for which claims have not yet been reported. Short-duration contract loss estimates rely on actuarial observations of ultimate loss experience for similar historical events. Measurement of long-duration insurance liabilities (such as guaranteed renewable term, whole life and long-term care insurance policies) also is based on approved actuarial methods that include assumptions about expenses, mortality, morbidity, lapse rates and future yield on related investments. Historical insurance industry experience indicates that a greater degree of inherent variability exists in assessing the ultimate amount of losses under short-duration property and casualty contracts than exists for long-duration mortality exposures. This inherent variability is particularly significant for liability-related exposures, including latent claims issues (such as asbestos and environmental related coverage disputes), because of the extended period of time — often many years — that transpires between when a given claim event occurs and the ultimate full settlement of such claim. This situation is then further exacerbated for reinsurance entities (as opposed to primary insurers) due to coverage often being provided on an "excess-of-loss" basis and the resulting lags in receiving current claims data.

We continually evaluate the potential for changes in loss estimates with the support of qualified reserving actuaries and use the results of these evaluations both to adjust recorded reserves and to proactively modify underwriting criteria and product offerings. For actuarial analysis purposes, reported and paid claims activity is segregated into several hundred reserving segments, each having differing historical settlement trends. A variety of actuarial methodologies are then applied to the underlying data for each of these reserving segments in arriving at an estimated range of "reasonably possible" loss scenarios. Factors such as line of business, length of historical settlement pattern, recent changes in underwriting standards and unusual trends in reported claims activity will generally affect which actuarial methodologies are given more weight for purposes of determining the "best estimate" of ultimate losses in a particular reserving segment. As discussed in the insurance section on page 52 and in note 19, reported claims activity at ERC related to prior year loss events, particularly for liability-related exposures underwritten in 1997 through 2001, has performed much worse than we anticipated. This trend was considered in the actuarial reserve study completed in the fourth quarter of 2002, resulting in a significant increase in recorded reserves. Following these actions, we have continued to monitor reported claims volumes relative to our revised expected loss levels. While for the majority of our lines of business, reported claims activity in 2003 was reasonably close to expected amounts, for certain lines of business the reported claims volumes exceeded our revised loss expectations. In response to this new data, we further increased our loss reserves in 2003. ERC continues its comprehensive efforts to apply more rigorous underwriting standards that began in 2002. Actuarial reserve studies and recorded reserves continue to be updated accordingly.

PENSION ASSUMPTIONS Pension benefit obligations and the related effects on operations are calculated using actuarial models. Two critical assumptions — discount rate and expected return on assets — are important elements of plan expense and asset/liability measurement. We evaluate these critical assumptions at least annually. Other assumptions involving demographic factors such as retirement age, mortality and turnover are evaluated periodically and are updated to reflect our experience. Actual results in any given year will often differ from actuarial assumptions because of economic and other factors.

The discount rate enables us to state expected future cash flows at a present value on the measurement date. We have little latitude in selecting this rate; it is the yield on high-quality fixed income investments at the measurement date. A lower discount rate increases the present value of benefit obligations and increases pension expense. To reflect market interest rate conditions, we reduced our discount rate at December 31, 2003, from 6.75% to 6.0%.

To determine the expected long-term rate of return on pension plan assets, we consider the current and expected asset allocations, as well as historical and expected returns on various categories of plan assets. We assumed that long-term returns on our pension plans were 8.5% in 2003 and 2002 and 9.5% in 2001.

Sensitivity to changes in key assumptions follows:

- Discount rate — A 75 basis point reduction in discount rate would increase pension expense in 2004 by $0.3 billion.

- Expected return on assets — A 50 basis point increase in the expected return on assets of our principal plans would decrease pension expense in 2004 by $0.2 billion.

Further information on our principal postretirement benefit plans is provided on page 46 and in notes 5 and 6.

OTHER LOSS CONTINGENCIES are recorded as liabilities when it is probable that a liability has been incurred and the amount of the loss is reasonably estimable. Disclosure is required when there is a reasonable possibility that the ultimate loss will exceed the recorded provision. Contingent liabilities are often resolved over long time periods. Estimating probable losses requires analysis of multiple forecasts that often depend on judgments about potential actions by third parties such as regulators.

CERTAIN SIGNIFICANT ACCOUNTING POLICIES do not involve the same level of measurement uncertainties as those discussed above, but are nevertheless important to an understanding of the financial statements. Policies related to revenue recognition, financial instruments and business combinations require difficult judgments on complex matters that are often subject to multiple sources of authoritative guidance. Certain of these matters are among topics currently under reexamination by accounting standard setters and regulators; based on their tentative conclusions, significant changes to GAAP, and therefore to certain of our accounting policies, are possible in the future. Also see note 1, Summary of Significant Accounting Policies, which discusses accounting policies that we have selected from acceptable alternatives.

OTHER INFORMATION

New Accounting Standards

In December 2003, the FASB modified FIN 46, *Consolidation of Variable Interest Entities* with FIN 46R, which amended FIN 46 and deferred its application in certain cases. Our adoption of FIN 46 on July 1, 2003, was unchanged by FIN 46R. However, on January 1, 2004, we will adopt FIN 46R, adding approximately $2.5 billion to our total assets and liabilities. No cumulative or significant future effect on our earnings or equity will result from this change.

Financial Measures that Supplement GAAP

We sometimes refer to data derived from consolidated financial information but not required by GAAP to be presented in financial statements. Certain of these data are considered "non-GAAP financial measures" under SEC regulations. Specifically, we have referred to:

- 2003 revenue and earnings growth excluding the operations of Power Systems,

- GE CFOA excluding progress collections for the three years ended December 31, 2003, and

- GE earnings before income taxes and accounting changes and the corresponding effective tax rate for the three years ended December 31, 2003.

We believe trends in the Power Systems segment may be so significant as to obscure patterns and trends of our businesses in total. For this reason, we believe that investors may find it useful to see the measures noted above.

(3) The paragraphs here comprise the auditor's report, which appears on page 43 of the annual report. This *unqual-ified* ("clean") auditor's report follows a standard format. The first two paragraphs describe the auditor's work. The third paragraph gives the opinion. The fourth and fifth paragraphs, which the auditor inserts when needed, alert the reader to changes or non-standard items in the financial statements. These include GE's voluntary inclusion of information about two of its component businesses in its financial statements. We discuss this information further at *6* and *18*. GE's additional disclosure falls outside the scope of GAAP, and so the auditor excludes these pages from its opinion in the third paragraph. In the fifth paragraph, the auditor provides assurance that these non-GAAP disclosures are reliable. See the Glossary at *auditor's report*.

(4) In this section of the Management Discussion and Analysis, GE explains how it develops and verifies critical estimates for its accounting. See our discussion of this section in the chapter on financial literacy. Although the MD&A lies outside the financial statements, we include this section because of its importance for understanding GE's accounting. We will refer back to parts of this section as we discuss the relevant parts of the financial statements.

(5) GE's income statement reports the results of operations for each of three years, 2001 through 2003.

(6) GE presents income statements for three economic entities. GAAP require the first set of columns ("General Electric Company and consolidated affiliates"). GE provides the other two sets of columns ("GE" and "GECS") because the financial services operations – GECS – so differ from the company's other operations, that management feels this disaggregated information will aid investors. See GE's discussion in its Note 1 on page 76 under "Financial statement presentation."

(7) GE owns a majority of the outstanding shares of each of its consolidated subsidiaries, but not all the shares of all consolidated subsidiaries. Some subsidiary shares belong to others, called the *minority interest*. See the Glossary at *minority interest*, *proprietorship theory*, and *entity theory*. The minority interest's share of subsidiary earnings does not belong to GE's shareholders. Hence GE's accounting, following *proprietorship theory*, includes the minority share in the "costs and expenses" it subtracts from revenues to compute income to GE's parent-company shareholders. Under *entity theory*, which views minority shareholders as owners in the consolidated entity, GE would compute consolidated income to all shareholders (in 2003: $15,292 = $15,002 + 290 million), and then separate the portion owned by minority shareholders ($290 million) from the portion owned by parent-company shareholders ($15,002 million). See also our comment *15*.

Note that the reduction in income for minority interest uses no cash. The Statement of Cash Flows on GE's pages 74 and 75 contains an adjustment for this non-cash charge against income. The item is too small, however, to appear separately in the Statement of Cash Flows, so GE places it in "All other operating activities."

(8) Provision usually means "estimated expense" in the U.S.; see the Glossary at *provision* for the contrast in this word's meanings in the U.S. and the U.K.

(9) In each of the years 2001 through 2003, GE changed some of its accounting methods, as we discuss further in our comment *37*. Here GE reports the cumulative after-tax effect of each year's changes. Generally, the cumulative effect records the amount needed to update GE's balance sheet as if it had always followed the new accounting method. For example, in 2003 GE changed its accounting for variable interest entities, resulting in a cumulative effect of –$372 million, and for asset retirements, resulting in a cumulative effect of –$215 million. These two changes total the reported amount, –$587 million.

(10) GE reports diluted and basic earnings per share (EPS), as required by *SFAS No. 128*. Basic EPS is simply net income divided by the average number of shares outstanding during the year. Diluted EPS adjusts for the potential dilutive effects of instruments such as employee stock options, convertible bonds and convertible preferred shares. GE has the former, not the latter two. See GE's Notes 8 and 25. GE first reports EPS before this year's accounting changes for comparability with the preceding year, and then reports EPS after the changes.

(11) The FASB refers to all changes in owners' equity other than transactions with owners as *comprehensive income*. *SFAS No. 130* requires companies to display a statement explaining comprehensive income with the same prominence as the income statement, but does not specify the form of that statement. In this statement, presented directly below the income statement, GE shows changes in shareowners' equity during each of the years 2001 through 2003. GE reports net cash outflows of $5,520 million in 2003 on transactions with shareholders, including dividends, share issues, and purchases or sales of treasury stock. See GE's Note 24 on page 98 and our comment *67*. GE reports com-

STATEMENT OF EARNINGS ⑤

		General Electric Company and consolidated affiliates		
For the years ended December 31 (In millions; per-share amounts in dollars)		2003	2002	2001
REVENUES				
Sales of goods		$ 49,963	$ 55,096	$ 52,677
Sales of services		22,391	21,138	18,722
Other income (note 2)		602	1,013	234
Earnings of GECS before accounting changes		—	—	—
GECS revenues from services (note 3)		60,536	54,963	54,783
Consolidated, liquidating securitization entities (note 29)		695	—	—
Total revenues		134,187	132,210	126,416
COSTS AND EXPENSES (note 4)				
Cost of goods sold		37,189	38,833	35,678
Cost of services sold		14,017	14,023	13,419
Interest and other financial charges		10,432	10,216	11,062
Insurance losses and policyholder and annuity benefits		16,369	17,608	15,062
Provision for losses on financing receivables (note 13)		3,752	3,084	2,481
Other costs and expenses		31,727	29,229	28,665
Minority interest in net earnings of consolidated affiliates ⑦		290	326	348
Consolidated, liquidating securitization entities (note 29)		507	—	—
Total costs and expenses		114,283	113,319	106,715
EARNINGS BEFORE INCOME TAXES AND ACCOUNTING CHANGES ⑧		19,904	18,891	19,701
Provision for income taxes (note 7)		(4,315)	(3,758)	(5,573)
EARNINGS BEFORE ACCOUNTING CHANGES		15,589	15,133	14,128
Cumulative effect of accounting changes (note 1) ⑨		(587)	(1,015)	(444)
NET EARNINGS		$ 15,002	$ 14,118	$ 13,684
PER-SHARE AMOUNTS (note 8)				
Per-share amounts before accounting changes				
Diluted earnings per share		$ 1.55	$ 1.51	$ 1.41
Basic earnings per share ⑩		$ 1.56	$ 1.52	$ 1.42
Per-share amounts after accounting changes				
Diluted earnings per share		$ 1.49	$ 1.41	$ 1.37
Basic earnings per share		$ 1.50	$ 1.42	$ 1.38
DIVIDENDS DECLARED PER SHARE		$ 0.77	$ 0.73	$ 0.66

CONSOLIDATED STATEMENT OF CHANGES IN SHAREOWNERS' EQUITY ⑪

(In millions)	2003	2002	2001
CHANGES IN SHAREOWNERS' EQUITY (note 24)			
Balance at January 1	$ 63,706	$ 54,824	$ 50,492
Dividends and other transactions with shareowners	(5,520)	(6,382)	(7,529)
Changes other than transactions with shareowners			
Increase attributable to net earnings	15,002	14,118	13,684
Investment securities—net	549	1,303	(306)
Currency translation adjustments—net	5,123	1,000	(562)
Derivatives qualifying as hedges—net	320	(1,157)	(955)
Total changes other than transactions with shareowners	20,994	15,264	11,861
Balance at December 31	$ 79,180	$ 63,706	$ 54,824

The notes to consolidated financial statements on pages 76–113 are an integral part of these statements.

	GE			GECS		
	2003	2002	2001	2003	2002	2001
	$47,767	$51,957	$49,057	$ 2,228	$ 3,296	$ 3,627
	22,675	21,360	18,961	—	—	—
	645	1,106	433	—	—	—
	7,754	4,626	5,586	—	—	—
	—	—	—	61,356	55,403	55,229
	—	—	—	695	—	—
	78,841	79,049	74,037	64,279	58,699	58,856
	35,102	35,951	32,419	2,119	3,039	3,266
	14,301	14,245	13,658	—	—	—
	941	569	817	9,869	9,935	10,598
	—	—	—	16,369	17,608	15,062
	—	—	—	3,752	3,084	2,481
	9,870	9,131	8,637	22,342	20,343	20,320
	181	183	185	109	143	163
	—	—	—	507	—	—
	60,395	60,079	55,716	55,067	54,152	51,890
	18,446	18,970	18,321	9,212	4,547	6,966
	(2,857)	(3,837)	(4,193)	(1,458)	79	(1,380)
	15,589	15,133	14,128	7,754	4,626	5,586
	(587)	(1,015)	(444)	(339)	(1,015)	(169)
	$15,002	$14,118	$13,684	$ 7,415	$ 3,611	$ 5,417

In the consolidating data on this page, "GE" means the basis of consolidation as described in note 1 to the consolidated financial statements; "GECS" means General Electric Capital Services, Inc. and all of its affiliates and associated companies. Transactions between GE and GECS have been eliminated from the "General Electric Company and consolidated affiliates" columns on page 70.

STATEMENT OF FINANCIAL POSITION

At December 31 (In millions)	General Electric Company and consolidated affiliates	
	2003	2002
ASSETS		
Cash and equivalents	$ 12,664	$ 8,910
Investment securities (note 9)	120,724	116,862
Current receivables (note 10)	10,732	10,681
Inventories (note 11)	8,752	9,247
Financing receivables (investments in time sales, loans and financing leases)—		
net (notes 12 and 13)	226,029	198,060
Insurance receivables—net (note 14)	27,053	31,585
Other GECS receivables	9,545	11,432
Property, plant and equipment (including equipment leased to others)—		
net (note 15)	53,382	49,073
Investment in GECS	—	—
Intangible assets—net (note 16)	55,025	46,180
Consolidated, liquidating securitization entities (note 29)	26,463	—
All other assets (note 17)	97,114	93,214
TOTAL ASSETS	**$647,483**	**$575,244**
LIABILITIES AND EQUITY		
Short-term borrowings (note 18)	$134,917	$138,775
Accounts payable, principally trade accounts	19,824	18,874
Progress collections and price adjustments accrued	4,433	6,706
Dividends payable	2,013	1,895
All other current costs and expenses accrued	15,343	15,577
Long-term borrowings (note 18)	170,004	140,632
Insurance liabilities, reserves and annuity benefits (note 19)	136,264	135,853
Consolidated, liquidating securitization entities (note 29)	25,721	—
All other liabilities (note 20)	41,357	35,236
Deferred income taxes (note 21)	12,647	12,517
Total liabilities	562,523	506,065
Minority interest in equity of consolidated affiliates (note 22)	5,780	5,473
Common stock (10,063,120,000 and 9,969,894,000 shares outstanding		
at year-end 2003 and 2002, respectively)	669	669
Accumulated gains/(losses)—net		
Investment securities	1,620	1,071
Currency translation adjustments	2,987	(2,136)
Derivatives qualifying as hedges	(1,792)	(2,112)
Other capital	17,497	17,288
Retained earnings	82,796	75,553
Less common stock held in treasury	(24,597)	(26,627)
Total shareowners' equity (notes 24 and 25)	79,180	63,706
TOTAL LIABILITIES AND EQUITY	**$647,483**	**$575,244**

The sum of accumulated gains/(losses) on investment securities, currency translation adjustments, and derivatives qualifying as hedges constitutes "Accumulated nonowner changes other than earnings," as shown in note 24, and was $2,815 million and $(3,177) million at year-end 2003 and 2002, respectively.

The notes to consolidated financial statements on pages 76–113 are an integral part of this statement.

	GE		GECS	
	2003	2002	2003	2002
	$ 1,670	$ 1,079	$ 11,273	$ 7,918
	380	332	120,344	116,530
	10,973	10,973	—	—
	8,555	9,039	197	208
	—	—	226,029	198,060
	—	—	27,053	31,585
	—	—	11,901	12,984
	14,566	13,743	38,816	35,330
	45,308	36,929	—	—
	30,204	23,049	24,821	23,131
	—	—	26,463	—
	30,448	30,167	67,629	64,082
	$142,104	$125,311	$554,526	$489,828
	$ 2,555	$ 8,786	$132,988	$130,126
	8,753	8,095	13,440	12,608
	4,433	6,706	—	—
	2,013	1,895	—	—
	15,343	15,577	—	—
	8,388	970	162,540	140,836
	—	—	136,264	135,853
	—	—	25,721	—
	18,449	16,621	22,828	18,441
	1,911	1,927	10,736	10,590
	61,845	60,577	504,517	448,454
	1,079	1,028	4,701	4,445
	669	669	1	1
	1,620	1,071	1,823	1,191
	2,987	(2,136)	2,639	(782)
	(1,792)	(2,112)	(1,727)	(2,076)
	17,497	17,288	12,268	12,271
	82,796	75,553	30,304	26,324
	(24,597)	(26,627)	—	—
	79,180	63,706	45,308	36,929
	$142,104	$125,311	$554,526	$489,828

In the consolidating data on this page, "GE" means the basis of consol-idation as described in note 1 to the consolidated financial statements; "GECS" means General Electric Capital Services, Inc. and all of its affiliates and associated companies. Transactions between GE and GECS have been eliminated from the "General Electric Company and consolidated affiliates" columns on page 72.

STATEMENT OF CASH FLOWS ⑳

For the years ended December 31 (In millions)		2003	2002	2001
		General Electric Company and consolidated affiliates		
CASH FLOWS—OPERATING ACTIVITIES				
Net earnings		$ 15,002	$ 14,118	$ 13,684
Adjustments to reconcile net earnings to cash provided				
from operating activities				
Cumulative effect of accounting changes		587	1,015	444
Depreciation and amortization of property, plant and equipment	㉑	6,956	6,511	5,873
Amortization of goodwill		—	—	1,252
Earnings (before accounting changes) retained by GECS		—	—	—
Deferred income taxes		1,127	2,414	1,426
Decrease (increase) in GE current receivables		534	(409)	197
Decrease (increase) in inventories		874	(87)	(485)
Increase (decrease) in accounts payable		802	227	4,676
Increase (decrease) in GE progress collections	㉒	(2,268)	(5,062)	3,446
Increase in insurance liabilities and reserves		1,679	9,454	8,194
Provision for losses on financing receivables		3,752	3,084	2,481
All other operating activities		1,244	(1,264)	(8,296)
CASH FROM OPERATING ACTIVITIES		30,289	30,001	32,892
CASH FLOWS—INVESTING ACTIVITIES				
Additions to property, plant and equipment		(9,767)	(14,056)	(16,394)
Dispositions of property, plant and equipment		4,945	6,357	7,591
Net increase in GECS financing receivables	㉓	(14,273)	(18,082)	(13,837)
Payments for principal businesses purchased		(14,407)	(21,570)	(12,429)
Investment in GECS		—	—	—
All other investing activities		10,599	(15,111)	(5,742)
CASH USED FOR INVESTING ACTIVITIES		(22,903)	(62,462)	(40,811)
CASH FLOWS—FINANCING ACTIVITIES				
Net increase (decrease) in borrowings (maturities of 90 days or less)		(11,107)	(17,347)	20,482
Newly issued debt (maturities longer than 90 days)	㉔	67,545	95,008	32,071
Repayments and other reductions (maturities longer than 90 days)		(43,155)	(40,454)	(37,001)
Net dispositions (purchases) of GE shares for treasury		726	(985)	(2,435)
Dividends paid to shareowners		(7,643)	(7,157)	(6,358)
All other financing activities		(9,998)	3,873	2,047
CASH FROM (USED FOR) FINANCING ACTIVITIES		(3,632)	32,938	8,806
INCREASE (DECREASE) IN CASH AND EQUIVALENTS DURING YEAR	㉕	3,754	477	887
Cash and equivalents at beginning of year		8,910	8,433	7,546
Cash and equivalents at end of year		$ 12,664	$ 8,910	$ 8,433
SUPPLEMENTAL DISCLOSURE OF CASH FLOWS INFORMATION				
Cash paid during the year for interest		$(10,561)	$ (9,654)	$(11,125)
Cash recovered (paid) during the year for income taxes		(1,539)	(948)	(1,487)

The notes to consolidated financial statements on pages 76–113 are an integral part of this statement.

	GE			GECS	
2003	2002	2001	2003	2002	2001
$15,002	$14,118	$13,684	$ 7,415	$ 3,611	$ 5,417
587	1,015	444	339	1,015	169
2,277	2,199	1,919	4,679	4,312	3,954
—	—	545	—	—	707
(4,319)	(2,661)	(3,625)	—	—	—
389	1,005	564	738	1,409	862
585	(486)	207	—	—	—
909	(149)	(881)	(35)	62	396
676	708	364	666	(880)	4,804
(2,268)	(5,062)	3,446	—	—	—
—	—	—	1,679	9,454	8,194
—	—	—	3,752	3,084	2,481
(913)	(590)	530	2,215	(556)	(8,688)
12,925	10,097	17,197	21,448	21,511	18,296
(2,158)	(2,386)	(2,876)	(7,609)	(11,670)	(13,518)
—	—	—	4,945	6,357	7,591
—	—	—	(14,273)	(18,082)	(13,837)
(3,870)	(8,952)	(1,436)	(10,537)	(12,618)	(10,993)
—	(6,300)	(3,043)	—	—	—
236	203	1,508	9,788	(15,234)	(7,741)
(5,792)	(17,435)	(5,847)	(17,686)	(51,247)	(38,498)
(6,704)	7,924	327	(4,035)	(34,687)	23,634
7,356	66	1,303	59,939	96,044	30,752
(277)	(1,229)	(950)	(42,878)	(39,225)	(36,051)
726	(985)	(2,435)	—	—	—
(7,643)	(7,157)	(6,358)	(3,435)	(1,965)	(1,961)
—	—	—	(9,998)	10,173	5,090
(6,542)	(1,381)	(8,113)	(407)	30,340	21,464
591	(8,719)	3,237	3,355	604	1,262
1,079	9,798	6,561	7,918	7,314	6,052
$ 1,670	$ 1,079	$ 9,798	$ 11,273	$ 7,918	$ 7,314
$ (248)	$ (155)	$ (358)	$(10,313)	$ (9,499)	$(10,767)
(2,685)	(2,331)	(1,616)	1,146	1,383	129

In the consolidating data on this page, "GE" means the basis of consolidation as described in note 1 to the consolidated financial statements; "GECS" means General Electric Capital Services, Inc. and all of its affiliates and associated companies. Transactions between GE and GECS have been eliminated from the "General Electric Company and consolidated affiliates" columns on page 74.

prehensive income of $20,994 million for 2003, comprising $15,002 million in net earnings, and three smaller non-earnings components. The non-earnings components – investment securities, currency translation adjustments and derivatives qualifying as hedges – all concern current-year revaluations of items on GE's balance sheet that GE excludes from current earnings, but will report in earnings in later years. See our comments *16* and *54*.

(12) This statement contains two balance sheets, one at the end of 2003 and the second a year earlier, for each of the three economic entities: GE, GECS and consolidated, as we described in our comment *6*.

(13) Following Financial Accounting Standards Board (FASB) *Interpretation Number* (*FIN*) 46, in 2003 GE began recognizing its interest in certain entities that previously had been off-balance-sheet. Through its GECS unit, GE created these entities to issue asset-backed securities, and provides the majority of their financial support, although it has no legal access to their assets. GE separates these assets and their related liabilities from its other operations, both because of the restricted legal access and because GE plans to discontinue activity in such entities that it must recognize on the balance sheet. See the glossary at *off-balance-sheet financing*, *securitization* and *special-purpose entity*, GE's Note 29, and our comments *72* and *73*.

(14) GE uses the completed contract method of recognizing revenue from long term construction contracts; see our comment *29*. As GE incurs costs on these contracts it makes journal entries such as:

Work in Process Inventory for Long Term Contracts.	X	
Various Assets and Liabilities		X
To record cost of construction activity.		

Some of GE's long-term construction contracts provide that the customer shall make progress payments to GE as GE performs the work. GE does not recognize revenue until it completes all work on the contract, so when GE receives cash it makes a journal entry such as:

Cash	Y	
Progress Collections (*or* Advances) from Customers on Long-Term Contracts.		Y
To record cash received and to set up the corresponding liability.		

When GE prepares the balance sheet, it nets the amounts in the inventory accounts, X (debit balance), against the amounts in the liability accounts, Y (credit balance). If cash collections exceed the amounts in the inventory account, as here, then GE records the difference, Y – X, as a liability. GE shows this liability under the title "Progress collections." On contracts where the amounts in the inventory account exceed the cash collections, the difference X – Y appears as an asset under a title such as "Contract costs incurred in excess of billings." *ARB No. 45* requires this netting of costs incurred against cash collections, with excesses shown separately. On many of its contracts, GE collects cash before completion of construction only for engineering costs incurred in preparation to undertake construction. GE expenses these engineering costs, rather than accumulating them in Work in Process inventory accounts. Thus, GE has no asset account to net against the liability, so GE uses the title "Progress collections" rather than the more typical "Billings on uncompleted contracts in excess of related costs." The "price adjustments accrued" represent amounts that GE expects to pay in the future for which it will not receive reimbursement from the buyer under the contract.

(15) This account represents the minority shareholders' equity in the consolidated affiliates. Refer to the Glossary at *minority interest*, and to our comment *7* for a description of the related income statement item. GE's shareholders may view this equity belonging to the minority as a liability, because the minority shareholders' claims to affiliates' assets diminish the net assets available to GE shareholders. From the point of view of the consolidated entity, the minority shareholders' interest is part of total owners' equity. Thus, whether one believes that minority interest is a liability or an item of owners' equity depends upon whether one views the financial statements as prepared for the shareholders of GE (the *proprietorship theory*) or for all potential readers (the *entity theory*). Note that GE avoids the issue here by classifying minority interest neither with liabilities nor with owners' equity.

(16) The "Accumulated gains/(losses) – net" represent shareowners' equity in gains and losses not yet recorded in net earnings arising from revaluations of assets and liabilities. These items correspond to the non-earnings components of *comprehensive income*. See our comment *11*.

(17) GE uses the *cost method* of accounting for *treasury stock* and shows the cost of its own shares acquired on the market as contra to all of owners' equity. Refer to the Glossary, and our comment *68*.

(18) In the middle set of columns, GE uses the *equity method* to account for its subsidiary, General Electric Capital Services (GECS). Because GE has owned 100 percent of GECS since it organized the subsidiary, GE's investment (asset) account for GECS is the mirror image of GECS's owners' equity accounts. See GECS's balance sheet on page 73 near the call-out for our comment *19*. Consider the following example transactions.

(1) GE makes an investment in GECS by sending it cash:
     GE debits the investment account and credits cash;
     GECS debits cash and credits a contributed capital account.

(2) GECS earns income:
     GECS debits various net asset accounts and (after closing entries) credits retained earnings;
     GE, using the equity method, debits the investment account and credits income.

(3) GECS declares and pays a dividend:
     GECS debits retained earnings and credits cash;
     GE, using the equity method, debits cash and credits the investment account.

(19) *SFAS No. 94* requires firms to consolidate majority-owned and controlled subsidiaries. In compliance with this standard, GE consolidates GECS in its first set of columns on page 72, where all GECS's assets and liabilities appear on the consolidated balance sheet. In consolidation, GE adds $45,308 (= $554,526 – $504,517 – $4,701) million of net assets to its parent-company balance sheet at December 31, 2003, shown in the middle set of columns on page 73. GE simultaneously eliminates the account "Investments in GECS." Notice that GECS's owners' equity equals GE's equity-method investment in GECS, as we explained in comment *18*.

     GE's consolidated retained earnings in the first set of columns, however, equal the retained earnings in the second set of columns where GE accounts for GECS using the equity method. This equality results from the fact that, under the equity method, the parent records its share (in this case, 100 percent) of unconsolidated subsidiaries' income.

     Consolidating GECS affects the financial statements' appearance. Below, we show two key financial ratios calculated from year-end account balances. See the Glossary at *return on assets* and *debt-equity ratio* for definitions.

RATIOS: GENERAL ELECTRIC AND GE CAPITAL SERVICES, 2003
(For Authors' comment (19). Dollar amounts are in millions)

Using the Equity Method for GECS
(from the middle set of columns)

Rate of Return on Beginning-of-Year Assets:

$$\frac{\$15,002 + \$181^a + (.65 \times \$941)^b}{\$125,311}$$

$$= \frac{\$15,795}{\$125,311} = 12.60\%$$

Year-end Debt-to-Total Equities Ratio:

$$\frac{\$61,845}{\$142,104} = 43.52\%$$

Consolidating GECS
(from the first set of columns)

Rate of Return on Beginning-of-Year Assets:

$$\frac{\$15,002 + \$290^a + (.65 \times \$10,432)^b}{\$575,244}$$

$$= \frac{\$22,073}{\$575,244} = 3.84\%$$

Year-end Debt-to-Total Equities Ratio:

$$\frac{\$562,523}{\$647,483} = 86.88\%$$

a. Minority interest in net income, from the income statement.
b. Interest expense, multiplied by .65 (= 1.00 – .35 federal tax rate) to place it on an after-tax basis.

---

(20) GE presents cash flow statements for three entities, GE, GECS and consolidated, as it did with the income statements and balance sheets. The cash flow statement starts with net earnings as shown in the income statement on page 70 or 71. The following twelve lines adjust net earnings for non-cash components of revenues and expenses, to derive cash flow from operations. This presentation, known as the *indirect method* (see the Glossary), derives operating cash flow indirectly by adjusting income. The acceptable alternative format, the *direct method*, would show operating cash collections, less operating cash expenditures, and requires no adjustments.

㉑ The first five adjustments show subtractions for revenues and other credits to income that did not produce cash or working capital, and additions for expenses and other charges against income that did not use cash or working capital.

The cumulative effect of accounting changes, discussed by GE in its Note 1 and in our comments *9* and *37*, alters the appearance of the financial statements but causes no inflow or outflow of cash. GE adds this effect back, removing the deduction from net earnings, to derive operating cash flow.

Depreciation and amortization expenses reduce net income without using cash currently. Hence, GE adds this amount back to net income to derive cash provided by operations. The firm used cash sometime in the past when it acquired the depreciable or amortizable assets; see "Additions to property, plant, and equipment," at our comment *23*, below.

Under the equity method, GE includes all earnings of GECS in income. GECS income produced a larger investment balance on GE's balance sheet, while the dividend reduced the investment balance; see our comment *18*. In 2003, GECS earned $7,754 (= 7,415 + 339) million before the cumulative effect of accounting changes, and paid dividends of $3,435 million. We adjust GECS's earnings for the cumulative effect of accounting changes here because GE accounted for those changes in the step we described two paragraphs above. The difference between income and dividends from GECS, $4,319 (= $7,754 – $3,435) million, provided no cash to GE and therefore the parent company subtracts this amount from net income to derive cash from operations.

Income tax expense for each of the three years exceeded the amount of income taxes payable. See the discussion at GE's Notes 7 and 21, and our comments *51* and *63*. Because GE used less cash for income taxes than it reported as income tax expense, it must add the amount of expense not using cash to derive cash from operations.

㉒ The next seven adjustments to net earnings show the increases and decreases in working capital accounts. The Statement of Cash Flows classifies cash flows into three types: operating activities, financing activities, and investment activities. *SFAS No. 95* requires that working capital items appear in the operating section, although one could argue that companies invest cash to acquire inventory, just as they do to acquire plant and equipment. Similarly, one could argue that companies obtain financing when they save cash by letting accounts payable increase, just as when they borrow from a bank.

Increases in accounts receivable represent the amounts by which sales on account exceeded cash collections from customers. Conversely, decreases in accounts receivable represent the amount by which cash collections exceeded sales on account. Thus, we adjust net income, which includes sales, for this difference to derive cash flow.

Increases in inventories use cash, just as increases in property and plant do. Conversely, decreases in inventories provide funds.

Increases in accounts payable defer cash payments to future periods, decreasing the use of cash in this period. Conversely, decreases in accounts payable require cash payments.

Early in 2005, GE restated its 2003 and 2002 consolidated cash flow numbers, moving GECS receivables that financed purchases of GE products from the investing section to the operating section for the consolidated entity. GECS considers these long-term receivables as investments, just as a bank would consider loans receivable. For the consolidated entity, however, they represent receivables associated with sales of products, and so belong in operations. The effect was to reduce 2003 consolidated operating cash inflow by $1.06 billion, and reduce investing cash outflow by the same amount.

㉓ Acquisition of new property, plant and equipment, for growth and to replace the old as it wears out, represents the primary use of cash for most non-financial companies most of the time. The amounts invested in property plant and equipment will appear on the income statement in future periods as depreciation charges. GE uses cash when it acquires long-term assets, and its income decreases in later periods when it uses the assets. In 2003, GE spent more cash acquiring entire businesses, reported as "Payments for principal businesses purchased," than it did maintaining and expanding existing plant and equipment. Its other major category of investment, "Net increase in GECS financing receivables," represents loans to others through its GECS unit.

㉔ GE, following *SFAS No. 95*, views all borrowing, whether short-term or long-term, as financing. Notice that on the balance sheet, GE classifies borrowings into "short-term" (due within one year) versus "long-term" (due after one year), while on the cash flow statement it classifies them as "maturities of 90 days or less," versus "more than 90 days." In doing so, GE takes advantage of a provision of *SFAS No. 95* that allows it to report only net cash flows for short-maturity (three months or less), high-turnover borrowing. Nevertheless, *ARB No 43* requires manufacturers like GE to divide current from non-current assets and liabilities on the balance sheet at one year. GE reports information in its Note 26 that allows the analyst to distinguish borrowings with maturities between 91 and 365 days (classified here as long-term) from those with maturities beyond one year. For borrowings maturing in more than 90 days, GE separates cash provided by new borrowings from cash used to reduce old borrowings. We prefer the separate disclosure, because the net amount provides no information about the amount of actual borrowings and repayments during the period.

㉕ GE demonstrates that the net cash flow, the sum of cash flows from operating, investing and financing activities ($3,754 million for the consolidated entity in 2003), exactly explains the change in the "Cash and equivalents" account on the balance sheet on page 72.

㉖ APB *Opinion No. 22* requires that all annual reports include a summary of significant accounting policies used, so the analyst can learn which accounting alternatives the company has chosen. Most firms provide this summary in the first footnote to their financial statements, as GE does.

㉗ GE explains its consolidation policy and three-entity presentation. See our comments *6, 18* and *19*. The "'one-line' basis" refers to the *equity method* (see the Glossary).

㉘ Consolidated financial statements present information about a group of affiliated companies as if the group were one economic entity. Consequently, GE must eliminate from reported financial statements all within-group transactions, such as borrowing and lending, or purchases and sales of assets between companies in the consolidated group. The consolidated financial statements present information only about transactions with parties outside the consolidated group.

㉙ Here GE describes when it recognizes revenue in its different lines of business. The first paragraph describes reasonably straightforward sales. Subsequent paragraphs describe GE's policies on more complex sales, where one sale transaction may have multiple components. For example, GE may sell a piece of medical equipment, and also provide its installation and servicing for a period of time after the sale. For information on how GE monitors and revises the estimates mentioned here, see the Critical Accounting Estimates – Revenue Recognition on Long-Term Agreements section on GE's page 66 below our callout *4*.

㉚ See *effective interest method* and *amortized cost* in the Glossary.

㉛ GE uses accelerated depreciation for financial reporting, an unusual choice among U.S. corporations. Most corporations use accelerated depreciation for tax reporting but straight-line depreciation for financial reporting. See *sum-of-the-years'–digits depreciation* in the Glossary.

㉜ See *allowance method* in the Glossary.

㉝ GECS holds large dollar values of marketable debt and equity securities. GE follows *SFAS No. 115*, which requires it to classify these securities into three categories: *trading, available for sale*, and *held to maturity.* See the Critical Accounting Estimates – Investments section on GE's page 66 below our callout *4*, and GE's Note 9.

㉞ GE uses a *lower-of-cost-or-market* valuation basis for inventories, with "market" defined as *net realizable value*. The company uses the *LIFO* cost flow assumption for U.S. inventories. Most foreign governments do not allow LIFO for tax purposes, so GE gains no clear advantage from using LIFO outside the U.S. See our comments *56* and *57*.

㉟ *Goodwill* results from GE's past acquisitions of other companies, in which it used purchase accounting. (See the Glossary under *purchase method* and *pooling-of-interests method*.) On the acquisition date, GE recorded the difference between the purchase price and the current value of identifiable net assets acquired as an intangible asset called "goodwill." GE explains here that, beginning in 2002, it ceased amortizing goodwill and began testing it annually for impairment, following *SFAS No. 142*. See the Critical Accounting Estimates – Goodwill and Other Identified Intangible Assets section on GE's page 67 below our callout *4*, GE's Note 16 and our comment *61*.

㊱ Insurance represents a substantial component of GE's business, in terms of both revenues and assets. Here GE describes its accounting in this business. See also the Critical Accounting Estimates – Insurance Liabilities and Reserves section on GE's page 67 below our callout *4*, and GE's Notes 14 and 19, which we have not reproduced.

㊲ Here GE describes changes in accounting policies that it implemented during the years represented in these financial statements. Each change has a cumulative effect from adjusting the balance sheet in the year of the change, which companies report separately on the income statement, and ongoing effects as GE implements the new accounting thereafter, which we generally cannot observe separately. In 2003, the cumulative effect of GE's consolidation of certain variable interest entities reduced net earnings by $372 million, while its recognition of future legal obligations relating to nuclear fuel reduced net earnings by another $215 million, for a total reduction of $578 million. See our comment *9*.

NOTES TO CONSOLIDATED FINANCIAL STATEMENTS

NOTE 1

SUMMARY OF SIGNIFICANT ACCOUNTING POLICIES

Consolidation

Our financial statements consolidate all of our affiliates — companies that we control and in which we hold a majority voting interest. In 2003, as we describe on page 79, we added certain non-affiliates that we do not control to our consolidated financial statements because of new accounting requirements that require consolidation of entities based on holding qualifying residual interests.

Associated companies are companies that we do not control but over which we have significant influence, most often because we hold a shareholder voting position of 20% to 50%. Results of associated companies are presented on a "one-line" basis.

Financial statement presentation

We have reclassified certain prior-year amounts to conform to this year's presentation.

Financial data and related measurements are presented in the following categories:

- GE This represents the adding together of all affiliates other than General Electric Capital Services, Inc. (GECS), whose operations are presented on a one-line basis.

- GECS This affiliate owns all of the common stock of General Electric Capital Corporation (GE Capital) and GE Global Insurance Holding Corporation (GE Global Insurance Holding), the parent of Employers Reinsurance Corporation (ERC). GE Capital, GE Global Insurance Holding and their respective affiliates are consolidated in the GECS columns and constitute its business.

- CONSOLIDATED This represents the adding together of GE and GECS.

Effects of transactions between related companies are eliminated. Transactions between GE and GECS are immaterial and consist primarily of GECS services for material procurement and trade receivables management, aircraft engines and medical equipment manufactured by GE that are leased by GECS to others, buildings and equipment leased by GE from GECS, and GE investments in GECS commercial paper.

Preparing financial statements in conformity with generally accepted accounting principles requires us to make estimates and assumptions that affect reported amounts and related disclosures. Actual results could differ from those estimates.

Sales of goods and services

We record sales of goods when a firm sales agreement is in place, delivery has occurred and collectibility of the fixed or determinable sales price is reasonably assured. If customer acceptance of products is not assured, sales are recorded only upon formal customer acceptance.

Sales of goods in the Consumer & Industrial, Advanced Materials and Infrastructure businesses typically do not include multiple product and/or service elements, in contrast with sales in certain of the businesses referred to below. Consumer lighting products and computer hardware and software are often sold with a right of return. Accumulated experience is used to estimate and provide for such returns when we record the sale.

Sales of goods in the Transportation, Healthcare, Energy and certain Infrastructure businesses sometimes include multiple components and sometimes include services such as installation. In such contracts, amounts assigned to each component are based on that component's objectively determined fair value, such as the sales price for the component when it is sold separately or competitor prices for similar components. Sales are recognized individually for delivered components only if undelivered components are not essential to functionality of delivered components, fair values of delivered components have been objectively determined, and the delivered components have value to the customer on a standalone basis. However, when undelivered components are inconsequential or perfunctory and not essential to the functionality of the delivered components (like certain training commitments), we recognize sales on the total contract and make provision for the cost of the incomplete elements.

We record sales of product services and certain power generation equipment in accordance with contracts. For long-term product services agreements, we use estimated contract profit rates to record sales as work is performed. For certain power generation equipment, we use estimated contract profit rates to record sales as major components are completed and delivered to customers. Estimates are subject to revisions; revisions that affect an agreement's total estimated profitability result in an immediate adjustment of earnings. We provide for any loss when that loss is probable. We expense costs to acquire or originate sales agreements as incurred.

Sales by NBC are recorded when advertisements are broadcast, with provision made for any shortfalls from viewer commitments ("make goods") based on specific contracts and independent viewer census information.

GECS revenues from services (earned income)

We use the interest method to recognize income on all loans. Interest on time sales and loans includes origination, commitment and other non-refundable fees related to funding (recorded in earned income on the interest method). Nonearning loans are loans on which we have stopped accruing interest at the earlier of the time at which collection of an account becomes doubtful or the account becomes 90 days past due. We recognize interest income on nonearning loans either as cash is collected or on a cost-recovery basis as conditions warrant. We resume accruing interest on nonearning, non-restructured Commercial Finance loans only when (a) payments are brought current according to the loan's original terms and (b) future payments are reasonably assured. When we agree to restructured terms with the borrower, we resume accruing interest only when reasonably assured that we will recover full contractual payments, and pass underwriting reviews equivalent to those to which we subject new loans. We resume accruing interest on nonearning Consumer Finance loans only upon receipt of the third consecutive minimum monthly payment or the equivalent. Specific limits restrict the number of times any particular type of delinquent loan may be categorized as non-delinquent and interest accrual resumed.

We record financing lease income on the interest method to produce a level yield on funds not yet recovered. Estimated unguaranteed residual values of leased assets are based primarily on periodic independent appraisals of the values of leased assets remaining at expiration of the lease terms. Significant assumptions we use in estimating residual values include estimated net cash flows over the remaining lease term, results of future remarketing, and future component part and scrap metal prices, discounted at an appropriate rate.

We recognize operating lease income on a straight-line basis over the terms of underlying leases.

Fees include commitment fees related to loans that we do not expect to fund and line-of-credit fees. We record these fees in earned income on a straight-line basis over the period to which they relate. We record syndication fees in earned income at the time related services are performed unless significant contingencies exist.

See below and page 78 for a discussion of income from investment and insurance activities.

Depreciation and amortization

(31) The cost of GE manufacturing plant and equipment is depreciated over its estimated economic life. U.S. assets are depreciated using an accelerated method based on a sum-of-the-years digits formula; non-U.S. assets are depreciated on a straight-line basis.

The cost of GECS equipment leased to others on operating leases is amortized on a straight-line basis to estimated residual value over the lease term or over the estimated economic life of the equipment. See note 15.

Losses on financing receivables

(32) Our allowance for losses on financing receivables represents our best estimate of probable losses inherent in the portfolio. Our method of calculating estimated losses depends on the size, type and risk characteristics of the related receivables.

Our consumer loan portfolio consists of homogeneous card receivables, installment loans, auto loans and leases and residential mortgages. The allowance for losses on these receivables is based on ongoing statistical analyses of our historical experience adjusted for the effects of economic cycles.

Our allowance for losses on our commercial and equipment loan and lease portfolios is based on relevant observable data that include, but are not limited to, historical experience; loan strati-

fication by portfolio and, when applicable, geography; collateral type; credit class or program type; size of the loan balance; and delinquency. In certain commercial loan and lease portfolios, we review all loans based on a number of monitored risk factors other than size, including collateral value, financial performance of the borrower, aging and bankruptcy. We stratify portfolios in which we believe that it is informative to differentiate between small and large balance loans depending on geography and portfolio. For loans deemed individually impaired, we determine allowances using the present values of expected future cash flows. If repossession is expected to be a source of repayment, we estimate the fair value of that collateral using independent appraisals when necessary.

Delinquencies are the clearest indication of a developing loss, and we monitor delinquency rates closely in all of our portfolios. Experience is not available with new products; therefore, while we are developing that experience, we set loss allowances based on our experience with the most closely analogous products in our portfolio. When we repossess collateral in satisfaction of a commercial loan, we write the receivable down against the allowance for losses. We transfer the asset to "Other assets" and carry it at the lower of cost or estimated fair value less costs to sell.

Cash and equivalents

Debt securities with original maturities of three months or less are included in cash equivalents unless designated as available for sale and classified as investment securities.

Investment securities   (33)

We report investments in debt and marketable equity securities, and equity securities at our insurance affiliates, at fair value based on quoted market prices or, if quoted prices are not available, discounted expected cash flows using market rates commensurate with credit quality and maturity of the investment. Substantially all investment securities are designated as available for sale with unrealized gains and losses included in shareowners' equity, net of applicable taxes and other adjustments. We regularly review investment securities for impairment based on criteria that include the extent to which the investment's carrying value exceeds its related market value, the duration of the market decline, our ability to hold to recovery and the financial strength and specific prospects of the issuer of the security. Unrealized losses that are other than temporary are recognized in earnings. Realized gains and losses are accounted for on the specific identification method.

Inventories   (34)

All inventories are stated at the lower of cost or realizable values. Cost for substantially all of GE's U.S. inventories is determined on a last-in, first-out (LIFO) basis. Cost of other GE inventories is determined on a first-in, first-out (FIFO) basis. GECS inventories consist of finished products held for sale. Cost is determined on a FIFO basis.

Intangible assets

As of January 1, 2002, goodwill is no longer amortized but is tested for impairment using a fair value approach, at the "reporting unit" level. A reporting unit is the operating segment, or a business one level below that operating segment (the "component" level) if discrete financial information is prepared and regularly reviewed by management at the component level. We recognize an impairment charge for any amount by which the carrying amount of a reporting unit's goodwill exceeds its fair value. We use discounted cash flows to establish fair values. When available and as appropriate, we use comparative market multiples to corroborate discounted cash flow results. When a business within a reporting unit is disposed of, goodwill is allocated to the gain or loss on disposition using the relative fair value methodology.

We amortize the cost of other intangibles over their estimated useful lives unless such lives are deemed indefinite. Amortizable intangible assets are tested for impairment based on undiscounted cash flows and, if impaired, written down to fair value based on either discounted cash flows or appraised values. Intangible assets with indefinite lives are tested annually for impairment and written down to fair value as required.

Before January 1, 2002, we amortized goodwill over its estimated period of benefit on a straight-line basis; we amortized other intangible assets on appropriate bases over their estimated lives. No amortization period exceeded 40 years. When an intangible asset's carrying value exceeded associated expected operating cash flows, we considered it to be impaired and wrote it down to fair value, which we determined based on either discounted future cash flows or appraised values.

 GECS insurance accounting policies

Accounting policies for GECS insurance businesses follow.

PREMIUM INCOME. We report insurance premiums as earned income as follows:

- For short-duration insurance contracts (including property and casualty, accident and health, and financial guaranty insurance), we report premiums as earned income, generally on a pro-rata basis, over the terms of the related agreements. For retrospectively rated reinsurance contracts, we record premium adjustments based on estimated losses and loss expenses, taking into consideration both case and incurred-but-not-reported (IBNR) reserves.

- For traditional long-duration insurance contracts (including term and whole life contracts and annuities payable for the life of the annuitant), we report premiums as earned income when due.

- For investment contracts and universal life contracts, we report premiums received as liabilities, not as revenues. Universal life contracts are long-duration insurance contracts with terms that are not fixed and guaranteed; for these contracts, we recognize revenues for assessments

against the policyholder's account, mostly for mortality, contract initiation, administration and surrender. Investment contracts are contracts that have neither significant mortality nor significant morbidity risk, including annuities payable for a determined period; for these contracts, we recognize revenues on the associated investments and amounts credited to policyholder accounts are charged to expense.

LIABILITIES FOR UNPAID CLAIMS AND CLAIMS ADJUSTMENT EXPENSES represent our best estimate of the ultimate obligations for reported claims plus those IBNR and the related estimated claim settlement expenses for all claims incurred through December 31 of each year. Specific reserves — also referred to as case reserves — are established for reported claims using case-basis evaluations of the underlying claim data and are updated as further information becomes known. IBNR reserves are determined using generally accepted actuarial reserving methods that take into account historical loss experience data and, as appropriate, certain qualitative factors. IBNR reserves are adjusted to take into account certain additional factors that can be expected to affect the liability for claims over time, such as changes in the volume and mix of business written, revisions to contract terms and conditions, changes in legal precedents or developed case law, trends in healthcare and medical costs, and general inflation levels. Settlement of complex claims routinely involves threatened or pending litigation to resolve disputes as to coverage, interpretation of contract terms and conditions or fair compensation for damages suffered. These disputes are settled through negotiation, arbitration or actual litigation. Recorded reserves incorporate our best estimate of the effect that ultimate resolution of such disputes have on both claims payments and related settlement expenses. Liabilities for unpaid claims and claims adjustment expenses are continually reviewed and adjusted; such adjustments are included in current operations and accounted for as changes in estimates.

DEFERRED ACQUISITION COSTS. Costs that vary with and are directly related to the acquisition of new and renewal insurance and investment contracts are deferred and amortized as follows:

- Short-duration contracts — Acquisition costs consist of commissions, brokerage expenses and premium taxes and are amortized ratably over the contract periods in which the related premiums are earned.

- Long-duration contracts — Acquisition costs consist of first-year commissions in excess of recurring renewal commissions, certain variable sales expenses and certain support costs such as underwriting and policy issue expenses. For traditional long-duration insurance contracts, we amortize these costs over the respective contract periods in proportion to either anticipated premium income, or, in the case of limited-payment contracts, estimated benefit payments. For investment contracts and universal life contracts, amortization of these costs is based on estimated gross profits and is adjusted as those estimates are revised.

We review deferred acquisition costs periodically for recoverability considering anticipated investment income.

PRESENT VALUE OF FUTURE PROFITS. The actuarially determined present value of anticipated net cash flows to be realized from insurance, annuity and investment contracts in force at the date of acquisition of life insurance policies is recorded as the present value of future profits and is amortized over the respective policy terms in a manner similar to deferred acquisition costs. We adjust unamortized balances to reflect experience and impairment, if any.

(37) **Accounting changes**

We adopted Financial Accounting Standards Board (FASB) Interpretation No. (FIN) 46, *Consolidation of Variable Interest Entities*, on July 1, 2003, and consolidated certain entities in our financial statements for the first time. New balance sheet captions, "Consolidated, liquidating securitization entities," included $36.3 billion of assets and $35.8 billion of liabilities at transition related to entities involved in securitization arrangements. Given their unique nature and the fact that their activities have been discontinued, they are classified in separate financial statement captions. Further information about these entities is provided in note 29. In addition, $14.1 billion and $1.0 billion were added to "Investment securities" and "Other GECS receivables," respectively, at transition for investment securities related to guaranteed investment contracts (GICs) issued by Trinity, a group of sponsored special purpose entities. The related GIC liabilities of $14.7 billion, consolidated at transition, are displayed in "Insurance liabilities, reserves and annuity benefits." As issuance of GICs by these entities is likely to continue in the future, we have displayed these investment securities in financial statement captions consistent with like items of our Insurance businesses. Our consolidation of these entities resulted in a $372 million after-tax accounting charge ($0.04 per share) to net earnings and is reported in the caption "Cumulative effect of accounting changes." This charge resulted from several factors. For entities consolidated based on carrying amounts, the effect of changes in interest rates resulted in transition losses on interest rate swaps that did not qualify for hedge accounting before transition. Losses also arose from the FIN 46 requirement to record carrying amounts of assets in certain securitization entities as if those entities had always been consolidated, requiring us to eliminate certain previously recognized gains. For certain other entities that we were required to consolidate at their July 1, 2003, fair values, we recognized a loss on consolidation because their liabilities, including the fair value of interest rate swaps, exceeded independently appraised fair values of the related assets.

Statement of Financial Accounting Standards (SFAS) 143, *Accounting for Asset Retirement Obligations*, became effective for us on January 1, 2003. Under SFAS 143, obligations associated with the retirement of long-lived assets are recorded when there is a legal obligation to incur such costs. This amount is accounted for like an additional element of cost, and, like other cost elements, is depreciated over the corresponding asset's useful life. SFAS 143 primarily affects our accounting for costs associated with the future retirement of facilities used for storage and production of nuclear fuel. On January 1, 2003, we recorded a one-time, non-cash transition charge of $330 million ($215 million after tax, or $0.02 per share) which is reported in the caption "Cumulative effect of accounting changes."

In 2002, we adopted SFAS 142, *Goodwill and Other Intangible Assets*, under which goodwill is no longer amortized but is tested for impairment using a fair value methodology. Using the required reporting unit basis, we tested all of our goodwill for impairment as of January 1, 2002, and recorded a non-cash charge of $1.204 billion ($1.015 billion after tax, or $0.10 per share). All of the charge related to Equipment & Other Services. Factors contributing to the impairment charge were the difficult economic environment in the information technology sector and heightened price competition in the auto insurance industry. No impairment charge had been required under our previous goodwill impairment policy, which was based on undiscounted cash flows.

Also in 2002, we adopted the stock option expense provisions of SFAS 123, *Accounting for Stock-Based Compensation*. A comparison of reported and pro-forma net earnings, including effects of expensing stock options, follows. (38)

(In millions; per-share amounts in dollars)	2003	2002	2001
Net earnings, as reported	**$15,002**	$14,118	$13,684
Earnings per share, as reported			
Diluted	**1.49**	1.41	1.37
Basic	**1.50**	1.42	1.38
Stock option expense included in net earnings	**81**	27	—
Total stock option expense(a)	**315**	330	296
PRO-FORMA EFFECTS			
Net earnings, on pro-forma basis	**14,768**	13,815	13,388
Earnings per share, on pro-forma basis			
Diluted	**1.47**	1.38	1.33
Basic	**1.47**	1.39	1.35

(a) As if we had applied SFAS 123 to expense stock options in all periods. Includes amounts we actually recognized in 2003 and 2002 earnings.

(38) No issue ever on the FASB's agenda has been more controversial than measuring and reporting the compensation cost of employee stock options. In 2002, GE voluntarily adopted *SFAS No. 123*'s recommended fair value accounting. *SFAS No. 123* allows companies to use either fair value or intrinsic value accounting in their financial statements, but requires them to disclose fair value information in their footnotes. In this table, GE provides the required disclosure of fair value compensation cost and *pro forma* income. Transition rules in *SFAS Nos. 123* and *148* allow GE to begin measuring fair value costs as if it had never granted options prior to 2002. The *pro forma* disclosure rules, on the other hand, have been in effect since 1995. Based only on options granted since 2002, GE included $81 million of stock option compensation expense in its 2003 net earnings. If it had based the expense on options granted since 1995, its earnings would have been $234 (= $315 – 81) million lower. See our comment *71* for a discussion of the fair value assumptions and compensation expense calculation.

(39) See *capital lease*, *sales-type lease* and *operating lease* in the Glossary. In these leases, GECS acts as lessor. Accounting views operating leases as *executory contracts* (see the Glossary). Although GECS has an assured right to receive payments and has already put the equipment in the hands of the users, it will not recognize revenue for the operating leases until it receives cash. In the financing leases, GE acts as lender and recognizes interest revenue over the lease term. See GE's Notes 12 and 15, and our comments comment *58* and *59*.

(40) *SFAS No. 2* requires GE to expense most research and development (R & D) costs, and to disclose the costs incurred during the year for R & D. Because GE does not identify R & D costs separately on its income statement on page 70 (they probably appear in "Other costs and expenses"), it reports them here. *SFAS No. 2* allows firms to capitalize reimbursable R & D costs they incur under contract. GE identifies the R & D costs that do not qualify for capitalization and therefore reduce current year income ($2,103 million in 2003) as Company-funded.

(41) In these operating leases, GE acts as lessee. Although GE can use the leased equipment and must make future payments, it recognizes neither an asset nor a liability. See the Glossary under *executory contracts*. *SFAS No. 13* requires companies with operating leases to report current rental expense and non-cancelable payable amounts for the next five years.

(42) GE computes costs for post-retirement benefits other than pensions similarly to pension costs, which we describe in comment *45*.

(43) Unlike pensions, non-pension post-retirement benefits have no law requiring companies to fund them in advance. Like most companies, GE funds these non-pension benefits only to the extent that it can deduct the amounts on its tax return. Consequently, its obligation exceeds the value of assets placed in trust to fund the future costs. GE reports this obligation under the caption "All other liabilities" on the balance sheet on its page 72.

(44) This note describes *defined benefit plans*, in contrast to *defined contribution plans*; see the Glossary.

In 2001, we adopted SFAS 133, *Accounting for Derivative Instruments and Hedging Activities*, as amended. Under SFAS 133, all derivative instruments are recognized in the balance sheet at their fair values. Further information about derivatives and hedging is provided in note 28. The cumulative transition effect of adopting this accounting change at January 1, 2001, was a $324 million ($0.03 per share) reduction of net earnings and $827 million reduction in equity.

Also in 2001, we adopted Emerging Issues Task Force (EITF) Issue 99-20. Under this consensus, impairment of certain retained interests in securitized assets must be recognized when (a) the asset's fair value is below its carrying value, and (b) it is probable that there has been an adverse change in estimated cash flows. The cumulative effect of adopting EITF 99-20 at January 1, 2001, was a one-time reduction of net earnings of $120 million ($0.01 per share).

NOTE 2

GE OTHER INCOME

(In millions)	2003	2002	2001
Licensing and royalty income	$135	$ 103	$ 75
Associated companies	118	(170)	(106)
Marketable securities and bank deposits	75	31	184
Bravo exchange	—	571	—
Global eXchange Services gain	—	488	—
Other items	317	83	280
Total	$645	$1,106	$ 433

NOTE 3

GECS REVENUES FROM SERVICES

(In millions)	2003	2002	2001
Premiums earned by insurance businesses	$18,646	$16,484	$15,634
Interest on time sales and loans	16,495	14,068	12,136
Operating lease rentals	7,199	6,879	6,762
Investment income	6,468	5,570	6,593
Financing leases	4,077	4,441	4,346
Fees	3,349	2,943	2,535
Other income	5,122	5,018	7,223
Total	$61,356	$55,403	$55,229

For insurance businesses, the effects of reinsurance on premiums written and premiums earned were as follows:

(In millions)	2003	2002	2001
PREMIUMS WRITTEN			
Direct	$11,640	$11,659	$ 9,958
Assumed	9,616	9,409	9,603
Ceded	(2,654)	(4,069)	(3,718)
Total	$18,602	$16,999	$15,843
PREMIUMS EARNED			
Direct	$11,433	$10,922	$ 9,912
Assumed	9,964	9,569	9,471
Ceded	(2,751)	(4,007)	(3,749)
Total	$18,646	$16,484	$15,634

NOTE 4

SUPPLEMENTAL COST INFORMATION

Total expenditures for research and development were $2,656 million, $2,631 million and $2,349 million in 2003, 2002 and 2001, respectively. The portion we funded was $2,103 million in 2003, $2,215 million in 2002 and $1,980 million in 2001.

Rental expense under operating leases is shown below.

(In millions)	2003	2002	2001
GE	$733	$773	$ 694
GECS	893	977	1,006

At December 31, 2003, minimum rental commitments under noncancelable operating leases aggregated $2,764 million and $4,354 million for GE and GECS, respectively. Amounts payable over the next five years follow.

(In millions)	2004	2005	2006	2007	2008
GE	$568	$466	$375	$298	$240
GECS	759	627	539	509	418

GE's selling, general and administrative expense totaled $9,870 million in 2003, $9,131 million in 2002 and $8,637 million in 2001. Capitalized interest is insignificant in 2003, 2002 and 2001.

We recorded restructuring charges of $270 million ($354 million including other related charges) in 2002 to rationalize certain operations and facilities of GE's worldwide industrial businesses. Major elements of these restructuring programs included costs for employee severance, lease termination, dismantlement, and other exit costs. These programs were essentially completed by the end of 2003.

NOTE 5

RETIREE HEALTH AND LIFE BENEFITS

We sponsor a number of retiree health and life insurance benefit plans (retiree benefit plans). Principal retiree benefit plans are discussed below; other such plans are not significant individually or in the aggregate.

PRINCIPAL RETIREE BENEFIT PLANS generally provide health and life insurance benefits to employees who retire under the GE Pension Plan (see note 6) with 10 or more years of service. Retirees share in the cost of healthcare benefits. Benefit provisions are subject to collective bargaining. These plans cover approximately 250,000 retirees and dependents. Our principal retiree benefit plans have a December 31 measurement date.

The effect on operations of principal retiree benefit plans is shown in the following table.

EFFECT ON OPERATIONS

(In millions)	2003	2002	2001
Expected return on plan assets	$ (159)	$(170)	$(185)
Service cost for benefits earned	307	277	191
Interest cost on benefit obligation	535	469	459
Prior service cost	191	96	90
Net actuarial loss recognized	127	78	60
Retiree benefit plans cost	$1,001	$ 750	$ 615

ACTUARIAL ASSUMPTIONS. The discount rate at December 31 was used to measure the year-end benefit obligations and the earnings effects for the subsequent year. Actuarial assumptions used to determine benefit obligations and earnings effects for principal retiree benefit plans follow.

ACTUARIAL ASSUMPTIONS

December 31	2003	2002	2001	2000
Discount rate [a]	6.0%	6.75%	7.25%	7.5%
Compensation increases	5	5	5	5
Expected return on assets	8.5	8.5	9.5	9.5
Healthcare cost trend rate [b]	10.5	13	12	10

[a] Weighted average discount rate for determination of 2003 costs was 6.4%.
[b] For 2003, gradually declining to 5% after 2010.

To determine the expected long-term rate of return on retiree life plan assets, we consider the current and expected asset allocations, as well as historical and expected returns on various categories of plan assets. We apply our expected rate of return to a market-related value of assets, which reduces the underlying variability in assets to which we apply that expected return.

We amortize experience gains and losses, as well as the effects of changes in actuarial assumptions and plan provisions, over a period no longer than the average future service of employees.

FUNDING POLICY for retiree health benefits is generally to pay covered expenses as they are incurred. We fund retiree life insurance benefits at our discretion. Under the provisions of these plans, we expect to contribute approximately $640 million in 2004 to cover unfunded healthcare benefits.

Changes in the accumulated postretirement benefit obligation for retiree benefit plans follow.

ACCUMULATED POSTRETIREMENT BENEFIT OBLIGATION (APBO)

(In millions)	2003	2002
Balance at January 1	$7,435	$6,796
Service cost for benefits earned	307	277
Interest cost on benefit obligation	535	469
Participant contributions	33	32
Plan amendments [a]	2,483	(60)
Actuarial (gain) loss	(416)	567
Benefits paid	(720)	(687)
Other	44	41
Balance at December 31 [b]	$9,701	$7,435

[a] For 2003, associated with changes in retiree benefit plans resulting from collective bargaining agreements that extend through June 2007.
[b] The APBO for the retiree health plans was $7,514 million and $5,458 million at year-end 2003 and 2002, respectively.

Increasing or decreasing the healthcare cost trend rates by one percentage point would have had an insignificant effect on the December 31, 2003, accumulated postretirement benefit obligation and the annual cost of retiree health plans. Our principal retiree benefit plans are collectively bargained and have provisions that limit our per capita costs.

NOTE 6

PENSION BENEFITS

We sponsor a number of pension plans. Principal pension plans are discussed below; other such plans are not significant individually or in the aggregate. Principal pension plans constitute about 90% of global pension assets and obligations.

PRINCIPAL PENSION PLANS are the GE Pension Plan and the GE Supplementary Pension Plan. These plans have a December 31 measurement date.

The GE Pension Plan provides benefits to certain U.S. employees based on the greater of a formula recognizing career earnings or a formula recognizing length of service and final average earnings. Benefit provisions are subject to collective bargaining. The GE Pension Plan covers approximately 508,000 participants, including 136,000 employees, 171,000 former employees with vested rights to future benefits, and 201,000 retirees and beneficiaries receiving benefits.

The GE Supplementary Pension Plan is an unfunded plan providing supplementary retirement benefits primarily to higher-level, longer-service U.S. employees.

Details of the effect on operations of principal pension plans, and the total effect on cost of principal postretirement benefit plans, follow.

EFFECT ON OPERATIONS

(In millions)	2003	2002	2001
Expected return on plan assets	$ 4,072	$ 4,084	$ 4,327
Service cost for benefits earned (a)	(1,213)	(1,107)	(884)
Interest cost on benefit obligation	(2,180)	(2,116)	(2,065)
Prior service cost	(248)	(217)	(244)
Net actuarial gain recognized	609	912	961
Income from pensions	1,040	1,556	2,095
Retiree benefit plans cost (note 5)	(1,001)	(750)	(615)
Net cost reductions from principal postretirement benefit plans	$ 39	$ 806	$ 1,480

(a) Net of participant contributions.

ACTUARIAL ASSUMPTIONS. The discount rate at December 31 was used to measure the year-end benefit obligations and the earnings effects for the subsequent year. Actuarial assumptions used to determine benefit obligations and earnings effects for principal pension plans follow.

ACTUARIAL ASSUMPTIONS

December 31	2003	2002	2001	2000
Discount rate	6.0%	6.75%	7.25%	7.5%
Compensation increases	5	5	5	5
Expected return on assets	8.5	8.5	9.5	9.5

To determine the expected long-term rate of return on pension plan assets, we consider the current and expected asset allocations, as well as historical and expected returns on various categories of plan assets. We apply our expected rate of return to a market-related value of assets, which reduces the underlying variability in assets to which we apply that expected return.

We amortize experience gains and losses, as well as the effects of changes in actuarial assumptions and plan provisions, over a period no longer than the average future service of employees.

FUNDING POLICY for the GE Pension Plan is to contribute amounts sufficient to meet minimum funding requirements as set forth in employee benefit and tax laws plus such additional amounts as we may determine to be appropriate. We have not made contributions to the GE Pension Plan since 1987; any such GE contribution would require payment of excise taxes and would not be deductible for income tax purposes. We will not make any contributions to the GE Pension Plan in 2004. We expect to pay approximately $100 million for GE Supplementary Pension Plan payments and administrative expenses in 2004.

BENEFIT OBLIGATIONS. Accumulated and projected benefit obligations (ABO and PBO) represent the obligations of a pension plan for past service as of the measurement date. ABO is the present value of benefits earned to date with benefits computed based on current compensation levels. PBO is ABO increased to reflect expected future compensation.

Changes in the PBO for principal pension plans follow.

PROJECTED BENEFIT OBLIGATION

(In millions)	2003	2002
Balance at January 1	$33,266	$30,423
Service cost for benefits earned (a)	1,213	1,107
Interest cost on benefit obligation	2,180	2,116
Participant contributions	169	158
Plan amendments	654	9
Actuarial loss (b)	2,754	1,650
Benefits paid	(2,409)	(2,197)
Balance at December 31 (c)	$37,827	$33,266

(a) Net of participant contributions.
(b) Principally associated with discount rate changes.
(c) The PBO for the GE Supplementary Pension Plan was $2.7 billion and $2.2 billion at year-end 2003 and 2002, respectively.

ABO balances for principal pension plans follow.

ACCUMULATED BENEFIT OBLIGATION

December 31 (In millions)	2003	2002
GE Pension Plan	$33,859	$29,698
GE Supplementary Pension Plan	1,619	1,296
Total	$35,478	$30,994

(45) GE's pension plans generated income in excess of costs in each of the years 2001 through 2003. Pension cost or income comprises three major components:

(1) *Return on plan assets* – GE funds its pension plans with cash, which a pension plan trustee invests in assets such as debt and equity securities. GE reports the allocation of its pension plan assets in a table on page 84, below our callout *49*. The returns on those assets reduce pension expense or increase pension income. *SFAS No. 87* requires that the *expected* return on pension plan assets, not the actual return, offset pension expense. In 2003, GE expects a return on assets of 8.5%; see the table at our callout *46*. The expected return contributes $4,072 million to pension income in 2003.

(2) *Service cost* – GE estimates the cost today of future pensions attributable to employees' work during the current year, and records this estimate as "Service cost for benefits earned." The estimate involves actuarial calculations of employee turnover and survival rates, and discounting for the time value of money that GE will pay in the future. GE's service costs, $1,213 million in 2003, decrease pension income and increase the *projected benefit obligation*, described in our comment *48*.

(3) *Interest cost* – Because GE records service costs as discounted values (see item (2) above), it accrues interest annually on its outstanding pension obligation, using the rate of interest implicit in the discounting. GE records the interest accrual as "Interest cost on benefit obligation." The 2003 interest cost, $2,180 million, decreases pension income and increases the projected benefit obligation, described in our comment *48*.

In addition to the above three major components, GE amortizes two items which we describe below in our comment *50*: prior service costs, and net actuarial gains or losses. These two items increase GE's pension income by $361 million in 2003.

GE combines its income from pensions with its cost of other retiree benefits to show a net cost reduction of $39 million in 2003. GE computes the cost of other retiree benefits in a manner similar to pension cost, and reports it in Note 5 near our callout *42*.

(46) GE uses these assumptions to compute its obligation and costs for pensions. During 2003, GE reduced the discount rate it uses to compute the projected benefit obligation from 6.75 percent to 6.00 percent. GE expects compensation to increase by 5% per year, and the invested plan assets to earn a 8.5 percent rate of return. In its MD&A discussion of Critical Accounting Estimates on its page 68, GE explains the basis for these assumptions.

(47) Federal law requires GE to fund its pension plan, i.e. to place assets with an independent trustee who will use them to satisfy obligations to employees in future. On its tax return, GE may deduct the amounts used to fund the pension plan only to the extent that the amounts satisfy legal funding requirements. Since 1987, GE's pension plan assets in its main U.S. pension plan have exceeded the amount required by law, so the company has made no contributions to this plan, and would receive no tax deduction if it did.

(48) Here GE shows how its projected pension obligation increased in each balance sheet year. GE's projected obligation to pay pension benefits increases with employee service, and as interest accrues on the existing obligation (see our comment *45* above). GE must return participants' contributions to them, so their contributions increase GE's obligation. When employee groups negotiate increases in their pension benefits, GE records the increase in its future obligation as "Plan amendments." "Actuarial loss" represents amounts by which GE's actual experience in the current year with factors like employee retirements, salary increases, mortality and interest rates differ from its assumptions. Finally, GE reduces its future obligation by paying benefits owed to retirees.

(49) GE reports how its pension plan assets increased or decreased in each of the balance sheet years. Compare the actual gain (loss) on plan assets to the expected return that GE incorporates into earnings, at our callout *45*. GE always expects a positive return on assets, but actual returns can be negative, as they were in 2002. Pension plan assets also increase with GE's or employees' (participants') contributions. The item "employer contributions," adding $105 million to pension assets in 2003, represent GE payments under its unfunded Supplementary Pension Plan. [We know this because we have asked GE, not because the disclosure makes it clear.] GE also discloses how its pension plans invest the assets.

Changes in the fair value of assets for principal pension plans follow.

FAIR VALUE OF ASSETS

(In millions)	2003	2002
Balance at January 1	$37,811	$45,006
Actual gain (loss) on plan assets	8,203	(5,251)
Employer contributions	105	95
Participant contributions	169	158
Benefits paid	(2,409)	(2,197)
Balance at December 31	$43,879	$37,811

The GE Pension Plan's assets are held in trust, as follows:

PLAN ASSET ALLOCATION

	2003		2002
December 31	Target allocation	Actual allocation	Actual allocation
Equity securities	51-63%	60%	56%
Debt securities	21-27	20	26
Real estate	4-8	7	6
Private equities	5-11	7	7
Other	3-7	6	5
Total		100%	100%

Plan fiduciaries set investment policies and strategies for the GE Pension Trust. Long-term strategic investment objectives include preserving the funded status of the trust and balancing risk and return. The plan fiduciaries oversee the investment allocation process, which includes selecting investment managers, commissioning periodic asset-liability studies, setting long-term strategic targets and monitoring asset allocations. Target allocation ranges are guidelines, not limitations, and occasionally plan fiduciaries will approve allocations above or below a target range.

Trust assets are invested subject to the following policy restrictions: short-term securities must be rated A1/P1 or better; investments in real estate—7% of trust assets at year end—may not exceed 25%; other investments in securities that are not freely tradable—11% of trust assets at year end—may not exceed 20%. GE common stock represented 6.3% and 6.0% of trust assets at year-end 2003 and 2002, respectively, and is subject to a statutory limit when it reaches 10% of total trust assets.

Our recorded assets and liabilities for principal pension plans are as follows:

PREPAID PENSION ASSET/(LIABILITY)

December 31 (In millions)	2003	2002
Funded status[a]	$ 6,052	$ 4,545
Unrecognized prior service cost	1,571	1,165
Unrecognized net actuarial loss	7,588	8,356
Net asset recognized	$15,211	$14,066
Amounts recorded in the Statement of Financial Position:		
Prepaid pension asset	$17,038	$15,611
Supplementary Pension Plan liability	(1,827)	(1,545)
Net asset recognized	$15,211	$14,066

[a] Fair value of assets less PBO, as shown in the preceding tables.

NOTE 7

PROVISION FOR INCOME TAXES

(In millions)	2003	2002	2001
GE			
Current tax expense	**$2,468**	$2,833	$3,632
Deferred tax expense from			
temporary differences	**389**	1,004	561
	2,857	3,837	4,193
GECS			
Current tax expense (benefit)	**720**	(1,488)	517
Deferred tax expense from			
temporary differences	**738**	1,409	863
	1,458	(79)	1,380
CONSOLIDATED			
Current tax expense	**3,188**	1,345	4,149
Deferred tax expense from			
temporary differences	**1,127**	2,413	1,424
Total	**$4,315**	$3,758	$5,573

GE and GECS file a consolidated U.S. federal income tax return. The GECS provision for current tax expense includes its effect on the consolidated return.

Consolidated current tax expense includes amounts applicable to U.S. federal income taxes of $1,555 million, $137 million and $2,514 million in 2003, 2002 and 2001, respectively, and amounts applicable to non-U.S. jurisdictions of $1,304 million,

$1,061 million and $1,225 million in 2003, 2002 and 2001, respectively. Consolidated deferred tax expense related to U.S. federal income taxes was $685 million, $2,112 million and $1,455 million in 2003, 2002 and 2001, respectively.

Deferred income tax balances reflect the effects of temporary differences between the carrying amounts of assets and liabilities and their tax bases and are stated at enacted tax rates expected to be in effect when taxes are actually paid or recovered. See note 21 for details.

We have not provided U.S. deferred taxes on cumulative earnings of non-U.S. affiliates and associated companies that have been reinvested indefinitely. These earnings relate to ongoing operations and, at December 31, 2003, were approximately $21 billion. Because of the availability of U.S. foreign tax credits, it is not practicable to determine the U.S. federal income tax liability that would be payable if such earnings were not reinvested indefinitely. Deferred taxes are provided for earnings of non-U.S. affiliates and associated companies when we plan to remit those earnings.

Consolidated U.S. income before taxes and the cumulative effect of accounting changes was $11.2 billion in 2003, $12.0 billion in 2002 and $13.9 billion in 2001. The corresponding amounts for non-U.S.-based operations were $8.7 billion in 2003, $6.9 billion in 2002 and $5.8 billion in 2001.

A reconciliation of the U.S. federal statutory tax rate to the actual tax rate is provided below.

RECONCILIATION OF U.S. FEDERAL STATUTORY TAX RATE TO ACTUAL TAX RATE

	Consolidated			GE			GECS		
	2003	2002	2001	**2003**	2002	2001	**2003**	2002	2001
Statutory U.S. federal income tax rate	**35.0%**	35.0%	35.0%	**35.0%**	35.0%	35.0%	**35.0%**	35.0%	35.0%
Increase (reduction) in rate resulting from:									
Inclusion of after-tax earnings of GECS									
in before-tax earnings of GE	—	—	—	**(14.7)**	(8.5)	(10.7)	—	—	—
Amortization of goodwill	—	—	1.0	—	—	0.8	—	—	0.9
Tax-exempt income	**(1.1)**	(1.2)	(1.3)	—	—	—	**(2.4)**	(5.1)	(3.8)
Tax on international activities									
including exports	**(9.0)**	(10.6)	(5.4)	**(4.3)**	(5.2)	(3.2)	**(10.8)**	(22.5)	(6.7)
Americom/Rollins goodwill	—	—	(1.1)	—	—	—	—	—	(3.2)
All other—net	**(3.2)**	(3.3)	0.1	**(0.5)**	(1.1)	1.0	**(6.0)**	(9.1)	(2.4)
	(13.3)	(15.1)	(6.7)	**(19.5)**	(14.8)	(12.1)	**(19.2)**	(36.7)	(15.2)
Actual income tax rate	**21.7%**	19.9%	28.3%	**15.5%**	20.2%	22.9%	**15.8%**	(1.7)%	19.8%

50. GE's "Funded status" shows that its pension assets exceed its projected benefit obligation by $6,052 million at the end of 2003. The other two balances accumulate adjustments to the pension calculations over time. Plan amendments, sometimes called "prior service costs," reflect changes in the projected obligation (see our comment *48*) because GE amended the pension plan, and the amendment applies retroactively to employees' past service. This can happen, for example, because of organized labor contract renegotiation. GE amortizes this balance into pension cost over employees' remaining service lives (see our comment *45*). "Unrecognized net actuarial loss" accumulates the differences between GE's assumptions and its actual experience in return on pension plan assets (see our comment *49*), and factors used to compute the projected benefit obligation (see our comment *48*). When this balance exceeds ten percent of the asset or obligation measured at the beginning of the year, *SFAS No. 87* requires GE to amortize the excess into pension cost or income (see our comment *45*).

51. This schedule shows the details of income tax expense, which GE calls a "provision." The schedule's bottom line equals the total provision for income taxes reported on the statement of earnings. GE derives its income tax expense by first reporting the portion currently payable, and then adjusting for *temporary differences* (see the Glossary, GE's Note 21 on page 97, and our comments *63* and *64*).

52. The SEC requires disclosure of pretax income disaggregated into domestic and foreign sources. From information in these paragraphs, the analyst can compute an effective foreign tax rate for 2003 of 15 percent (= $1,304/$8,700). Compare this with the overall effective rate discussed in our comment *53*.

53. The SEC requires GE to disclose how the reported income tax expense rate differs from the statutory U.S. federal tax rate of 35 percent. The 21.7 percent effective tax figure for 2003, which GE calls the "Actual income tax rate," results from dividing income tax expense of $4,315 million by pretax income, $19,904 million. The reasons that the effective tax rate differs from the U.S. statutory rate include the following.

    (1) GE's 2003 income statement on page 71, using the *equity method*, includes $7,754 million of *after-tax* income from GECS, yet the subsidiary's income appears before GE's income tax calculation. Because GE and GECS file a consolidated tax return, GE pays no further taxes on the income from GECS. The reported reduction in tax rate, 14.7 percent in 2003, derives from GE's statutory federal tax rate applied to the GECS portion of its reported pre-tax income, or 35% x $7,754/$18,446 = 14.7%.

    (2) The IRS disallows any tax deduction for amortization of goodwill acquired before August 11, 1993. This permanent difference reduces shareholder net income, increasing the effective tax rate relative to the statutory rate. It applies only to years prior to 2002, when *SFAS No. 142* required companies to discontinue amortizing intangible assets with indefinite lives, like most goodwill. See GE's Note 1 near our callout *35*, GE's Note 16 and our comment *61*

    (3) Some of GECS's income, for example income on state and municipal bonds, is tax-exempt at the federal level — a *permanent difference*. This decreases the effective tax rate, relative to the statutory rate.

    (4) GE's international activities reduce its effective tax rate because the IRS exempts some income from Foreign Sales Corporations from tax, and taxes other such income at lower rates than the statutory rate. See the Glossary at *FSC*.

    (5) In 2001, GE disposed of businesses that included goodwill for less than it paid for the businesses. The IRS allows a deduction for this realized loss at disposal. As we discussed in item (2) above, GE amortized some of the goodwill on its shareholder financial statements. The 2001 tax deduction therefore exceeds the financial statement expense, reducing GE's effective tax rate relative to the statutory rate.

54. GE reports the fair value of investment securities, $120,724 million at the end of 2003, on its consolidated balance sheet on page 72. Here it reports its *amortized cost* for these securities, and the unrealized gains and losses that reconcile amortized cost to estimated fair value. The unrealized gains and losses (net of tax) become part of owners' equity. See our comment *11*, GE's Note 1 near the call-out for our comment *33*, GE's Note 24 and our comment *67*. On GE's page 87, which we have not reproduced, the company reports additional information about its investments' performance in various investment categories.

55. The SEC requires firms to report concentrations of credit risk arising because they sell to a small number of customers, in a narrow industry or in a limited geographic region. *SFAS No. 131* requires disclosure about customers whose purchases represent 10 percent or more of a firm's revenues. GE discloses here that one large customer, the U.S. government, accounts for most of its Aircraft engine accounts receivable.

NOTE 8

EARNINGS PER SHARE INFORMATION

(In millions; per-share amounts in dollars)	2003 Diluted	2003 Basic	2002 Diluted	2002 Basic	2001 Diluted	2001 Basic
CONSOLIDATED OPERATIONS						
Earnings before accounting changes	**$15,589**	**$15,589**	$15,133	$15,133	$14,128	$14,128
Dividend equivalents—net of tax	**1**	**—**	13	—	12	—
Earnings before accounting changes for per-share calculation	**15,590**	**15,589**	15,146	15,133	14,140	14,128
Cumulative effect of accounting changes	**(587)**	**(587)**	(1,015)	(1,015)	(444)	(444)
Net earnings available for per-share calculation	**$15,003**	**$15,002**	$14,131	$14,118	$13,696	$13,684
AVERAGE EQUIVALENT SHARES						
Shares of GE common stock outstanding	**10,019**	**10,019**	9,947	9,947	9,932	9,932
Employee compensation-related shares, including stock options	**56**	**—**	81	—	120	—
Total average equivalent shares	**10,075**	**10,019**	10,028	9,947	10,052	9,932
PER-SHARE AMOUNTS						
Earnings before accounting changes	**$ 1.55**	**$ 1.56**	$ 1.51	$ 1.52	$ 1.41	$ 1.42
Cumulative effect of accounting changes	**(0.06)**	**(0.06)**	(0.10)	(0.10)	(0.04)	(0.04)
Net earnings per share	**$ 1.49**	**$ 1.50**	$ 1.41	$ 1.42	$ 1.37	$ 1.38

NOTE 9

 ### INVESTMENT SECURITIES

December 31 (In millions)	2003 Amortized cost	2003 Gross unrealized gains	2003 Gross unrealized losses	2003 Estimated fair value	2002 Amortized cost	2002 Gross unrealized gains	2002 Gross unrealized losses	2002 Estimated fair value
GE								
Debt—U.S. corporate	$ 350	$ —	$ (28)	$ 322	$ 350	$ —	$ (86)	$ 264
Equity	42	18	(2)	58	86	10	(28)	68
	392	18	(30)	380	436	10	(114)	332
GECS								
Debt								
U.S. corporate	50,779	2,558	(684)	52,653	55,489	2,416	(1,490)	56,415
State and municipal	12,707	382	(23)	13,066	12,147	358	(45)	12,460
Mortgage-backed	13,441	271	(93)	13,619	12,285	438	(46)	12,677
Asset-backed	12,471	250	(84)	12,637	7,081	126	(32)	7,175
Corporate—non-U.S.	14,720	557	(89)	15,188	13,396	529	(230)	13,695
Government—non-U.S.	8,558	169	(65)	8,662	8,147	291	(62)	8,376
U.S. government and federal agency	1,611	58	(19)	1,650	1,678	67	(18)	1,727
Equity	2,593	393	(117)	2,869	4,333	165	(493)	4,005
	116,880	4,638	(1,174)	120,344	114,556	4,390	(2,416)	116,530
Total consolidated	$117,272	$4,656	$(1,204)	$120,724	$114,992	$4,400	$(2,530)	$116,862

NOTES TO CONSOLIDATED FINANCIAL STATEMENTS

NOTE 10

GE CURRENT RECEIVABLES

December 31 (In millions)	2003	2002
Advanced Materials	$ 927	$ 1,082
Consumer & Industrial	1,111	1,426
Energy	3,788	3,883
Healthcare	2,024	1,411
Infrastructure	400	363
NBC	938	891
Transportation	1,993	2,021
Corporate items and eliminations	278	349
	11,459	11,426
Less allowance for losses	(486)	(453)
Total	$10,973	$10,973

Receivables balances at December 31, 2003 and 2002, before allowance for losses, included $6,746 million and $6,269 million, respectively, from sales of goods and services to customers, and $226 million and $304 million, respectively, from transactions with associated companies.

Current receivables of $444 million at year-end 2003 and ⑤⑤ $344 million at year-end 2002 arose from sales, principally of aircraft engine goods and services, on open account to various agencies of the U.S. government, which is our largest single customer. About 4% of our sales of goods and services were to the U.S. government in 2003, 2002 and 2001.

NOTE 11

INVENTORIES

December 31 (In millions)	2003	2002
GE		
Raw materials and work in process	$4,530	$4,894
Finished goods	4,376	4,379
Unbilled shipments	281	372
	9,187	9,645
⑤⑥ Less revaluation to LIFO	(632)	(606)
	8,555	9,039
GECS		
Finished goods	197	208
Total	$8,752	$9,247

LIFO revaluations increased $26 million in 2003, compared with decreases of $70 million in 2002 and $169 million in 2001. Included in the 2003 change was an increase of $3 million that resulted from higher LIFO inventory levels. Included in the 2002 and 2001 changes were decreases of $21 million and $8 million, ⑤⑦ respectively, that resulted from lower LIFO inventory levels. Net costs increased in 2003 and decreased in 2002 and 2001. As of December 31, 2003, we are obligated to acquire certain raw materials at market prices through the year 2023 under various take-or-pay or similar arrangements. Annual minimum commitments under these arrangements are insignificant.

NOTE 12

GECS FINANCING RECEIVABLES (INVESTMENTS IN TIME SALES, LOANS AND FINANCING LEASES)

December 31 (In millions)	2003	2002
COMMERCIAL FINANCE		
Equipment	$ 63,737	$ 64,618
Commercial and industrial	39,383	36,512
Real estate	20,171	21,041
Commercial aircraft	12,424	11,397
	135,715	133,568
CONSUMER FINANCE		
Non-U.S. installment, revolving credit and other	34,440	23,655
Non-U.S. residential	19,593	9,731
Non-U.S. auto	18,668	15,113
U.S. installment, revolving credit and other	16,545	14,312
Other	5,431	3,225
	94,677	66,036
Equipment & Other Services	1,893	3,956
	232,285	203,560
Less allowance for losses (note 13)	(6,256)	(5,500)
Total	$226,029	$198,060

GECS financing receivables include both time sales and loans and financing leases. Time sales and loans represents transactions in a variety of forms, including time sales, revolving charge and credit, mortgages, installment loans, intermediate-term loans and revolving loans secured by business assets. The portfolio includes time sales and loans carried at the principal amount on which finance charges are billed periodically, and time sales and loans carried at gross book value, which includes finance charges.

Investment in financing leases consists of direct financing and leveraged leases of aircraft, railroad rolling stock, autos, other transportation equipment, data processing equipment and medical equipment, as well as other manufacturing, power generation, commercial real estate, and commercial equipment and facilities.

(56) GE uses the LIFO cost flow assumption for inventories, but manages its inventories, as most sensible businesses do, on FIFO, using the older materials and finished goods before the newer. It keeps its records internally on a FIFO basis, and reports here the FIFO cost of 2003 year-end inventories, $9,187 million. GE makes an adjustment at year-end to convert the internal records to LIFO, by debiting Cost of Goods Sold and crediting Ending Inventory for $632 million. Some business analysts call this amount the "LIFO reserve," but we prefer GE's more descriptive caption.

The IRS does not allow companies using LIFO for tax purposes to disclose in the financial statements what income would have been under FIFO. The SEC, however, requires the disclosure of beginning and ending inventories as they would have been under FIFO, if these amounts differ significantly from the LIFO amounts. The SEC's required disclosure allows the analyst to compute pretax income had GE used FIFO, rather than LIFO. As of December 31, 2003, GE has reported $632 million less in *cumulative* pretax income than it would have under FIFO. As of January 1, 2003, GE had reported $606 million less in cumulative pretax income than it would have under FIFO. This difference increased by $26 (= $632 – $606) million during 2003. Hence, 2003 pretax income would have been $26 million higher if GE had used FIFO. We show details of this calculation in the accompanying exhibit. Generally, companies choose LIFO if it will typically result in smaller pretax income, thereby reducing the tax bill.

INVENTORY DATA: GENERAL ELECTRIC COMPANY AND CONSOLIDATED AFFILIATES, 2003
(For Authors' comment (56). Dollar amounts are in millions.)

	LIFO Cost-Flow Assumption (Actually Used)	+	Excess of FIFO over LIFO Amount	=	FIFO Cost-Flow Assumption (Hypothetical)
Beginning Inventory.....................	$ 9,247[a]		$ 606		$ 9,853
Plus: Purchases[b]	36,694		0		36,694
Cost of Goods Available for Sale	$45,941		$ 606		$46,547
Less: Ending Inventory	8,752		632		9,384
Cost of Goods Sold	$37,189		($ 26)		$37,163
Sales of Goods........................	$49,963		$ 0		$49,963
Less: Cost of Goods Sold	37,189		($ 26)		37,163
Gross Margin on Sales	$12,774		26		$12,800

[a] Amounts shown in **boldface** appear in GE's financial statements and notes.
[b] Computation of Purchases:

Purchases	=	Cost of Goods Sold	+	Ending Inventory	–	Beginning Inventory
$36,694	=	$37,189	+	$8,752	–	$9,247

(57) See the Glossary at *LIFO inventory layer*, particularly the last sentence. In 2002 and 2001, GE decreased its inventory by selling more items than it acquired, while in 2003 it increased its inventory by acquiring more items than it sold. Under LIFO, in 2002 we assume that GE sold all the items it acquired, plus some items from beginning inventory. If GE had purchased sufficient amounts at year-end to avoid selling from old layers, these purchases would have cost more than the old layers assumed sold, cost of goods sold would have been higher and income for the period would have been lower. GE tells us that its 2002 pretax income is $21 million larger because it dipped into old LIFO layers. The rest of the 2002 $70 million decrease in LIFO revaluation (and $70 million increase in pretax income) results from declines in GE's cost of items for inventory during the year.

(58) GECS acts as the lessor in many equipment leases that provide financing to the equipment user, called *direct financing* and *leveraged leases* (see the Glossary). In these leases, GECS retains title to the leased equipment, but the equipment does not appear on its balance sheet. Instead, GECS records an "Investment in financing leases" equal to the discounted present value of future payments receivable on the lease, plus the present value of the equipment's expected residual value after the lease term. For some of these leases, a third party provides some financing, while GE retains the "equity" interest.

(59) In Note 15, GE discloses the original cost of its property, plant and equipment. In addition to the equipment leased to others under financing leases described in GE's Note 12 and our comment *58*, GECS leases most equipment that appears on its balance sheet to others under *operating leases* (see the Glossary).

As the sole owner of assets under direct financing leases and as the equity participant in leveraged leases, GECS is taxed on total lease payments received and is entitled to tax deductions based on the cost of leased assets and tax deductions for interest paid to third-party participants. GECS is generally entitled to any residual value of leased assets.

Investment in direct financing and leveraged leases represents net unpaid rentals and estimated unguaranteed residual values of leased equipment, less related deferred income. GECS has no general obligation for principal and interest on notes and other instruments representing third-party participation related to leveraged leases; such notes and other instruments have not been included in liabilities but have been offset against the related rentals receivable. The GECS share of rentals receivable on leveraged leases is subordinate to the share of other participants who also have security interests in the leased equipment.

NET INVESTMENT IN FINANCING LEASES

December 31 (In millions)	Total financing leases		Direct financing leases		Leveraged leases	
	2003	2002	2003	2002	2003	2002
Total minimum lease payments receivable	$ 87,400	$ 88,640	$57,929	$56,779	$ 29,471	$ 31,861
Less principal and interest on third-party nonrecourse debt	(22,144)	(24,249)	—	—	(22,144)	(24,249)
Net rentals receivable	65,256	64,391	57,929	56,779	7,327	7,612
Estimated unguaranteed residual value of leased assets	9,733	9,807	6,058	6,032	3,675	3,775
Less deferred income	(13,496)	(13,947)	(9,720)	(9,998)	(3,776)	(3,949)
Investment in financing leases	61,493	60,251	54,267	52,813	7,226	7,438
Less amounts to arrive at net investment						
Allowance for losses	(830)	(861)	(734)	(759)	(96)	(102)
Deferred taxes	(10,250)	(9,763)	(5,793)	(5,559)	(4,457)	(4,204)
Net investment in financing leases	$ 50,413	$ 49,627	$47,740	$46,495	$ 2,673	$ 3,132

CONTRACTUAL MATURITIES

(In millions)	Total time sales and loans	Net rentals receivable
Due in		
2004	$ 55,044	$16,490
2005	28,020	13,272
2006	23,249	10,148
2007	13,951	6,883
2008	12,650	4,066
2009 and later	37,878	14,397
Total	$170,792	$65,256

We expect actual maturities to differ from contractual maturities.

"Impaired" loans are defined by generally accepted accounting principles as large balance loans for which it is probable that the lender will be unable to collect all amounts due according to original contractual terms of the loan agreement. An analysis of impaired loans follows.

December 31 (In millions)	2003	2002
Loans requiring allowance for losses	$ 940	$1,140
Loans expected to be fully recoverable	1,355	845
	$2,295	$1,985
Allowance for losses	$ 378	$ 397
Average investment during year	2,193	1,747
Interest income earned while impaired [a]	33	16

[a] Recognized principally on cash basis.

NOTE 15

PROPERTY, PLANT AND EQUIPMENT
(INCLUDING EQUIPMENT LEASED TO OTHERS)

December 31 (In millions)	Estimated useful lives	2003	2002
ORIGINAL COST			
GE			
Land and improvements	8(a)	$ 861	$ 623
Buildings, structures and related			
equipment	8-40	8,369	8,398
Machinery and equipment	4-20	24,184	22,264
Leasehold costs and manufacturing			
plant under construction	1-10	2,228	1,964
		35,642	33,249
GECS (b)			
Buildings and equipment	1-40	4,792	4,731
Equipment leased to others			
Aircraft	6-19	23,065	20,053
Vehicles	3-12	16,600	13,349
Railroad rolling stock	3-30	3,356	3,376
Mobile and modular	3-20	3,164	2,994
Construction and manufacturing	3-25	1,562	1,326
All other	2-35	3,025	3,004
		55,564	48,833
Total		$91,206	$82,082
NET CARRYING VALUE			
GE			
Land and improvements		$ 814	$ 587
Buildings, structures and related			
equipment		4,332	4,375
Machinery and equipment		7,547	7,083
Leasehold costs and manufacturing			
plant under construction		1,873	1,698
		14,566	13,743
GECS			
Buildings and equipment		2,827	2,893
Equipment leased to others			
Aircraft (c)		19,093	17,030
Vehicles		9,745	8,481
Railroad rolling stock		2,220	2,309
Mobile and modular		1,814	1,632
Construction and manufacturing		1,120	1,010
All other		1,997	1,975
		38,816	35,330
Total		$53,382	$49,073

(a) Estimated useful lives excluding land.

(b) Included $1.8 billion and $1.4 billion of assets leased to GE as of December 31, 2003 and 2002, respectively.

(c) Commercial Finance recognized impairment losses of $0.2 billion in 2003 and 2002 recorded in the caption "Other costs and expenses" in the Statement of Earnings to reflect adjustments to fair value based on current market values from independent appraisers.

Amortization of GECS equipment leased to others was $4,224 million, $3,919 million and $3,461 million in 2003, 2002 and 2001, respectively. Noncancelable future rentals due from customers for equipment on operating leases at year-end 2003 are due as follows:

(In millions)	
Due in	
2004	$ 5,267
2005	4,662
2006	3,426
2007	2,373
2008	1,661
After 2008	5,673
Total	$23,062

(60) GE uses *accelerated depreciation* for its U.S. depreciable assets. GECS uses accelerated depreciation for some of its own property, plant and equipment, but *straight-line depreciation* for all assets leased to others. GE uses the term *amortization* to describe depreciation of leased equipment. See the Glossary, and GE's Note 1 on page 77 at the call-out for our comment *31*. If a firm depreciates an asset costing $1,000 on a straight-line basis by $100 per year and has a net carrying value of $600 at year-end, then the asset has accumulated depreciation of $400 (= $1,000 – 600), and must be four (= $400/$100) years old. The analogous computation for GECS at year-end 2003 indicates that the leased assets have accumulated amortization of $14,783 million (= ($55,564-4,792)-($38,816-2,827) million), and the leases began roughly 3.5 (= $14,783/$4,224) years ago. Two facts complicate performing this computation for GE: (1) GE uses accelerated, not straight-line depreciation, so accumulated depreciation builds up at a faster rate than under straight-line depreciation; and (2) GE does not report depreciation expense on these assets separately. On its cash flow statement on page 75, GE reports depreciation combined together with amortization of intangibles at $2,277. In Note 16, (see our comment *61*) GE reports that its accumulated amortization on intangibles increased by $556 (= $5,759 – 5,203) million. From these facts we estimate GE's depreciation expense at $1,721 (= $2,277 – 556) million. The asset age computation indicates GE spent the dollars on its assets roughly 12.2 (= ($35,642 – 14,566) / $1,721) years before the balance sheet date. Because GE uses accelerated depreciation, however, we can conclude that GE spent dollars for plant on average less than 12.2 years prior to the end of 2003.

(61) See GE's Note 1 at the call-out for our comment *35*. GE acquired new intangibles in several categories, including Goodwill, during 2003. Consolidated accumulated amortization increased by $1,181 (= $10,057 – 8,876) million in 2003, due to amortization expense and dispositions. GE reports in Note 16 that it disposed of $658 million of PVFW. We infer that GE disposed of servicing assets from the declines in their "Gross carrying amounts."

(62) In Note 20, GE describes items included in the catch-all "All other liabilities." At year-end 2003, the balance sheet on page 72 shows $41,357 million in this category, of which $10,380 million represent accrued costs for various employee benefits. See GE's Notes 5 and 6 and our comments *45* through *50* for a description of the accounting for deferred employee benefits. GE also reports its involvement in clean-up of hazardous waste sites, and describes its policy for accruing liabilities for estimated future costs. Although GE values most long-term liabilities based on the present value of estimated future net cash payments, the company values clean-up liabilities at the undiscounted minimum of the range of possible future costs. GE does not disclose the amount it has accrued, probably because of concern that the disclosure could affect future negotiations with insurance companies and regulators.

(63) Under *SFAS No. 109*, deferred tax liabilities arise when a firm reports revenues to shareholders sooner, or reports expenses to shareholders later, than it reports those items to the IRS. Conversely, deferred tax assets arise when the firm reports revenues to shareholders later, or reports expenses to shareholders sooner, than it reports those items to the IRS. See the Glossary at *temporary differences*. This note shows the deferred tax assets and liabilities for GE and GECS, and the aggregate deferred tax liability for the consolidated company. The net consolidated position is a deferred tax liability of $12,647 million at December 31, 2003.

(64) GE's deferred tax assets and liabilities arise primarily from four items: Provisions for expenses, Retiree insurance plans, GE pensions and Depreciation. We discuss each of these in turn in this comment.

"Provisions for expenses" include bad debt expense and warranty expense. GE uses an *allowance method* (see the Glossary) to recognize bad debt expense and warranty expense for shareholder reporting. The estimated expenses under the allowance method do not, however, qualify as tax deductions. As we explain below, this generates a temporary difference between shareholder and tax net income, which causes GE to record a deferred tax asset. We illustrate the accounting with warranty costs; bad debt expense works similarly.

As GE sells products carrying warranties, it makes the following entry recognizing the estimated liability for future repairs and replacements:

Estimated Warranty Expense (Provision)	X	
Estimated Warranty Liability		X
Entry for expected warranty costs made in the period of sale.		

NOTES TO CONSOLIDATED FINANCIAL STATEMENTS

NOTE 16

INTANGIBLE ASSETS

December 31 (In millions)	2003	2002
GE		
Goodwill	**$25,960**	$20,044
Capitalized software	**1,678**	1,559
Other intangibles	**2,566**	1,446
	30,204	23,049
GECS		
Goodwill	**21,527**	19,094
Present value of future profits (PVFP)	**1,562**	2,457
Capitalized software	**800**	894
Other intangibles	**932**	686
	24,821	23,131
Total	**$55,025**	$46,180

GE intangible assets were net of accumulated amortization of $5,759 million in 2003 and $5,203 million in 2002. GECS intangible assets were net of accumulated amortization of $11,515 million in 2003 and $10,603 million in 2002.

INTANGIBLE ASSETS SUBJECT TO AMORTIZATION

December 31 (In millions)	Gross carrying amount	Accumulated amortization	Net
2003			
PVFP	$ 4,571	$ (3,009)	$1,562
Capitalized software	4,911	(2,433)	2,478
Servicing assets[a]	3,539	(3,392)	147
Patents, licenses and other	2,721	(806)	1,915
All other	1,095	(417)	678
Total	$16,837	$(10,057)	$6,780
2002			
PVFP	$ 5,261	$ (2,804)	$ 2,457
Capitalized software	4,269	(1,816)	2,453
Servicing assets[a]	3,582	(3,240)	342
Patents, licenses and other	1,665	(675)	990
All other	556	(341)	215
Total	$ 15,333	$ (8,876)	$ 6,457

[a] Servicing assets, net of accumulated amortization, were associated primarily with serviced residential mortgage loans amounting to $14 billion and $33 billion at December 31, 2003 and 2002, respectively.

Indefinite-lived intangible assets were $758 million and $585 million at December 31, 2003 and 2002, respectively, and principally comprise U.S. Federal Communication Commission licenses and cable affiliation agreements.

Consolidated amortization expense related to intangible assets, excluding goodwill, for 2003 and 2002 was $1,407 million

and $1,999 million, respectively. The estimated percentage of the December 31, 2003, net PVFP balance to be amortized over each of the next five years follows.

2004	2005	2006	2007	2008
8.8%	8.2%	7.5%	6.9%	6.4%

Change in PVFP balances follow.

(In millions)	2003	2002
Balance at January 1	**$2,457**	$2,198
Acquisitions	**46**	494
Dispositions	**(658)**	—
Accrued interest[a]	**80**	83
Amortization	**(318)**	(369)
Other	**(45)**	51
Balance at December 31	**$1,562**	$2,457

[a] Interest was accrued at a rate of 4.3% and 3.5% for 2003 and 2002, respectively.

Recoverability of PVFP is evaluated periodically by comparing the current estimate of expected future gross profits to the unamortized asset balance. If such comparison indicates that the expected gross profits will not be sufficient to recover PVFP, the difference is charged to expense. No such expense was recorded in 2003 or 2002.

Amortization expense for PVFP in future periods will be affected by acquisitions, realized capital gains/losses or other factors affecting the ultimate amount of gross profits realized from certain lines of business. Similarly, future amortization expense for other intangibles will depend on acquisition activity and other business transactions.

The amount of goodwill amortization included in net earnings (net of income taxes) in 2001 was $499 million and $552 million for GE and GECS, respectively.

The effects on earnings and earnings per share of excluding such goodwill amortization from 2001 follow.

(In millions; per-share amounts in dollars)	2001		
	Consolidated	GE	GECS
Net earnings, as reported	$13,684	$13,684	$5,417
Net earnings, excluding goodwill amortization	14,735	14,735	5,969

	Diluted	Basic
Earnings per share, as reported	$ 1.37	$ 1.38
Earnings per share, excluding goodwill amortization	1.47	1.48

Our mortgage insurance business experienced favorable development during the three-year period, primarily reflecting continued strength in certain real estate markets and the success of our loss containment initiatives.

Financial guarantees and credit life risk of insurance affiliates are summarized below.

December 31 (In millions)	2003	2002
Guarantees, principally on municipal bonds and asset-backed securities	$ 1,190	$226,559
Mortgage insurance risk in force	146,627	101,530
Credit life insurance risk in force	25,728	23,283
Less reinsurance	(2,207)	(38,883)
Total	$171,338	$312,489

Certain insurance affiliates offer insurance guaranteeing the timely payment of scheduled principal and interest on municipal bonds and certain asset-backed securities. Substantially all of this business was conducted by Financial Guaranty Insurance Company (FGIC), which we sold in the fourth quarter of 2003. Other insurance affiliates provide insurance to protect residential mortgage lenders from severe financial loss caused by the non-payment of loans and issue credit life insurance designed to pay the balance due on a loan if the borrower dies before the loan is repaid. As part of their overall risk management process, insurance affiliates cede to third parties a portion of their risk associated with these guarantees. In doing so, they are not relieved of their primary obligation to policyholders.

NOTE 20

ALL OTHER LIABILITIES

This caption includes noncurrent compensation and benefit accruals at year-end 2003 and 2002 of $10,380 million and $8,826 million, respectively. Also included are amounts for deferred income, derivative instruments, interest on tax liabilities, product warranties and a variety of sundry items.

We are involved in numerous remediation actions to clean up hazardous wastes as required by federal and state laws. Liabilities for remediation costs at each site are based on our best estimate of undiscounted future costs, excluding possible insurance recoveries. When there appears to be a range of possible costs with equal likelihood, liabilities are based on the lower end of such range. Uncertainties about the status of laws, regulations, technology and information related to individual sites make it difficult to develop a meaningful estimate of the reasonably possible aggregate environmental remediation exposure. However, even in the unlikely event that remediation costs amounted to the high end of the range of costs for each site, the resulting additional liability would not be material to our financial position, results of operations or liquidity.

NOTE 21

DEFERRED INCOME TAXES

Aggregate deferred income tax amounts are summarized below.

December 31 (In millions)	2003	2002
ASSETS		
GE	$ 7,594	$ 6,817
GECS	9,948	7,584
	17,542	14,401
LIABILITIES		
GE	9,505	8,744
GECS	20,684	18,174
	30,189	26,918
NET DEFERRED INCOME TAX LIABILITY	$12,647	$12,517

Principal components of our net liability/(asset) representing deferred income tax balances are as follows:

December 31 (In millions)	2003	2002
GE		
Provisions for expenses [a]	$ (4,723)	$ (4,693)
Retiree insurance plans	(1,206)	(1,043)
Prepaid pension asset	5,963	5,464
Depreciation	1,714	1,536
Other—net	163	663
	1,911	1,927
GECS		
Financing leases	10,250	9,763
Operating leases	3,523	3,627
Deferred acquisition costs	1,501	1,494
Allowance for losses	(2,036)	(1,569)
Insurance reserves	(1,109)	(1,218)
Derivatives qualifying as hedges	(1,029)	(1,252)
AMT credit carryforward	(351)	(597)
Other—net	(13)	342
	10,736	10,590
NET DEFERRED INCOME TAX LIABILITY	$12,647	$12,517

[a] Represents the tax effects of temporary differences related to expense accruals for a wide variety of items, such as employee compensation and benefits, interest on tax liabilities, product warranties and other sundry items that are not currently deductible.

Later, when GE makes repairs and incurs warranty costs, it makes an entry like:

Estimated Warranty Liability	Y	
Assets Used and Liabilities Incurred		Y
To recognize cost of actual repairs and replacements.		

The repair, and therefore the second entry, often occurs in a year subsequent to the year of sale. The cost of providing the warranty services does not become a tax deduction until GE makes the repair. This creates temporary differences: GE subtracts an expense on the financial statements in one year but deducts it on the tax return in a later year. GE records the eventual benefit of deducting these accrued warranty costs on the tax return as a deferred tax asset. Following *SFAS No. 109*, GE estimates the future benefit as the U.S. statutory tax rate (35 percent in 2003) times the difference between Estimated Warranty Liability and its "tax basis" — the amount of Warranty Liability that would be measured using tax accounting. In this case, the tax basis equals zero because tax accounting never records a warranty obligation prior to incurring costs. GE therefore estimates the future tax benefit as 0.35 times the balance in the Estimated Warranty Liability, and records this future benefit as a deferred tax asset.

Similarly, GE accrues expenses for "Retiree insurance plans" and "GE pension" when employees provide labor services (see GE's Notes 5 and 6 and our comments thereon), but tax rules allow deductions only when GE pays out benefits or provides legally-required funding (see our comments *47* and *43*). The unfunded retiree insurance liability reported to shareholders has zero (or small) tax basis. The deferred tax asset for retiree insurance plans, approximately 35 percent times the unfunded liability, represents the future benefit GE will receive when it deducts the insurance payments on its tax return in years following 2003. From this, we can infer that GE carries a retiree insurance liability of approximately \$3,446 (=\$1,206 / .35) million at year-end 2003.

In contrast, GE's prepaid pension asset generates a deferred tax liability of \$5,963 million. This figure, 35 percent of the amount by which cumulative pension tax deductions have exceeded cumulative pension expenses reported to shareholders, indicates a gross cumulative difference of \$17,037 (= \$5,963 / .35) million. Compare this figure with the net prepaid pension asset GE reports in Note 6 near the call-out for our comment *50*. The balance in that schedule reconciles GE's cumulative pension plan funding, determined by allowable tax deductions, with various components of the cumulative pension expense reported to shareholders. See our comment *45* for further details of pension expense reported to shareholders.

GE uses *MACRS depreciation* (see the Glossary) for tax purposes, as U.S. tax law requires. This accelerated method uses reduced asset lives and declining-balance depreciation. GE also uses an accelerated method for shareholder reporting (see Note 1 at the callout for our comment *31*, as well as our comment *60*), but the reduced lives of MACRS make it the more accelerated of the two methods. Because GE depreciates assets faster for tax purposes than for shareholder reporting, the tax basis of GE's property, plant and equipment is smaller than its depreciated cost on the balance sheet. The deferred tax liability, measured as the difference between the tax basis and book value of these assets, multiplied by the statutory tax rate of 35 percent, represents the future tax cost GE will incur when its depreciation expense reported to shareholders exceeds its depreciation tax deduction. Using the method applied above, we can compute that the book value of GE's depreciable property, plant and equipment exceeds the tax basis by \$4,897 (= \$1,714 / .35) million. Using information from GE's Note 15, we compute the assets' tax basis as \$9,669 (= \$14,566 – \$4,897).

Notice that deferred tax "assets" and "liabilities" measure benefits GE will receive or costs GE will incur at some unspecified future time, which may be indefinitely far off. Nevertheless, GAAP require reporting *undiscounted* estimated amounts among GE's resources and obligations. We believe that deferred taxes do not fit the usual definitions of *asset* and *liability* (see the Glossary) and GAAP should not report them in this way, but those who set GAAP disagree.

⑥⑤ See the Glossary at *minority interest* and our comments *7* and *15*. Note 22 reveals that part of the minority interest in GECS's affiliates consists of *preferred shares* (see the Glossary), although the parent company, GECS, reports no preferred stock on its balance sheet on page 73.

NOTE 22

GECS MINORITY INTEREST IN EQUITY OF CONSOLIDATED AFFILIATES

 Minority interest in equity of consolidated GECS affiliates includes preferred stock issued by GE Capital and by affiliates of GE Capital. The preferred stock primarily pays cumulative dividends at variable rates. Value of the preferred shares is summarized below.

December 31 (In millions)	2003	2002
GE Capital	**$2,600**	$2,600
GE Capital affiliates	**1,841**	1,588

Dividend rates in local currency on the preferred stock ranged from 0.91% to 5.65% during 2003 and from 1.44% to 6.20% during 2002.

NOTE 23

RESTRICTED NET ASSETS OF GECS AFFILIATES

Certain GECS consolidated affiliates are restricted from remitting funds to GECS in the form of dividends or loans by a variety of regulations, the purpose of which is to protect affected insurance policyholders, depositors or investors. At December 31, 2003 and 2002, net assets of regulated GECS affiliates amounted to $46.7 billion and $43.7 billion, respectively, of which $37.0 billion and $37.8 billion, respectively, was restricted.

At December 31, 2003 and 2002, the aggregate statutory capital and surplus of the insurance businesses totaled $15.9 billion and $17.9 billion, respectively. Accounting practices prescribed by statutory authorities are used in preparing statutory statements.

NOTE 24

SHAREOWNERS' EQUITY

(In millions)	2003	2002	2001
COMMON STOCK ISSUED	$ **669**	$ 669	$ 669
ACCUMULATED NONOWNER CHANGES OTHER THAN EARNINGS			
Balance at January 1	**$ (3,177)**	$ (4,323)	$ (2,500)
Cumulative effect of adopting SFAS 133—net of deferred taxes of $(513)	**—**	—	(827)
Investment securities—net of deferred taxes of $505, $805 and $111 [a]	**799**	1,555	203
Currency translation adjustments—net of deferred taxes of $(1,447), $20 and $48	**5,119**	1,000	(562)
Derivatives qualifying as hedges—net of deferred taxes of $(448), $(822) and $(505)	**(803)**	(2,070)	(690)
Reclassification adjustments— Investment securities—net of deferred taxes of $(135), $(135) and $(274)	**(250)**	(252)	(509)
Currency translation adjustments	**4**	—	—
Derivatives qualifying as hedges—net of deferred taxes of $643, $207 and $397	**1,123**	913	562
Balance at December 31	**$ 2,815**	$ (3,177)	$ (4,323)
OTHER CAPITAL			
Balance at January 1	**$17,288**	$16,693	$15,195
Gains on treasury stock dispositions [b]	**209**	595	1,498
Balance at December 31	**$17,497**	$17,288	$16,693
RETAINED EARNINGS			
Balance at January 1	**$75,553**	$68,701	$61,572
Net earnings	**15,002**	14,118	13,684
Dividends [b]	**(7,759)**	(7,266)	(6,555)
Balance at December 31	**$82,796**	$75,553	$68,701
COMMON STOCK HELD IN TREASURY			
Balance at January 1	**$26,627**	$26,916	$24,444
Purchases [b]	**1,177**	2,851	4,708
Dispositions [b]	**(3,207)**	(3,140)	(2,236)
Balance at December 31	**$24,597**	$26,627	$26,916

[a] This category includes $(161) million and $(75) million, net of deferred taxes of $(85) million and $(42) million, in 2003 and 2002, respectively, for minimum pension liabilities on certain pension plans other than the principal pension plans.

[b] Total dividends and other transactions with shareowners reduced equity by $5,520 million, $6,382 million and $7,529 million in 2003, 2002 and 2001, respectively.

In December 2001, our Board of Directors increased the authorization to repurchase GE common stock to $30 billion. In 2003 we repurchased 12 million shares for a total of $0.3 billion. Through year-end 2003, 1,103 million shares having an aggregate cost of approximately $23.0 billion had been repurchased under this program and placed in treasury.

Common shares issued and outstanding are summarized in the following table.

SHARES OF GE COMMON STOCK

December 31 (In thousands)	2003	2002	2001
Issued	11,145,212	11,145,212	11,145,212
In treasury	(1,082,092)	(1,175,318)	(1,219,274)
Outstanding	10,063,120	9,969,894	9,925,938

GE has 50 million authorized shares of preferred stock ($1.00 par value), but has not issued any such shares as of December 31, 2003.

The effects of translating to U.S. dollars the financial statements of non-U.S. affiliates whose functional currency is the local currency are included in shareowners' equity. Asset and liability accounts are translated at year-end exchange rates, while revenues and expenses are translated at average rates for the period.

NOTE 25

OTHER STOCK-RELATED INFORMATION

We grant stock options, stock appreciation rights (SARs), restricted stock units (RSUs) and performance share units (PSUs) to employees under the 1990 Long-Term Incentive Plan as described in our current Proxy Statement. In addition, we grant options and RSUs in limited circumstances to consultants, advisors and independent contractors (primarily non-employee talent at NBC) under a plan approved by our Board of Directors in 1997 (the consultants' plan). There are outstanding grants under two separate shareowner approved option plans for non-employee directors; the last grant was made in 2002 and no further grants are expected to be made under these plans. With certain restrictions, requirements for stock option shares may be met from either unissued or treasury shares. RSUs give the recipients the right to receive shares of our stock upon the lapse of their related restrictions. Restrictions on RSUs lapse in various increments and at various dates after three years from grant to grantee retirement. Although the plan permits us to issue RSUs settleable in cash, we have only issued RSUs settleable in shares of our stock.

We measure the total cost of each stock option grant at the date of grant using a market-based option trading model. We recognize the cost of each stock option, SAR, RSU and PSU straight-line over its vesting period.

Stock options and stock-settled SARs expire 10 years from the date they are granted; options and SARs vest over service periods that range from one to five years.

All grants of GE options under all plans must be approved by the Management Development and Compensation Committee, which comprises entirely outside directors.

STOCK OPTION ACTIVITY

(Shares in thousands)	Shares subject to option	Average per share Exercise price	Average per share Market price
Balance at			
December 31, 2000	333,179	$21.03	$47.94
Options granted	60,946	41.15	41.15
Options exercised	(31,801)	10.04	43.95
Options terminated	(7,871)	39.02	—
Balance at			
December 31, 2001	354,453	25.08	40.08
Options granted	46,928	27.37	27.37
Options exercised	(29,146)	9.45	31.86
Options terminated	(10,177)	38.14	—
Balance at			
December 31, 2002	362,058	26.26	24.35
Options granted	8,261	31.19	31.19
Options exercised	(43,829)	9.45	27.59
Options terminated	(10,643)	38.98	—
Balance at			
December 31, 2003	315,847	$28.30	$30.98

STOCK COMPENSATION PLANS

December 31, 2003 (Shares in thousands)	Securities to be issued upon exercise	Weighted average exercise price	Securities available for future issuance
APPROVED BY SHAREOWNERS			
Options	314,579	$28.31	(a)
RSUs	28,074	(b)	(a)
PSUs	250	(b)	(a)
SARs (c)	(d)	(c)	(a)
NOT APPROVED BY SHAREOWNERS			
Options	1,268	24.37	(e)
RSUs	3,867	(b)	(e)
Total (f)	348,038	$28.30	130,622

(a) Under the 1990 Long-Term Incentive Plan, 0.95% of the company's issued common stock (including treasury shares) as of the first day of each calendar year during which the Plan is in effect becomes available for awards in that calendar year. Total shares available for future issuance under the 1990 Long-Term Incentive Plan amounted to 105.9 million shares.

(b) Not applicable.

(c) During 2003, approximately 3.8 million SARs were granted at a weighted average exercise price of $31.41.

(d) Determined at vesting based on the difference between the exercise price and market price.

(e) Total shares available for future issuance under the consultants' plan amount to 24.7 million shares.

(f) In connection with various acquisitions, there are an additional 1.9 million options outstanding, with a weighted average exercise price of $20.89.

66 APB *Opinion No. 12* requires the disclosure of all changes in owners' equity accounts.

67 This section recapitulates the information in the statement of changes in shareowners' equity at the bottom of page 70, with more detail. See also our comment *11*, GE's Note 1 near the call-out for our comment *33*, GE's Note 9 and our comment *54*.

68 A company may recognize neither gain nor loss on transactions in its own shares (called *treasury shares*). GE uses correct accounting, but the term "gain" may mislead. When GE reissues previously acquired treasury shares, the difference between the cost of those shares and their re-issue price appears, not on the income statement, but in the "Other capital" account. If GE acquires treasury shares for an outlay of $1,000 and then reissues them for $1,200, then the entries would be:

Common Stock Held in Treasury	1,000	
Cash		1,000
To record acquisition of treasury shares.		

Cash	1,200	
Common Stock Held in Treasury		1,000
Other Capital		200
To record reissue of treasury shares for an amount greater than outlay to acquire them.		

If the firm receives proceeds on reissue of $800, not $1,200, then in the second entry it debits $200 to the "Other capital" account instead of crediting the account.

69 *ARB No. 43* requires disclosure of the details of employee stock option plans and currently outstanding options. This table shows that the exercise prices of stock options GE granted in 2001 through 2003 equal the market prices on the grant dates. Under the *intrinsic value* method prescribed by *APB Opinion No. 25*, which GE used prior to 2002, these options have zero (= market price at grant date – exercise price) compensation cost. Since 2002, GE uses the *fair value* method recommended, but not required, by *SFAS No. 123*. GE has disclosed the fair value in its footnotes, as required, since 1995. The fair value disclosures appear in Note 1 (see our comment *38*), while the assumptions underlying their calculation appear later in Note 25. See our comment *71*.

70 At the end of 2003, the market priced GE common shares at $30.98 per share. The 214,285,000 options exercisable at the end of 2003 have an average exercise price of $24.63. If employees exercised all these options, the present owners' equity would be diluted approximately $1,361 million [= ($30.98 – $24.63) x 214,285,000] in comparison to GE's issuing the same number of new shares at the year-end market price. Alternatively, the proceeds from employees' exercising these options at year-end, $5,278 (= $24.63 x 214.285) million, could repurchase 170,363,000 (= $5,278 million / $30.98 per share) shares at the year-end market price. The net increase in outstanding GE shares, with no net cash inflow to GE, would be about 43,922,000 (= 214,285,000 – 170,363,000) shares, about 0.4 percent of the 10,063 million shares actually outstanding at year-end. Dilution calculations like these underlie the diluted earnings per share calculations in GE's Note 8.

71 *SFAS No. 123* requires firms to disclose the fair value of options granted to employees, along with the assumptions underlying the fair value. GE uses the Black-Scholes option pricing model, and in this table reports the values it has assumed for the model's parameters. Higher option values result from assuming longer times until exercise, higher volatility, lower dividend yield and higher interest rates. The 2003 grant-date option fair value, $9.44, equals 30.3 percent of the grant-date market price of a share, $31.19 (from the table near our callout *69*). This proportion exceeds the corresponding values computed for 2002 and 2001, 28.2 and 29.5 percent respectively, primarily because GE assumes higher expected volatility. Notice, from Note 1 near our callout *38*, that in 2003 GE deducts stock option compensation expense of $81 million, which exceeds the $77.984 (= $9.44 x 8.261) million fair value of the options GE granted in 2003. Following *SFAS No. 123*, GE computes the options' fair value at the grant date, and amortizes this value into compensation expense over the options' vesting period. Because GE elected to begin using the fair value method in 2002, the $81 million in 2003 compensation cost results from amortizing GE's 2002 and 2003 option grants. If we assume GE's options vest over five years, and GE granted its 2003 options in the middle of the year, we can estimate its 2003 compensation cost using values from values in Note 25 as follows. The options granted in 2002, from a fair value of $362.753 (= $7.73 x 46.928) million, generate annual amortization of $72.551 (= $362.753 / 5) million. The 2003 options, amortized over only half the year, generate 2003 amortization of $7.798 (= ($77.984 / 5) x 0.5) million. The sum of these two yields $80.349 million, roughly the amount GE deducted in 2003, per its Note 1 near our callout *38*.

Outstanding options and SARs expire on various dates through December 11, 2013.

The following table summarizes information about stock options outstanding at December 31, 2003.

STOCK OPTIONS OUTSTANDING

(Shares in thousands)	Outstanding			Exercisable	
Exercise price range	Shares	Average life (a)	Average exercise price	Shares	Average exercise price
$ 6.67–13.23	61,303	1.0	$ 9.05	61,303	$ 9.05
13.48–26.42	71,992	3.5	19.96	71,705	19.94
26.65–35.48	70,106	8.5	29.79	10,570	28.02
35.79–43.17	60,992	5.8	39.54	42,909	38.96
43.75–57.31	51,454	7.3	47.55	27,798	47.72
Total	315,847	5.2	$28.30	214,285	$24.63

At year-end 2002, options with an average exercise price of $18.75 were exercisable on 214 million shares; at year-end 2001, options with an average exercise price of $14.73 were exercisable on 209 million shares.

(a) Average contractual life remaining in years.

OPTION VALUE INFORMATION (a)

(In dollars)	2003	2002	2001
Fair value per option (b)	$9.44	$7.73	$12.15
Valuation assumptions			
Expected option term (years)	6.0	6.0	6.0
Expected volatility	34.7%	33.7%	30.5%
Expected dividend yield	2.5%	2.7%	1.6%
Risk-free interest rate	3.5%	3.5%	4.9%

(a) Weighted averages of option grants during each period.

(b) Estimated using Black-Scholes option pricing model.

NOTE 26

SUPPLEMENTAL CASH FLOWS INFORMATION

Changes in operating assets and liabilities are net of acquisitions and dispositions of principal businesses.

"Payments for principal businesses purchased" in the Statement of Cash Flows is net of cash acquired and includes debt assumed and immediately repaid in acquisitions.

"All other operating activities" in the Statement of Cash Flows consists primarily of adjustments to current and noncurrent accruals and deferrals of costs and expenses, adjustments for gains and losses on assets, increases and decreases in assets held for sale, and adjustments to assets.

Non-cash transactions include the following: in 2003, the acquisition of Osmonics, Inc. for GE common stock valued at $240 million; in 2002, the acquisition of Interlogix, Inc. for GE common stock valued at $395 million and the acquisition of Bravo for GE common stock and other investment securities valued at $335 million and $886 million, respectively; and in 2001, the acquisition of Imatron Inc. for GE common stock valued at $205 million.

NOTE 29

SECURITIZATION ENTITIES

We securitize financial assets in the ordinary course of business to improve shareowner returns. The securitization transactions we engage in are similar to those used by many financial institutions. Beyond improving returns, these securitization transactions serve as funding sources for a variety of diversified lending and securities transactions. Historically, we have used both supported and third-party entities to execute securitization transactions funded in the commercial paper and term bond markets.

The following table represents assets in securitization entities both consolidated and off-balance sheet.

December 31 (In millions)	2003	2002
Receivables secured by:		
Equipment	$15,616	$13,926
Commercial real estate	16,713	14,168
Other assets	9,114	12,000
Credit card receivables	8,581	11,292
GE trade receivables	3,249	2,841
Other trade receivables	—	693
Total securitized assets	$53,273	$54,920
On-balance sheet assets in securitization entities (a)	$26,463	$ —
Off-balance sheet (b)(c)		
Supported entities	5,759	42,222
Other	21,051	12,698
Total securitized assets	$53,273	$54,920

(a) Related credit and liquidity support amounted to $18.4 billion, net of $5.3 billion of participated liquidity and arrangements that defer liquidity beyond 2005. This amount includes credit support, in which we provide recourse for a maximum of $8.6 billion at December 31, 2003.

(b) Liabilities for recourse obligations related to off-balance sheet assets were $0.1 billion and $0.3 billion at December 31, 2003 and 2002, respectively.

(c) At December 31, 2003 and 2002, related credit and liquidity support amounted to $3.1 billion and $27.5 billion, respectively, net of participated liquidity and arrangements that defer liquidity beyond one year which amounted to $2.4 billion and $13.6 billion, respectively. These amounts include credit support of $5.5 billion and $17.2 billion at December 31, 2003 and 2002, respectively.

Securitized assets that are on-balance sheet were consolidated on July 1, 2003, upon adoption of FIN 46, *Consolidation of Variable Interest Entities.* Although we do not control these entities, consolidation was required because we provided a majority of the credit and liquidity support for their activities. A majority of these entities were established to issue asset-backed securities, using assets that were sold by us and by third parties. These entities differ from others included in our consolidated statements because the assets they hold are legally isolated and are unavailable to us under any circumstances. Use of the assets is restricted by terms of governing documents, and their liabilities are not our legal obligations. Repayment of their liabilities depends primarily on cash flows generated by their assets. Because we have ceased

transferring assets to these entities, balances will decrease as the assets repay. Given their unique nature the entities are classified in separate financial statement captions, "Consolidated, liquidating securitization entities."

We continue to engage in off-balance sheet securitization transactions with third-party entities and to use public market, term securitizations. Further information about these activities is provided on page 108.

On-balance sheet arrangements

The following tables summarize the revenues, expenses, assets, liabilities and cash flows associated with consolidated securitization entities.

(In millions)	2003
REVENUES (a)	
Interest on time sales and loans	$513
Financing leases	129
Other	53
Total	$695
EXPENSES (a)	
Interest	$393
Costs and expenses (b)	114
Total	$507

(a) Entities consolidated on July 1, 2003.

(b) Includes minority interest expense of $20 million.

December 31 (In millions)	2003
ASSETS	
Cash	$ 684
Debt securities	1,566
Financing receivables (a)(b)	21,877
Other	2,336
Total	$26,463
LIABILITIES	
Short-term borrowings (c)	$22,842
Long-term notes payable (d)	1,948
Other liabilities	517
Minority interest	414
Total	$25,721

(a) Included $0.9 billion of retained interests associated with securitized assets now consolidated.

(b) At July 1, 2003, the carrying amount of financing receivables was recorded net of a previously recorded recourse obligation of $0.1 billion.

(c) Primarily commercial paper with original maturities less than one year. Average interest rate of 1.1%, including the effect of interest rate swaps designated and effective as hedges.

(d) Weighted average rate of 2.0%; matures between 2005 and 2007.

⑫ Like many financial institutions, GECS obtains cash through *securitization* of pools of financial assets, often using *special purpose entities* that it creates to facilitate the transaction. Tension in GAAP over asset securitizations concerns whether the securitization constitutes a sale or collateralized borrowing. Prior to 1996, a firm wishing to securitize assets would determine whether its securitization transaction, in its entirety, satisfied criteria for a sale. If it did not, then the firm would account for the transaction as secured borrowing. In 1996, the FASB introduced the financial components approach in *SFAS No. 125*, under which a firm could sell parts of a pool of assets (for example, the principal repayments from a pool of mortgages), while retaining other portions, including the residual risks. *SFAS No. 140*, which superceded *SFAS No. 125* in 2001, continues the financial components approach.

Asset securitizations can occur without special purpose entities, but many involve these vehicles. Tension in GAAP over these entities concerns who controls and/or benefits from it, and therefore who should consolidate it. *FIN 46*, an FASB interpretation and clarification of existing GAAP, requires GE to consolidate some special purpose entities, termed *variable interest entities* (VIEs). Before 2003, GE treated these as separate third-party entities. From this table we learn that the newly-consolidated VIEs hold 49.7% (= $26,463 / $53,273) of GE's securitized assets. In the accompanying text, GE announces its intention to cease using these consolidated entities for future securitizations, although not to cease securitizations. Future securitizations may involve special purpose entities that GE creates, but GE will structure them so that they do not meet the *FIN 46* criteria for consolidation.

⑬ Here GE provides additional detail about its newly-consolidated entities. From these disclosures we observe that the VIEs had relatively high leverage. In this table, the ratio of total liabilities to total assets exceeds 97% (= $25,721 / $26,463). GE reports in the footnotes to this table that the assets include $900 million that GE retained – that is, assets that would not have belonged to the VIEs if they had remained third-party entities – and that GE supported the VIEs' liabilities with a $100 million "recourse obligation," or guarantee against losses. Removing these two items from the assets and liabilities, respectively, indicates that the VIEs' liabilities exceeded their assets (($25,721 – $900) / ($25,721 – $100) = 100.2%). Thus, the VIEs likely rely on GE's support for their continued existence. In its Note 1 near our callout *37*, GE reports that on consolidating these entities it recognized $372 million in cumulative after-tax losses.

⑭ GE provides information on its securitizations that remain off-balance sheet. In 2003, GE reported gains on sales of $1,394 million, offset by losses of $1,160 million in the fair value of interests it retained. GE's 2003 year-end on-balance sheet assets and liabilities associated with the off-balance sheet securitizations net to $2,738 million, approximately 10.2% (= $2,738 / ($5,759 + $21,051)) of the associated securitized assets, which GE reports on its page 107 near our callout *72*. GE does not disclose the liabilities of these entities, which it regards as separate.

⑮ Following *SFAS No. 140*, GE discloses the assumptions it used to determine the fair value of the receivables it securitized in 2003. Because GE securitizes several different types of assets, each with its own risks, the company reports assumptions for each type separately. In the right-hand column of the same page, GE reports the sensitivity of its valuation of retained interests to similar assumptions. Because GE discloses (on its page 108 near our callout *74*) only the aggregate value of the retained interests, and not the value disaggregated by type, these disaggregated disclosures of sensitivities have limited value to the reader.

The portfolio of financing receivables consists of loans and financing lease receivables secured by equipment, commercial real estate and other assets; credit card receivables; and trade receivables. Examples of these assets include loans and leases on manufacturing and transportation equipment, loans on commercial property, commercial loans, and balances of high credit quality accounts from sales of a broad range of products and services to a diversified customer base. Under terms of credit and liquidity support agreements with these entities, when predefined triggers are met related to asset credit quality or a put is exercised by beneficial interest holders, we may be required to repurchase financing receivables. Upon such repurchases, the underlying receivable is classified as "Financing receivables" (disclosed in note 12).

"Financing receivables" includes $3,827 million of direct financing leases, an analysis of which follows.

December 31 (In millions)	2003
DIRECT FINANCING LEASES	
Total minimum lease payments receivable	$4,192
Estimated unguaranteed residual value of leased assets	14
Less deferred income	(379)
Investment in financing leases	$3,827

A schedule of changes in the financing receivables balance since we adopted FIN 46 follows.

(In millions)	2003
Balance at July 1	$31,395
Net collections	(9,150)
Net write-offs	(42)
Credit and liquidity support repurchases	(54)
All other	(272)
Balance at December 31	$21,877

Although we expect actual maturities to differ from contractual maturities, the following table summarizes the contractual maturities of financing receivables in our consolidated securitization entities.

CONTRACTUAL MATURITIES

(In millions)	Total time sales and loans	Net rentals receivable
Due in		
2004	$ 4,810	$1,329
2005	1,317	1,001
2006	1,325	636
2007	1,104	330
2008	965	130
2009 and later	8,529	766
Total	$18,050	$4,192

(In millions)	2003
CASH FLOWS—INVESTING ACTIVITIES [a]	
Net collections	$ 9,150
Other	225
Total	$ 9,375
CASH FLOWS—FINANCING ACTIVITIES [a]	
Newly issued debt	$ 157,593
Repayments and other reductions	(167,354)
Total	$ (9,761)

[a] Entities consolidated on July 1, 2003.

Derivatives included in consolidated securitization entities consist principally of pay fixed, receive variable interest rate swaps. These swaps are designated, and effective, as hedges of fixed rate assets (fair value hedges) or variable rate liabilities (cash flow hedges). Risk management objectives are consistent with those described in note 28. Ineffectiveness recognized on fair value hedges was zero; ineffectiveness recognized on cash flow hedges was insignificant. No amounts were excluded from the measure of ineffectiveness of either fair value or cash flow hedges.

Off-balance sheet arrangements

As discussed on page 107, assets in off-balance sheet securitization entities amounted to $26.8 billion and $54.9 billion at December 31, 2003 and 2002, respectively.

Additional information about securitization transactions follows.

(In millions)	2003	2002	2001
Gross gains	$ 1,394	$ 1,796	$2,193
Reduction of retained interest in revolving facilities, before replenishment	(1,160)	(1,029)	(866)
Net	$ 234	$ 767	$1,327

Amounts recognized in our financial statements related to sales to off-balance sheet securitization entities are as follows:

December 31 (In millions)	2003	2002
Retained interests	$2,663	$3,283
Servicing assets [a]	150	340
Recourse liability	(75)	(261)
Total	$2,738	$3,362

[a] Included mortgage servicing rights related to an amortizing pool of mortgages associated with a business exited in 2000. As of December 31, 2003, the net carrying value of remaining mortgage servicing rights relating to these former operations was $115 million.

- RETAINED INTERESTS. When we securitize receivables, we determine fair value based on discounted cash flow models that incorporate, among other things, assumptions including loan pool credit losses, prepayment speeds and discount rates. These assumptions are based on our experience, market trends and anticipated performance related to the particular assets securitized. Subsequent to recording retained interests, we review recorded values quarterly in the same manner and using current assumptions. We recognize impairments when carrying amounts exceed current fair values.

- SERVICING ASSETS. Following a securitization transaction, we retain responsibility for servicing the receivables, and are therefore entitled to an ongoing fee based on the outstanding principal balances of the receivables. Servicing assets are primarily associated with residential mortgage loans. Their value is subject to credit, prepayment and interest rate risk.

- RECOURSE LIABILITY. Certain transactions require credit support agreements. As a result, we provide for expected credit losses under these agreements and such amounts approximate fair value.

The following table summarizes data related to securitization sales that we completed during 2003.

(In millions)	Equipment	Commercial real estate	Other assets	Credit card receivables
Cash proceeds from securitization	$5,416	$3,082	$ 2,009	N/A
Proceeds from collections reinvested in new receivables	N/A	N/A	$14,047	$11,453
Weighted average lives (in months)	29	72	106	7
ASSUMPTIONS AS OF SALE DATE [a]				
Discount rate	6.6%	11.5%	6.4%	11.2%
Prepayment rate	10.1%	10.8%	4.6%	15.0%
Estimate of credit losses	1.6%	1.6%	0.2%	10.8%

[a] Based on weighted averages.

Key assumptions used in measuring the fair value of retained interests in securitizations and the sensitivity of the current fair value of residual cash flows to changes in those assumptions are noted in the following table. These assumptions may differ from those in the previous table as these relate to all outstanding retained interests as of December 31, 2003.

(In millions)	Equipment	Commercial real estate	Other assets	Credit card receivables
DISCOUNT RATE [a]	6.5%	10.7%	7.7%	10.9%
Effect of:				
10% Adverse change	$(10)	$ (14)	$(30)	$ (8)
20% Adverse change	(20)	(27)	(57)	(25)
PREPAYMENT RATE [a]	11.0%	4.1%	1.0%	15.4%
Effect of:				
10% Adverse change	$ (5)	$ (1)	$ (7)	$ (33)
20% Adverse change	(11)	(3)	(14)	(62)
ESTIMATE OF CREDIT LOSSES [a]	2.0%	1.9%	0.1%	9.9%
Effect of:				
10% Adverse change	$ (2)	$ (8)	$ (2)	$ (46)
20% Adverse change	(3)	(16)	(4)	(91)
Remaining weighted average lives (in months)	43	112	64	7
Net credit losses	$ 5	$ —	$ 14	$443
Delinquencies	52	52	4	139

[a] Based on weighted averages.

GUARANTEE AND REIMBURSEMENT CONTRACTS. We provide protection to certain counterparties of interest rate swaps entered into by securitization-related entities related to changes in the relationship between commercial paper interest rates and the timing and amount of the payment streams. These arrangements provide protection for the life of the assets held by the SPE but generally amortize in proportion to the decline in underlying asset principal balances. The notional amount of such support is $0.3 billion; fair value of the related assets was $1 million at year-end 2003.

Corporate Scandals: The Accounting Underpinnings

Kathleen Fitzgerald
Roman L. Weil
Graduate School of Business // University of Chicago

Corporate Accounting Scandals Rock Public Confidence
SEC Charges Former Tyco Officers With Fraud
WorldCom Controller Pleads Guilty
Myers Admits to Falsifying Numbers, Says He Acted at His Superiors' Behest
Fraud Suit Names KPMG And Partners
How Executives Prospered as Global Crossing Collapsed
Fun-House Accounting: The Distorted Numbers at Enron
'You Wuz Robbed!'

Hardly a week goes by without the press commenting on the state of financial reporting. Accounting scandals have captured the attention of government enforcement agencies (the Securities and Exchange Commission), standard setters (the Financial Accounting Standards Board and the International Accounting Standards Board), investment banking companies, venture capital companies, corporate boards, and family members concerned with their retirement funds and investment activities. The accounting issues discussed in the financial press can confuse the accounting novice. The details can overwhelm even accounting professionals.

Fraudulent accounting practices impose real costs on individuals and the economy as a whole. Companies that report that they are restating their financial statements in order to correct errors or irregularities in previously issued financial statements often experience a significant drop in their market capitalization within moments of such a disclosure. The United States Government Accountability Office (formerly the U.S. General Accounting Office) reported in October of 2002 that of the 689 cases it analyzed from January 1, 1997, to March 26, 2002, the stock price of a company making an initial restatement announcement fell by almost 10 percent, on average, from the trading day before to the day after the announcement (the immediate impact). Unadjusted losses in the market capitalization of companies issuing initial restatement announcements totaled over $100 billion, ranging from about $4.6 billion in 1997 to about $28.7 billion in 2000. The report further documents that losses

over 60 trading days before and after the restatement announcements appear to have had an even greater negative impact on stock prices.[1] For example, Cendant Corporation lost $14.7 billion or 47 percent of its market cap-
italization. After their respective restatements, Microstrategy lost $11 billion, Waste Management lost $4.76
billion, and Sunbeam lost $3.64 billion. Investors bear these losses and the economy as a whole suffers as these
revelations undermine investor confidence.

This chapter explains the earnings management fundamentals behind the current scandals. Earnings management occurs when managers use judgment in financial reporting and in structuring transactions to alter
financial reports to either mislead some stakeholders about the underlying economic performance of the company or to influence contractual outcomes that depend on reported accounting numbers.[2]

We discuss earnings management that results in fraudulently reported earnings by management, and discuss
earnings management that results in *low quality*, but not technically fraudulent, earnings. We refer to *fraudulent*
financial reporting as "intentional or reckless conduct, whether [by] act or omission, that results in materially
misleading financial statements."[3] Fraudulent financial reporting refers to using accounting not allowed by
Generally Accepted Accounting Principles (GAAP). *Low quality earnings* do not reflect future earnings potential; which some people call non-sustainable earnings. When we use the term *low-quality reporting*, we mean
using rules within GAAP.

The discussion proceeds as follows:

- We describe the current financial reporting environment, which includes the incentives that management
  has to engage in deceitful or misleading practices.
- We explain the main areas where management can focus efforts to achieve its desired results and the
  existing regulatory enforcement to restrain management in these areas. You will realize that some of
  these regulatory controls do not work well because of the subjectivity in management's financial reporting decisions.
- We analyze the specific methods management uses to manipulate financial reports in order to deceive the
  public, illustrating these with recent accounting scandals.
- Finally, we discuss the auditor responsibilities, analyses used to detect fraud, and recent reforms to corporate America's financial reporting practices.

CURRENT FINANCIAL REPORTING ENVIRONMENT

Accounting scandals have become a regular part of the business landscape and we expect them to continue.
Accounting fraud is not new, but only recently have billions of dollars of market value disappeared as investi-
gators have uncovered corporate malfeasance. Further, in these instances, management, board members, and
accountants spend many more millions of dollars to defend and settle shareholder lawsuits connected with mis-
representations. Some executives even serve time in prison for their activities and many more have their professional lives ruined.

Recent History

Although many of the publicized scandals became public only recently, as early as September 1998, Chairman
Arthur Levitt of the Securities Exchange Commission signaled his concerns and suspicions in his speech, "The
Numbers Game".[4] By that time, evidence of erosion in the quality of financial reporting had begun to appear.
In hindsight, we know that the SEC was aware of fraud by Waste Management and Sunbeam, but had not com-
pleted its cases against these companies. In this speech, Mr. Levitt called for an end to the practice of earnings

---

[1]United States General Accounting Office Report to the Chairman, Committee on Banking Housing, and Urban Affairs, U.S. Senate.
"Financial Statement Restatements: Trends, Market Impacts, Regulatory Responses, and Remaining Challenges." October 2002.
[2]Healy, P.M. and J.M.Wahlen. 1999. "A Review of the Earnings Management Literature and its Implications for Standard Setting." Accounting
Horizons (December): 365–383.
[3]Report of the National Commission on Fraudulent Financial Reporting, October 1987.
[4]http://www.sec.gov/news/speech/speecharchive/1998/spch220.txt

management and a return to the practice of providing transparent and comparable financial statements. In his speech, he discussed five common accounting practices that companies had been misusing. They were:

1. **Big Bath Charges**

   See the Glossary. This term dates back at least to the 1930's, when Benjamin Graham used it in his classic book, *Security Analysis*. Companies that take a big bath overstate current expenses (e.g., restructuring charges), by recording expenses early to make the books look unfavorable now, resulting in better future earnings reports.[5] Management hopes that the market will not incrementally penalize the company's valuation for the extra bad news. Then later, management can artificially boost income in hopes that the market will incrementally reward the extra income.

2. **Creative Acquisition Accounting**

   Mr. Levitt pointed out that one company purchasing another can create an effect similar to the *big bath* by incorrectly overestimating the part of the acquisition cost it classifies as *in-process research and development*. This is the portion of the purchase price allocated to the cost of existing R&D efforts not yet found to be worthless or valuable. GAAP require companies to write off to expense any amounts so classified immediately after an acquisition. Similar to the big bath charges, described above, creative acquisition accounting makes future earnings artificially higher and enables the write off to appear separately from ordinary income items, artificially boosting the apparent earnings quality.

3. **Miscellaneous Cookie-Jar Reserves**

   Mr. Levitt noted that companies overestimate liabilities for warranties, loan losses or sales returns, and overestimate allowances for accounts receivable. By doing so, management can inflate expenses in good times and reduce them during bad times. This has the effect of smoothing earnings, and gives management the power to ensure it achieves its accounting objectives. This is sometimes referred to as "making its numbers," another way of saying that management reports numbers it believes the marketplace expects to see.[6]

   Management's Response Invokes Conservatism. Management sometimes excuses all the first three accounting actions as being *conservative*, which is generally thought to be a good thing in accounting. Conservatism is, in fact, an underlying accounting principle.[7] It is often a fuzzy distinction when an accounting practice is fraudulent, outside GAAP, or merely low quality reporting but within GAAP guidelines. Consider, for example, Waste Management's fraudulent extension of the depreciable life of its garbage trucks beyond reason. Management might argue that depreciation is part of GAAP and that its use of long lives for garbage trucks was not fraudulent, but merely aggressively within GAAP. Those executives facing criminal charges for fraudulent financial reporting will care about the distinction and which side of the line between outside GAAP [fraud] and inside GAAP [low-quality reporting] the practice falls.

---

[5]We shall repeat this thought again, as the reader of financial statements should never forget: Over long-enough time spans, income is cash flow in less cash flow out, other than transactions with owners. So, as long as cash flow does not change, income over the time span will be a constant, with manipulations affecting the timing of reporting to the periods within the span. Hence, recording excess expense today, wrongly reducing income, necessarily means reporting higher income later.

[6]See the preceding footnote. Management, by making expense artificially high (or low) today can, at its discretion, make future income appear low (or high).

[7]No authoritative definition of conservatism exists. In its most extreme form, conservatism is interpreted as "anticipate no gains, but anticipate all losses". FASB Concepts Statement 2 (SFAC 2), *Qualitative Characteristics of Accounting Information*, rejects that form of conservatism: "Conservatism in financial reporting should no longer connote deliberate, consistent understatement of net assets and profits." SFAC 2 reads, "Conservatism is a prudent reaction to uncertainty to try to ensure that uncertainties and risks inherent in business situations are adequately considered. Thus, if two estimates of amounts to be received or paid in the future are about equally likely, conservatism dictates using the less optimistic estimate; however, if two amounts are not equally likely, conservatism does not necessarily dictate using the more pessimistic amount rather than the more likely one. Conservatism no longer requires deferring recognition of income beyond the time that adequate evidence of its existence becomes available or justifies recognizing losses before there is adequate evidence that they have been incurred." The pre-SFAC 2 interpretation of conservatism is admonished by the International Accounting Standards Committee (IASC) in International Accounting Standard No. 1, Disclosure of Accounting Policies: "Uncertainties inevitably surround many transactions. This should be recognized by exercising prudence in preparing financial statements. Prudence does not, however, justify the creation of secret or hidden reserves."

We like to remind our students that *conservative* means *biased*, biased in the particular direction of reporting lower cumulative income, lower assets totals, and lower retained earnings, but nevertheless biased. A conservative estimate is purposefully inaccurate—off the mark. Often, circumstances suggest making a conservative estimate, but in financial reporting it can lead to fraud.

4. **Materiality Thresholds**

   Mr. Levitt reported that some companies have intentionally recorded errors within a limited range defined by materiality considerations. GAAP define materiality in terms of what influences or makes a difference to a decision-maker. The FASB takes the position that "no general standards of materiality could be formulated to take into account all the considerations that enter into an experienced human judgment," but that the Board may give quantitative materiality criteria in specific standards, as appropriate.[8] The typical accounting standard specifies the materiality threshold and allows that, "The provisions of this Statement need not be applied to immaterial items." The manipulating manager intentionally commits an accounting error, but keeps the amount within traditional materiality ranges.[9] Although these errors violate GAAP, management argues that the amount is immaterial, so it doesn't matter. Some auditors acquiesced in this manipulation, until the SEC expressly prohibited it.

5. **Revenue Recognition**

   A company might recognize revenue before it completes the sale or before it delivers the product to the customer or when the customer still has the option to cancel the sale. GAAP require that the seller wait to recognize revenue until it has delivered the goods to the customer and the customer has no right of return or if there is right of return, the seller can estimate the amounts of expected returns with reasonable precision.

In 1998, Chairman Levitt seemed more concerned with low quality earnings than with actual fraud; he indicated that he believed management used the above tools to manipulate the accounting numbers so that the share prices would remain high or not decline as much as they otherwise would. As time passed, earnings management turned into fraud for many companies. (The law does not draw a clear line between the two. The distinction often involves the intent of the wrong-doer, which is more difficult to prove than that the wrong, itself, occurred.) We will now discuss how management used these tools and others to deceive internal and external auditors, directors, regulators, investors, analysts, creditors, suppliers, and employees.

Who is Watching the Shop?

Who bears the blame when companies commit accounting fraud? Why do companies have so much opportunity to manage earnings or commit fraud? Doesn't someone have responsibility for monitoring management and making sure that it fairly presents the financial statements? What role do the internal auditors play? External auditors? Audit committees? Boards of directors? Analysts? Regulators? If some of these participants had been alert and knew what to look for, they would likely have identified some fraud earlier. We will identify several causes of the collective failures to spot fraud[10]:

---

[8]*FASB Concepts Statement No. 2*, Qualitative Characteristics of Accounting Information, paragraph 131. Concepts Statement No. 2 states that the omission or misstatement of an item in a financial report is material if, in the surrounding circumstances, a reasonable person, relying on the report, would probably have changed a judgment had the company included or corrected the item.

[9]Why would management have an incentive to do this? Imagine, as was true for many years, that auditors considered an accounting adjustment immaterial if its effect on income was less than 10 percent of reported income. Imagine the CFO learns that reported earnings per share will be only $1.90, but that analysts are expecting $2.00, and that to report anything less will cause the stock price to drop. The CFO fudges income by $.15 per share, raising it to $2.05. The auditor excuses the fudge on the grounds that it is immaterial. The SEC has since clarified its meaning of materiality to stop this practice. SAB 99 says that exclusive reliance on quantitative benchmarks to assess materiality in preparing financial statements is inappropriate; misstatements are not immaterial simply because they fall beneath a numerical threshold. The SEC says its interpretation merely clarifies long-standing law, but some critics, say the SEC made new law when it defined materiality in this way. We do not think the SEC made new law with its clarifications.

[10]Congress has addressed several of these failures in recent legislation.

Conflicts of Interest

- Most internal audit departments report to management with the result that internal auditors have incentives to satisfy management goals in order to keep their positions, bonuses, and promotion prospects.
- External auditors receive payment from the companies they audit. In addition, they earn a significant percentage of their fees by procuring consulting engagements for the same company. They have an incentive to satisfy management.
- Analysts work for brokerages that seek banking business from the companies, business such as underwriting (that is, managing for a fee) stock or bond issuances. Analysts like to get timely information from these companies. Brokerages that have employed analysts who spoke badly about companies generally do not receive profitable banking business from those companies; nor do they receive timely information.

Ignorance

- Many individuals on the boards of directors, even on audit committees, simply don't have the accounting literacy needed to monitor management.[11] Audit committee members have not, historically, been independent or financially literate, so these committees failed to adequately represent shareholder interests. As a result of new legislation, they will likely be better educated and more vigilant in their approach.
- Relations among Management, the Board of directors, and Audit committees have previously reflected some cronyism. Many of the members have been mutual friends and served on each other's Boards or Committees. Strong friendships have reduced the incentive to investigate thoroughly the accounting practices of each other, which may violate standards of independence and prohibitions on conflict of interest, rather than reflect pure ignorance.

Not Enough Time

- Board members appear not to have taken enough time for appropriate understanding of financial reporting issues.
- Audit committee members have not properly understood their roles, failing to address both information they should understand and how well they should understand it.
- The SEC hasn't enough resources, including time, to review the accounting practices and financial statements of every company. For example, the SEC had not reviewed Enron Corporation for at least three years before it went bankrupt in 2001.

Even with many gatekeepers to the final financial reports, a management team, determined to deceive, could do so. Why would management want to deceive?

MANAGEMENT INCENTIVES TO REPORT FRAUDULENT EARNINGS

Management has many incentives and opportunities to distort their financial reports. These include:

Raising funds for investment through the issue of shares of stock

Suppose that management wants to invest in a new project, but the company does not have enough cash on hand to finance the project. Companies can raise cash by issuing shares of stock on the market. When all else is equal, the higher the company's reported earnings, the more likely that investors will pay more to purchase shares. Companies getting ready for an Initial Public Offering (IPO) want to show high and growing earnings to capture a higher price per share issued. A documentary that aired on U.S. public tele-

---

[11]These frauds occurred in spite of the existence of audit committees at the affected companies. According to a report issued by the National Commission on Fraudulent Financial Reporting (the "NCFFR Report") in 1987, 69 percent of the companies pursued by the SEC in enforcement cases for fraudulent reporting between 1981 and 1986 had audit committees. Some of our own research suggests that audit committee members do not, as individuals, understand the critical accounting judgments management must make to prepare the financial statements, so that they cannot recognize accounting manipulations. See R.L. Weil, "Audit Committee Financial Literacy: A Work Not Yet in Progress," working paper from the University of Chicago, Graduate School of Business, 2002, and "Audit Committees Can't Add," *Harvard Business Review*, May 2004, pp 21 ff.

vision (PBS) in January 2002 claimed that venture capital firms and investment banks manipulated many of the IPOs in the 1990's to pocket billions of dollars at the expense of smaller investors.[12] By disseminating false information about future expected earnings, companies created demand for their stocks at inflated prices. While PBS did not provide evidence to support the claims, more rigorous research done by John M. Friedlan (1994) uncovered evidence consistent with companies managing earnings upwards in the latest accounting period prior to an IPO.[13]

Raising funds with debt financing or obtaining more favorable terms on existing debt financing

If the company would rather borrow funds to finance a project, it must show the potential creditors (e.g., banks or other lenders) that the company can make its debt service payments. When a company borrows from the bank, the borrower usually must meet certain financial criteria before the lender will provide funds. These criteria often take the form of ratios, such as the debt-to-equity ratio or the interest-coverage ratio. Companies trying to refinance their debt have similar requirements. So, if a company needs to borrow, management has an incentive to dress up the financial reports. Improving the balance sheet reduces the debt-equity ratio, while boosting income makes interest coverage ratios look better. Most actions designed to benefit one of these, accomplish the other because of the articulation of the balance sheet and the income statement.

Dispelling negative market perceptions

If the company has been doing so poorly that interested parties worry about the viability of the company, management has an incentive to demonstrate the company's improving health. Interested parties include shareholders, employees, the Board of Directors, suppliers, other creditors, and potential lenders.

Demonstrating compliance with financing covenants

A company must meet certain financial requirements, typically stated in terms of financial statement ratios, before a bank will lend to it. The company must keep its financial health sufficiently robust that it meets these requirements, known as *debt covenants*, throughout the term of the loan. If the company violates the covenants, the bank usually has the right to call the loan. Given that covenant violations can impose heavy costs on the company, management has an incentive to avoid them. Research in this area has found evidence consistent with management using income-increasing techniques when the company's financials approach covenant violations.[14]

Meeting company goals and objectives

If the company has publicly stated goals or objectives, then management has an incentive to make sure the numbers reflect those projections. To miss a projection usually results in a negative reaction in the market. Research shows that missing earnings by a little can cause the stock price of a company to drop a lot. It has found that the ratios of market price to reported earnings (the price-earnings multiples) decline significantly when earnings decrease after a previous pattern of increases.[15] This suggests an additional target of showing increasing earnings in every period which might be accomplished by smoothing or managing the reported income stream.

Meeting bonus targets

Management has an incentive to manipulate earnings to maximize the compensation of its executives through salary and bonuses. One might expect that management will try to manipulate earnings upward if the company is close to reaching target earnings levels that will result in a bonus to executives. When, however, the company will miss its target in any event, management has incentive to make earnings lower

---

[12]http://www.pbs.org/wgbh/pages/frontline/shows/dotcon/
[13]Friedlan, John M., "Accounting Choices of Issuers of Initial Public Offerings", *Contemporary Accounting Research*, 17, 1-31.
[14]DeFond, M. and J. Jiambalvo, 1994, "Debt Covenant Violation and Manipulation of Accruals", *Journal of Accounting and Economics*, 17, 145–176.
[15]Finn, M. W., J.A. Elliott and M. E. Barth. "Market Rewards Associated with Patterns of Increasing Earnings". 1999. *Journal of Accounting Research*, Vol. 37 Issue 2; pp. 387–413.

than otherwise would occur, taking a big bath now, in order to make easier achieving higher earnings in a later period. Taking a big bath in one period makes it easier to reach earnings targets in the future. Research by Paul Healy and by the team of Gaver, Gaver and Austin find evidence consistent with this theory.[16]

Management has significant financial interest in the company

Besides incentives arising from bonus plans, managers often have significant financial interests in the company, such as providing personal guarantees for the debt of the company. Whenever managers have a personal financial stake dependent on the performance of the company, they have incentive to enhance the numbers.

Increasing dividend or partnership distributions

Generally, earnings levels constrain dividend policies and partnership distributions. If a company wants to increase dividends or distributions, then it must usually report increased earnings. Meeting the financial thresholds required for increasing dividends or partnership distributions can tempt management to increase earnings.

Executing mergers and acquisitions

Companies often finance mergers or acquisitions with their own shares. The market will likely value shares higher when the company reports higher earnings. If the market thinks that the company has done well, and will continue to do well, then the price of the shares will likely exceed levels that will occur if the company reports lower earnings. The higher the price of the shares, the fewer shares the company must give up to raise a given dollar sum. Therefore, manipulation of earnings, if it increases share price, lowers the cost of acquiring a company.

Different companies will have different reasons for wanting to improve the appearance of the financial reports. Other incentives exist: e.g., lowering the value of the company just prior to a management buyout, reducing taxes by shifting income to lower-tax rate years, and reducing (increasing) regulatory costs (benefits). The savvy financial statement analyst will recognize when the company has greater incentive to engage in manipulations or fraudulent activity (e.g., right before an IPO). Once one recognizes *when* management has incentive to engage in such activities, it is easier to think about how management might manipulate earnings. What line items in the statements might management manipulate? What GAAP and securities laws might management violate when it uses these tools?

SPECIFIC METHODS TO MANIPULATE FINANCIAL REPORTS

This section illustrates the methods that management has used to commit fraud and the tools management has used to distort the financial results that it reports.

Given that management can choose accounting practices from a set of policies required by GAAP, one should expect it to choose approaches to maximize the market value of the company. While management generally will try to achieve these goals through transparent financial reporting (that is, reporting with full disclosure of techniques and the related judgments), management has the ability to achieve these two goals either by committing fraud or by opportunistically choosing accounting policies. We consider instances in which management exceeded the acceptable limits for managing earnings, and instances in which management has approached the acceptable limit in choosing its accounting practices for the financial reports provided to the public.

Managers can manipulate four key items to achieve accounting goals. These four items are:

- Revenue
- Expenses and Assets

---

[16]Healy, P.M. "The Effect of Bonus Schemes on Accounting Decisions," *Journal of Accounting and Economics* (April 1985), pp. 85–107. Gaver, J.J., K.M. Gaver, and J. Austin. "Additional Evidence on Bonus Plans and Income Measurement". *Journal of Accounting & Economics*. (February 1995), pp. 3–28.

- Liabilities
- Disclosures

For each, we discuss the guidance governing its proper accounting , describe how management can break the rules to achieve its earnings goals, and provide examples of management manipulations.

SEC Cases of Accounting Restatements

The SEC provided the following summary of accounting restatements over a five-year period from July 1998 through June 2002.[17]

Improper Accounting Practice	Number of Enforcement Matters Involving Each Practice
Improper Revenue Recognition	126
Improper Expense Recognition	101
Improper Accounting in Connection with Business Combinations	23
Inadequate Disclosures in MD&A and Elsewhere	43
Failure to Disclose Related Party Transactions	23
Inappropriate Accounting for Non-monetary and Roundtrip Transactions	19
Improper Accounting for Foreign Payments in Violation of the FCPA	6
Improper Use of Off-balance Sheet Arrangements	3
Improper use of Non-GAAP Financial Measures	2

Revenue

Revenue is usually the largest single amount in a financial statement. The summary of SEC cases above indicates that revenue recognition is the single largest cause of financial statement restatements. Consequently, the issues involving revenue recognition are essential to understand.

A study commissioned by the Committee of Sponsoring Organizations (COSO) of the Treadway Commission analyzed instances of fraudulent financial reporting alleged by the SEC in the Accounting and Auditing Enforcement Releases (AAERs) issued during the 11-year period between January 1987 and December 1997. The researchers looked at 200 companies involved in fraudulent reporting and found that over half the frauds involved overstating revenues by recording revenues prematurely or fictitiously, which typically results in overstated receivables. The remainder of the frauds involved overstating assets by understating allowances for uncollectible receivables, overstating the value of inventory, property, plant and equipment and other tangible assets, and recording assets that did not exist.

Before December 1999, GAAP's only conceptual requirements for revenue recognition appeared in the Financial Accounting Standards Board's (FASB) Statements of Financial Accounting Concepts. A disparity arose between the general concepts and the detailed guidance provided for specific transactions in the authoritative literature because no conceptual standard for revenue recognition existed. The literature comprises pronouncements with differing degrees of authority such as Accounting Principles Board (APB) Opinions, FASB

---

[17]To address concerns raised by these restatements, and to restore public trust in the U.S. financial markets, Congress passed the Sarbanes-Oxley Act of 2002, which the President signed into law on July 30, 2002. Section 704 of the Sarbanes-Oxley Act directs the SEC to study enforcement actions over the five years preceding its enactment in order to identify areas of issuer financial reporting that are most susceptible to fraud or inappropriate earnings management. Over the study period, the Commission filed 515 enforcement actions for financial reporting and disclosure violations. The study, issued in January 2003, included 164 corporations and 705 individuals. SEC Report Pursuant to Section 704 of the Sarbanes-Oxley Act of 2002.

Statements, American Institute of Certified Public Accountants (AICPA) Audit and Accounting Guides, AICPA Statement of Positions (SOPs), FASB Interpretations, Emerging Issues Task Force (EITF) Issues, and Securities and Exchange Commission (SEC) Staff Accounting Bulletins. Standard setters developed this literature on an ad hoc basis in response to needs of specific transactions or industries for detailed implementation guidance. Each pronouncement focuses on a specific practice problem. The result is that as a group, the pronouncements do not provide consistent guidance.[18] In December 1999, the SEC issued SAB 101, *Revenue Recognition in Financial Statements* in an attempt to align conceptual guidance and practice. The FASB expects to issue, in 2005, pronouncements that will further define appropriate practices. Until then, GAAP require that revenue recognition principles follow, first, the guidance in SAB 101, and then the FASB Concept Statements.

FASB *Statement of Financial Accounting Concepts 5*: Recognition and Measurement in Financial Statements of Business Enterprises sets forth revenue recognition criteria and required disclosures, including timing of disclosure, for information incorporated into financial statements. It focuses on the statements of earnings and comprehensive income and addresses measurement issues related to recognition. It requires that management measure revenues by the exchange value of the assets or liabilities involved. It states that management should recognize the revenue only after the transaction has met both of the following criteria:

- Revenue is realized or realizable
  Revenue is considered *realized* only when the seller has exchanged goods or services, merchandise, or other assets for cash or claims to cash. Revenue is considered *realizable* only when the seller can readily convert related assets received or held (e.g., accounts receivable) to known amounts of cash or claims to cash.
- Revenue is earned
  The seller may recognize revenue only after it has delivered goods or produced goods or rendered services or performed other activities that constitute its ongoing major or central operations.

SEC Staff Accounting Bulletin: No. 101—Revenue Recognition in Financial Statements summarizes the staff's views in applying GAAP to financial reporting and, once issued, becomes part of GAAP. The staff provided guidance on revenue recognition because, in part, of the revenue recognition issues that registrants encounter. The staff said that revenue generally is realized or realizable and earned only when a transaction meets all of the following four criteria:

- Persuasive evidence of an arrangement with a buyer exists
- Delivery has occurred or services have been rendered to the buyer
- The seller's price to the buyer is fixed or determinable
- Collectibility is reasonably assured

These four criteria amplify the criteria for revenue recognition set forth in FASB *Statement of Financial Accounting Concepts No. 5*. The second, third, and fourth criteria resemble the two criteria—realized or realizable and earned—stated above. What's new? The SEC staff focuses on the existence of an arrangement with the buyer. The arrangement may take the form of a contract, or prior business dealings with a particular customer, or customary business practices by a company and its industry. The arrangement sets forth the responsibilities of the company and its customers with respect to the nature and delivery of goods or services, the risks assumed by the buyer and seller, the timing of cash payments and similar factors. Having an arrangement in place permits more informed observations and judgments as to the SEC staff's second, third, and fourth criteria.

Commonly Used Methods for Misrepresenting Revenues

Management misrepresents the actual revenues of the company for a given period with:

- Inflated revenues, including phantom sales and improper classification of revenues
- Mis-estimations of contra revenue accounts

---

[18]FASB Proposal for a New Agenda Project. Issues Related to the Recognition of Revenues and Liabilities.

- Reporting revenue gross as an agent rather than net as a principal
- Reporting revenue gross in advertising barter transactions rather than as net
- Shifting revenues across reporting periods through either channel stuffing or manipulating completion estimates in applying percentage of completion accounting

Overstating revenues increases Net Income. Management can overstate revenues in several ways. First, consider the fraud of complete fabrication—saying there are revenues when the company did not make the sale. Management can record false journal entries—either recording fictitious sales to existing customers or to fictitious customers. Recording a fictitious sale results in recording a fictitious debit, typically to Accounts Receivable. Auditors must check the amounts of Accounts Receivable, so these frauds should not escape notice for long. Moreover, creating revenue requires creating Cost of Goods [or Services] Sold and the recordkeeping manipulations to fudge inventories require steps auditors can detect.

Despite the difficulties in creating fictitious sales, some companies have been accused of committing this fraud. One example of allegations involves Cendant Corporation. Cendant Corporation resulted from a December 1997 merger between CUC International, Inc. and HFS Incorporated. The Securities and Exchange Commission alleged that CUC made top-side adjustments[19] beginning in the 1980's, which continued until its discovery and disclosure by Cendant in April 1998. The Commission filed a civil enforcement action for two top former officers of CUC alleging that they directed a massive financial fraud while selling on personal account. The SEC alleged that these two officers:

- earned millions of dollars by selling personal shares at inflated prices while they perpetrated the fraud, and
- reviewed and managed schedules listing fraudulent adjustments to be made to CUC's quarterly and annual financial statements.
- At the end of each of the company's first three fiscal quarters and fiscal year end, senior managers took the company's actual results for the quarter and compared them with the quarterly analyst expectations.
- The senior managers directed mid-level financial reporting managers at CUC corporate headquarters to add whatever amounts were needed in order to bring CUC's quarterly income up to analyst expectations.
- In conjunction with these income statement changes, the managers cosmetically altered certain CUC balance sheet items. For example, they increased the reported cash amount to one more consistent with the income statement line items.
- To conceal the scheme, at year-end they repeatedly used unsupported post-closing journal entries carrying effective dates spread retroactively over prior months.
- CUC made sure that each major expense category bore approximately the same percentage relation to revenues as in the quarter before.
- CUC senior management used the adjustments to artificially increase income and earnings, defrauding investors by creating the illusion of a company that had ever-improving earnings and making millions for themselves along the way. For the period 1995 to 1997, it inflated pre-tax operating income reported to the public by an aggregate amount of over $500 million.[20]

Over 40 years ago, management of Equity Funding engaged in overstating revenues by fabricating insurance policy sales. It evaded the auditors' detection by fabricating fictitious insurance policy files, quickly on demand, as the auditors asked for proof that a given policy existed. This was a billion dollar fraud with thousands of fictitious transactions that outside auditors should have caught. As the story goes, the company was having computer problems at the close of the financial year in 1964. The president instructed his employees to make up the bottom line to show about $10 million in profits and calculate the other figures consistent with that result. The transactions to generate that amount never materialized, but management kept the financial statements as

---

[19]*Top-side adjusting entries* refer to those not done in the ordinary course of end-of-period adjustments, but at the end of the process. The word *top* sometimes means that top management recorded the entry and sometimes means that the auditor prepared the entry on its top file, the file of final adjustments, not in detailed working papers. Not all top-side changes result from management entries, but the fraudulent ones typically do.

[20]Accounting and Auditing Enforcement Release ("A.A.E.R.") No. 1372 (February 28, 2001) and AAER 1272 (June 14, 2000).

they were. This gave management the idea to keep the stock price up by manufacturing false insurance policies. In time, they became greedier, and began selling these fake policies to other insurance agencies. In 1972, the head of data processing calculated that by the end of decade, at current rates of fabrication, Equity Funding would have insured the entire population of the world. Its assets would surpass the gross national product. The scheme fell apart only when an angry employee, forced to work overtime, reported it to the authorities.[21]

Because creating fictitious revenue requires creating the asset accounts (debits) to match the faked credits, most cases of overstated revenue do not result from management's creating the revenues with false customers or fake accounts receivable. A more sophisticated (and harder-to-detect) way to manipulate earnings shifts authentic revenues between time periods. Although the auditors may detect these schemes while performing their analytical and confirmation procedures, the manipulating management may be able to persuade its vendors and customers to go along with a scheme and provide misleading information to the auditors. These practices are known as *bill-and-hold sales*, and using *side letters*. We describe these practices and provide examples of their use and modifications.

Bill-and-Hold Sales

Legitimate bill-and-hold sales require that the buyer request the transaction be on a bill-and-hold basis, that the buyer must have a substantial business purpose for ordering the goods on a bill-and-hold basis; and that the risks of ownership must pass to the buyer.[22] Fraudulent management might get permission from the customer to ship, promising not to bill the customer until next period and giving the customer its usual grace period to pay, starting from that later date, next period.

Side Letters

A sales staff eager to boost their own sales commissions might send a letter, called a *side letter*, to the customer stating that the customer will accept the shipment and if asked, confirm that it ordered the goods, but that the seller will not send an invoice until later, and the customer need not pay until later or can return the goods for full credit. Even honest management has a hard time locating these letters issued by dishonest sales staff. Management must be alert for this practice and deal severely with employees it finds issuing them. Some in management have said they disapprove of side letters, but do not enforce the policy. A bill-and-hold sale may involve a side letter, but in typical usage, the term *side letter* is applied only when the seller has shipped the goods.

Use and Modifications of These Practices

Bill-and-Hold Sales

The SEC settled with management at ElectroCatheter for alleged fraudulent financial reporting involving bill-and-hold sales in the mid 1980's. Its management engaged in so many fake bill-and-hold sales, that by the end, it was marking goods in its warehouse that were allegedly sold to customers but were of a type of goods these customers never bought or would buy. For example, one customer, a hospital, purchased only catheters. To generate a given dollar volume selling low-priced catheters created work for the fraudsters, who had to physically tag the sold goods. So, to save time, management said that the customer had bought high-priced computers, which enabled it, in a given time interval, to generate fake sales in higher amounts than if it had generated fake sales of catheters.

Channel Stuffing

Channel stuffing, (a form of bill-and-hold sales), is a fraudulent activity that accelerates sales revenue into earlier periods. If the customer decides later to return the goods, this practice results in recording revenues that never occur. Channel stuffing artificially inflates sales and earnings figures.[23] Assume a company ordinarily waits to record revenue until it ships goods previously ordered by the customer. A company engaging in chan-

---

[21]"The Equity Funding Fraud", NetworkWorldFusion.com, by M.E. Kabay, January 21, 2002
[22]*In the Matter of Stewart Parness*, Exchange Act. Rel. No. 23507, A.A.E.R. No. 108 (August 5, 1986).
[23]Note that the company also inflates the balance sheet by increasing accounts receivable for the same amount.

nel stuffing will ship goods not yet ordered but record them as sales, as though a real customer had ordered them. The Sunbeam case illustrates an allegation of this practice:

> *"Two of the suits allege that the company failed to disclose an 'early buyout' program that allowed retailers to purchase grills in November and December, keep them in Sunbeam warehouses and not pay for them until June. The allegation is that the program, sometimes called channel-stuffing, masked declining grill sales."*

> —David Sedore, "Five more class actions target Sunbeam," *Palm Beach Daily Business Review*

In its May 2001 Sunbeam filing, the Securities and Exchange Commission states, "The undisclosed or inadequately disclosed acceleration of sales through 'channel-stuffing' materially distorted the Company's reported results of operations and contributed to the inaccurate picture of a successful turnaround." More specifically, the Commission alleged that beginning with the first quarter of 1997, Sunbeam achieved its sales goals, in large part, by offering its customers discounts and other incentives to place their purchase orders before the period when they would otherwise have done so. Since many customers who wished to take advantage of these inducements could not burden their warehouses with out-of-season merchandise, Sunbeam offered to hold product for a customer until the customer requested delivery. Sunbeam typically paid the costs of storage, shipment, and insurance on the product. Moreover, the customers often retained the right, through explicit agreement or established practice, to return unsold product to Sunbeam for full refund or credit. In the second quarter of 1997, Sunbeam recognized $14 million in sales revenue and over $6 million in income from bill-and-hold sales, with no disclosure of this practice in its quarterly filing on Form 10-Q.[24]

In its *A.A.E.R. No. 1467*, the SEC describes other forms of alleged revenue-enhancing fraud in a case involving McKesson HBOC, Inc.[25]

Holding Books Open After the Close of a Reporting Period

By holding the books open after the close of a reporting period, a company may inappropriately include revenues not realized and earned in the current period. The SEC prosecuted Sirena Apparel Group ("Sirena"), a women's swimwear manufacturer, located in Los Angeles County, for this. In its filing, the Commission alleged that the CEO and CFO instructed Sirena personnel to hold open the March 1999 fiscal quarter until Sirena had reached its sales target for that period. The perpetrators held the quarter open by periodically resetting the date on Sirena's computer clock to March 30 or March 31. The result was that they held the quarter ending March 1999 open until April 12, 1999. The filing alleged that the two executives ordered Sirena personnel to create false shipping records to conceal their scheme. The CEO settled the action against him by consenting to a permanent injunction, without admitting or denying the allegations in the complaint, and he agreed to pay a civil penalty in the amount of $30,000.[26]

Overestimating Revenues When Using the Percentage of Completion Method

Companies may recognize as revenue in a given period a percentage of the total contract price when they use the percentage-of-completion method of recognizing revenue. The company can base the percentage on the ratio of actual costs incurred during the period to total estimated costs for the entire product or project [see Glossary at *cost-to-cost*]. A company may use this method only when it can reliably estimate progress toward completion of a contract and the collection of cash is likely. Thus, management must be able to reliably estimate the total costs required to complete the contract for the contract to qualify for the percentage of completion practice. Management must be able to reliably estimate any additional contract revenue (above the original contract price) and costs to be incurred related to cost overruns and changes requested by the customer.

---

[24] A.A.E.R. No. 1393 (May 15, 2001)
[25] Report Pursuant to Section 704 of the Sarbanes-Oxley Act of 2002
[26] A.A.E.R No. 1325 (September 27, 2000)

For example, the company agrees to pay a builder a long-term contract with a total price of $100,000. The builder incurs contract costs of $20,000 in one period out of an estimated total cost of $80,000. The company should record 25 percent [= $20,000/$80,000] of the contract price, or $25,000 [= .25 × $100,000], as revenue in the current period.

If management would like to accelerate revenues, then it may either underestimate the total amount of costs it expects to incur for the project or overestimate the amount of revenues that it expects to receive. Suppose, in the example above, that the builder expects total costs to complete the project to be $80,000, but wants to increase revenues for the period when he incurred the costs of $20,000. By underestimating the expected total cost of the project, the builder can increase revenues. For example, say that the builder declares that the estimated total costs will be $62,500 rather than the $80,000 he expects. The company will recognize 32 percent [= $20,000/$62,500] of the contract price, or $32,000 [= .32 × $100,000] as revenue in the current period. Since expenses stay the same at $20,000, net earnings for this period are increased by $7,000 [= $32,000 − $25,000]. Alternatively, the builder could predict that the contract price would increase to $110,000 because of change orders increasing costs during the current period, which he thinks he is sure to collect. Now the ratio is $30,000/$110,000 or 27 percent, which means he will recognize revenues of $30,000 [= .27 × $110,000] and net earnings for this period increase by $5,000 [= $30,000 − $25,000].

Critics have alleged that Halliburton Corporation, one of the world's largest oil services, construction, and engineering firms, improperly applied the percentage of completion rules by overestimating the amount of total revenues (i.e., contract price) it expected to receive. Halliburton uses the percentage-of-completion method to account for long-term contracts. Starting in 1998, Halliburton changed its accounting methods to include a portion of costs generated by change orders in expected receipts, hence boosting the amount of revenue recognized for each increment of work done on the contract. The lawsuits against Halliburton claim that it should not have included these expected cost recoveries in expected receipts because management could not reliably estimate the probable amounts. Halliburton claims that not including these expected cost recoveries is misleading to financial statement users. Further, management at Halliburton did not include the total dollar amount of the cost recoveries; it included only the portion it expected to collect. Management estimated the portion of the costs it expected not to recover. Whatever the merits of the arguments about the legitimacy of Halliburton's change in accounting methods, we agree with those who found that the disclosures of the changes were not transparent.

Misclassifying Revenue Streams

The accounting practices for multiple-element, or bundled arrangements, provide opportunity for fraudulent manipulations. Consider a single sale combining the two elements of software and technical support service. SOP 97-2 allows a seller to recognize revenue on the software part of the sale combining software and service elements only if the customer can purchase the software separately from the services and only after the seller deducts revenue attributable to the service element from the total.[27]

MicroStrategy, a software company, began deriving its revenues in 1996 from product licenses, fees for maintenance, technical support, training, consulting, and development services. The SEC investigated MicroStrategy for improperly accounting for its multiple-element arrangements. The Commission alleged that MicroStrategy improperly separated product license sales from service elements and characterized the revenue in multiple-element transactions as product or software revenue, recognizing it at the time of the transaction. For example, in the fourth quarter of 1998, MicroStrategy negotiated a $4.5 million transaction with ShopKo Stores, Inc., to provide software licenses as well as consulting and development services and a warrant permitting ShopKo to purchase 50,000 shares of MicroStrategy common stock. Although the product and service development depended on each other, MicroStrategy accounted for the software product as though the sale did not depend on the service and warrant obligations. In addition, MicroStategy recognized the entire $4.5 million as software product license revenue, allocating no revenue to the extensive service obligations or to the warrant.[28]

---

[27] AICPA Statement of Position (SOP) 97-2, Software Revenue Recognition.
[28] A.A.E.R. No. 1350 (December 14, 2000)

Xerox Corporation ran into similar trouble with its accounting for lease arrangements, which typically involve a single quoted price for maintenance and supplies as well as use of a copying machine. On April 11, 2002, the SEC filed a civil fraud injunctive action against Xerox Corporation alleging that Xerox employed a variety of undisclosed accounting actions to meet or exceed Wall Street expectations and disguise its true operating performance.[29] The complaint alleged that several of the accounting actions related to Xerox's accounting for lease arrangements wrongly boosted income. Revenue from Xerox's customer leases typically has several components: equipment, servicing, supplies, and a finance charge implicit for spreading the payments over time. Under GAAP, Xerox should book the revenue from the amount allocated to the capital lease of the equipment at the beginning of the lease, but should spread the revenue for the other items over the life of the lease. According to the complaint, Xerox relied on accounting actions to justify shifting more of the receipts to the equipment, so that it could recognize a greater portion of that revenue immediately. The SEC alleged that Xerox wrongly accelerated recognition of equipment revenue by over $3 billion and increased its pre-tax earnings by approximately $1.5 billion over the four-year period from 1997 through 2000.[30]

Gross vs. Net Revenue Recorded in Transactions

When should companies recognize revenue at the gross invoice amount or the net amount retained? This issue arises for internet companies and other new businesses where some analysts believe they should base share price valuations on revenues per share, not earnings nor cash flow per share, because these latter two are negative for many new companies. For example, Hotwire collects $200 from a customer who rents a car online, keeps $15 and remits $185 to Avis. Similarly, Priceline collects $280 from a customer who purchases a discounted airline ticket to fly on Delta, keeps $15 and remits $265 to Delta. Should companies like Hotwire and Priceline recognize revenues based on the full price the customers pay for the products? Or, should they recognize only the portion they get to keep from these sales.[31] The accounting rules require that only if the company assumes the risks and rewards of owning the product can it report gross amounts as revenues. If it acts merely as agent or broker, it must report only the net collections as revenues.

This issue arises for start-up companies because investors have appeared to value these companies based on revenues, rather than earnings or cash flows. While reported net earnings do not depend on whether the company reports revenues net or gross, some financial advisors believe that the presentation of the financial statement affects the stock price. The result is that in order to increase revenues, companies try to qualify for gross reporting requirements. Priceline operates the ultimate in just-in-time inventory management by taking ownership of the ticket it sells for a fraction of a second. The company works out an agreement with the airline for specific flights and seats that it can sell at an agreed upon price. Only when the customer places an order does Priceline buy the ticket from the airline which Priceline then sells immediately to the customer who has been waiting on-line briefly for the transaction to complete. This arrangement qualifies the entire amount collected as revenue, not just Priceline's net revenue. It seems to us that it flaunts the ordinary rule that the seller must own the item it sells before it can report the gross, not the net, amount as revenue. The owner who reports the gross revenue ordinarily bears the risks and rewards of ownership. The Priceline model allows Priceline to avoid all the risk of ownership.

Round-tripping Transactions

A round-tripping transaction has the same effect as inflating revenue without changing net income. It is a transaction where one company sells goods or services to the buyer that the buyer doesn't need while making arrangements to purchase the same or equivalent assets back for the same cost. This transaction allows both companies to book revenue from the deal. Some Internet companies in the late 1990's and early 2000's used this revenue

---

[29]Securities and Exchange Commission v. Xerox Corporation, Civil Action No. 02-CV-2780 (DLC) (S.D.N.Y.) (April 11, 2002)
[30]A.A.E.R. No. 1542 (April 11, 2002)
[31]Priceline and Amazon report gross revenues as they actually take possession of the tickets and books, while Ebay reports net revenues, never actually taking possession of the goods sold. Priceline reported 1999 gross revenue of $482.4 million with net revenue of $72.8 million. If they reported only on net revenues, they would have had margins similar to Ebay's rather than Amazon's.

increasing practice. Some of these schemes became complex as several companies were involved in the round-tripping transactions in order to hide the bogus activities more easily. While this practice does not usually increase the net earnings amount, it does inflate revenues, which can lead to inflated stock prices if analysts use revenue-based pricing models to value share prices.

The SEC and Justice Department probed round-trip deals by America Online Inc. and two of its partners. AOL has said it will restate revenues of $190 million based on its round-trip deals and could restate an additional $400 million more that the SEC has called into question.[32] The SEC investigated round-trip transactions at Unify Corporation, a manufacturer and seller of database management software. In May 2002, the SEC filed a complaint against two former executives of Unify Corporation, alleging that, in several instances, the two executives engaged in round-tripping, by causing Unify to provide funds to its customers who, in turn, bought Unify products, with no reasonable expectation that the customers would repay the funds, other than through product purchases.[33] In some instances, Unify made an investment in other companies, which then used most or all of the invested funds to purchase Unify products. In others, Unify contracted for services from other companies, but these companies provided no services, and simply used funds from Unify to buy Unify product.[34]

Barter Transactions

Here's an old story.

> Husband: We just had a great day; I sold the dog for $10,000. Wife: Great; where's the money? Husband: I didn't get any money; I swapped the dog for two $5,000 cats.

If you get the point of that story—that barter transactions can have arbitrary dollar amounts attached to them—you understand the accounting problem. Barter transactions exist when two or more companies enter into a non-cash transaction to exchange goods or services with each other. They represent another method for inflating revenue without changing net income and were popular with Internet companies in the late 1990's and early 2000's. A typical transaction, often seen in the last decade, involves the swap of advertising among Internet companies: Company A sells Company B $10,000 of banner advertising [creating revenue for Company A] and in turn pay for it by purchasing two $5,000 links on Company B's web site. No cash changes hands. Some companies inflate revenue by recognizing equal revenue and expense amounts to account for these transactions. This does not affect earnings, but inflates revenues when companies overestimate the value of the goods or services provided and received. Analysts, who estimate share values based on revenue streams, rather than earnings, will over-value the company if the financial statements do not reflect the details of these transactions.

The SEC investigated Critical Path, Inc. for improperly recognizing revenue from barter transactions. The commission alleged that in order to meet consensus earnings estimates by analysts who followed the company, Critical Path's president engaged in, or oversaw, several fraudulent revenue transactions in the third quarter of 2000. The largest misstated transaction involved a barter transaction with a software company. Critical Path had made plans to purchase some software; then it increased the order by $3.6 million in return for the software vendor becoming a revenue-producing customer of Critical Path's. The SEC alleged that in violation of GAAP,[35] Critical Path did not appropriately establish the fair value of either the software it received or the software it sold to the other company. In the end, Critical Path permanently reversed the amount.[36]

---

[32]"Culture of Loopholes Bred Corporate Abuse; Tricks of the 1990's are Focus of Accounting Reform", by Carrie Johnson. *The Washington Post*. April 18, 2003.

[33]This transaction has the effect of causing the cash to make a round trip from Unify to the customers and back, while Unify gives the customer some product. Ordinarily, this would be an income-decreasing activity for a seller, because it has, effectively, given away some of its product. This product, however, is software and has no, or near-zero, incremental cost.

[34]Litigation Release No. 17522 (May 20, 2002)

[35]Accounting Practice Bulletin 29, Accounting for Non Monetary Transactions

[36]A.A.E.R. 1503 (February 5, 2002)

Expense, Asset, and Liability Recognition

The opportunities that management has to manipulate expense and asset recognition provide another tool for fraudulent reporting. The Financial Accounting Standards Board (FASB) *Statement of Financial Accounting Concepts No. 5* sets forth the requirements for expense and asset recognition.

Expense Recognition

In double-entry record keeping, the accounting model interlocks these two kinds of fraud—expenses that are too small require that net assets are too large (i.e., assets overstated or liabilities understated). Sometimes management commits fraud by purposefully overstating expenses (and liabilities) resulting in taking a *big bath*; see Glossary. Accounting income is cash-flow in less cash-flow out over long-enough time spans, other than transactions with owners. If a company knows it will report a poor financial result, sufficiently bad that the market will likely respond by punishing the company's share price, the company is inclined to make the bad result appear even worse than it is because the penalty in reduced value is likely to be less than proportionate to the artificially depressed income. In the future, the company's results will appear artificially better than actual to the extent that it can make the current results artificially worse than they actually are.

A company generally recognizes expenses when it consumes an asset's economic benefits in delivering or producing goods, rendering services, or other activities that constitute its ongoing operations. It recognizes losses when it judges that previously recognized assets have lost future benefits, losses sufficiently large to pass the test for impairments.[37] A business sometimes recognizes expenses in the period when it incurs costs or in a later period when it matches them to revenues recognized during the later period. The general distinctions for costs are:

- **Product costs:** Expenses, such as cost of goods sold, match with revenues. The company recognizes them when it recognizes the associated revenues.
- **Period costs:** The company recognizes many expenses, such as selling and administrative expenses, during the period when it spends cash or incurs liabilities.
- **Allocated costs:** The company allocates costs, such as plant assets and insurance, with systematic and rational procedures to the periods during which it expects the related assets to provide benefits. This allocation process is known as *amortization*, and is called *depreciation* for physical assets.[38]
- **Loss or lack of future benefit:** The company will recognize a loss when it decides that previously expected future economic benefits of an asset have declined enough to pass the impairment test.

Asset Recognition

Assets are probable future benefits controlled by the company as a result of a past transaction. On first recognizing an asset in the balance sheet, the company generally records the asset's cost, based on current exchange prices on the date of acquisition. Once the company recognizes the asset, it will continue to record the asset at its initial amount until an event occurs that meets the criteria to record a change, which includes sale or other disposal of the asset, and changes in the expected future benefits reflected in amortization and impairment charges.

Commonly used methods for misrepresenting the amount of expenses, assets and liabilities

Fraudsters manipulate earnings by understating expenses, which overstates net assets. Lowering expenses increases net income. A fraudster can lower expenses in the current period by, for example, capitalizing costs that the company should expense or lengthening the depreciable life of assets beyond their economic life. Increasing the estimated salvage value of a depreciable asset beyond its expected life results in reducing current depreciation charges and overstating the balance sheet amount for the depreciable asset. Underestimating bad debt expense overstates the asset for net accounts receivable. Underestimating warranty expense understates liabil-

---

[37]See the Glossary for the contrast between *expense* and *loss* and for the details of the *impairment* test.
[38]Amortization and depreciation are processes of cost allocation, not of asset valuation.

ities. Capitalizing costs that the company should expense overstates assets. To capitalize a cost means to put it on the balance sheet as an asset and then amortize it over time. Alternatively, the cost can be expensed in the period incurred.

In this section, we provide examples of the following:

- Improper capitalization of assets or deferral of expenses
- Overstating ending asset values
- Improper use of restructuring reserves or manipulating recorded liabilities
- Improper use of asset reserves
- Failure to record asset impairments

Improper capitalization of assets or deferral of expenses

WorldCom, a major global communications provider with operations in 65 countries, appears to have capitalized costs it should have expensed. In a civil action against WorldCom, the SEC alleged that by transferring certain costs to asset accounts, rather than expensing them in the period incurred, WorldCom violated GAAP and falsely portrayed itself as a profitable business during 2001 and the first quarter of 2002. The SEC alleges that senior management approved and directed this practice, which overstated income before income taxes and minority interests by approximately $3.055 billion in 2001 and $797 million during the first quarter of 2002.[39] In this fraud, WorldCom removed operating expenses by paying fees to lease the phone networks and computer services of other companies, removing these fees from WorldCom's income statement, and putting them on its balance sheet as computer and leasing assets. [40]

WorldCom's internal audit team discovered the fraud when it received tips from other employees. After investigating and finding numerous instances of wrongdoing, on June 14, 2002, the internal audit team contacted WorldCom's audit committee, who asked management for documentation supporting its accounting treatment. Management provided none and on June 25, WorldCom representatives announced that it had inflated profits by $3.8 billion over the previous five quarters. Within a day or two, trading in WorldCom shares had halted and plaintiffs' lawyers had filed civil suits alleging fraud. Less than six weeks later, on July 21, WorldCom filed for bankruptcy.[41]

The SEC accused Waste Management, Inc., a company specializing in waste collection, of massive earnings management fraud similar to WorldCom's alleged fraud. The Commission alleged that, beginning in 1992 and continuing into 1997, the most senior officers of Waste Management engaged in a scheme to falsify and misrepresent Waste Management's financial results in order to enrich themselves and keep their jobs.[42] They understated depreciation expense on their garbage trucks by extending their useful lives and assigning unsupported and inflated salvage values to those trucks; they assigned arbitrary and significant salvage values to other assets that previously had zero salvage value; and they improperly capitalized a variety of expenses. All of these practices have the concurrent effect of overstating asset values and retained earnings on the balance sheet.

---

[39]SEC Litigation Release No. 17588 (June 27, 2002); A.A.E.R. No. 1585 (June 27, 2002)

[40]Imagine the following transaction. A company wants to rent a warehouse for Year 3, but doesn't need it for Years 1 and 2. The company is willing to pay up to $40,000 today to lock in the warehouse for that one-year period starting two years from today. It finds a landlord who will rent a suitable warehouse for three years starting today at $1,000 per month, $36,000 in total. The landlord requires full payment for the three-year rent in advance. The company judges that renting the warehouse for three years is a bargain relative to what it expected to pay. It pays $36,000 today, setting up an asset for Advances to Owner of Warehouse. One year from today, the question becomes what the carrying amount of the Advance to Owner should be? We think it should be $36,000 because the future benefits contemplated on acquisition of the original lease have not diminished, the cost to secure the services wanted were cheaper to acquire with a three years lease. Many accountants would disagree with us and mechanically require that $12,000 of expense are recognized for the first year, and show the asset at $24,000. Some newspaper accounts suggest that the WorldCom situation parallels this example: WorldCom paid for multiple years of capacity in advance to secure capacity several years later. Should WorldCom have recorded the expense at the end of the first year for capacity it had rented for that year even though it didn't need or want that capacity at that time? We don't know enough about the facts to be able to answer that question, but we can easily conceive circumstances that suggest the continuing capitalization of the cost was proper.

[41]Presentation: The WorldCom Fraud, 2003, AICPA, Inc., New York, New York.

[42]A.A.E.R. No. 1532 (March 26, 2002)

The SEC alleged that the company's long-time auditor, Arthur Andersen LLP, which repeatedly issued unqualified reports on the company's materially false and misleading annual financial statements, aided defendants in their fraud. According to the Commission, Andersen annually presented Company management with Proposed Adjusting Journal Entries that would correct errors, fixing the understated expenses and overstated earnings in the Company's financial statements. The executives refused to make the adjustments, but entered into a secret agreement with Andersen to correct the accumulated errors over ten years and to change the underlying accounting practices, but to do so only in future periods.[43] In May of 2001, Andersen agreed with the SEC that it would not support this practice in the future.

In the fall of 2001, Enron collapsed with some evidence suggesting that Arthur Andersen's partners had connived with Enron management in the accounting for Enron's complex transactions. Following within half a year of the resolution of the Waste Management irregularities, the Enron practices led the Justice Department to file criminal charges against Andersen. Andersen ultimately went out of business as a result of these charges.

Overstating ending asset values
In the preceding examples, management understated expenses, which inevitably led to overstated net assets. Here is an example where management overstated assets, which led to understated expenses. The SEC alleged that Rite Aid, one of the nation's largest drugstore chains, failed to record $8.8 million in shrinkage (the general name for disappearance of inventory through shoplifting, embezzlement, theft, breakage, and evaporation) for stores in which it conducted physical inventories and failed to record $5.0 million in shrinkage for stores in which it had not conducted physical inventories.[44] As a result, Rite Aid's balance sheet showed $13.8 million of inventory that it did not possess.

By increasing ending inventory, Rite Aid understated its cost of goods sold and overstated its income before tax by the same amount:

Cost of Goods Sold = Beginning Inventory + Purchases − Ending Inventory.

Improper use of restructuring reserves or manipulating recorded liabilities
Many companies record restructuring reserves,[45] which estimate the costs of restructuring, for activities such as closing down plants or changing product lines, which include items like severance pay for laid-off employees and costs to cancel leases. GAAP require companies to recognize some losses of this sort, with attendant liabilities, when it can estimate that it will incur such costs. While GAAP require companies to record the losses and liabilities (reserves), the process invites abuse. Some management cannot resist the opportunity to overestimate future costs, artificially increasing reserve requirements, so that they can either reverse the reserves into future earnings that are short of earnings targets or simply report fewer expenses in the future. The effect of both practices is to make future earnings look better at the expense of current earnings. This practice embodies the ideas of *big bath* and *cookie-jar reserves* that Arthur Levitt identified in his speech that we described earlier.

The SEC investigated Xerox Corporation, Sunbeam Corporation, and W.R. Grace & Company for engaging in improper use of restructuring reserves. The SEC alleged that Xerox manipulated its reserves in order to meet market expectations by maintaining $396 million in cookie jar reserves, which it periodically released into earnings to improve operating results artificially.[46] The SEC alleged that Sunbeam created cookie jar

---

[43] According to the Commission, in the end, Waste Management did not even comply with the agreement because it would have prevented the company from meeting earnings targets; *ibid*.

[44] A.A.E.R. No. 1579 (June 21, 2002)

[45] See the Glossary for *reserves*. No other word in accounting causes so much confusion for financial statement readers. In accounting, a reserve always has a credit balance, but many people think of them as debits, often in the form of assets. Reserves can represent asset contra accounts (Reserve for Bad Debts better called *Allowance for Bad Debts*, Reserve for Depreciation, better called *Accumulated Depreciation*) or liabilities (as here, Restructuring Reserves means Estimated Liabilities for Restructuring Costs to be Incurred) or, occasionally, owners' equity accounts. Sometimes, users mean credits, say for future income, not appearing on the financial statements at all, as in hidden reserves.

[46] A.A.E.R. No. 1542 (April 11, 2002)

reserves in 1996 to increase its reported loss, and then reversed these excess reserves into income during 1997.[47] The SEC alleged that W.R.Grace recorded liabilities through the deferral of income, in order to build cookie jar reserves, which it later used to meet earnings estimates.[48]

Improper use of asset reserves

The matching principle in GAAP requires that a company expense costs incurred to earn revenue in the same period for which it recognizes the revenue. For example, companies that make sales on credit will not receive cash from all the customers. Accordingly, management must make an estimate of the amount of sales for which it will never receive cash and reduce the balance sheet amount of accounts receivable for that amount. To bring about this reduction, companies charge bad debt expense on the income statement and reduce the accounts receivable account by a corresponding amount in a contra asset account often called the *allowance for bad debts* or the *allowance for uncollectible receivables*, or, regrettably, *bad debt reserves*. The company estimates the appropriate balance in this account either by the percentage of sales or by the aging method, both of which use historical information obtained by management. Because management estimates this balance, it has the opportunity manipulate the amount to achieve earnings targets or expectations.

The SEC investigated Allegheny Heath Education and Research Foundation, healthcare provider in Pennsylvania, for inappropriately manipulating its bad debt allowances. The SEC alleged that Allegheny masked its deteriorating financial condition by failing to increase its bad debt allowances to account for uncollectible accounts receivable by approximately $100 million.[49]

Similarly, in early 2003, several analysts alleged that Sears understated the expected losses on its credit card receivables, overstating assets and income, even after the company increased its allowance for future uncollectible credit-card debts by $189 million in October of 2002 and increased its write-offs of uncollectible accounts by $33 million for the same period.

Failure to record asset impairments

A company must recognize an impairment loss if it cannot recover the carrying amount of a long-lived asset from its undiscounted cash flows under SFAS No. 144, *Accounting for Impairment or Disposal of Long-Lived Assets*. If management judges the asset to be impaired, then management must write down the carrying amount for the asset on the balance sheet by the amount of the difference between the carrying amount and fair value of the asset. The accounting matches that asset write down with a corresponding impairment loss recognized on the income statement in the period in which management recognizes the asset's impairment. Failure to do so overstates the assets and net income of the company.

Management must use judgment to answer the questions, "Have an asset's expected cash flows diminished and, if so, by how much?" Accordingly, management may manipulate its company's financial results by

- choosing to ignore impairments of assets in times when the company is in danger of missing its earnings estimates
- recording false impairments of assets in times when the company will overshoot its estimates
- writing down the assets as part of a business combination.

The first of these has a straightforward effect—overstate assets and income by the amount of the omitted impairment. The second and third practices have subtle effects on the income statement. In the second, by recording false impairments, current year earnings are lower, but future years, earnings are higher because of artificially lower depreciation on the assets. This effect resembles the cookie-jar reserves, the artificially large credit balance in the accumulated depreciation account. While we have not seen the term applied to this fraud, the term applies here as well. If the company recorded the impairment with a direct credit to the asset account, with the effect of reducing it, the reserve becomes *hidden*. The third practice requires an understanding of purchase accounting principles and goodwill impairments that we omit here.

---

[47]A.A.E.R. No. 1395 (May 15, 2001)
[48]A.A.E.R. No. 1140 (June 30, 1999)
[49]A.A.E.R. No, 1283 (June 30, 2000)

The SEC alleged that CUC (later, Cendant) participated in all three types of these deceptive practices for impairments. The SEC alleged that for years ended January 31, 1996, and January 31, 1997, management inflated CUC operating income by avoiding charges that it should have recognized as impairment losses. When the company merged with HFS to become Cendant in December 1997, management created fraudulent estimated liabilities for future merger costs, often called *merger reserves*. Merger reserves resemble reserves resulting from restructuring charges and serve many of the same purposes. Management creates liabilities based on its representations that the company will incur these costs in the future. The liabilities provide estimates of expenditures management expects to make as a result of a business combination.[50] Management makes an estimate of the amount of the expenditures, expensing the full amount and setting up the reserve at the time of the estimate. Often, management has no clear idea of which items will result in future charges or write downs since the activity generating the liability has not yet occurred. Some in management take the opportunity to inflate the estimate [like a big bath where they report too much expense or loss now to enable reporting too much profit later, hoping the future boost to market price exceeds the current reduction]. If management has created merger reserves larger than necessary, it can later inappropriately charge items such as plant and equipment impairments, non-recoverable receivable amounts, and obsolete inventory costs against the reserve.

At the time of merger, CUC apparently overestimated the amount of merger costs by the amount of assets that it wanted to write down as impaired. By offsetting the asset write-downs against the merger reserves,[51] the financial statements showed the write-downs as unusual charges, not as ordinary, or operating, expenses, on the income statement. Thus, for assets already impaired, CUC would permanently avoid classifying ultimate write downs as operating expenses, and when it eventually took the asset write downs, it would overstate them, allowing Cendant to report smaller operating expenses in the future and larger future income.

Liability Recognition

Liabilities are probable future sacrifices of economic benefits arising from present obligations of a particular entity to transfer assets or provide services to other entities in the future as a result of past transactions or events.[52] The initial amount recorded for a liability uses a measurement based on current exchange prices on the date of recognition. Most liabilities are monetary, requiring payments of specific amounts of cash, while some are nonmonetary, requiring the delivery of goods or services. Monetary liabilities due within one year or less appear at the amount of cash the company expects to pay to discharge the obligation. If the payment dates extend more than one year into the future, a monetary liability appears at the present value of the future cash outflows.

When the company receives cash in advance from a customer for the future delivery of a good or service, the nonmonetary liability to deliver the goods and services appears on the balance sheet at the amount of cash received. Sometimes, the company has an obligation to deliver a good or service but has not received an explicit cash amount in return for taking on that performance obligation. Then, the related nonmonetary liability appears on the balance sheet at the estimated cost of providing the goods or services. An example of this type of liability is estimated costs for warranty services, where the customer paid a single price for the goods and the related warranty. The seller cannot disentangle the cash receipts into the amounts received for the goods and the amounts received for the warranty. If the seller can allocate the single receipt into components, it will record the nonmonetary liability using that allocation. An example is the sale of a TV and warranty contract in a single price where the seller also separately offers the two items for sale.

---

[50]EITF 94-3 permits merger reserves for (a) the recognition as a liability today of future expenditures for involuntary termination benefits to be paid to employees and (b) the recognition of a liability today for future expenditures that are directly associated with a plan to exit an activity—provided those expenditures will have no future economic benefit and provided four conditions laid down by the EITF are met. EITF 95-3 expands on 94-3 to say that, in a business combination, expenditures to relocate employees may also be recognized as a liability at the time of the business combination, in addition to the employee termination benefits and exit costs covered by 94-3.

[51]Rather than debit an expense or loss account, debit the liability for merger reserves.

[52]This definition comes from *SFAC No. 6*. See the Glossary; we think one will understand better the distinctions between liabilities and obligations that are not liabilities by defining a liability to be an obligation for a definite (or reasonably definite) amount due at a definite (or reasonably definite) time arising from a transaction that is not an executory contract (a mere exchange of promises).

One troublesome question of liability recognition relates to *contingent obligations*. Contingent obligations require some future event to occur before accounting can establish the existence or amount, or both, of a liability. Examples of contingent liabilities include unsettled lawsuits and loan guarantees. In both cases, the company does not clearly have an obligation and even if it does, the amount is not clear until either the case is settled or the loan goes into default. GAAP requires the recognition of a liability only when the payment is probable; i.e., greater than 80 or 85 percent.

A typical accounting entry to record a liability credits the liability and debits the expense. If a company understates liabilities, it typically understates expenses, overstates income, and understates the debt-equity ratio. Sometimes the recording of a liability matches the recording of an asset (as in recording a financing lease), where omitting the liability has no immediate effect on reported income, but does distort the debt-equity ratio, making it appear smaller than it should.

Commonly used methods for understating liabilities

Many liabilities require a management estimate. For example, when a company sells products with a warranty attached, management must estimate the amount of future warranty costs the company will incur on these products, and record an expense and a liability in the period of the sale. Management bases the estimate on experience and expected changes in the business environment. Whenever accounting requires a management judgment, it provides opportunity for earnings management or fraud.

Another way management reduces stated liabilities involves constructing transactions so that the obligations stay off the balance sheet. Raising funds without showing the resulting obligations on the balance sheet is referred to as off-balance-sheet ("OBS") financing. The most common (non-fraudulent) OBS financings arise from some leasing activities and by raising funds with debt incurred by related entities that the reporting company does not have to consolidate. Instances of the latter involve joint ventures, partnerships, or less-than-majority-owned subsidiaries. From 1990 until recently, accounting jargon referred to these entities as special purpose entities ("SPEs"), but now the FASB calls them *variable interest entities* ("VIEs").

This section provides examples of the following types of liability manipulation:

- Improper estimation of liabilities, sometimes called *reserves*
- Improper use of off-balance-sheet arrangements
- Improper estimation of pension liabilities
- Improper (non-) recognition of contingent liabilities

Improper estimation of liabilities, sometimes called *reserves*

Companies that sell products with attached warranties must recognize, at the time of sale, an estimated warranty liability that results in reducing income and increasing liabilities for the estimated cost of fulfilling the promises given in the warranty. Some call this a *warranty reserve*, but you will understand it better if you think of it as a liability for Estimated Costs of Future Warranty Repairs.

The amount of this estimated expense results from management's past experience and its expectations of future changes. If the amount is underestimated, the result is to decrease expenses and increase net income. The SEC has alleged that Signal Tech, a publicly traded defense contractor, improperly understated its estimated warranty expenses. The Commission alleged that in March 1998, an executive for one of Signal Tech's divisions prepared a handwritten list of improper adjustments and directed his accounting staff to enter them directly into the general ledger. These adjustments took the form of unsupported reductions to

- estimated expenses on the income statement
- balance sheet liabilities for estimated contract losses ($210,000)
- balance sheet liabilities for estimated warranty costs ($121,000)
- balance sheet amounts estimated for excess and obsolete inventory ($100,000) [53]

---

[53]SEC Civil Action No. CO 2 - 01467

By underestimating the anticipated expenses for these activities, Signal Tech reported higher income and shareholder equity for the period.

Improper use of off-balance-sheet arrangements

Companies use off-balance-sheet arrangements to provide financing, liquidity, market or credit risk support or to engage in leasing or hedging or research and development. These arrangements may involve the use of special purpose entities, now called *VIEs (variable interest entities)* by the FASB. The misuse of these types of structures has only recently come to the attention of the general public, mostly as a result of the collapse of Enron. Since then, the FASB has developed new financial accounting standards to deal with these structures.

Prior to the new standards being implemented, the main violation occurred when companies failed to consolidate the financial results of affiliates which they should have consolidated.[54] The accounting rules for when a parent must consolidate an affiliate involve considerations of ownership and control, but applying those rules in practice presented management with opportunities for manipulation and bending of the rules.

Even before the Enron collapse, the SEC had investigated The PNC Financial Services Group, Inc. (PNC) for this type of inappropriate use of off-balance-sheet arrangements.[55] A press release issued on July 18, 2002, regarding the Cease and Desist Order given by the SEC to PNC, said

> *The SEC's administrative Order found that in 2001, PNC endeavored to remove approximately $762 million of volatile, troubled or underperforming loans and venture capital investments from its financial statements by transferring them to three special purpose entities that were specially created to receive these assets and in which PNC held a substantial interest. PNC failed to consolidate the special purpose entities on its second and third quarter financial statements filed with the Commission even though the entities failed to meet the requirements under generally accepted accounting principles (GAAP) for non-consolidation. In connection with its improper accounting for its interest in the three special purpose entities, PNC also made materially false and misleading disclosures in certain press releases and in quarterly reports filed with the Commission for the second and third quarters of 2001 about its financial condition, earnings and exposure to the risks of its commercial lending activities.*

In that same press release, an SEC official stated, "Today's action demonstrates that the Commission will closely scrutinize transactions with special purpose entities. Public companies engaged in transactions with special purpose entities not only must rigorously comply with GAAP, but also must assure that they accurately portray the material elements of the economic risks and realities that they face as a result of these transactions."

Soon thereafter, the SEC investigated Adelphia Communications Corporation ("Adelphia"), a large cable television provider, for deceptive off-balance-sheet arrangements. The SEC alleged that senior management caused Adelphia to fraudulently exclude over $2.3 billion in bank debt by deliberately shifting those liabilities onto the books of Adelphia's off-balance-sheet, unconsolidated affiliates. Similar to PNC, these affiliates did not qualify for nonconsolidation under GAAP. Adelphia went one step further, though, and created fictitious documents to give the false appearance that it had repaid the debts, rather than transfer them to unconsolidated entities controlled by the founder, CEO, and Chairman of Board of Directors, John J. Rigas. [56]

Following Adelphia, the SEC cited Dynegy, Incorporated and its use of its special purpose entity, Alpha. Internal Dynegy documents suggest that Alpha's principal purpose was to address the "disconnect . . . between book and cash earnings" and to improve "quality of earnings"—*i.e.*, to create the appearance that Dynegy's operations generated more cash than they did.[57] Dynegy reported a $300 million loan from Alpha (which had

---

[54]A consolidated balance sheet is, approximately, the sum of two separate balance sheets. If an entity borrows funds, it will record a liability. If a parent company can avoid consolidating the balance sheet of an affiliated company that does borrow funds, the liability will appear on the balance sheet of the borrowing affiliate, but not on the consolidated balance sheet of the parent.

[55]SEC Report Pursuant to Section 704 of the Sarbanes-Oxley Act of 2002

[56]A.A.E.R., No., 1599 (July 24, 2002)

[57]A.A.E.R., No., 1631 (September 24, 2002)

effectively borrowed these funds from a syndicate of lenders, through other entities), as operating cash flow on the statement of cash flows. Dynegy should have reported this transaction as financing cash flow. This case particularly worried analysts as they had considered cash from operations to be both a key indicator of the financial health of a company and difficult to manipulate. As a result, analysts began to understand that companies were using SPEs to manipulate the placement of items in the statement of cash flows.

Improper estimation of pension liabilities

The amount of a company's pension expense can differ from the amount of cash it contributes to its pension fund. Recognizing pension expense requires a debit to expense with a credit to a liability account. Funding pension liabilities requires a debit to the liability account and a credit to cash transferred to the pension fund. This issue here is the amount of pension expense a company recognizes—the amount by which it reduces income in the current period.

The amount a company recognizes as pension expense depends on factors such as employee demographics, the expected rate of return on existing pension assets, anticipated wage increases, assumptions made about the return on invested pension assets, and the rate the company uses to discount future liabilities.[58] Overestimating the discount rate will understate liabilities on the balance sheet. An assumed higher rate of return for earnings on invested pension assets will decrease the amounts of expense the company will record for any given year. So, higher estimates of interest rates and rates of return reduce both the amounts of pension liabilities and the current pension expenses. In October 2002, Standard and Poor's downgraded its credit rating for General Motors because of its increasing pension liabilities. Executives would rather have higher, not lower, ratings, which allows a management interested in manipulating the result to adjust the assumptions related to pension expenses to its advantage. In 2002, Lockheed Martin announced that its pension plan would reduce net income by as much as $100 million, rather than increase the bottom line as it had done in an earlier period.[59] Although there was no fraud here, this illustration shows the effect of such information on the value of the company's shares. Executives are cognizant of this impact and may intentionally hide this information from the public.

Improper (non-)recognition of contingent liabilities [60]

Contingent obligations arise from lawsuits, loan guarantees, environmental exposures, and repurchase agreements. Management must record the potential obligation as a liability when it is probable that the company has incurred the liability and when management can reasonably estimate its amount. If it is only "reasonably possible" that the potential obligation will become a liability, management must disclose the contingency in the footnotes to the financial statements.

Almost all large corporations report contingencies for ongoing civil litigation. A complex example of a contingency arose when Enron's unconsolidated partnerships (special purpose entities) issued bonds, which required the parent entity Enron to issue shares of its common stock to the bondholders under certain conditions, such as a downgrade in the bonds' ratings. Because Enron did not consolidate the bond-issuing entity, it did not fully disclose the nature of the contingency. As Enron's share prices declined, the bond indentures potentially required Enron to issue shares to the bondholders, which potentially increased the number of shares outstanding, which caused further decline in the market value of the shares, which process continued until Enron shares became worthless. The evidence available to us suggests that Enron should have consolidated those SPEs and should have disclosed the nature of the contingencies. Such disclosure, alone, would not have made the collapse of Enron less likely, but would likely have caused Enron management to abandon this form of raising funds and not to have issued the bonds in the first place.

---

[58]The discounting of future cash outflows allows raising the rate for discounting future liabilities decreasing the present value of the associated liabilities. Management records long-term liabilities, such as pension obligations, at the present value of future cash outflows.
[59]"Culture of Loopholes Bred Corporate Abuse", by Carrie Johnson. The Washington Post. Friday, April 18, 2003.
[60]Many financial statement preparers and users refer to *contingent liabilities*. We deplore this usage, because by its very nature a liability appears in the balance sheet, while a contingency, a potential obligation and liability, does not. We prefer to use the word *liability* only when the item appears on the balance sheet, so we use *contingency* when the potential obligation is not yet a liability. You should be aware that many financial statements use the term *contingent liability* for items not in the balance sheet.

Disclosures Recognition

Disclosure refers to any information the company provides to the public beyond the basic financial statements, including notes to the financial statements, other information in the annual report (e.g., the Management Discussion and Analysis), press releases, and conference calls. The GAAP and SEC rules regulating disclosures apply to the following:

- Accounting Policies
- Related Parties
- Commitments and Contingencies
- Risks and Uncertainties
- Nonmonetary Transactions

We discuss the types of information that companies must disclose and the regulation governing this disclosure, including how companies must both prepare and report the information. Then, we show how companies violate these requirements.

What information must reporting companies disclose?

Under *Accounting Principles Board Opinion No. 22* (APB 22), "Disclosure of Accounting Policies", companies must provide the financial statement user with a description of the significant accounting policies the company adopts. The accounting policies a company adopts affect the presentation of its financial position, changes in financial position, and results of operations. Accordingly, the usefulness to readers of financial statements for making economic decisions about the reporting entity depends upon the reader's understanding of the entity's accounting policies.[61]

For example, one company may use straight-line depreciation for its depreciable assets, while another uses accelerated depreciation. One company may use a LIFO cost flow assumption for inventories while another uses a FIFO cost flow assumption. Without this information, financial statement users would find it difficult if not impossible to compare financial statements of different companies using different accounting policies to prepare their statements. Recently, the SEC has begun to require companies to describe the critical accounting judgments management has to make to prepare the financial statements. A financial institution will discuss its procedures for estimating the amounts of loan losses, while a commercial company will discuss how it estimates the amount of bad debts. A retail company will discuss methods of estimating ending inventory valuations, while a manufacturing company using plant assets will discuss methods of estimating depreciable lives and salvage values.

Companies must provide information about the significant risks and uncertainties they face. In December 1994, the AICPA's Accounting Standards Executive Committee issued Statement of Position (SOP) 94-6, "*Disclosure of Certain Significant Risks and Uncertainties.*" This pronouncement requires non-governmental entities that prepare financial statements in conformity with GAAP to disclose risks and uncertainties that could significantly affect the amounts reported in those financial statements. This pronouncement provides more detailed practical guidance than does the FASB's *Statement of Financial Accounting Concepts No. 1*, which states that the purpose of financial accounting is to "provide information that is useful to present and potential investors and creditors and other users in making rational investment, credit, and similar decisions." SOP 94-6 requires disclosures in the following areas:

- the nature of operations
- the use of estimates in the preparation of financial statements
- certain significant estimates
- current vulnerability due to certain concentrations, such as having a disproportionate amount of business with a single customer or with many customers in a single foreign country

Reporting the nature of operations is straightforward, but understanding the other three areas requires further discussion. Many fraudulent activities relate directly to management estimates for items such as allowance

---

[61]Accounting Principles Board Opinion, No. 22. (April 1972)

for bad debts, estimated warranty liabilities, contingencies, and estimated costs to complete mergers. The relevant disclosure for GE reads,

> *Accounting policies discussed in this section are those that we consider to be critical to an understanding of our financial statements because their application places the most significant demands on our ability to judge the effect of inherently uncertain matters on our financial results. For all of these policies, we caution that future events rarely develop exactly as forecast, and the best estimates routinely require adjustment.*

This disclosure communicates the uncertainties inherent in measuring assets, liabilities, revenues, and expenses while alerting the reader that future events may differ from those anticipated by management when it prepared the financial statements. Management accused of preparing fraudulent financial statements often points to this disclosure in defense of its actions.

Where does this information appear?

While some of this disclosure appears in the required notes to the financial statements in SEC filings such as the 10-K or the annual report, much of it appears in the Management Discussion and Analysis (MD&A) and the Letter to Shareholders. Companies provide further disclosures through press releases and conference calls. Item 303 of Regulation S-K, issued by the SEC, "Management's Discussion and Analysis of Financial Condition and Results of Operations," requires the MD&A to provide investors with "information that the registrant believes to be necessary to an understanding of its financial condition, changes in financial condition and results of operations." The section of the MD&A discussing forward-looking information often leads to allegations of manipulation or fraud by management. Management must provide information regarding the possible future effects of the most important *existing* currently known demands, risks, uncertainties, events, conditions and trends. It may include forward-looking information about the possible effects of *anticipated* future demands, events, conditions, and trends. This forward-looking information may take the form of pro-forma financial information [see Glossary for definition].

Misleading or fraudulent disclosure

- Most alleged misleading or fraudulent disclosure involves: inaccurate estimates by management of asset and liability amounts, amounts for contingencies, and pension discount rates or investment return amounts
- failure by management to advise financial statement users of possible risks to the company
- management dissemination of misleading financial information through the use of non-GAAP pro-forma information.

An example of inaccurate estimations by management of asset amounts is the case of Waste Management, discussed earlier. Examples of the other two fraudulent disclosure practices follow.

Non-disclosure of possible risks

The SEC entered an enforcement action for inadequate MD&A disclosure in 1992 *In the Matter of Caterpillar, Inc.* (SEC Release No. 34-30532). In that action, the SEC found that Caterpillar had failed to comply with the reporting requirements of the Securities Exchange Act of 1934 (the "Exchange Act"). Caterpillar failed to disclose the concerns of its board of directors that the dramatic increase in revenues experienced in the company's Brazilian unit in 1989, which significantly contributed to the company's earnings, resulted from the combined effects of Brazil's currency hyper-inflation and international exchange rates, and would not likely recur. The Caterpillar case illustrates that when management knows of adverse trends and uncertainties, it must disclose its concerns.[62] The SEC said, that by omitting this information from its MD&A, management, "left investors with an incomplete picture of Caterpillar's financial condition and results of operations and denied them the opportunity to see the company 'through the eyes of management'."

---

[62]"SEC Presses for Expanded MD&A Disclosure," by A. John Murphy, Jr., and Charles S. Kaufman. March 29, 2002. Sheppard, Mullin, Richter, and Hampton LLP.

Non-GAAP pro forma information

Pro forma financial statements refer to presentations in which management shows how financial statements would appear had events not occurred or, less often, shows the financial results of events occurring that hadn't actually happened. Pro forma statements have long had a valid use in business forecasting and budgeting. For example, management might forecast, "If sales grow at 10 percent next year and the cost of goods sold remains 65 percent of sales while administrative expense ratios remain the same as the previous year, the income statement for the year will show . . . ." This would be a pro forma income statement useful in internal budgeting and planning. As a result, the term *pro forma statements* has an honorable past. The term now has less benign uses.

In recent years, companies have issued pro forma statements showing how the statements would have looked had there been no asset impairments or had two companies, which have not yet merged, been operating together with projected efficiencies from the merger.

The use of non-GAAP pro forma information has prompted the SEC to issue a warning regarding the release of pro forma information to the public.[63] In its statement, the SEC cautioned against providing misleading pro-forma information. Specifically, the Commission reminded the reader that the antifraud provisions of securities laws apply to a company issuing pro forma information, thus companies should be particularly mindful of their obligation not to mislead investors who use the information. It stated that, "a presentation of financial results that is addressed to a limited feature of a company's overall financial results (for example, earnings before interest, taxes, depreciation and amortization), or that sets forth calculations of financial results on a basis other than GAAP, raises particular concerns." Such statements mislead investors when the company does not clearly disclose the basis of presentation. Effective March 2003, the SEC adopted a new disclosure regulation, Regulation G, which required public companies that disclose or release non-GAAP financial measures to include a presentation of the most directly comparable GAAP financial measure or reconciliation of the non-GAAP financial measure to the GAAP counterpart.[64]

In its first enforcement action addressing the abuse of pro forma earnings figures, the SEC alleged in January 2002 that Trump Hotels & Casino Resorts, Inc. (Trump), made misleading statements in its third-quarter 1999 earnings release. The SEC found that the release cited pro forma figures that presented purportedly positive operations results without disclosing that an unusual, one-time gain had caused these results rather than profitable, ongoing operating activities. The error was further compounded when the company excluded one-time losses from the calculation. The results would have shown a decline in both revenues and net income had Trump excluded from the quarterly pro forma results both the unusual gain and the one-time charge, which would have failed to meet analysts' expectations.[65] An SEC official stated, "In this case, the method of presenting the pro forma numbers and the positive spin the Company put on them were materially misleading. The case starkly illustrates how pro forma numbers can be used deceptively and the mischief that they can cause." The SEC found that Trump violated Section 10(b) of the Exchange Act its Rule 10b-5 and ordered the company to cease and desist from violating those provisions.

AUDITOR RESPONSIBILITY FOR DETECTING FRAUD

Earlier, we asked, "Who is watching the shop?" The auditors have the responsibility for attesting that management has prepared the financial statements in accordance with GAAP.

Now, we ask, "Are the auditors responsible for detecting fraud?" Management prepares the financial statements. The rules of the game could make the auditors responsible for checking every assertion implied by these statements. Auditors know how to do these checks—to search systematically for fraud—but these audits would cost more than ten times as much as audits now done under Generally Accepted Auditing Standards, called *GAAS audits*. It is accepted practice that auditors should be skeptical in reviewing financial statements but not assume that management is dishonest, which keeps the auditing costs reasonable. The generally accepted prac-

---

[63]http://www.sec.gov/rules/other/33-8039.htm
[64]http://www.sec.gov/rules/final/33-8176.htm
[65]A.A.E.R. No. 1499 (January 16, 2002)

tice is "trust, but verify." This approach implies that auditors will not be as likely to find fraud as when their retention specifies that they are to search for it or that, at the end of the audit, the auditor will be confident there is no fraud. GAAS do not require, nor even suggest, that the auditors will question management on every item. GAAS state that due professional care requires that the auditor exercise professional skepticism. Professional skepticism is an attitude that includes a questioning mind and a critical assessment of audit evidence. The standards go on to state that an auditor should neither assume that management is dishonest nor assume unquestioned honesty. In exercising professional skepticism, the auditor should not be satisfied with less than persuasive evidence because of belief that management is honest.[66]

Professional guidance regarding the auditor's responsibility to detect errors and fraud includes the following paragraph,

> *The auditor has a responsibility to plan and perform the audit to obtain reasonable assurance about whether the financial statements are free of material misstatement, whether caused by error or fraud. Because of the nature of audit evidence and the characteristics of fraud, the auditor is able to obtain reasonable, but not absolute, assurance that material misstatements are detected. The auditor has no responsibility to plan and perform the audit to obtain reasonable assurance that misstatements, whether caused by error or fraud, that are not material to the financial statements are detected.[67]*

This guidance makes the auditors responsible for attaining *reasonable assurance* that the statements are free of material misstatements. In practice, after the world discovers that management has committed fraud, the auditors cannot easily show that the evidence entitled them to be reasonably assured there was no fraud, but that in spite of their reasonable assurance, fraud was there and escaped notice. The professional guidance quoted above doesn't help us figure out how the auditors should design their tests or their decision rules for stopping further digging into the facts underlying the financial statements. For this, we have the Statement on Auditing Standards (SAS) No. 99, *Consideration of Fraud in a Financial Statement Audit.* SAS 99 provides the auditor with defining characteristics of fraud, discusses the meaning and importance of professional skepticism, suggests procedures for obtaining the information needed to identify the risks of material misstatement. It provides guidance on how the auditor should identify these risks, respond to the results of the assessment, and evaluate the audit evidence.[68]

In practice, after the fact, one cannot easily decide whether material misstatements resulted from error or from fraud, because of the inherent flexibility in GAAP and the need for management estimation in many regards. Apart from the blatant misappropriation of assets—as in the case of Tyco—proving that management intended to deceive the public requires more evidence than most investigations can find. Still, over the years, practitioners have developed successful analytical procedures for detecting fraud.

SIGNS OF TROUBLE

Investors, regulators, management, and auditors all want to prevent fraud or detect it once it is committed. We have discussed the actions management can take to commit fraud and how these affect the financial statements. We have discussed the responsibilities of auditors to detect fraud. In this section, we discuss how financial statement users might identify fraudulent activities.

The financial statement user should understand the environment conducive for fraud. We have discussed specific situations in which management might become aggressive and engage in fraudulent financial reporting. *SAS No. 99* documents three general conditions often present when fraud occurs:

---

[66]"Fraud in a financial statement audit: what every auditing student should know about SAS 99", A Student Educational Manual Provided by the American Institute of CPAs, by Kurt Pany and Ray Whittington. (December 2002)

[67]AU sec. 110, par 2

[68]You can find further discussion of the auditor's responsibility by visiting the AICPA website at http://www.aicpa.org/members/div/auditstd/index.htm. The Sarbanes-Oxley Act established the Public Company Accounting Oversight Board (PCAOB), which now regulates auditors and the auditor process. The PCAOB has only recently begun its operations and its standards appear at http://www.pcaobus.org/pcaob standards.asp.

- incentive or pressure
- opportunity
- attitude and rationalization

Incentive or pressure

Incentives and pressure are powerful motivators. If a company is operating in a declining industry, management may try to offset the lower demand by misstating the financial statements. If management has special performance incentives, such as a CFO who is about to retire and whose retirement pay depends on reported income in the last year before retirement, or management whose bonuses depend on accounting income, management may modify the financial statements to enhance the results. When top management pressures lower-level executives to achieve the forecasted target, fraudulent reporting can result, especially when top management has a practice of publicly committing to aggressive or unreasonable forecasts.

Opportunity

Opportunity opens possibilities that executives might never have considered. When a company has effective controls but its accounting requires management judgments that are hard to document, such as the need to estimate future warranty costs or environmental contingencies, opportunity arises. For example, estimates of loan losses critically affect the income reported in the banking industry, but rarely in the magazine industry. Estimates of estimated liabilities for civil penalties are likely to impact both the tobacco and chemical industries, but may have little effect on the computer industry.

Attitude and Rationalization

 Management may adopt an attitude of acceptance when it can rationalize or justify its fraudulent activities. An example would be when management believes future years will be more profitable and inflated results now will keep the company from bankruptcy.

The financial statement user must identify whether the business environment could nurture fraudulent activities and, then, where in the financial statements evidence of these activities might appear. When fraud seems possible, the financial statement user should execute more detailed financial statement diagnostics to assess whether management has presented accurate financial results.[69] These diagnostics usually come in the form of financial statement ratios which the user compares either to results for the same company in prior years (time-series analyses) or to the results of different companies or an industry average for the same year (cross-sectional analyses).[70] These ratios will not provide conclusive evidence for or against earnings manipulation, but the results provide a starting point from which the financial statement user may decide to focus extra effort.

Fraudulent activities affect income in one of two ways. The first increases net income by increasing current revenues or decreasing current expenses. The second decreases net income by decreasing current revenues or increasing current expenses. The diagnostic ratios we suggest can detect both types of fraud. The financial statement user should look for inconsistencies across time or across companies in either direction.

Most of the ratios used to detect overstated and understated revenues have net sales in the denominator (numerator) and some other item of interest in the numerator (denominator). Examples include:

- Cash Flow from Operations [CFO/Net Sales]
- Bad Debt Expense/Net Sales
- Warranty Expense/Net Sales

Unexplained differences in these ratios across time or across companies in the same industry signal the need for further investigation. By *unexplained*, we mean differences that the user cannot attribute to typical growth rates for the company or for the industry or to changes in the business environment such as a recession or some other macroeconomic condition or to a change in business strategy. Consider the first ratio, CFO/Net Sales. An unexplained decrease (increase) in this ratio may signify overstated (understated) revenue. Notice that the second two ratios have an expense in the numerator and revenue in the denominator. Unexplained changes in these ratios require more investigation to decide whether misstated expenses or revenues caused them.

---

[69]Obviously, internal auditors will have much greater access to management and the internal financial documents of the company. We confine our discussion here to information available to users *outside* of the company.
[70]Industry averages are available on the Internet.

The financial statement user can implement simple ratios, such as bad debt expense/net sales or warranty expense/net sales, to detect inconsistencies in expense recognition. Misstated expenses usually mean misstated assets or liabilities. Expenses that result mainly from management judgment, such as pension expense, depreciation expense, bad debt expense or warranty expense, merit special review. The carrying values of the assets need testing for impairment. The notes provide clues to ascertain the existence of off-balance-sheet liabilities. Calculate turnover ratios, such as inventory and accounts receivable turnover. These ratios reveal combined balance sheet and income statement effects of financial statement preparation and provide an additional perspective on possible inconsistencies.

The process of detecting potential fraud by financial statement users outside a company is time consuming and can be frustrating because you may pursue blind alleys, situations where ratios or other signals suggest investigation but non-fraudulent reasons exist for the results. Comparisons with other industry indicators can mislead as some legitimate companies have such unstable operating results that the time series of diagnostics provides no information. Alternatively, companies in new industries do not have time series over which to perform your diagnostics or may not have any comparison companies. Regardless, using these analytic diagnostics provides a useful start in understanding financial statements.

Analytic Diagnostics to Discover Accounting Fraud

We have discussed the sorts of actions management takes to commit fraud and how these affect the financial statements. One action shows two kinds of accounting fraud affecting income:

- Make current periods look better than they should be accelerating or inventing revenue or by delaying expenses with fraudulent debits to an asset account; or
- Make bad current periods look worse in order to make future periods look better with the booking of fraudulent expenses and special charges, which create fake liabilities, which the fraudster can reverse in the future with credits to income statement accounts.

There are, of course, no easy answers to how to detect fraud early. Successful financial analysts often use diagnostics like these we illustrate. Our examples focus on the first sort of fraud above, where the fraudster makes current income look better than it should, but will work as well for the second kind. They will not help in the diagnosing of fraudulent consolidation policy affecting on-balance-sheet debt.

We recommend that a serious analyst develop several years of diagnostic ratios based on quarterly data and construct similar data series for comparable companies, typically companies in the same industry. The goal is to define benchmarks against which to compare the studied company's results with an intent to find signals that point to the need for investigation.

We illustrate the computations for three years. In practice, analysts prefer to use quarterly data over a five-year period to provide a more accurate data series.

These exhibits, found in Appendix A on page 197 show how the ordinary turnover ratios and the ratio of cash flow from operations to net income can help the analyst focus on potential fraud.

1. Exhibit 1 shows three years of operations for a profitable, growing company built on the following assumptions used to generate the financial statements:
   a. Sales growth of 10 percent per year
   b. Cost of goods sold is 65 percent of sales
   c. Receivables turnover of 6, implying that the company collects its receivables, on average, two months after the sale
   d. Payables turnover of 12, implying that the company pays its suppliers, on average, one month after purchase[71]

---

[71]In most growing, successful businesses, the company finds itself paying its suppliers faster than it receives cash from its customers, creating a chronic cash shortage. Most new business managers find themselves surprised and in a panic. A new business should anticipate this chronic shortage of cash and make arrangements for long-term financing to solve the problem. Short-term borrowings from a bank will cover the situation, because financing receivables is a permanent need, in spite of the fact that it looks short term. Many bankers do not like to provide long-term financing.

    e. General and administrative expense growth at 8 percent per year

    f. Property, plant, equipment and depreciation charges of 7 percent per year

    g. Interest rate on long-term borrowings of 8 percent per year

    f. Income taxes of 40 percent of taxable income

    g. Dividends declared each year of 55 percent of after-tax income

    h. Long-term debt and owners' equity to total assets ratio of 60 percent

        We show three years of operating and cash flow data for this company and show standard financial ratios at the bottom. This set of financial statements illustrates a normal, non-fraudulent base case.

2. Exhibit 2 shows results when, in Year 3, the company has an unexpected bad event, increasing pre-tax expenses [and expenditures] by $100. For our purposes, the cause of the extra $100 expense is not important; we show it as an increase in administrative expenses.

        Look at the diagnostic ratios, at the bottom. The profitability ratios show the expected declines, but the turnover ratios do not change.

3. Exhibit 3 shows what happens when management attempts to cover-up fraud by inflating revenues.[72] Management increases revenues by $100, but takes no other steps. This feeble manipulation shows itself immediately because the balance sheet doesn't balance. No competent fraudster would attempt such a blatant fraud because anyone financially-minded will know that a balance sheet must have equal amounts of assets and sources of funds (liabilities plus owners' equity). The word *signal* appears in the appropriate place to call your attention to the fraud signal. This exhibit reminds you of the elegance and power of double-entry record keeping.

4. Exhibit 4 shows the results of a more sophisticated fraud. It invents fake sales and matches those credits with inflated receivables (debits). It records the increase in income taxes, as well. The diagnostics—receivables turnover ratio and ratio of cash flow from operations to income—signal something worth investigating. This fraud overstates Accounts Receivable, so that a thorough audit of that account might detect the fraud, as well. GAAS audits might easily overlook one such fake receivable because they do not pretend to examine them all in ordinary circumstances. Note the signals, which some call *red flags*.

5. Exhibit 5 shows still more sophistication. The salesperson who generates the bogus sale sends a side letter to the customer and has the company ship goods not yet ordered. The salesman gets permission from the customer to ship, saying the company will not bill the customer until the next period and that the customer will get its usual grace period to pay the bill starting from that later date in the next period. This letter is a *side letter*.[73] An auditor's confirmation of accounts receivable will no longer detect this fraud unless the auditor specifically asks, and the customer fully responds, about the conditions of side letters.

        Still, the turnover ratios—both inventory and receivables—and the ratio of operating cash flow to income signal something unusual, worth investigating.

6. Exhibit 6 shows another common fraud—over-valuing ending inventory, which reduces cost of goods sold and boosts income. The inventory turnover ratio and ratio of operating cash flow to income signal something worth investigating.

These exhibits show that the turnover and cash-flow-to-income ratios for a company committing fraud will go awry. They do not show the false positives—ratios gone awry when a company is not committing fraud. Hence, the analyst can use the ratios to decide where to focus extra effort. These ratios provide a starting point but are not conclusive evidence of fraud.

---

[72]In this exhibit and the following ones, we show both the non-fraud financial statements and the fraudulent ones.

[73]Even honest management has a hard time locating these. Management must be diligent and deal severely with employees found to be issuing side letters.

Accounting Magic

Generally accepted accounting principles permit alternative treatments for certain accounting events. The treatment a company chooses affects the financial statements that the company issues. This section shows how alternative accounting treatments of identical events can lead to reported income figures that differ, perhaps surprisingly, from each other.[1]

The Scenario

On January 1, two companies start in business. The two companies engage in identical activities but account for them differently. Conservative Company chooses the accounting alternatives that will minimize its reported income while High Flyer Company chooses the alternatives that will maximize its reported income. Both companies choose, where permitted, accounting methods that will minimize income taxes. The following events occur during the year.

1. Both companies issue common stock to raise funds necessary to commence a merchandising business.
2. Both companies purchase $6,000,000 of equipment that they assume will have zero salvage value and useful life of 8 years.
3. Both companies make the following purchases of merchandise inventory:

Date	Units Purchased		Unit Price		Cost of Purchase
January 1	85,000	@	$60	=	$ 5,100,000
May 1	95,000	@	$63	=	5,985,000
September 1	100,000	@	$68	=	6,800,000
Total	280,000				$17,885,000

4. During the year, both companies sell 210,000 units at an average price of $100 each so that each realizes sales revenues of $21,000,000.
5. During the year, both companies have selling, general and administrative expenses, excluding officers' salaries, of $3,350,000.

---

[1] The idea and title for this example come from an article by Leonard Spacek, "Business Success Requires an Understanding of Unsolved Problems of Accounting and Financial Reporting," Arthur Andersen Pamphlet (September 25, 1959), pp. 19–28. Since the time Spacek prepared his illustration, generally accepted accounting principles have changed, but several of the alternatives we illustrate he illustrated, too.

6. At the end of the year, both companies award officers options to purchase shares of common stock, as bonuses for jobs well done. These supplement the $350,000 paid to them during the year in salaries. Comparable options have market value of $150,000.

Accounting Alternatives

At the end of the year both companies prepare financial statements. Both must decide how to report the various events that occurred during the year. The companies made the following decisions, all generally acceptable.

Inventory Cost Flow Assumption. During the year, both companies purchased more goods than they sold. Each company must make an assumption about the cost of goods sold it will show on the income statement and, simultaneously, about the cost of ending inventory it will show on the balance sheet. Conservative Company makes a last-in, first-out (LIFO) cost flow assumption while High Flyer Company makes a first-in, first-out (FIFO) assumption.

Because the beginning inventory is zero, the cost of goods available for sale by each company equals the purchases of $17,885,000 during the year. Both companies have 70,000 units in ending inventory. Conservative Company, using LIFO, reports a cost of goods sold of $13,685,000 (= $17,885,000 − 70,000 × $60) while High Flyer Company reports a cost of goods sold of $13,125,000 (= $17,885,000 − 70,000 × $68).

Income tax regulations require a company to use LIFO in its financial statements if it uses LIFO for its tax return. High Flyer wants to report high income, so does not use LIFO in its financial statements and, therefore, forgoes the savings in taxes from using LIFO on its tax returns.

Depreciation. Conservative Company depreciates its equipment using the double-declining-balance method on its financial statements while High Flyer Company uses the straight-line method. Conservative Company takes a full year of depreciation in the year it acquires equipment, while High Flyer Company uses a half-year convention under which it takes only one-half year of depreciation in the first year. (The modified accelerated cost recovery system, MACRS, used by both companies for income tax reporting effectively requires that both take one-half year of depreciation on their tax returns.) Conservative Company therefore reports depreciation expense of $1,500,000 (= 2 × 1/8 × $6,000,000) while High Flyer Company reports depreciation expense of $375,000 (= 1/8 × $6,000,000 × 1/2).

Officers' Bonuses. Conservative Company reports expense of $150,000 for the stock options awarded to officers, while High Flyer Company reports no expense for its officers' stock options. GAAP now require firms to expense options such as this, but as this book goes to press, the rules have not yet taken effect and, see discussion on pages 189–90, the Congress and lobbyists are attacking this rule. We show a difference in accounting treatment so you can see how the accounting treatments differ, even though these differences may disappear during the year 2006. Generally accepted accounting principles recommend, but do not require, that the firm to show the fair market value of qualified stock options granted to employees as an expense.[2] If the officers later exercise the options, both companies will record the cash received (i.e., the options' exercise price times the number of shares issued) as paid-in capital, but High Flyer will never record compensation expense for the options. The IRS allows no deduction on the firm's tax return when the employee earns the options, but allows a compensation expense tax deduction when the employees exercise the options. The deductible amount is the difference between the exercise price of the options and the market value of the shares issued.

Published Income Statements

Income Tax Calculation. We assume a combined federal and state income tax rate of 40 percent. Both companies show deductions for MACRS depreciation of equipment on the income tax return different from the depreciation expense reported to shareholders. Conservative Company also shows an expense for stock option compensation that does not appear its its tax return. Both are *temporary differences*. That is, in subsequent

---

[2]*SFAS No. 123 (revised 2004) Share Based Payment: Accounting for Stock-Based Compensation* has been the most-debated issue ever on the FASB's agenda. See our section "Accounting for the Cost of Employee Stock Options," elsewhere in this book. As this book goes to press, the FASB requires the expensing of stock options.

years, the companies may report on their tax returns amounts different in opposite directions from the amounts they report to shareholders. Consequently, each company reports deferred income taxes on its income statement and deferred tax assets or liabilities on its balance sheet.

High Flyer Company reports smaller depreciation on the income statement than the amount of depreciation claimed on the tax return and will have deferred tax credits on its balance sheet. (Most published annual reports reflect this situation for depreciation.) Conservative Company reports larger depreciation and larger compensation expense on the income statement than the amounts it claims on the tax return and will have deferred tax assets on its balance sheet. (This phenomenon arises for Conservative's depreciation because the company depreciates only one item of equipment and because the first-year conventions for tax reporting and financial reporting differ.) The following equation holds for both companies (dollar amounts are in thousands):

	Income Tax Expense		Income Tax Payable		Deferred Tax Credits		Deferred Tax Debits
Conservative Company:	$786	=	$966	+	$0	−	$180
High Flyer Company:	$1,520	=	$1,190	+	$330	−	$0

Deferred tax credits either increase a deferred tax liability or decrease a deferred tax asset, and the reverse is true of deferred tax debits. In this case, Conservative Company shows a deferred tax asset of $180,000, and High Flyer Company shows a deferred tax liability of $330,000.

The income statements for both companies appear on page 180. As a result of its conservative treatment of accounting alternatives, Conservative Company reports net income and earnings per share about half of High Flyer Company's. Both companies used generally accepted accounting principles and each would receive a clean opinion from its auditor.

Comparisons of Cash Flows

Until the two companies paid their income taxes, they were alike in all economically significant respects. Because High Flyer Company wished to report higher net income, it paid $224,000 (= $1,190,000 − $966,000) more in income taxes than did Conservative Company. Thus, after tax payments, Conservative Company, in a real sense, is wealthier than is High Flyer. Conservative Company ends the year with $224,000 more cash (or other net assets), than does High Flyer.

You might find it instructive to construct statements of cash flows for each of the two companies. You will find that Conservative Company generates $224,000 (= tax savings) more cash from operations than does High Flyer.

Managing Reported Earnings

The simple illustration for Conservative Company and High Flyer Company does not exhaust the set of choices available to a firm to manage its earnings. Managing earnings refers to a process of taking deliberate steps within the constraints of generally accepted accounting principles to bring about a desired level of reported earnings. This section describes some of the techniques for managing earnings and offers arguments for and against an earnings-management policy.

Techniques for managing earnings divide into three categories:

(1) selection of accounting principles,
(2) application of accounting principles, and
(3) timing of asset acquisitions and dispositions.

Next, we give some examples of actions in each of these categories.

180   **ACCOUNTING MAGIC**

Accounting Magic Comparative Income Statements
For the Year Ending December 31
(Amounts in Thousands Except Per Share Amounts)

	Conservative Company		High Flyer Company	
	Financial Statement	Tax Return	Financial Statement	Tax Return
Sales Revenues	$21,000	$21,000	$21,000	$21,000
Expenses				
Cost of Goods Sold	$13,685	$13,685	$13,125	$13,125
Depreciation on Equipment	1,500	1,200[a]	375	1,200[a]
Officers' Compensation:				
Salaries	350	350	350	350
Stock Options	150	0	0	0
Other Selling, General and				
Administrative Expenses	3,350	3,350	3,350	3,350
Expenses Before Income Taxes	$19,035	$18,585	$17,200	$18,025
Income Before Taxes	$ 1,965	$ 2,415	$ 3,800	$ 2,975
Income Tax Expense[b]	786		1,520	
Net Income	$ 1,179		$ 2,280	
Earnings Per Share in Dollars (500,000 Shares Outstanding)	$ 2.36		$ 4.56	

[a]Amounts based on MACRS, 5-year class; 20 percent of cost is deducted in the first year: .20 × $6,000 = $1,200.
[b]Computation of Income Tax Expense:

Income Before Taxes	$ 1,965	$ 2,415	$ 3,800	$ 2,975
Income Tax Expense on Current Income (at 40 percent)	$ 786		$ 1,520	
Income Tax Currently Payable		$ 966		$ 1,190
Income Taxes Deferred by the Timing Difference from Depreciation:				
Dr. = .40 × ($1,200 − $1,500)	$ (120)			
Cr. = .40 × ($1,200 − $375)			$ 330	
Income Taxes Deferred by the Timing Difference from Stock Options:				
Dr. = .40 × ($0 − $150)	$ (60)			

Selection of Accounting Principles
1. Revenue recognition—percentage of completion, completed contract, time of sale, installment.
2. Inventory cost-flow assumption—FIFO, LIFO, weighted average.
3. Depreciation method—straight-line, declining-balance, sum-of-the-years'-digits.
4. Leases—operating, capital.
5. Corporate acquisitions—purchase, pooling of interests.
6. Mineral resource activities—successful-efforts costing, full costing.

Application of Accounting Principles
1. Estimates of degree of completion of contracts on which the percentage-of-completion method is used.
2. Estimates of service lives and salvage values of depreciable assets.
3. Estimates of uncollectable rate on accounts receivable.
4. Estimate of cost of warranty plans.
5. Treatment of indirect costs as product costs versus period expenses.
6. Classification of common stock investments as trading securities or as available-for-sale securities.

7. Selection of actuarial cost basis for pension plan.
8. Selection of interest rates for capitalized leases and for pension accounting.

Timing of Asset Acquisitions and Dispositions

1. Timing of discretionary expenditures for research and development, advertising, and maintenance costs, which become expenses in the period when the firm incurs costs.
2. Timing of the sale of property, plant, and equipment or of investments to accelerate or delay the recognition of a gain or loss.
3. Accelerating or delaying shipments of merchandise to customers at the end of a period.

These lists, although not exhaustive, indicate the variety of avenues available to management to manage earnings.

Arguments About Managing Earnings

Whether accounting magic matters to the reader of financial statements depends on the answers to two questions. First, do managers select accounting techniques strategically? Second, do managers or their firms gain anything by making strategic choices? Arguments on both sides of these questions, particularly the latter, vary both as to their underlying logic and to the evidence cited to support the position. We present the arguments here in as unbiased a manner as possible so that readers can make up their own minds.

Strategic Choices. Even if managers could make all accounting decisions with the sole objective of reporting economic reality faithfully, they would face complex choices. Managers face conflicting goals and objectives when they make financial reporting decisions. For example, in choosing between LIFO and FIFO, a manager must decide what aspect of economic reality matters most. Nearly all firms manage their inventories internally using FIFO, and FIFO typically creates a more realistic balance sheet because the FIFO ending inventory amount reflects current costs. Managers cannot manipulate FIFO income with end-of-year purchases as they can LIFO, which may reassure investors. On the other hand, LIFO creates a more realistic income statement, because the LIFO cost of goods sold number reflects current costs. LIFO gives a tax savings[3] to firms facing increasing input prices, as our example illustrates, which leaves investors with more wealth. Last and not at all least, LIFO results in lower net income when used by firms with increasing inventory costs, as our example illustrates.

The LIFO/FIFO decision is the only accounting choice that affects both the firm's current tax bill and reported earnings. Many anecdotes and some academic studies, however, support the argument that managers make accounting decisions with the intent or hope of reporting higher earnings. Aside from changes to LIFO, most firms' voluntary (i.e., not mandated by changes in GAAP) changes of accounting procedure result in higher earnings. Firms that make these changes have lower sales and earnings growth than other firms, on average, prior to making a change. When a change in GAAP mandates an accounting change, firms whose earnings increase most as a result of the new GAAP are most likely to adopt the new method before the rules require them to do so.[4] While this evidence does not prove that managements make accounting choices for strategic reasons, it suggests such a conclusion.

Capital Market Efficiency. One widely-accepted view holds that earnings management is futile because capital markets are efficient. When market prices adjust quickly, fully and in an unbiased manner to publicly available information, one cannot construct trading strategies based on observable data that consistently make money, and earnings management merely wastes valuable managerial time. Early theoretical and empirical stud-

---

[3]More precisely, LIFO defers income taxes, sometimes for long periods of time. Because taxes paid later have smaller economic cost that taxes paid sooner, LIFO does save taxes measured in present value of cash flows.
[4]See Morton Pincus and Charles Wasley, "The Incidence of Accounting Changes and Characteristics of Firms Making Accounting Changes," *Accounting Horizons* (June 1994): 1–24, and the references listed therein.

ies provided support for the efficiency of capital markets.[5] For example, several studies examined the effects of changes in accounting methods on stock prices, and found that changes in accounting methods with no real or economic effects (that is, those that do not affect cash flows) appear to have little effect on stock prices.[6] Using information from the financial statements and notes, investors can distinguish changes with real effects from those without, and react accordingly.

Proponents of the contrary view, namely that capital markets are not fully efficient, acknowledge this work but counter with two observations. First, the empirical work on market efficiency looks at average results for large numbers of firms. Because stock returns vary around these averages, in many cases the market has not priced securities efficiently for particular firms at particular times. Proponents of non-efficiency point to examples where the market prices of particular firms' shares decreased dramatically after analyses of the firms' (previously disclosed) accounting procedures appeared in the financial press.[7] Proponents of efficient capital markets counter that examples selected after the fact cannot disprove market efficiency, because trading opportunities require one to predict *future* stock prices.

The second observation of the non-efficient-market proponents is that later studies provide evidence that capital markets do not adjust fully to available information, even in aggregate. Several recent studies document successful trading strategies for large portfolios of firms based on financial statement data, and suggest that stock prices reflect a naïve understanding of accounting information.[8]

If capital markets are fully efficient, then earnings management cannot produce a capital market advantage. On the other hand, if capital markets are not efficient in all cases, then by managing earnings, firms may take advantage of inefficiencies and obtain capital at a lower cost than if they do not practice earnings management. In this case, investors do not necessarily allocate the economy's capital resources in a socially optimal way.

Management Incentives and Survival. Over sufficiently long time periods, net income equals cash-in minus cash-out, other than transactions with owners. Some corporate managers acknowledge that, because of this eventual reckoning, earnings management will not benefit the firm in the long run. They point out, however, that the long run comprises a series of short-run periods during which shareholders, creditors, and boards of directors make decisions based in part on accounting data. (See *agency theory* in the Glossary.)

Financial contracts—such as bond indenture agreements and executive compensation contracts—often use accounting earnings as triggers for transactions and, thereby, provide managers with incentives to manage the reported numbers in the short run. For example, bond covenants frequently contain financial ratio constraints

---

[5]See Eugene F. Fama, "Efficient Capital Markets: A Review of Theory and Empirical Work," *Journal of Finance* (May 1970): 383–417; Nicholas J. Gonedes and Nicholas Dopuch, "Capital Market Equilibrium, Information-Production and Selecting Accounting Techniques: Theoretical Framework and Review of Empirical Work," *Studies on Financial Accounting Objectives: 1974*, Supplement to Vol. 12, *Journal of Accounting Research*: 48–129; and Robert S. Kaplan, "Information Content of Financial Accounting Numbers: A Survey of Empirical Evidence," in: *Symposium of Impact of Accounting Research in Financial Accounting and Disclosure on Accounting Practice*, ed. by T. Keller and R. Abdel-khalik (Durham: Duke University Press, 1978). See also Thomas R. Dyckman and Dale Morse, *Efficient Capital Markets and Accounting: A Critical Analysis*, 2nd ed. (Englewood Cliffs, N.J.: Prentice-Hall, 1986).

[6]See, for example, Ray Ball, "Changes in Accounting Techniques and Stock Prices," *Empirical Research in Accounting: Selected Studies, 1972*, Supplement to Vol. 10, *Journal of Accounting Research*: 1–38; Robert S. Kaplan and Richard Roll, "Investor Evaluation of Accounting Information: Some Empirical Evidence," *Journal of Business* (April 1972): 225–257; Shyam Sunder, "Relationship Between Accounting Changes and Stock Prices: Problems of Measurement and Some Empirical Evidence," *Empirical Research in Accounting: Selected Studies, 1973*, Supplement to Vol. 11, *Journal of Accounting Research*: 1–45. A more recent study on the same topic is Bala G. Dharan and Baruch Lev, "The Valuation Consequences of Accounting Changes: A Multi-year Examination," *Journal of Accounting, Auditing and Finance* (Fall 1993): 475–494.

[7]For several examples, see Abraham J. Briloff, *More Debits Than Credits* (New York: Harper & Row, 1976). For an analysis of these examples see George Foster, "Briloff and the Capital Market," *Journal of Accounting Research* (Spring 1979): 262–274.

[8]See the papers published in *Current Studies on The Information Content of Accounting Earnings*, Supplement to Vol. 27, *Journal of Accounting Research*, especially Victor L. Bernard and Jacob K. Thomas, "Post-earnings-announcement Drift: Delayed Price Response or Risk Premium?" (1989): 1–36; Robert N. Freeman and Senyo Tse, "The Multiperiod Information Content of Accounting Earnings: Confirmations and Contradictions of Previous Earnings Reports," (1989): 49–79; and Jane A. Ou and Stephen H. Penman, "Accounting Measurement, Price-Earnings Ratio, and the Information Content of Security Prices," (1989): 111–144. See also Jeffery S. Abarbanell and Brian J. Bushée, "Abnormal Returns to a Fundamental Analysis Strategy," *The Accounting Review* (January 1998): 19-46.

(see the Glossary at *bond indenture* and *ratio*), which use reported accounting numbers. If an accounting change prevents violation of one of these constraints, the firm may avoid costly renegotiation with its creditors.[9] Likewise, corporate boards often link managers' bonus provisions to earnings performance. If managers can manipulate earnings numbers, they may be able to affect their own compensation.[10]

Managers sometimes prefer lower earnings for strategic reasons. For example, firms facing political or regulatory scrutiny, labor contract negotiations or substantial legal damage judgments may benefit if they can appear less profitable.[11] If managers propose a management buyout (a transaction in which managers buy the company from shareholders) they may be able to negotiate a lower buy-out price if the company appears unprofitable. Several studies suggest that managers use discretion in applying accounting procedures to reduce earnings when faced with strategic concerns like these.[12]

Corporate managers observe that, since other firms practice earnings management, their survival dictates that they do so as well. Shareholders, they argue, do not want to see wide, unexpected fluctuations in earnings from year to year. To smooth out these fluctuations and create the impression that management has operations under control, they continue, requires earnings management. In saying this, managers espouse the view that investors and creditors use accounting data naïvely, ignoring differences in accounting choices. Regardless of whether investors and creditors are naïve in using accounting numbers, if managers *believe* that it is true, then such managers have an incentive to manage earnings, and financial statement readers will find their accounting choices to be informative.

[9]See Messod D. Beneish and Eric Press, "Costs of Technical Violation of Accounting-Based Debt Covenants," *The Accounting Review* (April 1993): 233–257; and Amy Patricia Sweeney, "Debt-covenant Violations and Managers' Accounting Responses," *Journal of Accounting and Economics* (May 1994): 281–308.

[10]See Paul M. Healy, "The Effect of Bonus Schemes on Accounting Decisions," *Journal of Accounting and Economics* (April 1985): 85–107; and Paul M. Healy, Sok-Hyon Kang and Krishna Palepu, "The Effect of Accounting Procedure Changes on CEOs' Cash Salary and Bonus Compensation," *Journal of Accounting and Economics* (April 1987): 7–34. Interestingly, the latter paper finds that boards of directors appear not to adjust compensation formulas for accounting method changes.

[11]See Jennifer J. Jones, "Earnings Management During Import Relief Investigations," *Journal of Accounting Research* (Autumn 1991): 193–228; Steven C. Hall and William W. Stammerjohan, "Damage Awards and Earnings Management in the Oil Industry," *The Accounting Review* (January 1997): 47–65; and Kimberly Galligan Key, "Political Cost Incentives for Earnings Management in the Cable Television Industry," *Journal of Accounting and Economics* (November 1997): 309–337;

[12]See Linda Elizabeth DeAngelo, "Accounting Numbers as Market Valuation Substitutes: A Study of Management Buyouts of Public Stockholders," *The Accounting Review* (July 1986): 400–420; and Woody Y. Wu, "Management Buyouts and Earnings Management," *Journal of Accounting, Auditing and Finance* (Fall 1997): 373–389.

Tension in Reporting Income—Geography of the Income Statement and Implications for Valuation

Why do management and investors care about the placement of items in the income statement—the geography of the income statement? This section explains.

Accountants and managers typically classify operations as either recurring or nonrecurring and as either core activities or peripheral activities. Here we investigate the importance of the distinction between recurring and nonrecurring. To focus on that distinction, we ignore the distinction between cash flows, which we use in the valuations, and reported income based on accruals. We discuss the distinction between cash flows and reported income in Accounting Magic.

Measurement of Value from Cash Flow Data

Refer to Exhibit 1, which derives the value of a hypothetical company from the present value of the cash flows from its individual activities, some recurring, some not. Think of the cash flows as being aftertax. Assume the discount rate appropriate for finding the present value of the cash flows is 10 percent per year.

The firm engages in six activities, numbered 1 through 6, shown in Exhibit 1.

Activity 1. The first activity generates $100 per year, with the cash flow at the end of year, indefinitely. The present value of this activity is $1,000 (= $100/.10).[1] Investors sometimes call this process of deriving value from a series of future cash flows capitalizing earnings. The analyst might say that the earnings of $100 have a price/earnings ratio of 10 or that the earnings "deserve [or carry] a multiple of 10."

Activity 2. The second activity generates $30 at the end of the first year, and a cash flow that grows by 6 percent per year thereafter. The present value of this activity is $750 [= $30/(.10 − .06)].[2] The price/earnings ratio

---

[1]The present value of a perpetuity, an infinite series of future cash flows, of $1 per period received at the end of the period is $1/r, where r is the discount rate. The price/earnings ratio is the reciprocal of the discount rate. In the example, where the discount rate is 10 percent per period, then the price/earnings ratio is 10.

[2]See the preceding footnote. If the cash flow starts at $1 per year and grows at rate g per year, then the present value of the growing cash flows is $1/(r − g).

Exhibit 1

MEASUREMENT OF VALUE FROM INCOME DATA
Cash Flows Occur at the End of Each Period

Activity	End of Period									Present Value of Activity using Discount Rate = 10%
	1	2	3	4	5	6	7	8	...	
1 Recurring	$100	$100	$100	$100	$100	$100	$100	$100	...	$1,000.00
2 Recurring, But Grow at 6% Per Year	30	32	34	36	38	40	43	45	...	750.00
3 Cyclic	115	0	115	0	115	0	115	0	...	602.38
4 Nonrecurring	120	0	0	0	0	0	0	0	...	109.09
5 Recurring	−40	−40	−40	−40	−40	−40	−40	−40	...	(400.00)
6 Nonrecurring	−70	0	0	0	0	0	0	0	...	(63.64)
Present Value [=Fair Market Value] of Entire Firm										**$1,997.84**

(or multiple) for these cash flows is 25, because of their growth. Those interested in higher stock prices want investors to think of the company as a growth stock, because investors put higher values on growing-earnings companies than on stable-earnings companies.

Activity 3. The third activity is cyclic, generating $115 per year at the end of each odd-numbered year. The present value of this activity is $602.38.[3]

Activity 4. The fourth activity is nonrecurring, generating a single cash flow of $120 at the end of the first year, with present value of $109.09 (= $120/1.10) at the start of the first year.

Activity 5. The fifth activity, an expenditure (outflow), uses $40 of cash each year, at the end of each year. The present value of this activity is −$400.

Activity 6. The sixth activity, a single expenditure (outflow), uses $70 cash at the end of the first year and has present value of −$63.64 (= −$70/1.10).

The value of the firm is the sum of the present values of its individual activities, $1,998 in Exhibit 1. Note that most, more than 97 percent, of the value of this firm in this example comes from the recurring activities. In deriving firm values, investors generally care about recurring activities more than nonrecurring ones.

Presentation in the Income Statement

Exhibit 2 shows income of $255 for the year in the boxes on the left. How are investors to deduce the value of the company from this one year's income statement? They can't. This firm is too complex for even a sophisticated user to derive the value from a single column of data, without further information.

A manipulating manager who wanted to maximize the market value of this firm would want the external investor to view the firm as shown—good news is recurring, bad news in nonrecurring. If an investor believed that, then such an investor would estimate the firm value at approximately $3,500—using a price/earnings ratio of 10 on the seemingly recurring income of $365 and a one-time subtraction of the nonrecurring loss of $110.

---

[3]Think of this series of cash flows as a perpetuity with $115 per period, but each period is two years long. Then, when the discount rate is 10 percent per year, the discount rate for a two-year period must be 21 percent [= (1.10 × 1.10) − 1]. The cash flows from Year 2 onwards have present value of $547.62 (= $115/.21) at the start of Year 2 and present value of $497.84 (=$547.62/1.10) at the start of Year 1. The $115 cash flow received at the end of Year 1 has present value of $104.54 (=$115/1.10) at the start of Year 1. The entire series has present value of $602.38 at the start of Year 1.

Exhibit 2

PRESENTATION OF INFORMATION IN INCOME STATEMENT

Income Statement For Year		But, Manipulating Managers Would Like You to Think	So that You Derive Values From:	Rather than From:
Activity 1	$100	Recurring	$100	Recurring
Activity 2	30	Recurring and Growing ...	30	Recurring and Growing
Activity 3	115	Recurring	115	Cyclic Recurring
Activity 4	120	Recurring	120	Nonrecurring
			$365 = Total Recurring	
Activity 5	−40	Nonrecurring	−40	Recurring
Activity 6	−70	Nonrecurring	−70	Nonrecurring
			($110) = Total Nonrecurring	
Net Income ..	$255			

By using Multiple on Recurring Income But not for Nonrecurring Income:

$$\text{Value} = \$365/.10 - \$110 = \$3,540$$

Firm with These Activities Would Likely Report in a Format Such as This:

Recurring Operations	
Revenues	$245
Expenses	(40)
Earnings from Recurring Operations ...	$205
Non-recurring items, net ..	50
Earnings	$255

Growing activities, such as Activity 2, present a problem to the analyst in valuations. No matter how management classifies Activity 2 in the income statement, it cannot convey in the statement itself how the analyst should value that activity. The MDA section of the report, where management can explain and expand on the firm's activities, gives management the forum for explaining that such activities are growth opportunities and giving the analysts evidence that they should take the expected growth into the valuations.

In practice, neither management nor analysts can so easily classify activities as in this illustration, designed to teach the importance of the recurring/nonrecurring difference. In practice, management has some discretion in classifying activities as recurring or nonrecurring. For example, a company might say that the write-down of a particular asset is nonrecurring because the asset is unique and by definition the firm can write it down only once. The same company might, however, acknowledge that it has many unique assets and different lines of business and that write-downs of some of these can be expected each year in the future.

Some companies report bad news—losses—as special charges, a label designed to evoke the thought of nonrecurring in the mind of the reader. For example, WMX Technologies (formerly named Waste Management) reported special charges for six consecutive years, without indicating that these might continue year to year. Over this six-year period, WMX reported net income of about $2 billion; these special charges totaled about $1.5 billion. As this book goes to press the SEC is engaged in litigation with the former top executives of WMX to recover their ill-gotten compensation—amounts the executives earned from bonuses and other payments based on reported income.

Sensitivity of Market Values to Growth and Discount Rates

Market valuations based on price/earnings (P/E) multiples can change. P/E multiples for cash flows (or earnings) change as discount rates and growth rates change. Exhibit 3 shows you how sensitive market valuations are to these changes.

Exhibit 3
P/E RATIOS IMPLIED BY VARIOUS COMBINATIONS OF GROWTH AND DISCOUNT RATES

$$1/(r - g)$$

Growth Rate [g] =	Discount Rate [r] = 8%	10%	12%	15%	20%
0.0%	12.5	10.0	8.3	6.7	5.0
0.5%	13.3	10.5	8.7	6.9	5.1
1.0%	14.3	11.1	9.1	7.1	5.3
1.5%	15.4	11.8	9.5	7.4	5.4
2.0%	16.7	12.5	10.0	7.7	5.6
2.5%	18.2	13.3	10.5	8.0	5.7
3.0%	20.0	14.3	11.1	8.3	5.9
3.5%	22.2	15.4	11.8	8.7	6.1
4.0%	25.0	16.7	12.5	9.1	6.3
5.0%	33.3	20.0	14.3	10.0	6.7

Suppose the Federal Reserve raises interest rates so that the discount rate goes from 10% to 12%.

Congress proposes new regulations which analysts believe will lower growth in the economy from 4% to 3%.

How much will the stock market change?

Assume that, initially, the discount rate is 10 percent per year and that investors expect earnings to grow at 3 percent per year. Note that the P/E multiple is 14.3. That is, if investors expect earnings to recur and to grow at 3 percent per year, they will value the company at 14.3 times earnings. Each dollar of initial earnings, expected to grow, will add $14.30 to market value of the firm.

Now assume that the discount rate increases to 12 percent per year, say because the Federal Reserve increases interest rates or world tension increases uncertainty about the future of financial markets. Assume, further, that the investors expect growth rates of earnings to decrease to 2.5 percent per year, say because of expectation of increased government regulation. Note that the P/E multiple drops to 10.5. This means the value of the firm is only $10.50.

Under these conditions, one would observe that the market value of the firm would drop by more than 25 percent (= $1.0 - 10.5/14.3$).

Accounting for the Cost of Employee Stock Options: A Tale from Silicon Valley

Within the last two decades, no subject has caused more controversy in accounting than the accounting for the cost of employee stock options. When it issued *SFAS No. 119* in 1995, FASB said that this issue threatened to end standard-setting in the private sector and that the debate had ceased to be rational. The debate rages as this book goes to press. The FASB proposes to require the expensing of options, while various industry groups oppose such a requirement.

Some firms, such as GE, grant to employees the right to buy a specified number of shares of the firm's stock at a fixed price, called the *exercise price*, usually the price on the day the firm awards the options to the employee, say, $10 per share. The employee, typically, has several years to decide whether to exercise the option—that is, give up the option and cash in return for the shares. If the stock price rises above the exercise price, say to $18 per share, then the employee can give up the option and $10 in return for a share with current market value of $18.

Such options have value to employees who receive them and many companies, particularly the high-tech Silicon Valley companies, award such options to employees in lieu of higher cash wages. GE computes the value of the options it grants employees and discloses that information in its notes, page 79 of the 2003 annual report, reproduced on page 121 of this book. Employees have been happy to take such options as part of their compensation in hopes that the employer's shares will skyrocket in value, enriching the employee.

The accounting issue has been: how much should the employer firm, such as GE, charge to expense in the period when it awards an option to its employees. The FASB proposed a method for computing such amounts of expense and proposed requiring that firms report such amounts as expense. Some members of Congress pressured the FASB into not enacting its proposals.

The issue remains controversial. As this book goes to press, the FASB has already issued rules requiring firms to show in the computation of net income a compensation expense for the cost of options granted to employees that period. Industry lobbies Congress and the SEC to delay the impending implementation of these rules. The newly proposed chairman of the SEC, Congressman Chris Cox, has, before the President nominated him as Chairman, publicly criticized these rules, as well.

The cost to the firm of awarding the option can never exceed the market value of the share itself on the date of the award. This is true because the firm can always, on that day, go out into the market to buy a share for the current market price, holding that share until the employee exercises the option.

At the height of the debate, chief financial officers (CFOs) from Silicon Valley lobbied against the FASB proposal. We believed that many of those CFOs did not understand the FASB proposal, nor its consequences. Consequently, at a private seminar on the subject at which one of us taught, we administered the following quiz to the Silicon Valley CFOs. Answer the quiz for yourself, before reading on.

Multiple Choice Quiz:

Below appear excerpts from an article in the Viewpoint Section of the *San Francisco Examiner* [a popular Silicon Valley newspaper] by Michael Rothschild.

> *For example, if StartUp Inc. recruits the brilliant software designer Joe Bithead ... by offering him the option to buy 10,000 shares of StartUp's stock at its current price of a penny a share, what's the value of Joe's grant? If StartUp goes belly up, as 80 percent of new high-tech firms do, the grant is worthless. .... If, on the other hand, after five years of struggle, StartUp manages to create a successful product and outperforms its competitors, the company's stock might sell for $10 a share on the public market. For a penny each, Joe can buy the 10,000 shares. .... He unloads them in the market for a $100,000 profit.*

The accounting question is, What cost, if any, does StartUp incur on day 1 of the grant to Bithead of an option to acquire 10,000 shares five years hence for $.01 per share? StartUp shares currently trade in public stock markets. On the date of grant the market price is $.01 per share. Because the word *cost* has so many meanings (see *cost terminology* in the Glossary), make the question operational and specific by considering the following.

Imagine that you are the financial executive of StartUp and that Goldman Sachs offers to relieve you of the obligation to deliver the shares to Bithead. That is, Goldman will take a payment from you today and will deliver the shares to Bithead if he exercises the options but will do nothing otherwise, except keep your cash. How much are you willing to pay Goldman *today* to relieve you of your obligation to Bithead? That is, you pay Goldman now and they later deliver shares to Bithead if he exercises his options. No one can be sure of the exact answer, given the sketchy data, but which of the following ranges do you think most likely?

a. $0 to $10.

b. $10 to $100.

c. $100 to $1,000.

d. $1,000 to $10,000.

e. $10,000 to $100,000.

f. Some other answer.

[End of Quiz.]

Have you decided on your answer? The answer must be either *a* or *b*. The cost per option cannot exceed one penny per share, for otherwise StartUp would merely buy the shares on the open market, rather than pay Goldman Sachs to relieve StartUp of the burden. The total cost of the options awarded to Bithead, then, cannot exceed $100 (= 10,000 shares × $.01 per share). We think the answer is likely to be in the range of $15 - $40 for these shares, so we would answer *b*.

The Silicon Valley CFOs answered as follows: a = 3, b = 3, c = 6, d = 8, e = 5, and f = 1. That is, only six of the 26 participating got the answer right, which means that 20 of the 26 got it wrong. In the following discussion, we pointed out that these officers should probably understand the cost of options better than they did before arguing so hard against the proposed accounting. It's no wonder that a CFO would dislike the proposed accounting for options which the CFO thinks cost $10,000 when they actually cost no more than $100. About 25 percent of the Silicon Valley CFOs had beliefs that much in error.

Give Financial Literacy a Chance: Leave No Audit Committee Behind

Recent recommendations for the oversight of accounting and corporate governance will entail more regulation. We doubt that more regulation will get us where we want to be—we have too much already. Here, we suggest that we will get where we want to be when we let corporate audit committees take control of the interaction between accounting, internal controls, and governance.

In 1999, the Blue Ribbon Committee on Improving the Effectiveness of Corporate Audit Committee of the New York Stock Exchange and the National Association of Securities Dealers, suggested that publicly traded companies have audit committees with at least three independent directors who are financially literate. Such literacy, they said, "signifies the ability to read and understand fundamental financial statements, including a company's balance sheet, income statement and cash flow statement." The Blue Ribbon Committee likely erred in using the term *financial literacy*, not the narrower term *accounting literacy* in referring to the ability to read the financial statements for reasons we explain below.

By the end of December 1999, the NYSE had added to its listing requirements the following:

(b) **Each member of the audit committee shall be financially literate,** as such qualification is interpreted by the company's Board of Directors in its business judgment, or must become financially literate within a reasonable period of time after his or her appointment to the audit committee; and ....

The NASD has a similar listing requirement.

What is financial literacy? Start with what passes for a joke in accounting: the understanding that every number on the balance sheet, except one, involves a judgment. Which one? Cash you say? No; what about the bid-asked spread on conversion of foreign currency, say Mexican pesos, into dollars at the balance sheet date. Number of shares outstanding you say? No; long-time auditor and friend Bob Elliott of KPMG pointed out that in the Penn Central bankruptcy, he could not measure the number of shares outstanding. The only certain number on the balance sheet is its date.

The SEC recognizes that all the financial numbers require judgments. It requires registrants' management to describe the critical accounting judgments and estimates it must make in order to prepare the financial statements. Here's my current proposal for audit committee financial literacy.

First, to be financially literate, you must understand the transactions that cause management to have to make the judgment or estimate. Another way to say this is: you must understand how the company expects to make money. I'll illustrate by using GE management's disclosure of its critical accounting policies and estimates, which starts on page 118 of this book.

GE mentions pension issues in its note, in the left-hand column of its page 68, on page 106 of this book. Now, understand the transactions that cause management to have to make a judgment about pensions carrying value.

GE contributes cash to pension funds for employees. The funds invest the cash and sell the investments later when time comes to make pension payments to employees. GE must estimate the present value of the liabilities for future pension payments. GE tells us that the earnings rate on the investments and the discount rate for the liabilities affect its reported numbers.

Now, the second component of financial literacy: What choices among accounting methods and estimates must management make in reporting on those transactions? In GE's case management must make two sorts of choices to current pension expense, for the asset earnings rate and the liability discount rate. GE tells us that it has relatively little discretion in estimating the discount rate for liabilities. Let's consider the choice management must make about the earnings rate on the invested assets.

GE might use the historical rate of return on stocks or on bonds or on a combined portfolio. It might use historical averages covering the period since the 1920's (about as early as you can go and get good historical data) or the last decade or the last year. These averages vary widely—from around 3 percent up to over 12 percent.

Third, the next leg of financial literacy: what did management choose and why? GE chose 8.5 percent. It tells us how it derived that number but not why it used that particular derivation.

Fourth, and most important: A **financial literate** needs to understand the implications for financial reporting of management's choice. For example, choosing 8.5 percent, rather than 9.5 percent as GE chose in an earlier year, increases the amount of pension expense for the current year. The financial literate needs to know how management can manipulate the earnings rate to manage reported income. I'd like to have the audit committee understand the implications of management choices for potential manipulation of financial reporting.

We think the financially literate audit committee member should understand the transactions underlying the critical accounting judgments and estimates, the accounting issues for those transactions, why management chose as it did, and the implications of those choices for potential income manipulation.[1] We'd say that a financial literate does not qualify for board membership on that basis alone. We could say financial literacy is necessary, but not sufficient, to hold audit committee membership.

Many current board members believe these criteria for literacy are too tough. Their arguments are: I know I'm good enough to be on this audit committee and I can't do all that. It's too much to ask; I deserve to here; therefore, the criteria are wrong.

We've identified a cause of what's gone wrong with the accounting profession and its interaction with governance. We haven't demanded enough from our audit committee members who, then, can't demand enough from the auditors. The outside accountants have had their primary intellectual relation with the CFO, and not with the audit committee. Experience suggests that when the audit partner can discuss accounting matters with someone who understands the accounting issues and their causes, then, the partner becomes more independent of management. When the committee allies with the auditor, the pair can better deal with management than the auditor has been able to alone.

In putting people on the audit committee, the selectors act as though they think general business savvy includes enough knowledge of accounting to get by. It doesn't. Several audit committee members who find the criteria too tough say, "And besides, I don't need to understand all that, because I know how to ask the tough questions."

We respond, "What good does it do you to know how to ask the tough questions if you don't know how to evaluate the answers?" So we have constructed a Tough Questions Quiz. See Exhibit 1. Every company who sells other than for cash, and that's most companies, has a problem of accounting for expected uncollectible accounts receivable. GE mentions its issues with respect to financing receivables on page 66 of its annual report, page 104 of this book. We think every audit committee member should be able to ask the CFO, "How do you know the

---

[1]We think all board members should understand the first of these. You might be surprised at how few do.

allowance for uncollectibles is adequate?" and then evaluate the answers. The Tough Questions Quiz gives eight possible answers, some complete, some bafflegab—the sort a CFO trying to put one over on you might try, and others OK as far as they go, but requiring the right follow-up questions. The median number of correct responses to this quiz is under half.

I want the audit committee member to have in his or her own head those four pieces of understanding, not necessarily on the day of joining, but soon thereafter. We need not make knowing these items prerequisite to joining, but to staying on.

What is the state of financial literacy? Over the past few years, we have administered a financial literacy quiz to about 1,000 attendees at our directors' educational programs offered at Chicago, Stanford, and Wharton.[2] We do not have a scientific sample because we promise the attendees anonymity if they will take the quiz, so the takers have self-selected themselves. You can see the quiz at: www.gore.survey

The median score over the 25 multiple choice questions is about 40 percent.[3] Only 6 percent understand when management actions to manipulate income are allowed. Fewer than 20 percent of the quiz takers understand that retained earnings are not assets, but sources of financing.

Audit Committees, at least the ones who voluntarily take our quiz, are not yet financially literate. Here's where I regret the label *financial literacy*, instead of the more precise *accounting literacy*. Many people who are financially literate in the sense of understanding corporate finance or investments or financial asset management are not accounting literate. Many of these feel wrongly labeled financially illiterate when they are merely not accounting literate.

We can get audit committees comprising the financially literate, but nominating committees will need to want to get there. Typically, management has had strong input to board membership and many in top management want other CEO's on the board, not necessarily those who are financially literate. The ideal board member has been the CEO with wisdom and vision, which are not likely correlates of financial literacy. We likely cannot populate audit committees with people who are both financially literate and have CEO vision. Boards will likely have to choose specialists, not generalists, in order to get three independent financially literate audit committee members and most won't have CEO vision. We'd prefer that CEO's be financially literate, but we observe many are not.

Second choice appears to have been sitting CFO's. Audit committee members say, "We're OK; one of our audit committee members is the CFO of another company." I think the evidence shows that not all CFO's are financially literate, although almost all could get there. There are at least five paths to CFO these days: up through the controller function, up through the treasurer function, up through operational management, recruited from investment banking, and recruited from public accounting. Only those who have come up the controller and public accounting routes have career paths requiring accounting literacy. The treasurer has spent a career in corporate finance—from whom and when to raise funds using what instruments; how to relate to financial analysts. The investment banker has spent a career on valuations and M&A activity. We don't mean that former treasurers and investment bankers are bad CFO's. CFO's do their best when they look forward; accounting often looks backward. Many CFO's have had career paths and main responsibilities that do not naturally give them the exposure to financial accounting. Hence, they do not come to financial literacy as a result of their career paths. Capable of getting there? Yes. There as a result of prior work? Not necessarily.

Look at past issues of *CFO Magazine*. Tally the career paths of the glamorous folks featured thereon. Note that most of them have been treasurers, not controllers. Don't take sustenance from the fact that your audit committee has a CFO without checking what that person knows about accounting.

Getting back to the audit committee, think football a minute. These people are the defense, maybe even the last line of defense. The audit committee plays a specialized role on defense. Its business is tackling or deflecting passes, not scoring touchdowns. They shouldn't be in the headlines.

So, we say give Financial Literacy a try.

---

[2]Some pages in the handouts [H: pp 12–16] describe a typical program—the next one, in fact. [Send us some directors.]
[3]See R.L. Weil, "Audit Committees Can't Add," *Harvard Business Review*, May 2004, 21–23.

Criteria for Financial [Accounting] Literacy for Audit Committee Members

Refer to Management Discussion and Analysis of the company's annual report, to the section describing the company's Critical Accounting Policies and Estimates.

1. Understand the *transactions* that require the judgments described. [We think all board members should understand how the company earns income, which we think means all board members should master this step.]
2. Understand the *accounting and measurement issues* for the policies and estimates.
3. Understand management's *choices* among policies and methods for making estimates and the reasons for them.
4. Understand the implications of management choices for *potential manipulation* of financial reporting.

Market Reaction to Improvements in Potential for Financial Literacy

Recent research suggests that large companies who improved the potential for financial literacy during the period 2000 through 2004 had share price increases larger than those of otherwise-similar companies that did not improve by over 4.5 percent per year. See the research by Douglas J. Coates, M. Laurentius Marais, and Roman L. Weil at

http://papers.ssrn.com/sol3/papers.cfm?abstract_id=680281

Tough Questions Quiz

A member of the Audit Committee asks the CFO [or auditor] a tough question: "How do you know the Reserve for Uncollectible Accounts is adequate?" Classify each of the following responses as

> [1] Unresponsive; for example, you might hear this from a CFO who doesn't know his business or is trying to trick you.
> [2] OK as far as it goes, but needs a follow-up question, which you must pose.
> [3] Satisfactory and complete.

a. I think it much more likely than not that the amount of cash and marketable securities is adequate to cover any cash shortage caused by customers' not paying what they owe.
b. I have checked the Bad Debt Expense for sales made this past period and found that amount reasonable.
c. I have performed an aging of all Accounts Receivable and found that amount reasonable.
d. I have performed an aging of Accounts Receivable for all sales this period and found that amount reasonable.
e. The Reserve amount bears the expected relation to the amount of the Allowance for Uncollectible Accounts.
f. We performed a detailed confirmation of receivables from customers whose accounts the firm wrote off as uncollectible this period found the decisions suitable under the circumstances.
g. We performed a detailed confirmation of receivables from customers whose accounts the firm has neither collected nor written off by the end of this period and found the decisions suitable under the circumstances.
h. I know the Reserve was correct at the end of last period and I checked the Bad Debt Expense for this period using a percentage of sales recommended for this class of customers by the top two credit reporting agencies.

Quiz Answers and Explanations

a. I think it much more likely than not that the amount of cash and marketable securities is adequate to cover any cash shortage caused by customers' not paying what they owe. [1] No. If you think this answer has anything to do with the right answer, you should review the meaning of Reserves.

b. I have checked the Bad Debt Expense for sales made this past period and found that amount reasonable. [2] OK as far as it goes. What about the adequacy of the Reserve [Allowance] for sales made before this past period; what did you do about those?

c. I have performed an aging of all Accounts Receivable and found that amount reasonable. [3] Complete.

d. I have performed an aging of Accounts Receivable for all sales this period and found that amount reasonable. [2] OK as far as it goes. What about the aging for the amounts uncollected at the start of this period?

e. The Reserve amount bears the expected relation to the amount of the Allowance for Uncollectible Accounts. [1] Tautological; smoke screen. Or [2] ask the question again substituting *Allowance for Uncollectibles* for *Reserve for Uncollectible Accounts*.

f. We performed a detailed confirmation of receivables from customers whose accounts the firm wrote off as uncollectible this period found the decisions suitable under the circumstances. [1] Irrelevant.

g. We performed a detailed confirmation of receivables from customers whose accounts the firm has neither collected nor written off by the end of this period and found the decisions suitable under the circumstances. [1] Smokescreen or, some might say: [2] OK as far as it goes, which isn't very far. This tells you about the write-offs this period, not about the adequacy of the balance sheet amount. "OK, now you've told me about that, what about the adequacy of the Reserve, itself?"

h. I know the Reserve was correct at the end of last period and I checked the Bad Debt Expense for this period using a percentage of sales recommended for this class of customers by the top two credit reporting agencies.   [3] OK.

Appendix A

Exhibit 1
Base Case with Normal Results

Balance Sheets

		Yr 0	Yr 1	End of Year Yr 2	Yr 3
Plug	Cash	$78.0	$83.6	$91.9	$104.5
Turnover x/yr	6 Accounts Receivable	152.0	166.7	183.3	201.7
Turnover x/yr	4 Inventory	150.0	162.5	178.8	196.6
Grow at	7% Plant & Equipment [Net]	500.0	535.0	572.5	612.5
	Total Assets	$880.0	$947.7	$1,026.4	$1,115.3
Turnover x/yr	12 Accounts Payable	51.0	54.2	59.6	65.5
D/OE =	0.67 Long Term Debt	331.6	357.4	386.7	419.9
(D+OE)/A =	0.60 Owners' Equity	497.4	536.1	580.1	629.9
	Total Sources of Financing	$880.0	$947.7	$1,026.4	$1,115.3

Income Statements

		Yr 1	Yr 2	Yr 3
Grow at	10% Sales	$1,000.0	$1,100.0	$1,210.0
.65 of Sales	0.65 Cost of Goods Sold	650.0	715.0	786.5
Grow at	8% Administrative Expenses	100.0	108.0	116.6
Grow at	7% Depreciation Expense	80.0	85.6	91.6
Interest rate	8% Interest Expense	26.5	28.6	30.9
	Pretax Income	$143.5	$162.8	$184.3
Y Tax rate =	40% Income Tax Expense	57.4	65.1	73.7
	Net Income [= Y]	$86.1	$97.7	$110.6
Dividend Payout Rate =	55% Dividends	47.3	53.7	60.8
	Add to Retained Earnings	$38.7	$44.0	$49.8

Statements of Cash Flows

	Yr 1	Yr 2	Yr 3
Income [= Y]	$86.1	$97.7	$110.6
Plus Depreciation	80.0	85.6	91.6
Less Increase Receivables	(14.7)	(16.7)	(18.3)
Less Increase Inventories	(12.5)	(16.3)	(17.9)
Plus Increase Payables	3.2	5.4	6.0
Cash Flow from Operations	$142.1	$155.8	$171.9
New Equipment Purchases	(115.0)	(123.1)	(131.7)
New Borrowing	25.8	29.3	33.2
Dividends	(47.3)	(53.7)	(60.8)
Total Increase in Cash	$5.6	$8.3	$12.6

Diagnostic Ratios

	Yr 1	Yr 2	Yr 3
Inventory Turnover per Year	4.16	4.19	4.19
Receivables Turnover per Year	6.28	6.29	6.29
Cash Flow from Operations/Y	1.65	1.59	1.55
Quick Ratio	1.54	1.54	1.59
Return on Assets	11.6%	12.1%	12.6%
Return on Owners' Equity	17.3%	18.2%	19.1%

Exhibit 2
Bad Result in Year 3: Expenses Increase Unexpectedly by $100.00

Balance Sheets

		Yr 0	Yr 1	Yr 2	Yr 3
				End of Year	
Plug	Cash	$ 78.0	$ 83.6	$ 91.9	$ 59.5
Turnover x/yr 6	Accounts Receivable	152.0	166.7	183.3	201.7
Turnover x/yr 4	Inventory	150.0	162.5	178.8	196.6
Grow at 7%	Plant & Equipment [Net]	500.0	535.0	572.5	612.5
	Total Assets	$ 880.0	$ 947.7	$ 1,026.4	$ 1,070.3
Turnover x/yr 12	Accounts Payable	51.0	54.2	59.6	65.5
D/OE = 0.67	Long Term Debt	331.6	357.4	386.7	401.9
(D+OE)/A = 0.60	Owners' Equity	497.4	536.1	580.1	602.9
	Total Sources of Financing	$ 880.0	$ 947.7	$ 1,026.4	$ 1,070.3

Income Statements

		Yr 1	Yr 2	Yr 3
Grow at 10%	Sales	$ 1,000.0	$ 1,100.0	$ 1,210.0
.65 of Sales	Cost of Goods Sold	650.0	715.0	786.5
Grow at 8%	Administrative Expenses	100.0	108.0	216.6
Grow at 7%	Depreciation Expense	80.0	85.6	91.6
Interest rate 8%	Interest Expense	26.5	28.6	30.9
	Pretax Income	$ 143.5	$ 162.8	$ 84.3
Y Tax rate = 40%	Income Tax Expense	57.4	65.1	33.7
	Net Income [= Y]	$ 86.1	$ 97.7	$ 50.6
Dividend Payout Rate = 55%	Dividends	47.3	53.7	27.8
	Add to Retained Earnings	$ 38.7	$ 44.0	$ 22.8

Statements of Cash Flows

	Yr 1	Yr 2	Yr 3
Income [= Y]	$ 86.1	$ 97.7	$ 50.6
Plus Depreciation	80.0	85.6	91.6
Less Increase Receivables	(14.7)	(16.7)	(18.3)
Less Increase Inventories	(12.5)	(16.3)	(17.9)
Plus Increase Payables	3.2	5.4	6.0
Cash Flow from Operations	$ 142.1	$ 155.8	$ 111.9
New Equipment Purchases	(115.0)	(123.1)	(131.7)
New Borrowing	25.8	29.3	15.2
Dividends	(47.3)	(53.7)	(27.8)
Total Increase in Cash	$ 5.6	$ 8.3	$ (32.4)

Diagnostic Ratios

	Yr 1	Yr 2	Yr 3
Inventory Turnover per Year	4.16	4.19	4.19
Receivables Turnover per Year	6.28	6.29	6.29
Cash Flow from Operations/Y	1.65	1.59	2.21
Quick Ratio	1.54	1.54	0.91
Return on Assets	11.6%	12.1%	6.7%
Return on Owners' Equity	17.3%	18.2%	8.7%

Exhibit 3
Bad Expenses in Year 3 and Management Attempts Cover-Up by Inflating Revenues Only

Feeble attempt to repair damage: Inflate revenues in Year 3 by $ 100.0
Observe Balance Sheet doesn't balance, so need to be more sophisticated.

Balance Sheets

		Yr 0	Yr 1	Yr 2	No Fraud in Year 3 Yr 3	Fraud in Year 3 Yr 3	
lug	Cash	$ 78.0	$ 83.6	$ 91.9	$ 59.5	$ 59.5	
6 urnover x/yr	Accounts Receivable	152.0	166.7	183.3	201.7	201.7	
4 urnover x/yr	Inventory	150.0	162.5	178.8	196.6	196.6	
7% row at	Plant & Equipment [Net]	500.0	535.0	572.5	612.5	612.5	
	Total Assets	$ 880.0	$ 947.7	$ 1,026.4	$ 1,070.3	$ 1,070.3	Signal
12 urnover x/yr	Accounts Payable	51.0	54.2	59.6	65.5	65.5	
0.67 D/OE =	Long Term Debt	331.6	357.4	386.7	401.9	401.9	
0.60 (D+OE)/A =	Owners' Equity	497.4	536.1	580.1	602.9	662.9	
	Total Sources of Financing	$ 880.0	$ 947.7	$ 1,026.4	$ 1,070.3	$ 1,130.3	Signal

Income Statements

		Yr 1	Yr 2	Yr 3	Yr 3
Grow at	10% Sales	$ 1,000.0	$ 1,100.0	$ 1,210.0	$ 1,310.0
.65 of Sales	0.65 Cost of Goods Sold	650.0	715.0	786.5	786.5
Grow at	8% Administrative Expenses	100.0	108.0	216.6	216.6
Grow at	7% Depreciation Expense	80.0	85.6	91.6	91.6
Interest rate	8% Interest Expense	26.5	28.6	30.9	30.9
	Pretax Income	143.5	162.8	84.3	184.3
Y Tax rate =	40% Income Tax Expense	57.4	65.1	33.7	73.7
	Net Income [= Y]	$ 86.1	$ 97.7	$ 50.6	$ 110.6
ividend Payout Rate =	55% Dividends	47.3	53.7	27.8	27.8
	Add to Retained Earnings	$ 38.7	$ 44.0	$ 22.8	$ 82.8

Statements of Cash Flows

	Yr 1	Yr 2	Yr 3	Yr 3
Income [= Y]	$ 86.1	$ 97.7	$ 50.6	$ 110.6
Plus Depreciation	80.0	85.6	91.6	91.6
Less Increase Receivables	(14.7)	(16.7)	(18.3)	(18.3)
Less Increase Inventories	(12.5)	(16.3)	(17.9)	(17.9)
Plus Increase Payables	3.2	5.4	6.0	6.0
Cash Flow from Operations	$ 142.1	$ 155.8	$ 111.9	$ 171.9
New Equipment Purchases	(115.0)	(123.1)	(131.7)	(131.7)
New Borrowing	25.8	29.3	15.2	15.2
Dividends	(47.3)	(53.7)	(27.8)	(27.8)
Total Increase in Cash	$ 5.6	$ 8.3	$ (32.4)	$ 27.6

Diagnostic Ratios

	Yr 1	Yr 2	Yr 3	Yr 3
Inventory Turnover per Year	4.16	4.19	4.19	4.19
Receivables Turnover per Year	6.28	6.29	6.29	6.81
Cash Flow from Operations/Y	1.65	1.59	2.21	1.55
Quick Ratio	1.54	1.54	0.91	0.91
Return on Assets	11.6%	12.1%	6.7%	12.1%
Return on Owners' Equity	17.3%	18.2%	8.7%	18.3%

Exhibit 4
Bad Expenses in Year 3 and Management Attempts Cover-Up by Inflating Revenues and Receivables

In Year 3, Expenses Increase Unexectedly by $ 100.0

Inflate revenues and receivables in Year 3 by $ 100.0

Management records income taxes on the bogus income.

Note that an auditor who confirms receivables will discover error.

Balance Sheets

		Yr 0		Yr 1		Yr 2		End of Year No Fraud in Year 3 Yr 3		Fraud in Year 3 Yr 3
Plug	Cash	$ 78.0	$	83.6	$	91.9	$	59.5	$	59.5
Turnover x/yr	6 Accounts Receivable	152.0		166.7		183.3		201.7		301.7 Signal
Turnover x/yr	4 Inventory	150.0		162.5		178.8		196.6		131.6 Signal
Grow at	7% Plant & Equipment [Net]	500.0		535.0		572.5		612.5		612.5
	Total Assets	$ 880.0	$	947.7	$	1,026.4	$	1,070.3	$	1,105.3
Turnover x/yr	12 Accounts Payable	51.0		54.2		59.6		65.5		79.5
D/OE =	0.67 Long Term Debt	331.6		357.4		386.7		401.9		401.9
(D+OE)/A =	0.60 Owners' Equity	497.4		536.1		580.1		602.9		623.9
	Total Sources of Financing	$ 880.0	$	947.7	$	1,026.4	$	1,070.3	$	1,105.3

Income Statements

		Yr 1		Yr 2		No Fraud in Year 3 Yr 3		Fraud in Year 3 Yr 3
Grow at	10% Sales	$ 1,000.0	$	1,100.0	$	1,210.0	$	1,310.0
.65 of Sales	0.65 Cost of Goods Sold	650.0		715.0		786.5		851.5
Grow at	8% Administrative Expenses	100.0		108.0		216.6		216.6
Grow at	7% Depreciation Expense	80.0		85.6		91.6		91.6
Interest rate	8% Interest Expense	26.5		28.6		30.9		30.9
	Pretax Income	$ 143.5	$	162.8	$	84.3	$	119.3
Y Tax rate =	40% Income Tax Expense	57.4		65.1		33.7		47.7
	Net Income [= Y]	$ 86.1	$	97.7	$	50.6	$	71.6
Dividend Payout Rate =	55% Dividends	47.3		53.7		27.8		27.8
	Add to Retained Earnings	$ 38.7	$	44.0	$	22.8	$	43.8

Statements of Cash Flows

		Yr 1		Yr 2		No Fraud in Year 3 Yr 3		Fraud in Year 3 Yr 3
	Income [= Y]	$ 86.1	$	97.7	$	50.6	$	71.6
	Plus Depreciation	80.0		85.6		91.6		91.6
	Less Increase Receivables	(14.7)		(16.7)		(18.3)		(118.3)
	Less Increase Inventories	(12.5)		(16.3)		(17.9)		47.1
	Plus Increase Payables	3.2		5.4		6.0		20.0
	Cash Flow from Operations	$ 142.1	$	155.8	$	111.9	$	111.9
	New Equipment Purchases	(115.0)		(123.1)		(131.7)		(131.7)
	New Borrowing	25.8		29.3		15.2		15.2
	Dividends	(47.3)		(53.7)		(27.8)		(27.8)
	Total Increase in Cash	$ 5.6	$	8.3	$	(32.4)	$	(32.4)

Diagnostic Ratios

	Yr 1	Yr 2	No Fraud in Year 3 Yr 3	Fraud in Year 3 Yr 3
Inventory Turnover per Year	4.16	4.19	4.19	5.49
Receivables Turnover per Year	6.28	6.29	6.29	5.40 Signal
Cash Flow from Operations/Y	1.65	1.59	2.21	1.56 Signal
Quick Ratio	1.54	1.54	0.91	0.75
Return on Assets	11.6%	12.1%	6.7%	8.4%
Return on Owners' Equity	17.3%	18.2%	8.7%	11.9%

Entries for Fabricated Transactions:

Dr. Accounts Receivable	100	
Cr. Sales		100
Dr. Cost of Goods Sold	65	
Cr. Inventory		65
Dr. Income Tax Expense	14	
Cr. Payables		14
Cr. Cash		-

Exhibit 5

Bad Expenses in Year 3 and Management Attempts Cover-Up by Inflating Revenues and Receivables with Side Letter

In Year 3, Expenses Increase Unexectedly by $ 100.0

Inflate revenues and receivables in Year 3 by $ 100.0

Management records cost of goods sold and income taxes on the bogus income.

Note that an auditor who confirms receivables will *NOT* discover error.

Balance Sheets

		Yr 0	Yr 1	Yr 2	No Fraud in Year 3	Fraud in Year 3
Plug	Cash	$ 78.0	$ 83.6	$ 91.9	$ 59.5	$ 59.5
Turnover x/yr	6	Accounts Receivable	152.0	166.7	183.3	201.7	301.7
Turnover x/yr	4	Inventory	150.0	162.5	178.8	196.6	131.6
Grow at	7%	Plant & Equipment [Net]	500.0	535.0	572.5	612.5	612.5
		Total Assets	$ 880.0	$ 947.7	$ 1,026.4	$ 1,070.3	$ 1,105.3
Turnover x/yr	12	Accounts Payable	51.0	54.2	59.6	65.5	79.5
D/OE =	0.67	Long Term Debt	331.6	357.4	386.7	401.9	401.9
(D+OE)/A =	0.60	Owners' Equity	497.4	536.1	580.1	602.9	623.9
		Total Sources of Financing	$ 880.0	$ 947.7	$ 1,026.4	$ 1,070.3	$ 1,105.3

(Balance Sheet labels — End of Year columns: Yr 0, Yr 1, Yr 2; No Fraud in Year 3; Fraud in Year 3)

Income Statements

			Yr 1	Yr 2	Yr 3 (No Fraud)	Yr 3 (Fraud)
Grow at	10%	Sales	$ 1,000.0	$ 1,100.0	$ 1,210.0	$ 1,310.0
.65 of Sales		Cost of Goods Sold	650.0	715.0	786.5	851.5
Grow at	8%	Administrative Expenses	100.0	108.0	216.6	216.6
Grow at	7%	Depreciation Expense	80.0	85.6	91.6	91.6
Interest rate	8%	Interest Expense	26.5	28.6	30.9	30.9
		Pretax Income	$ 143.5	$ 162.8	$ 84.3	$ 119.3
Y Tax rate =	40%	Income Tax Expense	57.4	65.1	33.7	47.7
		Net Income [= Y]	$ 86.1	$ 97.7	$ 50.6	$ 71.6
Dividend Payout Rate =	55%	Dividends	47.3	53.7	27.8	27.8
		Add to Retained Earnings	$ 38.7	$ 44.0	$ 22.8	$ 43.8

Statements of Cash Flows

	Yr 1	Yr 2	Yr 3 (No Fraud)	Yr 3 (Fraud)
Income [= Y]	$ 86.1	$ 97.7	$ 50.6	$ 71.6
Plus Depreciation	80.0	85.6	91.6	91.6
Less Increase Receivables	(14.7)	(16.7)	(18.3)	(118.3)
Less Increase Inventories	(12.5)	(16.3)	(17.9)	47.1
Plus Increase Payables	3.2	5.4	6.0	20.0
Cash Flow from Operations	$ 142.1	$ 155.8	$ 111.9	$ 111.9
New Equipment Purchases	(115.0)	(123.1)	(131.7)	(131.7)
New Borrowing	25.8	29.3	15.2	15.2
Dividends	(47.3)	(53.7)	(27.8)	(27.8)
Total Increase in Cash	$ 5.6	$ 8.3	$ (32.4)	$ (32.4)

Diagnostic Ratios

	Yr 1	Yr 2	Yr 3 (No Fraud)	Yr 3 (Fraud)
Inventory Turnover per Year	4.16	4.19	4.19	5.49 **Signal**
Receivables Turnover per Year	6.28	6.29	6.29	5.40 **Signal**
Cash Flow from Operations/Y	1.65	1.59	2.21	1.56 **Signal**
Quick Ratio	1.54	1.54	0.91	0.75
Return on Assets	11.6%	12.1%	6.7%	8.4%
Return on Owners' Equity	17.3%	18.2%	8.7%	11.9%

Entries for Fabricated Transactions:

Dr. Accounts Receivable	100	
Cr. Sales		100
Dr. Cost of Goods Sold	65	
Cr. Inventory		65
Dr. Income Tax Expense	14	
Cr. Payables		14
Cr. Cash		-

Exhibit 6
Bad Expenses in Year 3 and Management Attempts Cover-Up by Inflating Ending Inventory

In Year 3, Expenses Increase Unexpectedly by $ 100.0
Overvalue ending inventory to cover up by $ 100.0
Management records cost of goods sold and income taxes on the bogus income.
Note that an auditor who tests inventory will discover error.

Balance Sheets

		Yr 0	Yr 1	End of Year Yr 2	No Fraud in Year 3	Fraud in Year 3
Plug	Cash	$ 78.0	$ 83.6	$ 91.9	$ 59.5	$ 59.5
6 Turnover x/yr	Accounts Receivable	152.0	166.7	183.3	201.7	201.7
4 Turnover x/yr	Inventory	150.0	162.5	178.8	196.6	296.6
7% Grow at	Plant & Equipment [Net]	500.0	535.0	572.5	612.5	612.5
	Total Assets	$ 880.0	$ 947.7	$ 1,026.4	$ 1,070.3	$ 1,170.3
12 Turnover x/yr	Accounts Payable	51.0	54.2	59.6	65.5	105.5
0.67 D/OE =	Long Term Debt	331.6	357.4	386.7	401.9	401.9
0.60 (D+OE)/A =	Owners' Equity	497.4	536.1	580.1	602.9	662.9
	Total Sources of Financing	$ 880.0	$ 947.7	$ 1,026.4	$ 1,070.3	$ 1,170.3

Income Statements

		Yr 1	Yr 2	Yr 3 (No Fraud)	Yr 3 (Fraud)
10% Grow at	Sales	$ 1,000.0	$ 1,100.0	$ 1,210.0	$ 1,210.0
.65 of Sales	Cost of Goods Sold	650.0	715.0	786.5	686.5
8% Grow at	Administrative Expenses	100.0	108.0	216.6	216.6
7% Grow at	Depreciation Expense	80.0	85.6	91.6	91.6
8% Interest rate	Interest Expense	26.5	28.6	30.9	30.9
	Pretax Income	$ 143.5	$ 162.8	$ 84.3	$ 184.3
40% Y Tax rate =	Income Tax Expense	57.4	65.1	33.7	73.7
	Net Income [= Y]	$ 86.1	$ 97.7	$ 50.6	$ 110.6
55% Dividend Payout Rate =	Dividends	47.3	53.7	27.8	27.8
	Add to Retained Earnings	$ 38.7	$ 44.0	$ 22.8	$ 82.8

Statements of Cash Flows

	Yr 1	Yr 2	Yr 3 (No Fraud)	Yr 3 (Fraud)
Income [= Y]	$ 86.1	$ 97.7	$ 50.6	$ 110.6
Plus Depreciation	80.0	85.6	91.6	91.6
Less Increase Receivables	(14.7)	(16.7)	(18.3)	(18.3)
Less Increase Inventories	(12.5)	(16.3)	(17.9)	(117.9)
Plus Increase Payables	3.2	5.4	6.0	46.0
Cash Flow from Operations	$ 142.1	$ 155.8	$ 111.9	$ 111.9
New Equipment Purchases	(115.0)	(123.1)	(131.7)	(131.7)
New Borrowing	25.8	29.3	15.2	15.2
Dividends	(47.3)	(53.7)	(27.8)	(27.8)
Total Increase in Cash	$ 5.6	$ 8.3	$ (32.4)	$ (32.4)

Diagnostic Ratios

	Yr 1	Yr 2	Yr 3 (No Fraud)	Yr 3 (Fraud)	
Inventory Turnover per Year	4.16	4.19	4.19	2.89	**Signal**
Receivables Turnover per Year	6.28	6.29	6.29	6.29	
Cash Flow from Operations/Y	1.65	1.59	2.21	1.01	**Signal**
Quick Ratio	1.54	1.54	0.91	0.56	
Return on Assets	11.6%	12.1%	6.7%	12.1%	
Return on Owners' Equity	17.3%	18.2%	8.7%	18.3%	

We show this as a reduction in the expense for Cost of Goods sold as a negative debit although typically reductions in expenses are positive credits.

Entries for Fabricated Transactions:

Dr. Accounts Receivable	-	-
Cr. Sales		
Dr. Cost of Goods Sold	(100)	(100)
Cr. Inventory		(100)
Dr. Income Tax Expense	40	40
Cr. Payables		40
Cr. Cash		-